The Buying
of the
President
2004

The Buying
of the
President
2004

WHO'S REALLY BANKROLLING BUSH AND HIS
DEMOCRATIC CHALLENGERS—AND WHAT
THEY EXPECT IN RETURN

Charles Lewis
and
THE CENTER FOR PUBLIC INTEGRITY

Perennial
An Imprint of HarperCollinsPublishers

HarperCollins books may be purchased for educational, business, or sales promotional use. For information please write: Special Markets Department, HarperCollins Publishers Inc., 10 East 53rd Street, New York, NY 10022.

FIRST EDITION

Library of Congress Cataloging-in-Publication Data is available.
ISBN 0-06-054853-3

04 05 06 07 08 WBC / RRD 10 9

For my daughter, Cassie

Few men have virtue to withstand the highest bidder.
—*George Washington*

The flood of money that gushes into politics today is a pollution of democracy.
—*Theodore H. White*

The Investigative Team

EXECUTIVE DIRECTOR
Charles Lewis

MANAGING EDITOR
Bill Allison

DEPUTY MANAGING EDITOR
Teo Furtado

RESEARCH EDITOR
Peter Newbatt Smith

PROJECT MANAGER
Alex Knott

SENIOR WRITERS
Alan Green
Alex Knott
Charles Lewis
Robert Moore

WRITERS
Ben Coates
M. Asif Ismail
Laura Peterson
Brooke Williams

DATABASE EDITORS
Aron Pilhofer
Derek Willis

WEB DEVELOPER
Han Nguyen

SENIOR RESEARCHERS
Aubrey Bruggeman
Ben Coates
Daniel Lathrop
Katy Lewis
Adam Mayle

RESEARCHERS

Agustin Armendariz
Jessica Bartko
Colleen Coffey
Sarah Coffey
Maren Goldberg
Neil Gordon
Dar Haddix
Lisa Hirsch
Sara Hunt
Osita Iroegbu
Morgan Jindrich
Allison Kaminsky
Lisa Kays
Sholpan Kozhamkulova
Kara Kridler
Alexander Leonhardt
Julie Mañes
Katie McLeod
Jennifer Mehigan
Andrew Noyes
Meghan O'Donnell
Alicia Oman
Erin Quintana
Mark Reading-Smith
Reem Rifai
Susan Schaab
Brooke Sherman
Oscar Ayala Silva
Dawn Triemstra
Ed Turner
André Vérlöy
Derrick Wetherell
Katharine Widland
Amy Wojciechowski

THE CENTER FOR PUBLIC INTEGRITY

Cathy Sweeney
Barbara Schecter
Ann Pincus
Javed Khan
Nathan Kommers
Regina Russell
Renee Christopher

WE GRATEFULLY ACKNOWLEDGE FINANCIAL SUPPORT FOR THIS PROJECT FROM THE VICTOR ELMALEH FOUNDATION, EDITH AND HENRY EVERETT, AND THE POPPLESTONE FOUNDATION.

SPECIAL THANKS TO PROFESSOR WENDELL COCHRAN OF THE AMERICAN UNIVERSITY IN WASHINGTON, D.C., WHOSE JOURNALISM GRADUATE STUDENTS ASSISTED IN THE RESEARCH AS PART OF HIS CLASS

CONTENTS

The Buying
of the
President
2004

Introduction

Politics, Winston Churchill once said, "are almost as exciting as war, and quite as dangerous. In war you can only be killed once, but in politics many times." Frankly, most Americans these days would hope for a little less excitement in their politics. But the appalling attacks on September 11, 2001, resulting in the largest loss of civilian lives on U.S. soil in modern times, followed by mysterious anthrax assaults and wars in Afghanistan and Iraq—all in just two years—have if anything further blurred the line between politics and war. Our unending war on terrorism overshadowed the 2002 midterm elections. And as we now contemplate the 2004 presidential election, there is no better metaphor for how war and politics have merged than the indelible image of our commander in chief speaking to the world just moments after his dramatic fighter plane landing on the flight deck of an aircraft carrier just returning from war.

Of course, our domestic politics had already become intensely bitter, full-throated combat by the turn of the new century and millennium. We witnessed the first impeachment and Senate trial of a sitting U.S. president in more than a century—which was decided along substantially party lines. And we lived through the closest presidential election since 1876, in which Vice President Al Gore won the popular vote but Texas Governor George W. Bush won the electoral vote (though neither got 50 percent of the votes cast)—with the outcome of the disputed Florida voting, and the presidency, decided by the Republican-controlled U.S. Supreme Court.

Bush and Gore spent a world record $325 million on the 2000 election, and even when the carnage was over it wasn't over. Despite 36 days of surreal, contentious post-election chaos and scores of lawsuits and multimillion-dollar investigations by major news media organizations in Florida, 175,000 legally cast ballots were not counted. What really happened in Florida in 2000, where the state legislature was Republican and the governor was the president's brother, but the state supreme court and most of the local county election supervisors were Democrats? We'll never know for sure, but political Hatfields and McCoys will be fighting over it for generations.

Indeed, we have become, as respected conservative author Michael Barone put it, "the 49 percent nation." Bill Clinton won reelection in 1996 with 49.2 percent of the vote; Republicans held onto the House of Representatives in 1996, 1998, and 2000 with 48.9, 48.9, and 49.2 percent of the votes, respectively. Each of these numbers rounds off to 49 percent. "We haven't had such stasis in successive election results since the 1880s, which was also the last decade when a president was elected despite trailing in the popular vote and when the Senate was equally divided between the two major parties," Barone noted.

Ours is the most elaborate, lengthy, and costly process for selecting a national leader in the world. Every year, politicians, journalists, and political scientists talk about our peculiar endurance contest to ascertain whether a candidate is fit to govern, but nothing ever changes. In 1995, when the Center for Public

Integrity first investigated the major presidential candidates and political parties for *The Buying of the President*, former Republican congressman, presidential candidate, and cabinet secretary Jack Kemp told us that he personally dreaded the prospect of appearing at between 200 and 250 fundraising events the year *before* the election and spending "eighty percent of my time on the phone or at fundraisers, which most of [the presidential candidates] are doing. . . . You've got to be compulsive. . . . I don't criticize anybody who's going through this, but I'm glad I'm not. . . . I think the [presidential election] process is too long and too expensive."

In early 2003, two major Democratic presidential candidates facing potentially life-threatening health problems found it necessary to hawk donors for campaign contributions while still recuperating from major surgery.

Eight years later, the process is just as intense and wacky. In early 2003, for example, two major Democratic presidential candidates facing potentially life-threatening health problems found it necessary to hawk donors for campaign contributions while still recuperating from major surgery. Florida senator Bob Graham had an aortic valve replacement and double coronary artery bypass surgery, but within days he was on the phone dialing for dollars. Massachusetts senator John Kerry, in a hospital *just hours* after prostate cancer surgery—sore, bandaged, medicated, and forced to use a catheter tube to urinate—nonetheless felt compelled to send a personal e-mail to his campaign's financial backers, flatly reassuring them that "We have every reason to expect a complete, speedy recovery."

Both men and their aides understood that these unforeseen developments could seriously disrupt their political plans, throw the embryonic campaign off message and on the defensive from the onset, and dissuade donors from writing those all-important early checks in the so-called wealth primary, the private referendum held the year *before* any votes are cast anywhere, in which *thousands* of the richest Americans—one-tenth of 1 percent of the population—make the maximum allowable campaign contribution, now $2,000. Early, crucial, political momentum has a decidedly greenish hue. And the often-criticized, who-will-win "horse race" coverage of the presidential candidates by political reporters always starts with—besides public opinion polling—Federal Election Commission contribution reports revealing exactly which candidate is amassing the most cash.

One horse who surprised everyone out of the gate was Democratic senator John Edwards of North Carolina, who raised the most money in the first quarter of 2003. He somehow appeared at 175 fundraisers, putting him on an average of two a day for the year. Edwards and eight other major Democratic White House contenders—the most crowded field since 1976—cumulatively raised $26 million in the first quarter. In stark contrast, the incumbent Republican president, who didn't start his reelection campaign until the second quarter, raised $34.4 million—more than *all* of the major Democratic candidates combined. That included $21.7 million in a two-week, 14-fundraiser blitz. It started off one late spring night in 2003, at a stand-up, $2,000-a-person, lobbyist-laden Washington reception where hot dogs and nachos were served. The Bush-Cheney campaign would not disclose the names of almost 200 people who had cochaired the event, and each personally promised to collect $20,000 for the cause, and restricted media access to the grand hotel ballroom affair, which generated $3.5 million.

The recurring secrecy leitmotif aside, George W. Bush has altogether redefined the parameters of political fundraising. In the 2003–2004 election, he is expected to collect in the vicinity of $200 million. To put that number into perspective, consider that it is 62 percent higher than his record-shattering total of $125 million and *four times* more than Al Gore collected in the 2000 presidential election.

Running for president today is an all-consuming, two-year basic training program that includes hundreds of dehumanizing meet-and-greet, frozen-smile events, which culminate in a grueling 33-week stretch of campaigning in 45 state caucuses and primaries. By comparison, John F. Kennedy campaigned in just seven states back in 1960 before he was nominated. The survivor then gets to accept his party's nomination at the carefully choreographed-to-the-minute national convention with its thousands of delegates, hundreds of parties and events, and dozens of personal meetings, followed by at least 10 *additional* weeks of brutal national barnstorming in the full glare of local, national, and international journalists.

But the most demoralizing—and shameless—thing candidates have to do is to ask for money from thousands of strangers, virtually every day for more than a year. Why do they do it? Because they have to if they want their message to resonate with voters. At a time when television networks and local TV stations keep decreasing the amount of air time on actual political news, they keep getting richer from paid political ads. According to the Alliance for Better Campaigns, candidates, parties, and issue groups spent slightly more than $150 million in 1980 and more than $1 billion in 2002—so much, in fact, that they are now one of television's leading sources of revenue. Candidates can no longer depend on "free media" news coverage to get their word out, which means they *must* have sufficient funding to purchase campaign commercials. A candidate with no ads simply doesn't exist. A well-funded major presidential candidate necessarily has scores of paid campaign staffers, plus a phalanx of pollsters and media and other consultants.

But there is another reason candidates must make a headlong rush for the cash. As we mentioned in the 1996 and 2000 editions of *The Buying of the President*, the single most salient fact about the White House selection process—a discovery first made by Republican political fundraising consultant Stan Huckaby—is that in *every* presidential election since 1976, the candidate who has raised the most money at the end of the year preceding the election, and been eligible for federal matching funds, has become his party's nominee for the general election. At midnight on December 31, it was Carter and Ford who had amassed the most campaign cash in 1975, Carter and Reagan in 1979, Mondale and Reagan in 1983, Dukakis and G. H. W. Bush in 1987, Clinton and Bush in 1991, Clinton and Dole in 1995, and Gore and G. W. Bush in 1999.

All major presidential candidates and most national political reporters recognize that the top money chaser the year before the election almost assuredly will be the nominee of his political party. That means that the race for the White House is substantially decided *before* any actual votes are cast. The dirty little secret of American presidential politics is that the wealthiest interests essentially hold a private referendum the year before the election; otherwise respectable candidates who didn't put up sufficiently impressive cash numbers are often driven from the race and cast as "losers" who can't put together "an effective organization." By January of the presidential election year, the biggest money is already down on the next president of the United States, which effectively predetermines whom the nondonor public gets to vote on.

Consider 1995, for example. That year the eventual 1996 Democratic and Republican presidential nominees, Clinton and Dole, each raised about $26 million, both record amounts at the time. Of the 16,200 donors who contributed $1,000 to the Clinton-Gore reelection campaign, 94 percent gave their money in 1995. Similarly, of the 48,000 donors who contributed the maximum $1,000 to Republican presidential candidates, 83 percent contributed their cash in 1995. Prior to the 2000 campaign, no single presidential candidate had found more than roughly 19,000 donors contributing the maximum $1,000 contribution. That all changed in 1999–2000, when George W. Bush received 59,279 donations of $1,000, more than *triple* that of any previous contender.

Bush would go on to shatter all fundraising records in 1999. He raised $68,877,684—$230,360 a day—with no single check larger than $1,000. During the first four months of his active candidacy, Bush collected $37 million. The previous record had been Bill Clinton's in 1995, when he raised $26 million in seven months. No one raises that kind of cash casually or quickly, of course, and it certainly doesn't come from backyard barbecues and neighborhood bake sales. A contribution check of $1,000 isn't something the average American can write; most often, those who open their checkbooks are lawyers, lobbyists, or the vested economic interests they represent who want something in return from the government.

BUNDLING FOR BUSH

For two years, the Texas governor and his brilliant political advisors had been quietly, meticulously planning his charge for the White House, including issue briefings by experts flown in to Austin to give Bush personal tutorials. Prospective major donors, more than sixty of whom stayed overnight in the governor's mansion, were personally feted by Bush and his coterie of aides. When Bush publicly announced he was running for president in June

1999, and he and his candidacy burst into the national conscious-ness, most Americans had no idea just how fully prepared or extensive his campaign and its fundraising apparatus were. Four leading Republican candidates soon quit the race, months before the 2000 caucuses and primaries were even held, because of those extraordinary numbers, the gushy media coverage, and the overall aura of inevitability that began to surround his candidacy.

How did a state governor just starting his second term—an elected official for less than five years—pull off such a historic fundraising feat? Well, being the son of a former president with his own nationwide network of thousands of loyal donors obvi-ously didn't hurt. But the elder Bush never racked up anything close to his son's cash numbers. The answer lies, rather, with an unusual, secretive "Pioneer" fundraising system, for which the participants pledged in writing to each raise at least $100,000 by aggressively "bundling" together $1,000 checks from family, friends, and acquaintances. (For the 2004 election, the Bush campaign has introduced a new wrinkle to the bundling pro-gram: in addition to the $100,000 Pioneer fundraisers, it has added the $200,000 "Rangers.")

In litigation filed by the National Voting Rights Institute, John L. Oliver III, the national finance director of the 2000 Bush campaign, explained under oath how the Pioneer program worked. "If you raised $100,000, it was credited to your number," he said. "That was how you were made a Pioneer." Each contribu-tion received had an assigned tracking number, so that the Pioneer and his or her industry received "credit" for the money raised.

Another indication of how the program worked came in a May 27, 1999, letter from Bush Pioneer Thomas R. Kuhn to other fundraisers for a reception with the presidential candi-date. "As you know, a very important part of the campaign's out-reach to the business community is the use of tracking numbers for contributions. . . . Listing your industry's code does not prevent you, any of your individual solicitors or your state from receiving credit for soliciting a contribution. It does ensure that our *industry* is credited, and that your progress is listed among the other business/industry sectors," he wrote.

Now why would they want to receive credit? Clearly, many donors wanted first-in-line access to and influence with the prospective new administration. What is unusual about the Pioneer system is the unabashed directness of the transaction: You help us and we'll credit you and remember your loyalty and support later.

> How did a state governor just starting his second term—an elected official for less than five years—pull off such a historic fundraising feat?

Raising money this way has long been controversial because such exceptionally well organized bundling violates the spirit of limiting the size of contributions, which is one of the hallmarks of the post-Watergate campaign finance laws. "These documents reveal the disproportionate power gained by those who can bundle huge sums of hard money for political campaigns," said John Bonifaz, the executive director of the National Voting Rights Institute. "This offends the basic constitutional promise of political equality for all."

Direct contributions to federal candidates must, of course, be disclosed as required by law, but fundraising networks can have secret contribution tracking systems without being required to make their information public. We only got a glimpse into the Pioneer "innovation" because litigation surrounding the McCain-Feingold Bipartisan Campaign Reform Act required the Bush campaign to disgorge thousands of internal documents.

In 2000, the Bush campaign publicly disclosed the names of 212 Pioneer fundraisers. Three years later campaign documents show that the number was larger than 550.

Attorneys for Bush also asserted, in response to a subpoena in the autumn of 2002, that they were unable to locate specific information about the money collected by each Pioneer; in fact, so far they have only provided limited financial data on 212 Pioneers. This inability strains credulity. With such a meticulous, methodical pledge card and numeric tracking system, how could the Bush campaign, when pressed in potentially embarrassing litigation, say that they couldn't find the relevant information? In the highly sophisticated, overlapping worlds of politics, law, and public relations, this sounds only slightly better than "the dog ate my homework."

Craig McDonald, director of Texans for Public Justice, and an expert witness on behalf of the National Voting Rights Institute, testified that many of the Pioneers had special access to candidate Bush and subsequently were rewarded with government appointments; for example, his group found that 19 Pioneers (of the first acknowledged batch of 212) were appointed as ambassadors. At least one Pioneer, Elaine Chao, the wife of Republican senator Mitch McConnell of Kentucky, became a member of the President's cabinet. But what most disturbs McDonald is what he perceives as deliberate subterfuge. "It's time to end the secrecy over who bankrolled the Bush campaign," he said. "It just isn't believable that the president's campaign lost most of a $60 million fundraising list."

One of the Pioneers was Kenneth Lay, CEO of Enron, the Houston-based company that collapsed from massive fraud in late 2001. Lay, cochairman of former president Bush's 1992 reelection campaign, was credited with raising at least $112,050 for the George W. Bush campaign. Enron, both the company and its top officers, were Bush's top career patron in *The Buying of the President 2000*, indeed the top career patron by amount of *any* of the presidential candidates for that election. And through mid-2003, the disgraced, now bankrupt company remains by far Bush's top career corporate patron, with company and employee contributions of more than $597,000. In January 2002, when the Enron scandal burst into public view, President Bush—previously known to call his longtime Enron sponsor "Kenny Boy"—now started publicly referring to him as "Mr. Lay." The Center for Public Integrity's investigations into the various legislative favors sought by Enron dating back to the late 1980s and the hundreds of pages of correspondence between Lay and Bush while the latter was governor of Texas, detailed later in this book, reveal that the relationship between the two men was much deeper and richer than the White House has acknowledged.

In contrast, Gore raised more money than any Democratic presidential candidate in U.S. history, but ultimately Bush raised *two and a half times more* than Gore's total. At the end of 1999, Gore had amassed $30,777,121, or an average of $84,320 a day. And by Election Day, he had accumulated $49,427,800, not including matching funds, compared to Bush's jaw-dropping $125,410,986. But early in the campaign, armed with such an astonishing amount of campaign cash, Bush did something else no other front-runner candidate for his party's presidential nomination had ever done: he declared that he would now voluntarily opt out of the post-Watergate reforms on presidential campaign finance.

In July 1999, days after stunning the political world with his $37 million in receipts, Bush announced that he would forgo federal matching funds and the spending limits that accompany them. Framed for journalists as a defensive maneuver designed to counter the unlimited spending anticipated by billionaire GOP candidate Steve Forbes, Bush ignored the federal spending ceiling of nearly $50 million in the pre-convention phase of the election cycle, as well as the state-by-state spending caps. Ironically, the most significant advantage this bold maneuver gave him was not against Forbes but against Arizona senator John McCain in their infamous "OK Corral" showdown, the South Carolina primary.

McCain Poses a Threat

The battle in South Carolina epitomizes the profoundly disturbing state of American politics today. It shows how the power of money and the messages it can buy can overwhelm an otherwise popular, respected opponent by creating devastating false perceptions. Anyone who recalls Joe McGinniss's book, *The Selling of the President* (1968), knows that conjuring up positive and negative images untethered to reality is hardly new. Still, the most demoralizing lesson of the 2000 Republican South Carolina primary is that if your resources are superior enough, inconvenient facts can be rendered irrelevant. With saturation through paid advertising, phone banking, direct mailing, and e-mailing—compounded by a tepid, easily hoodwinked news media abrogating its truth-telling role—veracity itself is obscured and the public, bamboozled. In the end, as Mark Twain put it best, "A truth is not hard to kill and a lie told well is immortal."

An authentic American hero who was a prisoner of war in Vietnam for five and a half years, McCain had served two House terms and had just begun his third Senate term when he entered the 2000 presidential campaign. Since the mid-1990s, he had championed the issue of campaign finance reform, persistently going against the wishes of his own Republican Party; in turn, GOP Senate and House leaders killed it or kept it off the legislative agenda year after year. McCain's genuine fervor over the issue is fascinating, given how he came to it.

In 1989, the Arizona senator got caught up in the infamous national savings-and-loan scandal, known as the Keating Five affair. McCain and four other senators had over the years accepted $1.3 million in campaign contributions from Charles Keating, who owned Lincoln Savings and Loan. It later collapsed and was bailed out by taxpayers at a cost of $2.6 billion. McCain had received $112,000 in campaign contributions during his political career from Keating, his family, or his employees; in addition, in 1986 Keating had sold shares in a shopping center to McCain's wealthy wife and her father. The McCain family and their babysitter had also traveled on Keating's corporate jet nine times, including three trips to Keating's vacation estate in the Bahamas.

In his memoir, *Worth the Fighting For*, McCain writes that he and Keating "became friends almost from the moment we met. . . . He was quite obviously an important supporter of my ambitions. But more, I genuinely liked him and enjoyed being around him." The five senators—Alan Cranston, Dennis DeConcini, John Glenn, McCain, and Donald Riegle—had met at least once with federal regulators on Keating's behalf, which McCain would later describe as "the worst mistake of my life." The Senate Ethics Committee concluded that McCain had "exercised poor judgment" but that his actions had not been "improper nor attended with gross negligence." But it ruined the political careers of DeConcini, Cranston, and Riegle; none of them sought reelection and all three were seriously rebuked by their Senate colleagues.

The Keating Five affair was a life-changing event for McCain. He apologized publicly and often for his actions and won reelection to the Senate with 56 percent of the vote. But the episode was instructive. The moth had gotten too close to the flame and gotten burned. Keating, the longtime career patron of McCain's and a multimillionaire thrift operator desperately worried about being shut down by regulators, had become Keating, the friend. He expected a particular return on his years of investments, as he made personally, painfully clear to McCain. And to aggravate matters for the Arizona senator, Keating was publicly outspoken about hoping that his campaign contributions had bought influence with the five senators.

McCain was frank when he spoke to the Center for Public Integrity. "There's no doubt that the Keating Five [scandal] . . . brought home to me the importance of the appearance, as well as the reality, of corruption," he said. "The appearance of what I did caused the citizens that I represent to become disillusioned with me. And that to me was the worst thing I could do to them, because they had placed their confidence in me."

So McCain had an epiphany about the corruption of American politics and fought courageously, if unsuccessfully, in the second half of the 1990s for the campaign finance reform legislation he cosponsored with his Democratic colleague, Russell Feingold of Wisconsin. At the same time, for his reelection and presidential campaigns, he had to raise millions of dollars in campaign contributions from companies with business before the government, including the Senate Commerce Committee he chairs. As we found in *The Buying of the President 2000*, half of his top 10 career patrons were telecom or media companies. But McCain's disarming candor and outspokenness about the pervasive corruption of American politics placed him in an unusual position with the media and public, and when he entered the presidential race and the New Hampshire primary in 2000, cleaning up politics was his central issue.

By contrast, Bush was unostentatiously but unmistakably opposed to campaign finance reform and, as noted earlier, had publicly thumbed his nose at the post-Watergate state spending limits and matching funds. Moreover, his father had vetoed the last comprehensive campaign finance reform legislation passed by Congress in 1992.

As a presidential candidate with relatively modest funding, McCain had decided to strategically sidestep the earlier Iowa caucuses and put his limited chips on New Hampshire, South Carolina, Michigan, and Arizona, four primary states in four different regions of the country. With his "Straight-Talk Express" chartered campaign bus, he campaigned intensely in the "Live Free or Die" state, holding 114 town hall meetings. The New Hampshire crowds got larger as the crucial vote neared. On primary election night, February 1, he stunned the nation and the world by upsetting Bush, shellacking him by 19 points.

> **On primary election night, February 1, Senator John McCain stunned the nation and the world by upsetting Bush, shellacking him by 19 points.**

For McCain's excited followers, the euphoria and hope of the moment were palpable. "All of a sudden, John McCain was transformed from a political candidate into a kind of folk hero," said former New Hampshire senator and friend Warren Rudman. "People wanted to touch him. They wanted to bring their little children. They wanted his autograph." That night, McCain described the victory to his screaming supporters as "remarkable" and said, "My friends, a wonderful New Hampshire campaign has come to an end, but a great national crusade has just begun. . . . We have sent a powerful message to Washington that change is coming." In fact, in exit polling that day, 80 percent of the voters in the New Hampshire Republican primary supported campaign finance reform, and two-thirds of those voters saw McCain as being more likely to help bring reform than Bush. In response to the question, "Which candidate do you feel says what he truly believes?" voters favored McCain over Bush by a three-to-one margin, 50 percent to 17 percent.

McCain would later write in his memoir that the night he won the New Hampshire primary "was probably the most intoxicating moment of my political career."

Humiliated, Bush and his inner circle of stunned aides retreated to Texas to "retool," his word for what would happen next. With the unexpected loss, his usually high-flying, button-down campaign faced angry questions from its biggest donors about everything from political strategy to spending. One frustrated Bush Pioneer who had raised more than $100,000 for the campaign told the *Washington Post* what he had privately told campaign officials: "We've raised you $70 million. Why have you spent $50 million through the end of January to win 31 delegates?" The rattled campaign, the *Post* reported, "deputized some of its leading money men to reassure the finance troops."

Meanwhile, just hours after Bush's defeat, at a Republican National Committee "Team 100" meeting in Florida of soft-money donors who had each given at least $100,000 to the party, cochair Julie Finley reportedly told those assembled that if McCain were to win the GOP nomination and get his way with campaign finance reform and a ban on soft money, "We're out of business."

When the Center for Public Integrity asked her three years later to expand on those remarks, Finley told us, "If [McCain] had been the nominee because of his [reform] position with regard to soft money, or non-federal money rather, it would have been difficult for us to raise non-federal money because my assumption was he would not attend events that were for the purpose of raising non-federal money." She emphasized that she and her Republican Party colleagues "were neutral. Those of us who were running RNC programs were neutral. We did not solicit for any candidate." That, of course, would have been illegal. But the implicit message to major party donors couldn't be clearer, especially since roughly 80 percent of the Team 100 members were supporting Bush, according to RNC finance chairman Mel Sembler.

McCain quietly understood the darker implications of his victory and the powerful forces he had just unleashed. He wrote in his memoir: "I had won [in New Hampshire] by running against the Republican establishment and against Republican orthodoxy on issues from campaign finance reform to tax cuts. . . . Party leaders and loyalists weren't about to turn on a dime and embrace my candidacy and positions just because I had landed one good punch in a twelve-round fight. They were going to help George fight like hell in South Carolina, and the worse the beating I got, the happier they would be."

His worst fears were confirmed. Two and a half weeks later, McCain got clobbered, losing to Bush 53 to 42 percent. Even though he later won primaries in Michigan and his home state of Arizona, his national momentum hit a brick wall on that fateful South Carolina night of February 19. Most stunning, though, were the exit poll results. A majority of Republican voters told pollsters that George W. Bush was the "real reformer," not McCain.

The Bush Team Goes Offensive

How had the Bush campaign reversed attitudes and perceptions so quickly, creating "a perfect storm" that capsized McCain's momentum in just 19 days?

Just after the New Hampshire debacle, back in Texas, Bush aide Karen Hughes had recalled the governor's successful 1994 and 1998 state campaigns as a "reformer" there on such issues as crime, education, taxes, and tort reform. She suggested to Bush's chief political strategist Karl Rove—frustrated and publicly embarrassed by his own underestimation of McCain in

New Hampshire—and to Bush himself, that, in order to counter the McCain momentum, they immediately needed to change Bush's campaign message to the "reformer with results." They all agreed. Although campaign finance reform was a subject about which Bush historically had had political laryngitis—in fact, prior to the presidential campaign, as far as we can tell, he had *never* made a single political reform speech or proposal as governor of Texas—after his humiliating New Hampshire loss, Bush miraculously found the subject and his voice in South Carolina. The campaign pounded in this theme over and over again, via hundreds of saturation radio and TV ads and in the candidate's speeches, accompanied by new slogan banners.

At the same time, this "reformer with results" was aggressively shaking the law and lobbying firm money trees in our nation's capital, sending out fundraising memos to "Association Executives for Bush," and seeking help from major corporate lobbyist Pioneers Haley Barbour and Wayne Berman, former House members Tom Loeffler and Bill Paxon, and others. Bush also ran attack ads in South Carolina labeling McCain a Washington insider and hypocrite. It was true, as we noted earlier, that McCain was no stranger to Washington. But neither was Bush. In fact, throughout 1999, Bush's presidential campaign took in at least $526,600 from employees of Washington lobbying firms, while McCain netted $116,675, according to the Center for Responsive Politics, a nonprofit research organization.

As McCain's campaign manager Rick Davis told us, after Bush "had announced that he was the 'reformer with results,' then on the day of one of our debates, he actually released his own campaign finance plan. We were really struck by that. Because basically, he had been [going] around talking about how nobody cared about campaign finance, he wasn't for that and he thought it would hurt the parties and all of these kinds of things. Then, on the day of the debate, he releases a five- or six-page campaign finance plan that didn't do a whole lot." (His plan did not end, for example, the large six- and seven-figure soft-money checks to the political parties.) The whole turn-around, Davis said, "was really amazing to us."

But according to Furman University political scientist Danielle Vinson, who has studied the primary campaign very closely, the actual truth about the "real" reformer never penetrated the South Carolina voter consciousness. While reporters were skeptical of Bush's new "reformer with results" message, she said, the "problem was that they didn't question it in the press. They just didn't report that he was saying that he was a reformer with results. But all of his mailings were hammering on that and hammering on that. And so there was really no one to refute that other than McCain. And I don't think he really picked up on it very quickly."

> Throughout 1999, Bush's presidential campaign took in at least $526,600 from employees of Washington lobbying firms, while McCain netted $116,675.

That may be at least partly because McCain was distracted and on the defensive. Most remarkable to the Arizona senator and his aides was the vicious personal turn the presidential campaign took in South Carolina. Both candidates went negative, criticizing each other in ads. "We found ourselves in quite a dog fight," McCain's campaign manager told us. "I have been doing this since 1976, and it was the worst barrage of negativism that I have ever seen in a campaign. And it was immediate."

In fact, a bizarre array of single-issue groups appeared out of nowhere, angrily trashing McCain. Besides facing the best-funded presidential candidate in U.S. history with at least a 5-to-1 cash advantage, McCain also found himself up against aggressive statewide campaigns criticizing him daily, using e-mails, faxes, phone calls, mail, newspaper ads, and radio and TV commercials. The groups assailing McCain included the National Right to Life Committee, the South Carolina Citizens for Life, the Christian Coalition, the Keep It Flying political action committee dedicated to preserving the Confederate flag, the National Smokers Alliance, the National Rifle Association, Americans for Tax Reform, the English Language PAC, and several anti-immigration groups.

Political scientists William Moore and Danielle Vinson, who have meticulously analyzed the South Carolina primary, replayed every campaign and outside-group ad that hit the airwaves, and collected every known communication via the U.S. mail, e-mail, fax, and telephone, have concluded that "virtually all" of the issue advocacy campaigns waged by interest groups in the primary "attacked John McCain."

Bush advisor Rove had earlier enlisted Ralph Reed, the former executive director of the Christian Coalition and a corporate lobbyist, to galvanize the religious right on Bush's behalf. To avoid the glare of publicity an association with the controversial Reed might cause, Rove reportedly asked Enron before its meltdown to quietly put Reed on *its* payroll while he was assisting the Bush campaign. Reed denied a *New York Times* story of being hired by the Houston firm to campaign for Bush in a Rove-Enron Texas two-step. But his involvement and role in South Carolina was undeniable. Century Strategies, Reed's Atlanta-based lobbying and consulting firm, contacted hundreds of thousands of Christian conservatives in the state with negative mailings and phone calls: "[McCain] claims he's conservative, but he's pushed for higher taxes and waffled on protecting innocent human life."

In the South Carolina primary, the Christian Coalition is believed to have targeted 140,000 voters, sending a card in the mail two days before the primary entitled "10 Disturbing Facts About John McCain," which, among other things, noted that McCain was the sole Republican candidate "who sought and received the endorsement of the Log Cabin Republicans, a pro–homosexual rights group." The Bush campaign disseminated a recorded phone message in South Carolina from Ralph Reed's former boss, televangelist Pat Robertson of the Christian Coalition, who separately on television made a dark, mysterious reference to "some of those other things that are in John McCain's background."

But it wasn't just the Christian Coalition and anti-abortion groups going after McCain, although they may have been the most effective. A Baptist church in Kansas faxed a flyer decrying McCain's "Fag Army" to South Carolina radio stations. On primary election night, several individuals called radio talk shows saying that a group of psychiatrists had come to the conclusion that the Vietnamese had brainwashed former prisoner of war McCain and programmed him to destroy the Republican Party.

No one will ever know how many millions of dollars were spent in the South Carolina primary by Bush and those "independent" outside groups that helped him, as there is no federal law requirement to disclose their spending. McCain was restricted under federal election laws to direct campaign expenditures in South Carolina of $1.5 million; counting media ad buys in neighboring states that reached South Carolina voters, he probably spent roughly $3 million. He believes Bush and all of the forces aligned with him together may have spent as much as $20 million.

What particularly irked McCain, though, were the personal slurs and subterfuge. During his interview with the Center for Public Integrity, McCain talked about "the under-the-radar campaign. . . . The thousands of phone calls, 'Do you know the McCains have a Black baby? Do you know that Cindy McCain is a drug addict?' But it was hundreds of thousands of calls. I knew people who got four or five calls that said that. So, you know, I mean, it was an unprecedented amount of money, and we, I could feel in the last four or five days of the campaign, I could feel the air going out of the balloon."

McCain recalled one galling incident in which Richard Hand, a professor at Bob Jones University, sent out an e-mail slurring McCain. CNN reporter Jonathan Karl managed to obtain a copy and then interview its author. "You probably remember this story," McCain said. " 'Professor, you are sending out e-mails saying that John McCain has fathered illegitimate children.' 'Yes.' 'Well, what proof do you have that Senator John McCain fathered illegitimate children?' Answer: 'It's up to John McCain to prove that he *didn't* father illegitimate children.' That was on CNN. It was a CNN interview!"

The Center contacted Professor Hand, who refused to provide the e-mail, but in a conversation in which he wanted to know our personal religious beliefs and who we voted for in the 2000 election, he acknowledged writing the offensive missive. "It's done, it was a disaster. I am very sad, I am sad for any possible misunderstandings. . . . I didn't wish the limelight in the first place." However, he is unrepentant about his assertion that McCain fathered children out of wedlock and simply doesn't understand why the comment might be so objectionable. After all, he said, "Having a child in the secular world out of wedlock is not a damaging comment."

During the South Carolina primary, the ad hominem undercurrent began to eat away at McCain. Just moments before the South Carolina debate, as the two men were standing together uncomfortably, McCain confronted Bush about the onslaught of negative slurs. As authors James Moore and Wayne Slater reported, McCain said to Bush, shaking his head disapprovingly, "George."

Bush replied, "John. It's politics."

McCain retorted, "George, everything isn't politics." Later, during a commercial break, after McCain complained about the vicious, unfair mail and phone campaign by Bush's supporters against him, Bush proclaimed his innocence. The Texas governor "reached over to grasp his rival's hand and said the two should put their acrimony behind them."

"Don't give me that shit," McCain said, pulling away. "And take your hands off me." McCain's public persona to voters in South Carolina began to fray, reflecting his bitterness over the smears. "I responded by getting angry in my stump speeches and running negative ads about my opponent that only raised the toxic level of the primary," he wrote in his memoir. "There wasn't a damn thing I could do about the subterranean assaults on my reputation except to act in a way that contradicted their libel." But that, too, became unsatisfactory to him as a strategy. At one point—against the advice of his senior staff, who worried about allowing the savagery to go unanswered—McCain halted all of his negative campaign ads in an unsuccessful attempt to change the downward dynamic of the primary battle.

In the meantime, Bush let the outside groups do the dirty work against McCain and assumed a more positive, above-the-fray posture. Perhaps the most bitter irony for McCain is that South Carolina primary voters in exit polling felt McCain had been the most negative campaigner, not Bush.

John Weaver of the McCain campaign told political scientist David Magleby that he had "never seen a more negative environment" than the 2000 South Carolina primary. Trey Walker, another McCain campaign consultant, has termed what happened to McCain in South Carolina as "a jailhouse rape." McCain's deputy campaign manager Roy Fletcher said at a National Press Club forum months later, "I've never seen anything like it and I come from Louisiana."

"History will make the judgment," McCain told us. "Americans do not like sore losers. And for me to look back with anger, bitterness, and complaints, it is neither appropriate, nor, frankly, in keeping with the incredible experience. How many Americans get the chance to run for president of the United States?"

Karl Rove, Bush's political strategist; Karen Hughes, his now former White House aide; and Joe Allbaugh, the manager of his national presidential campaign who also ran the Bush campaign in South Carolina, all declined to answer our questions about what exactly happened in that fateful primary. (After serving under Bush as director of the Federal Emergency Management Agency, Allbaugh is now a highly paid Washington lobbyist, chairman of New Bridge Strategies, LLC, "a unique company that was created specifically with the aim of assisting clients to evaluate and take advantage of business opportunities in the Middle East following the conclusion of the U.S.-led war in Iraq.")

It strains credulity for most people to imagine that the many, disparate, conservative, Republican-leaning interest groups active in South Carolina against McCain did not coordinate their efforts or communicate in some way with the Bush campaign. Of course, in the 28-year history of the Federal Election Commission, there has been only one successful case brought against a campaign for coordinating "independent" expenditures.

Wayne Slater, the bureau chief of the *Dallas Morning News* in Austin who has followed the careers of George W. Bush and Karl Rove from their political beginnings in Texas, says that McCain's bushwhacking in South Carolina was the all-too-familiar handiwork of Rove. The negative "push polls" in South Carolina were similar to a "survey" Rove—simultaneously working for Philip Morris while also a political consultant to Governor Bush—had engineered back in Texas years ago to derail Attorney General Dan Morales in the tobacco litigation. The mysterious phone calls spreading innuendo were similar to what happened to Governor Ann Richards, defeated by Bush in 1994. And at the University of Texas, Rove actually *taught* negative campaigning, including the strategic advantages of "narrowcasting" to small constituencies under the larger public radar, using radio, mail, and phone calling almost immune from media coverage.

> **Both parties have learned that slashing campaigns by candidates and interest groups are immensely effective and can stop an opponent's momentum cold, with little accountability.**

What happened in South Carolina has larger implications beyond the 2000 election, of course. Outside groups and both parties have learned that slashing campaigns by candidates and interest groups are immensely effective and can stop an opponent's momentum cold, with little accountability. According to campaign finance experts David Magleby and J. Quin Monson in their nationwide study of this phenomenon, in 1998 and 2000, interest groups generated more direct mail, print and radio ads, and phone banks than the political parties themselves. Trying to get information about these groups, which are known by their Internal Revenue Service statute as "527" organizations, is a problematic adventure for anyone.

BUYING INFLUENCE, WITH LITTLE OVERSIGHT

The Center for Public Integrity found last year that 527 committees spent more than $430 million over a three-year period to influence elections and policy debates across the country. These shadowy political organizations provide a convenient way around a recent federal ban on soft money—unlimited contributions to the political parties—because they remain almost totally free from fundraising restrictions while engaging in election-related activity, such as issue ads, voter drives, political research, and contributions to state and local candidates. Due to their unique legal status, 527 committees are not subject to regulation by state elections officials or the Federal Election Commission, and may accept unlimited contributions from nearly any source—companies, labor unions, and single-interest groups. No group raised more cash than the American Federation of State, County and Municipal Employees, a labor union representing state and local government workers, which took in almost $36 million over three years. They are required to report their contributors and finances to the Internal Revenue Service.

The larger implications of these groups and their constitutionally permissible mischief are troubling. Their multimillion-dollar hyperactivity in election campaigns obfuscates the responsibility a candidate has for his own campaign, giving him or her "deniability" about the dirty politics being waged. Could that many conservative groups coincidentally, in unison, jump on one conservative candidate? In South Carolina and throughout the entire 2000 presidential election, did George W. Bush personally know that his political strategist might be aggressively engaging in character assassination in cahoots with party-faithful allies? Maybe the question should be, How could he *not* know? After McCain's angry exchange with Bush at the South Carolina primary debate, did the Texas governor go back to Rove and his staff and demand, "What the hell is going on here? This is unacceptable!" We don't know that either, but, for various reasons, that reassuring scenario seems implausible. Neither Bush nor Rove has ever acknowledged any responsibility for what happened there, and no "smoking gun" proof has ever been found directly implicating them, not that anyone is investigating.

Is there any *practical* difference, in terms of initial political expediency, between the directed ugliness that rattled McCain in South Carolina in 2000 and the "dirty tricks" in the 1972 presidential election and Watergate scandal that derailed the candidacy of Democratic front-runner Edmund Muskie, who broke down and cried publicly one snowy day in New Hampshire because of the pernicious sabotage? Politically, both candidates were successfully removed by their opponents, albeit roughly. Unquestionably, in Muskie's case, the nefarious conduct was of much greater dimension—the attacks were conceived and orchestrated from inside the Nixon White House and involved everything from infiltrating his campaign staff with spies pilfering internal documents to planting phony letters to embarrass the candidate politically.

But is it possible, three decades later, that today's political campaign operatives in both parties are merely more shrewd and careful? Especially now that they can discreetly encourage third-party "cutout" allies, who are well funded and more than willing to publicly skewer a perceived foe? If Watergate taught them anything, it was, most of all, not to leave any fingerprints. Best of all for the campaign, these groups slur and slash personal reputations in full public view, conveniently allowing the candidate to feign ignorance and assume a more dignified posture of civility and decorum.

We do know that Karl Rove reportedly organized conferences for young Republicans in 1973 on how to do campaign dirty tricks, and he was influenced and impressed by his friend and party consultant colleague, the late Lee Atwater, former president Bush's chief political strategist who was infamous for his ruthless, hardball tactics. Atwater, on his deathbed in 1991 after a public struggle with brain cancer, personally lamented his "reputation as a fierce and ugly campaigner . . . while I didn't invent negative politics, I am one of its most ardent practitioners."

Regarding the 1988 presidential election, he said in a *Life*

magazine article that, "In part because of our successful manipu-
lation of his campaign themes, George Bush won handily." Atwater apologized to Michael S. Dukakis for the "naked cruelty" of a
remark he had once made during the 1988 presidential campaign,
in which he said he "would strip the bark off the little bastard" and
"make Willie Horton his running mate." Horton, who is African
American, raped a White woman and stabbed her husband while
on a weekend furlough from a Massachusetts prison at the time
Dukakis was governor. Supporters of the Bush campaign, in an
infamous commercial, linked Dukakis to Horton and portrayed
him as soft on crime. Former president Bush never publicly apologized for that ad or for Atwater's vicious tactics.

Another mysterious mugging similar to McCain's in South
Carolina occurred in Georgia two years later to incumbent
Democratic senator Max Cleland, who lost his 2002 bid for
reelection amidst another vile personal campaign that also
involved "independent" outside groups entering the fray to
smear him. The slander was, Senator McCain told us, "run by
the same people, Ralph Reed. . . . The same outfit, the same
organizations, and I will never, ever get over them running a
picture of Max Cleland, Saddam Hussein, and Osama Bin
Laden, [this about] a man who left three limbs on the battlefield
in Vietnam. That's just something I will never get over."

Cleland, still seething nine months after his defeat following
the most outrageous commercial in the 2002 election, told the
Washington Post, "That was the biggest lie in America—to put me
up there with Osama bin Laden and Saddam Hussein and say I
voted against homeland security! I volunteered 35 years ago to
go to Vietnam and the guy I was running against got out of going
to Vietnam with a trick knee! I was an author of the homeland
security bill, for goodness sake!"

For John McCain, beyond the brutal 2000 South Carolina

primary, the insults and indignities continued. In New York, he faced more negative ads both from the Bush campaign and from yet another mysterious group close to the Texas governor. Earlier in February, the Republican Party bosses in New York, firmly behind Bush, had attempted unsuccessfully to prevent McCain from getting on the state GOP primary ballot. In protest, McCain staged a news conference in front of the Russian embassy and excoriated the "Stalinist politics" of the New York Republican Party. He separately went to federal court, and ultimately a judge allowed him to compete against Bush.

> **In New York, John McCain faced more negative ads both from the Bush campaign and from yet another mysterious group close to the Texas governor.**

In New York, the Bush campaign aired a political commercial that inaccurately warned voters that McCain had opposed federal funding for breast cancer research, which the *Buffalo News*, among other publications, denounced as "a particularly ugly smear." Even Bush himself later admitted as much. According to a *Washington Post* article in March 2000, "When asked if he personally believed that his opponent opposed breast cancer research, Governor Bush replied, 'No, I don't believe that.'"

But what drew most public criticism and discussion were the ads run by another outside hit-and-run group no one had ever heard of, a 527 organization called Republicans for Clean Air. Essentially existing only on paper, it consisted, basically, of two brothers who at the time were Bush's ninth most generous career patrons, sponsoring his political campaigns to the tune of $222,773 through mid-1999. Charles Wyly, a Bush Pioneer, and his brother Sam, had moved $2.5 million through Republicans for Clean Air, producing misleading ads about McCain's environmental record. While the Arizona senator will never be mistaken for Rachel Carson, Bush in the 2000 election had earned the disdain of virtually all of the nation's environmental groups. They saw him as a former oil man who as governor had done very little to improve standards in Texas, the state with the worst air pollution in the nation. Once again an outside stealth group, this time with barely a fig leaf of pretense regarding independence, was spending significant cash to diminish Bush's political opponent; once again the actual truth was obscured from voters.

Outside groups have been proliferating and spending more and more lavishly in American politics. According to the University of Pennsylvania Annenberg Public Policy Center, in 1995–1996 more than two dozen groups—political parties, labor unions, trade associations, business and ideological organizations—spent between $135 million and $150 million on issue advocacy ads. By the 2000 election cycle, there were at least 130 groups sponsoring 1,100 unique issue advocacy ads, at a cost of more than $500 million.

When Bush was confronted with the subterfuge on the CBS news program *Face the Nation*, and essentially given a chance to publicly repudiate the delusive ads, he instead punted, replying, "People have the right to run ads. They have the right to do what they want to do, under the, under the First Amendment in America." Does anyone doubt that the Wyly brothers would have pulled their Big Apple ads in a minute if Governor Bush had asked? More to the point, New York was the last important primary state, the Wyly coyotes had howled longer and louder than almost anyone for Governor Bush, and $2.5 million for political ads is serious money, even for millionaires. To suggest that the Wylys were disinterestedly trying to inform the public of John McCain's record strains credulity.

McCain, of course, lost his bid for the Republican presidential nomination in 2000 and Bush became the forty-third President of the United States. But in Washington McCain kept pushing the campaign finance legislation he and Feingold had been advocating for years. With the aid of the Enron, WorldCom, and other scandals, the Bipartisan Campaign Reform Act of 2002 was passed by both houses of Congress and signed into law by George W. Bush on March 27. The new law most notably bans unlimited donations to national political parties, those six- and seven-figure checks known as "soft money." In the 1999–2000 cycle, the two major parties raised about $500 million from corporations, labor unions, and wealthy individuals, double the amount raised four years earlier.

BCRA is the most significant change in the nation's campaign finance laws since the Federal Election Campaign Act was dramatically signed into law in 1974 by President Gerald Ford just weeks after the Watergate scandal had culminated in the resignation of Richard Nixon. "The times," Ford said, "demand this legislation." The new law created the Federal Election Commission, set campaign contribution and expenditure disclosure requirements, and specified limits on what individuals, political action committees, and party committees could give to federal campaigns.

Contrast that historic moment with the signing into law of the Bipartisan Campaign Reform Act of 2002. There was no White House ceremony and no speech by the president; instead, a White House spokeswoman told curious reporters that "the manner in which the president signed the campaign finance reform into law was consistent with his views on the legislation." John McCain, who had pushed the bill for seven long years, got a call at home from a White House underling notifying him that the legislation had just officially become law. Once again, Bush and his aides had stuck it to the Arizona senator.

Bush promptly left the Oval Office that morning and flew off on Air Force One to Greenville, South Carolina, for a $1 million fundraising event, then on to Atlanta and Texas to raise more campaign cash. How fitting that he would give a speech that day to rich contributors at an exclusive fundraising event—in South Carolina no less—while remaining publicly silent on the subject of corruption, having signed into law the first significant political reform legislation since the Watergate reforms a quarter of a century earlier. Although the White House quietly issued a written statement about the signing, there would be no sound bites from Bush that night on the network evening news on this subject.

Within weeks, the Republican National Committee became one of approximately 80 special interests suing in federal court to have the new law declared unconstitutional, on the grounds that it violates free speech. Everyone knows that the president, any president, is traditionally the real head of his national political party, controlling all its major decisions and initiatives from 1600 Pennsylvania Avenue. So the commander in chief reluctantly signed reform legislation clearly holding his proverbial nose, and almost at the same time authorized his national political party to attempt to nullify it legally. How many informed Americans know that the President's political party tried to nuke legislation he had actually just signed into law?

Leading the legal efforts to kill the McCain-Feingold legislation are Senator Mitch McConnell, Republican of Kentucky, the National Rifle Association, the American Civil Liberties Union, the AFL-CIO, the Chamber of Commerce, and many more. Leading counsel against the new law are former Clinton prosecutor Kenneth Starr and well-known First Amendment attorney Floyd Abrams. Meanwhile, the Democratic National Committee chose not to file a lawsuit lest Americans think it opposes cleaning up politics; instead it quietly authorized its general counsel in Washington, Joe Sandler, to represent the

California Democratic Party in its lawsuit filed together with the California Republican Party.

Within days of Bush signing the McCain-Feingold legislation on March 27, 2002, a phalanx of party lawyers and Washington lobbyists began successful efforts to eviscerate the new law at the Federal Election Commission. The FEC issued a 300-page rule-making document on how the new law would be implemented, weakening the ban on political party use of soft-money contributions.

> **How many informed Americans know that the president's political party tried to nuke legislation he had actually just signed into law?**

McCain was apoplectic that an unelected body would have the audacity to ignore and undermine a landmark law that had been debated and discussed for seven long years. "My beef with President Bush and the administration is not that he didn't have a bill signing—I could care less," he told us. "But I am deeply disturbed about the appointment of Mr. Toner, Mr. Mason, and Mr. Smith [as FEC Commissioners], who are outspoken opponents to any kind of reform and have therefore issued regulations which contradict both the intent and the letter of the law in the most corrupt fashion that I've ever observed." McCain, Feingold, and other reformers in Congress, not surprisingly, now have their sights set on a major overhaul of the FEC.

The McCain saga since early 2000 is instructive in what it reveals about the state of our democracy today. From being mugged in South Carolina to having his pockets picked back in Washington—his greatest legislative achievement as a U.S. senator snatched away by lawyers, lobbyists, and bureaucrats—John McCain has new scar tissue reminding him that the *real* powers that be are not on any ballot. They are accountable to no one. Recall Churchill's quote about war and politics that began this Introduction. McCain once almost died in a North Vietnamese prison, but in politics, he has been stabbed over and over.

What has happened to American politics? Not only is the money and the power behind it out of control, but there seems to be an increasing, vulgar coarseness to political discourse and public life even as "spin" and other manipulations of truth have become more subtle and sophisticated. This at a time when the very basics of democracy seem to be in trouble.

Roughly half the voting-age population, 100 million Americans, routinely do *not* participate at the polls. Nearly 40 percent of state legislative races have no opponents at all. The incumbent class of Congress has become ever more entrenched and arrogant. Only *19 of 469* people lost their reelection bids to the House and Senate in 2002, and half of them were members running against other members because of census redistricting; 90 percent of the races in the House did not even have significant competition.

To try to put it all in a broader perspective, we spoke with former president and recent Nobel Peace Prize laureate Jimmy Carter, who with his Carter Center has helped monitor and oversee democratic elections in 40 countries around the world.

"Our democracy will survive," Carter said. "We have a fine country and a fine system of government, there's no question about that. But there are incumbent major politicians in both parties that are in office because of a certain constituency with which they are knowledgeable and with which they have a good relationship. Otherwise they would not have won in the last election. . . . I think now the entire election process, including the nomination of candidates, is predicated to a major degree on how much money they can raise. And that involves appealing, in most cases, to special-interest groups who hope they can get a favor after the election is over."

Despite the McCain-Feingold legislation, which he supported, Carter said that "We've not made any real progress on the extremely distorting effect of high finance being requisite for any successful candidate. If you look at the list of candidates now who are prominently mentioned for president, almost all of them who have any chance at all are millionaires or multimillionaires. And this is not an accident. An average person like I was, just a peanut farmer back in 1976, you know, we won with practically no money because we campaigned all over the country and built up a grassroots organization. . . . It was very difficult for us to qualify with the $250 per person, 20 contributions in each state, and 20 states, to get matching funds. That was very difficult for me, and it was my middle son, Chip, who personally went to the states and begged people for those contributions that finally let us qualify. And [when] we hit the general election, we depended almost exclusively on the fund derived from the income tax check-off to run our campaign. . . .

"I think nowadays that would be absolutely impossible, which means that there's a criterion for success in American politics now—the Democratic or Republican Party—and that is extreme wealth or access to major wealth. And we are the only democratic nation in the world, in the western world, within which that blight or cancer is affecting our system."

Former presidents Carter and Gerald Ford chaired a bipartisan Election Reform Commission after the controversial 2000 election, which made numerous specific recommendations to Congress. Carter told us that "85 or 90 percent" of the commission's proposals for improvement were implemented, "which is very gratifying to me. . . . I don't think there is any doubt that some progress was made. . . . There will be steps forward and ultimately in uniformity of voter lists and registration, hopefully improvements in voting techniques." However, he also expressed disappointment that there still will not be a single voting system for the nation, and with thousands of counties, "each county in the past has had the authority to set up its voting technique and educate its people and to decide on the registration process, and so forth. It's not possible to educate politically ignorant people about the electoral process and how to mark a ballot and the issues involved if there's a wide diversity of voting machines or voting techniques or ballots."

To compound his frustration, "although President Bush pledged personally to me and President Ford that it would be completely financed, the amount of money that he requested in his upcoming budget is roughly one-third of what the legislation requires."

That is a worrisome concern, especially recalling that in the 2000 presidential election, we were unable to complete an election. Fidel Castro's Cuba offered to send "democracy educators" to help South Floridians conduct free and fair elections. A spokesman for corrupt Zimbabwe despot Robert Mugabe joked to reporters, "Maybe Africans and others should send observers to help Americans deal with their democracy."

What does our respected ex-president, who has monitored elections and democratic processes globally now for two decades, think about the Florida debacle?

While Carter believes there may have been "some deliberate efforts in some counties" to minimize the Black, almost always Democratic, vote, he said, "I can't look into the mind of the voting officials, but there was certainly no real effort made to assure that there was uniform opportunity regardless of economic status or race or ethnic background in the access to a fair and equitable voting procedure that would minimize errors and ensure accuracy in the vote count. People were deprived of their basic American rights as citizens to cast their ballots in a knowledgeable fashion and have assurance that their ballots would be counted accurately."

In our next chapter, we will try to better understand how exactly that happened, in the United States of America in the twenty-first century.

Equal Rights, Unequal Protection

Apostle Willie David Whiting walked into his usual polling place, the John Wesley United Methodist Church in Tallahassee, Florida, on Election Day, November 7, 2000, with his wife, son, and daughter.

Although Whiting was the head of another place of worship, the House of Prayer Church, he lived nearby and had voted at United Methodist many times in the past. According to county records, Whiting had been registered since 1992 and voted in 10 elections, including the preceding one.

After introducing himself to the polling clerk, the minister was startled when he was told that his "name was not in the record book," he said under oath before the U.S. Commission on Civil Rights two months later. Another polling clerk "then checked her master book, and she didn't find my name either, so she became concerned." She called the Leon County courthouse to check the voter registration records there, and the supervisor on the telephone asked to speak to Whiting directly.

Pastor Whiting was about to get the shock of his life.

"We have you listed as a convicted felon," the local elections official told him. "You have been purged from our system. You've lost all your civil rights."

Whiting had never been arrested or convicted of anything in his life and was astonished by what he heard. But he refused to be intimidated. "I asked him if I needed a lawyer. He said, 'Well, let me check further.' He went away from the phone and after a few minutes, he came back to the phone and said there's been a mistake. There is a Willie J. Whiting, born July 27, 1950, two days after I was, middle initial is 'J.'

"I said, 'Well, do we have the same social security number?' Couldn't answer that. 'Do we have the same driver's license number?' He then asked to speak back to the polling clerk again, and he gave her a number that she could give to me or give me a card to proceed to vote. So I did vote that night, but I was purged from the system."

Whiting had not received any prior notification, in the mail or otherwise, that his name had been stricken from the eligible voters list. When asked by one of the commissioners, "How did you feel when you were told that . . . you were a convicted felon and you no longer have your civil rights?" Whiting paused for a moment and then said, "Well, I reflected upon African American history, every last bit of it. So it didn't feel good. I was sling-shotted into slavery, that's how I felt. I thought of all the things that had happened to African Americans that I knew about. . . ."

Compounding Whiting's personal humiliation that day was the presence of his wife and children—and other people at the polling church—who'd observed the spectacle. "When you're approached like that, you know, you're taken aback, I mean you're taken. . . . My family didn't want to vote because they were not going to allow me to vote. But I encouraged them to go ahead and vote."

Whiting was by no means alone. The Kafkaesque nightmare he lived through visited untold thousands throughout the state of

Florida that infamous election day, especially in African American areas that traditionally vote overwhelmingly Democratic. The 2000 Florida debacle is instructive because of what it reveals about power and money and influence—because it reminded us all of the myriad ways in which politics can be manipulated and abused to achieve desired ends. And because of the fundamental questions it raises: How are public resources allocated? To what end? And who, if anyone, is accountable when important public policy decisions go terribly, embarrassingly wrong? Florida spotlighted how badly the civic engine of democracy itself—elections and the fair, efficient, trustworthy counting of votes—has fallen into disrepair. What's more, Florida is by no means an aberration: inadequate public funding, petty partisan politics, and a fundamental lack of political accountability afflict the administering of local elections all across this nation.

A Felonious List of Errors

Florida is just one of eight states in the country that permanently disenfranchise convicted felons who have completed all of their sentencing requirements, and the only state to include such denial in its constitution. As a result of this ban, 31 percent of African American men in Florida today are prohibited from voting. As required by law, state Division of Elections officials sent a "felons list" prepared by a private, contracted company to 67 county supervisors of elections. According to a 2002 report by the Organization for Security and Cooperation in Europe's Office for Democratic Institutions and Human Rights, that list contained "the names of 3,000 to 4,000 people who should not have been included, either because they had never committed a felony or because their voting rights had been restored." Some people vehemently believe that number is much higher. For example, before its civil litigation against the state contractor was settled out of court, the National Association for the Advancement of Colored People and their coplaintiffs were planning to present expert-witness testimony that 70,000 of the 94,000 possible felon names sent to county supervisors were erroneous.

In Willie Whiting's Leon County, which has one of the state's highest percentages of Black and other minority voters, the supervisor of elections was given a list of nearly 700 names of convicted felons to purge from the voting rolls. But he could confirm that only 34 people were actual felons. Some county supervisors diligently checked and verified the felon list, and some didn't. Some supervisors found the list so unreliable they stopped using it. One of them was Madison County elections supervisor Linda Howell, who found *herself* on the state list, and got a letter informing her that as a felon, she would not be able to vote in the election; she, of course, had never committed a felony. No one will ever know exactly how many legitimately registered, eligible voters were turned away at polling places throughout the state.

If this were a Raymond Chandler murder mystery, the crime scene could not look more suspicious, with Republican fingerprints everywhere. A Republican state legislature passed the felon purge law, which was implemented by a Republican secretary of state who also happened to be a state campaign cochair for Bush—her Republican governor boss's brother, the Republican presidential nominee. The law required that the state award a felon purge contract to a private company, which, it turns out, had strong ties to the Republican Party. And it so happened that the names stricken from the voter rolls would have voted overwhelmingly Democratic.

Equally incriminating was how the state of Florida knew that the way it was administering the felon purge law was deliberately broad and might prevent innocent Floridians from voting. George Bruder, at the time a senior vice president of Database

Technologies Inc. (DBT; since bought by ChoicePoint), testified that the company advised Florida elections officials to use narrow database matching criteria in creating the voter purge lists; otherwise, the state risked the strong likelihood of too many incorrect, nonfelon names turning up. However, he said under oath, "the state dictated to us that they wanted to go broader, and we did it in the fashion that they requested." Other company officials echo Bruder's testimony. In an interview with the Center for Public Integrity, company vice president James E. Lee said that DBT had told Florida officials "on any number of occasions" that "if you do [a broad data search], that this is going to be the result, meaning there would be more false positives, or people who weren't the real person you are looking for—their name would appear. . . . At the end of the day, it was [the state's] decision."

> **In Florida, some county supervisors diligently checked and verified the felon list, some didn't, and some supervisors found the list so unreliable they stopped using it.**

It gets worse. Training county supervisors on the central voter file and felon purge lists was not a priority, to put it charitably, and in April 2000, state Division of Elections officials notified DBT in an e-mail that they were "swamped with work" and that training workshops throughout the state were not "really necessary."

After hearing sworn testimony from more than 100 witnesses in public proceedings and reviewing more than 118,000 pages of documents in the only formal public investigation into what happened in Florida, the U.S. Commission on Civil Rights, which at the time was made up of six Democrats and two Republicans, concluded that African American voters were disproportionately "placed on purge lists more often and more erroneously than Hispanic or White voters." In Miami-Dade County, for example, more than 65 percent of the names on the purge list were African Americans, "who represented only 20.4 percent of the population."

Beyond the "felon follies," as one Florida newspaper described the infamously inept voter list scrubbing operation, the commission found that Blacks cast about 54 percent of the 180,000 spoiled (uncounted) ballots in Florida—even though they represented only about 11 percent of the state's voters. In an extensive statistical analysis of the Florida vote, the *New York Times* found that Black precincts had more than three times as many rejected ballots as White precincts, regardless of "whether the precinct used punch cards or paper ballots, whether the neighborhoods were rich or poor or the ballot was straight or butterflied." A political scientist asked by the *Times* to review its study, Philip Klinkner of Hamilton College, said, "It raises the issue about whether there's some way that the voting system is set up that discriminates against Blacks. . . . It raises questions about how they administer elections—where they put the best voting machines, how many poll workers they put out, what kind of education is done."

Published just weeks after that immeasurable seismic jolt to the national psyche we all know simply as September 11, important investigative stories by the *Times* and other publications about the controversial Florida vote were largely lost in the din. Still, anyone who sifts through the rubble of the Florida recount— the millions of words written and broadcast, the 65 lawsuits filed, and the various pronouncements by politicians—is left with a distinctly hollow feeling almost impossible to articulate.

AN ABSENCE OF OUTRAGE—OR APOLOGY

The tragedy of thousands of citizens being disenfranchised—the vast majority of them Black—was barely acknowledged by the political powers that be. Despite the bitter, take-no-prisoners partisan milieu, despite the spate of lawsuits threatened and real, despite the embarrassment over the internationally observed calamity of incompetence, Florida officials never apologized to the nation, or to anyone for that matter. The party of Lincoln, the Great Emancipator himself, was noticeably silent. There was and remains a disturbing absence of outrage. Shouldn't all Americans in the twenty-first century, regardless of ideology or party affiliation, be deeply concerned, indeed, personally offended, that thousands of our fellow citizens in Florida—and more than a million people nationwide—tried but were unable to exercise their right to vote in our democracy? Not that anyone can measure these things, but isn't it an even more egregious effrontery when so many legally cast *Black* votes were not counted, as civic participation was denied yet again to an already aggrieved segment of the population, the descendants of slavery and apartheid?

Consider the perspective of John Lewis, one of the civil rights movement's most courageous heroes, who for years stood steadfastly at Martin Luther King Jr.'s side despite being arrested and brutally beaten more than 40 times in nonviolent protest marches and sit-ins, now in his ninth term as a Democratic congressman from Georgia. "Thousands of people—and a great majority of these people happened to be people of color, low-income people—were denied the right to participate in the election process," he told the Center for Public Integrity. "And, when you have that, it becomes the greatest threat to our democracy. For me personally, it was very, very sad. Just a few short years ago, especially in the American South, 11 states in the old Confederacy—from Virginia to Texas—we were fighting for the right to vote. And, we won that right with the passage of the Voting Rights Act of 1965. Then you turn around a few years later, and . . . that right is not being just abused, but that right has been denied."

Lewis was taken aback by the number of people in Florida in 2000 who had never been arrested or put in jail or even charged with a crime who found themselves stricken from the voting rolls. "I remember there was one young mother who brought her child to see her vote, a young child. And then she got there, and she was told that her name was on the [felon] list, that she couldn't vote. And she cried and the child cried, couldn't see the mother participate in the electoral process.

"I think in some parts of Florida, like in other parts of the country, it was a deliberate, systematic effort to discourage people from participating. . . . It was not Sheriff Clark standing in Selma, Alabama, at the courthouse, with his billy club and his electric [cattle prod]. But what they did was done in a much more sophisticated way. You use the power of the mail, and computers, and other ways to tell people that they are not registered or that they cannot vote because of some crime they've committed, when they have not committed a crime."

> "Thousands of people—and a great majority of these people happened to be people of color, low-income people—were denied the right to participate in the election process."

Lewis pointed out that some Americans have fought for the right to vote for more than two centuries. He notes that the impediments to their inclusion have run the full gamut, from forced slavery and no vote to poll taxes and literacy tests in which a well-educated Black voter with a Ph.D. degree would be denied ballot access because he supposedly did not provide the correct answer to the question, "How many bubbles are there in a bar of soap?"

"What was happening in Florida, it was not a poll tax, it was not a literacy test, but it was very similar."

Ironically, former Florida secretary of state Katherine Harris, one of the major players in the recount mess, is a newly elected Republican member of Congress in Washington and therefore a "colleague" of Lewis. "One day she spoke to me because she went to school in Atlanta . . . and we had a chat about Georgia. But we never, ever mentioned the election. . . . People got reelected, they got rewarded, but no one said to these [disenfranchised] citizens, 'We're sorry, we apologize.' No one apologized on behalf of the state of Florida, or any of those counties. . . . You know, we make apologies for less, you know, if we happen to bump against someone, or if we happen to step on somebody's toe, you say, 'I'm sorry, will you accept my apology?' And here, the whole electoral process was threatened, and no one said anything, or paid any price for it."

SILENCE AFTER THE STORM

Among those who had little to say was Jeb Bush, brother of the new president and chairman of his Florida campaign, who was elected to a second term as governor of Florida in 2002. During his sworn testimony before the Commission on Civil Rights, he said he had no authority or responsibility—and took no action—over the 2000 election in Florida, instead pointing to the secretary of state and the 67 county supervisors. Governor Bush did not recall any conversations with Katherine Harris or, for that matter, his brother, regarding state preparations for the fateful election.

Harris was similarly aloof when called before the commission. At one point, she said, "Although by statute, I am the chief elections official, please understand the Florida Constitution created the election system founded upon local control. . . . In most areas, including those dealing with the interplay among supervisors and the Division [of Elections], the Division's authority is best described as ministerial." But her actions could hardly be called "ministerial" when she dramatically stopped the manual recount in Palm Beach County at 5 P.M., slamming the door once and for all on a few thousand elderly Jewish Democrats who had inadvertently voted for their worst nightmare, the controversial third-party presidential candidate and occasional defender of accused Nazis, Pat Buchanan? They had fallen victim to the poorly designed, now infamous butterfly ballot.

The governor's and the secretary of state's claims of disinterest sometimes stretch credulity, but it is true, though often overlooked, that the entire state elections system was usually not closely controlled by Jeb Bush, Katherine Harris, or the Republicans. Indeed, fully two-thirds of the county elections supervisors in Florida in 2000 were Democrats, including Theresa LePore, the well-intentioned Palm Beach official who had designed the butterfly ballot to help vision-impaired voters.

The fact is, democracy's short-circuit in Florida occurred throughout the state, victimizing Democrats, Republicans, and independents alike. For example, when the national news media prematurely and incorrectly declared Gore the winner in Florida before the polls had even closed in the conservative western Panhandle, voter turnout was suppressed and many GOP voters, possibly thousands of them, stayed home. In their congressional testimony months later, the television network executives were unctuously insincere, delivering contrite apologies after prematurely announcing election returns in every recent presidential election. Of course, what the networks did on Election Night 2000, announcing a winner (more than once, incorrectly) before thousands of voters had cast their ballots, may have been television's lowest moment since the quiz show scandals of the late 1950s. Republicans were also justifiably angry over the aggressive campaign by Gore's lawyers during the recount ruckus to disqualify absentee ballots by overseas military personnel, successfully challenging and eliminating 1,420 absentee ballots cast—40 percent of the statewide total—because they were, say, missing postmarks (which is not unusual from naval vessels at sea). No one in the Bush camp was more incensed about this than former secretary of defense Dick Cheney. "I have strong feelings about the right of our people in uniform to vote—and they, perhaps, above all others," he said. "They're out there putting their lives on the line for us. For the other camp to pursue a conscious strategy to try to disqualify their ballots, I thought, was bad form."

Still, while the media's intrusive incompetence that election night and the Gore lawyers' cynical maneuvers after the election were indeed offensive and kept well-intentioned voters from voting, they resulted from mundane, even understandable, impulses. The media acted out of competitive, nonpartisan, disastrous inadvertence; the lawyers, from ex post facto party electioneering entirely predictable in a razor-close, bitterly fought national contest.

The same cannot be said of state of Florida election officials. Whether they acted from rank, callous incompetence or cold-blooded political calculation, they were accused of keeping thousands of Democratic voters from casting their legal ballots. When asked about it under oath, Harris could barely answer many of the commission's sharp questions and repeatedly consulted her Division of Elections director, Clay Roberts. She never apologized or acknowledged the wholesale disenfranchisement of thousands of eligible voters, although she did grudgingly concede that "I suppose mistakes occur." She specifically mentioned Willie Whiting's attempt to vote but was able to put a positive spin on it. Ultimately, she said, "He was able to vote."

Sure, Harris agreed, more money could have and should have been spent on voter education in Florida. "If there is any silver lining about what has happened," she said, "it certainly is first and foremost voter education. I mean, there's never been a more extensive voter education scenario in the history of our country than I think what we've just incurred in the last five weeks, an extraordinary lesson in civics."

Jeb Bush was equally sanguine in his testimony. Before the election, he told the commissioners, no one "came to me and said, Governor Bush, we're going to have a very close election and we're going to spend 45 days having the entire world look at us and you're going to be counting, you know, pregnant chads and indented chads—no one that I'm aware of came to me and said we have a serious problem we need to deal with in advance of this."

As the highest elected official and chief executive for the state of Florida, Jeb Bush showed few signs during his testimony of being curious about, apologetic for, or disconcerted by the disenfranchisement of thousands of voters. The Center for Public Integrity searched but found no speeches or testimony in which the governor publicly lamented the loss of ballot access for so many people. He did tell the chair of the commission, Mary Frances Berry, "I'm delighted that you're here to sort out any of the discrepancies that might exist, so that we can work together to build a world-class election system for Floridians that might be a model for the rest of the country." To his critics, such sunny-boy breeziness in the face of one of the most notorious election days in U.S. history seems incongruous, even disingenuous. For thousands of frustrated would-be voters, democracy hit an iceberg and sank to new depths on his watch, and instead of taking personal responsibility or investigating the titanic election catastrophe, the governor mostly talked about the next new ship.

As governor, Bush is empowered to appoint special officers to investigate alleged violations of the elections laws, under sec. 102.109(1) of the Florida statute. When asked if he had appointed anyone, Bush answered, "No, I haven't." When asked "Do you intend to appoint any?" he responded, "If there is a reason to do so, I will." The governor cited separate Department of Justice and state attorney general investigations, in addition to the U.S. Commission of Civil Rights investigation, as the reasons any other inquiries would be unnecessary. The latter inquiry, when completed, "found a strong basis" for concluding that violations of the historic Voting Rights Act had occurred, urging specific follow-up by federal and state authorities. The commission voted 6 to 2, with its two Republican appointees dissenting.

> **Whether they acted from rank, callous incompetence or cold-blooded political calculation, Florida election officials were accused of keeping thousands of Democratic voters from casting their legal ballots.**

Not surprisingly, the commission's report itself reflected the deep political fault lines that so defined every stage of the Florida voting fiasco. In their dissent, for example, the two Republican members were scathing in their accusations of partisanship. "The Commission's report has little basis in fact," wrote Commissioners Abigail Thernstrom and Russell G. Redenbaugh. "[Its] central finding—that there was 'widespread disenfranchisement and denial of voting rights' in Florida's 2000 presidential election—does not withstand even a cursory legal or scholarly scrutiny. . . . By basing its conclusion on allegations that seem driven by partisan interests and that lack factual basis, the majority on the Commission has needlessly fostered public distrust, alienation and manifest cynicism. . . . What appears to be partisan passions not only destroyed the credibility of the report itself, but informed the entire process that led up to the final draft."

Harris echoed that theme in a written response to questions from the Center for Public Integrity. She contested the majority report's findings, particularly the notion that Florida's election-day problems had a racial dimension, rather than being the result of a broken down voting system that is not unique to Florida. "The flaws in Florida's elections system that the historically close 2000 presidential election revealed—uncounted ballots due to under-votes and overvotes, polling places and machines that were inaccessible to persons with disabilities, too few resources dedicated to voter education—had existed throughout our nation for decades," she wrote. "Very few media reports have emphasized that these concerns were not unique to Florida."

Harris cited the dissent of the two Republican members of the commission. "The commissioners who voted against the U.S. Commission on Civil Rights majority report stated in their dissent that, based on their analysis of Miami-Dade County's use of the [Database Technologies Inc.] list, 'the error rate for Whites was almost double that for Blacks.'"

She added, "Most important in light of the U.S. Commission on Civil Rights's libelous charges of racism, the *Palm Beach Post* (based on its in-depth study) confirmed the fact that we have always made clear: that DBT Online *did not use race* to match names on the voter roles with felons."

NO ONE TO CLAIM RESPONSIBILITY

The U.S. Department of Justice Civil Rights Division received 11,000 complaints of election irregularities in Florida and filed three relatively minor complaints in Orange, Osceola, and Miami-Dade counties, but could find no specific or systematic pattern of discrimination. The Civil Rights Division would not comment on the status of any cases it had brought. The Florida attorney general similarly could find no one to prosecute. And the governor's Task Force on Election Procedures, Standards and Technology was not created to assess blame or investigate allegations of systemic voter fraud, but instead issued a report with 35 recommendations, including, most important, the establishment of a uniform voting system in Florida.

In 2001, the Florida legislature passed and Governor Bush signed into law election reform legislation that more than tripled state funding for the Division of Elections, from $5.9 million in 2000 to $21.6 million. From fiscal year 1992 through 2000, the average allotment for administering democracy in Florida was $4.5 million.

The cochair of the Task Force on Election Procedures, Jim Smith, has served as attorney general and secretary of state, first as a Democrat and later as a Republican. "There is no question that Florida had run their elections very much on the cheap," he told the Center. "There was never enough money for voter education or training. . . . The idea of local residents coming down to their polling places with lemonade and cookies to help out on Election Day—those days are over!"

But Smith took issue with critics who'd suggested that the huge number of voting irregularities in Florida that year could not be coincidental, calling such speculation "grossly unfair." Because of Florida's "extremely decentralized system of elections" and the antiquated punch-card system, among other reasons, Governor Bush and Secretary of State Katherine Harris simply could not have deliberately manipulated or otherwise encouraged the suppression of the heavily Democratic Black vote even if they had wanted to, he said.

Smith said the task force, the governor, and the legislature all have "gone a long way to clean up the process." Regarding the new law in Florida, he said that past disqualifying problems such as "overvoting" (voting for more than one candidate for an office) now cannot occur with the new, improved, technologically superior machines. Of course, he added, mistakes will occur in any election with millions of people voting in widely disparate parts of the state. "It will never be a perfect process," he said. In other words, inevitably there will be votes cast but not counted. When asked to explain why Black voters were substantially more likely to be rejected at the ballot box than Whites, Smith matter-of-factly noted that many minority voters are poor and have less education. It is well established that "less-educated voters are more likely to make mistakes" in voting, he said.

Not surprisingly, blaming the victims doesn't exactly go over well with Blacks, who see such explanations as condescending and bigoted. But if we look more closely at voter education for a moment, the facts are clear: Florida elections officials did little before the 2000 election. As Leon County elections supervisor Ion Sancho complained to the U.S. Commission on Civil Rights, "Voter education could have greatly reduced the number of errors made by voters on Election Day. On November 7th, that was the day the piper came to collect his due, because Florida, as a state, spends not one dollar on radio and TV ads informing voters how to vote. This in a state that in the past has spent over $35 million in one year telling Floridians how to play the lottery."

When the Governor's Task Force made its recommendations, the controversial felon list "scrubbing" problem was clearly not a priority—and it remains substantially unaddressed today in Florida. And while outsourcing the painstaking but crucially sensitive data work on voter backgrounds has fallen into disfavor—the Florida legislature terminated the contract and the company it retained has abandoned the voter purge business—neither state nor county election authorities have the time, expertise, or capacity to vet prospective voters.

Looking back, the U.S. Commission on Civil Rights makes one thing clear: "widespread voter disenfranchisement—not the dead-heat contest—was the extraordinary feature in the Florida election." The commission concluded that the "serious and not isolated" problems Florida experienced during the 2000 presidential election "resulted in an extraordinarily high and inexcusable level of disenfranchisement, with a significantly disproportionate impact on African American voters." What caused this "foreseeable" debacle? The commission cited six culprits: "(1) a general failure of leadership from those with responsibility for ensuring elections are properly planned and executed; (2) inadequate resources for voter education, training of poll workers and for Election Day trouble-shooting and problem solving; (3) inferior voting equipment and/or ballot design; (4) failure to anticipate and account for the expected high volumes of voters, including inexperienced voters; (5) a poorly designed and even more poorly executed purge system; and (6) a resource allocation system that often left poorer counties, which often were counties with the highest percentage of Black voters, adversely affected."

> It is well established that "less-educated voters are more likely to make mistakes" in voting, the cochair of the Task Force on Election Procedures said.

The governor's response to the commission's report was less than congenial. His office, via a letter by General Counsel Charles Canady, called the commission's report "biased and sloppy . . . riddled with baseless allegations, faulty reasoning and unsupported conclusions." His letter also challenged many of the commission's findings, including that nasty matter of the substantial disenfranchisement of minority voters, suggesting that the commission had not significantly enough taken into account several variables such as "the voter's education level, the voter's experience with voting, the ballot design and the voting machine used."

Once again, as he had throughout the time it took for the 2000 presidential election to be belatedly decided, the Florida governor refused to accept any personal responsibility for decisions his administration made that contributed to the voting irregularities. That's still true today. Former state senator Kendrick Meek, an African American Democrat whom voters elected to the U.S. House of Representatives in 2002, talked to the Civil Rights Commission about the exasperation he and many others feel. "If the house is on fire and the fire department is across the street and they're not pulling their trucks out, but they show up after there are ashes talking now about how we can correct this in the future, even though we saw it burning—that's what happened here in Florida," he said. "There's just some things that you know. And my house has been burned down many times without the water."

POLITICAL MACHINERY AND VOTING MACHINES

While Blacks and others continue to seethe over the embers of 2000, and the two major political parties remain bitterly divided, Florida today has fancy new touch-screen voting machines. Alas, even these are fraught with controversy. For one thing, the new machines leave no paper trail of the votes, making it impossible to do a recount. It's hard to detect any tampering; without exit polling few could tell whether an election was rigged. And because the equipment is so high-tech, the Division of Elections often does not use its own employees to fix the machines, in many cases turning instead to the supplier, a private company, to make repairs.

Equally problematic is the process by which the Florida counties chose the supplier. It seems that the Florida Association of Counties exclusively endorsed Election Systems & Software, one of the handful of companies vying for the multimillion-dollar contracts to replace the state's antiquated voting machinery with touch-screen equipment. ES&S, which has been responsible for about 56 percent of the U.S. national vote in each of the last four presidential and congressional elections, has strong ties to the GOP.

One such link is with Senator Chuck Hagel, a Republican from Nebraska who, according to the biography on his Senate Web site, was president of McCarthy & Company and chairman of the board of American Information Systems prior to his election. McCarthy & Company is a subsidiary of the McCarthy Group Inc., a private merchant banking company based in Omaha, which also owns ES&S, which was formed by a merger of American Information Systems and Business Records Corporation. On his financial disclosure form, Hagel lists assets worth between $1 million and $5 million in the McCarthy Group, which he describes as an "excepted investment fund," which exempts him from disclosing the details of the investment, though this designation has been questioned. He did not disclose the fact that one of the McCarthy Group's subsidiaries was ES&S—meaning that his stake did not show up on his financial disclosure form.

In Florida, ES&S got the nod from the Association of Counties and received orders totaling more than $70 million in taxpayer money from 12 counties, including Miami-Dade. But the Florida Association of Counties got something in return as well: The group received about $300,000 in commissions (a much more polite term than kickbacks) for all of those orders. The association was happy, ES&S was happy, and so was Sandra Mortham, the lobbyist who represented them both. Mortham was paid a commission for every county that purchased the company's machines. She told the Associated Press that her actions were proper. "All I did was present the company to the association," she said.

Sandra Mortham, it turns out, served as Florida's secretary of state just before Katherine Harris, but was forced off the GOP state ticket because of political scandal. It was Mortham—not Katherine Harris—who authorized the hiring of Database Technologies Inc. in 1998, the ill-fated company contracted by the state to scrub voting rolls of ineligible voters, including felons. Mortham would not talk with the Center for Public Integrity. But after the election spectacle of 2000 in Florida, it is unseemly that a fallen, besmirched political actor got to profit from her past public service in the name of improving the democratic process. Not surprisingly, no official government body in the state had a problem with the transactions.

PAYING FOR THE RECOUNT

The public still remains largely in the dark about how the two parties and their presidential candidates waged their 36-day war for the White House after Election Day, or who paid for it. Several books have been written about that extraordinary drama, most of them penned in the heat of the moment or soon afterward. One less examined issue from that wild period is that, after perhaps the most harrowing election night ever, after raising a combined $325 million in campaign contributions during the most expensive presidential election in history, George W. Bush and Al Gore would have to go back and tap donors for more money for the inevitable recount. Immediately both camps started raising contributions and within a week the contribution checks started tumbling in.

Along with the contributions came questions about disclosure. The Federal Election Commission, responsible for enforcing federal campaign contribution laws, has limited jurisdiction over recount committees. In this gray zone, the two parties can raise unlimited amounts of cash from almost any source. However, while these groups do not have to disclose their donors or expenditures to the FEC, many campaign finance analysts believe that they had an obligation to report such figures to the Internal Revenue Service through 527 laws.

Such 527 committees—so named because of the section of the Internal Revenue Code that regulates them—have to disclose their transactions and contributors to the IRS in periodic cycles that mirror the FEC's filing timetables. By reporting to the IRS, these political committees are, in essence, declaring themselves as nonprofit organizations and are thus exempt from taxes on their revenues.

As the lawyers and political operatives began descending upon Florida, television and print journalists clamored to cover the intricacies of the recount and demanded access to contribution and expenditure information. But with so many possible pots of money to draw from in the final days and minutes of the battle for the grandest political prize in the world, the possibilities for usable cash were almost endless. Bush and Gore had at their disposal not only their recount and presidential campaign committees, but also congressional leadership political action committees and state and federal party committees, not to mention the myriad of in-kind services provided by unions, companies, and other interested parties. How could anyone determine how much was spent and for what?

We'll never know. In fact, when we do get an occasional glimpse at the truth, it reminds us how little we actually know. Who can forget the initial national news media coverage of a "riot" that succeeded in temporarily halting the Miami-Dade recounts on November 22, 2000? Two weeks later, veteran

Washington Post reporter and columnist Al Kamen was able to put names to the angry white yuppie faces, some shaking their fists in the air, all captured on film. What did Tom Pyle, Garry Malphrus, Rory Cooper, Kevin Smith, Steven Brophy, Matt Schlapp, Roger Morse, Duane Gibson, Chuck Royal, and Layna McConkey all have in common? These "penny-loafer protesters," as Kamen memorably dubbed them, were current or former aides to Republican members of Congress, who all somehow just happened to be on the nineteenth floor of the Clark Building in Miami that day. The out-of-towners reportedly had been mobilized at the behest of House majority whip Tom "The Hammer" DeLay, although he has never acknowledged his role in the affair.

No one has any illusions that the Democrats also weren't deeply involved in similar antics. But the efficiency of the Republican Rioters—who surfaced the same day Bush first appealed to the U.S. Supreme Court—underscores a larger conclusion reached by most close observers of *l'affaire Florida* from start to finish. As syndicated columnist Jim Hoagland put it, "the Bush legal and political teams dominated the battle for control of perception and procedure. They were far more focused, tough-minded and agile than were Al Gore's operatives." Spending more than four times more cash ($13.8 million for Bush to $3.5 million for Gore) than the other side certainly helped, but what we witnessed cannot be explained by money alone.

Beyond political gamesmanship, though, journalists and the public simply cannot ascertain the full extent of such maneuverings in public records or public statements, not to mention follow the money. Officially, under law, recount committees must file a statement of organization "within 24 hours of the date on which the organization is established." But the public was kept waiting.

The Gore camp quickly created the Gore/Lieberman Recount Committee and filed forms available on the Internet with the IRS on November 9, 2000, two days after the election. Forms disclosing contributions to Gore's recount efforts were submitted eight days later. In response to media pressure, the Bush campaign finally made some of its contributions publicly available the following month on the Republican National Committee's Web site.

> Recount committees must file a statement of
> organization "within 24 hours of the date on
> which the organization is established."
> But the public was kept waiting.

Since there are no campaign contribution restrictions on recount committees, both candidates could accept unlimited contributions. The campaign of Vice President Gore took full advantage of these loopholes to accept six-figure contributions from wealthy donors. The Gore/Lieberman Recount Committee accepted nine contributions of $100,000 or more from individual donors such as Mouse Systems founder Steven Kirsch ($500,000), movie producer Stephen Bing ($200,000), and actress Jane Fonda ($100,000). In fact, although Gore claimed to represent the middle class, our research shows that almost two out of three dollars used by his recount committee came from large donors giving $25,000 or more.

In contrast, the Bush-Cheney 2000, Inc-Recount Fund voluntarily limited the size of its contributions to $5,000 per person, and officials said it would not take contributions from political action committees. But the Center has found that the Bush campaign didn't stay within these self-imposed limits, accepting six donations above $5,000 and taking PAC money from one timber and two energy groups.

Not all the rules that Bush-Cheney 2000 broke were voluntary. After the public waited for close to five months for the Bush recount committee to file its first official form, DNC chairman Terry McAuliffe called for an investigation by the IRS, charging that Bush-Cheney 2000 was a 527 committee violating federal election laws. Ben Ginsberg, counsel to the Bush recount fund, denied that the group had to file as a 527 or was breaking any laws. But almost 15 months later, Bush-Cheney 2000 quietly reversed itself. Republican Party officials declared that the group was indeed a 527, even though the group had been grossly delinquent in disclosing its contributions and expenditures to the public. Violations for such IRS laws could have cost Bush's recount committee more than $8 million in back taxes and penalties based on its receipts.

But the Bush-Cheney campaign never paid a dime.

Ten weeks before the Bush-Cheney 2000 recount fund filed its forms, the IRS, now under a new Republican administration, declared a special amnesty program for 527 groups that were out of compliance. IRS officials said that the program was designed to help political groups that might have been confused with the reporting requirements and allowed them until July 15, 2002, to file delinquent forms. With only nine hours before the amnesty was due to expire, Bush-Cheney 2000 filed 1,063 pages of contributions and expenditures that the public had been legally entitled to a year and a half earlier. With the amnesty in place, the Bush campaign was not fined.

The Center for Public Integrity also found that the Bush-Cheney recount fund neglected to disclose more than 650 contributions totaling more than $540,000 in these initial late filings. By comparing lists of contributors posted to the Republican National Committee's Web site and the disclosure forms filed by Bush's campaign, the Center discovered hundreds of contributors who are not accounted for, including 40 donors who each gave $5,000. Among the many contributions the recount fund neglected to disclose was that of White House chief strategist Karl Rove.

It is unclear whether the committee knowingly left these donations off its initial disclosure forms, but the omissions account for nearly 10 percent of the total number of contributions. Such nondisclosure of contributions potentially carries stiff fines from the IRS that could amount to more than $190,000, even if the donations were omitted inadvertently.

These omissions became evident in February 2003, when the IRS posted still more delinquent filings from the Bush-Cheney fund—this time outside the window of an amnesty. These reports revealed $1.7 million in missing contributions and $29,000 in previously unreported expenditures. This unambiguous violation could, if the laws were enforced, cost Bush's 527 more than $610,000.

Missing donations weren't the only things out of compliance on the recount fund disclosure forms. The Center found that the 527 neglected to disclose the necessary information on most of its contributions. In fact, Bush-Cheney 2000 failed to disclose both the contributors' employer and occupation for 2,745 of the group's 8,225 donors—a third of its contributions. All told, the necessary filing information was missing or left blank for more than $2 million of the money the Bush campaign used to recount votes. According to the U.S. Postal Service, the post office box listed on the group's forms as a primary address doesn't even exist.

While the Bush-Cheney recount fund was guilty of flagrantly delinquent filing, the Gore-Lieberman recount committee used some of its money to keep up appearances and the illusion of power on behalf of the former vice president. As Gore mulled a White House run in late 2002, he used a campaign finance loophole to send $100,000 he had raised two years earlier for the

Florida recount to Iowa and New Hampshire in order to bolster his position in the first two states where presidential candidates must test their mettle.

> **All told, the necessary filing information was missing or left blank for more than $2 million of the money used by the Bush campaign to recount votes.**

IRS forms reveal disbursements on Oct. 24, 2002, to the Iowa Democratic Party Coordinated Campaign ($25,000), New Hampshire Senate Democratic Caucus ($20,000), New Hampshire Democratic Party ($30,000), and Iowa's Truman Fund ($25,000). The donations came ten days after Gore made a two-day trip to Iowa, where he attended fundraisers for Democratic candidates.

The Gore/Lieberman recount committee also gave $75,000 to the Florida Democratic Party; $50,000 to Victory 2002, the Coordinated Campaign for the Tennessee Democratic Party; and $10,000 to the Louisiana Democratic Party during the last two reporting periods of 2002.

Meanwhile, almost triple the cash in Florida raised and spent by the Republicans over the Democrats also resulted in triple the fun. Not only did Bush and his party capture Florida's 25 electoral votes, and thus the entire presidential election, but many of the lawyers and operatives sent by the Republicans into Florida in those frenetic days after election night were later rewarded with plum political jobs.

Another Center for Public Integrity analysis found that seven law firms, each providing more than $250,000 in legal services to the Bush-Cheney recount fund, later produced at least 14 senior political appointees and at least one judicial nominee. We found that appointees—including the solicitor general, the administrator of the relatively anonymous but influential Office of Federal

Procurement Policy, and the Commissioner of U.S. Customs—are former members of the seven law firms that were paid a combined $3.9 million for recount-related legal services.

Indeed, Gibson, Dunn & Crutcher, the top law firm in billings securing President Bush's recount result boasts three high-profile appointments to the executive branch, as well as the controversial appeals court nominee Miguel Estrada, whose rejection by Democratic procedural moves caused the president to call for reform of the judicial nomination process. Estrada, a partner at Gibson, Dunn & Crutcher, is one of the first Hispanics ever to serve as a clerk to the U.S. Supreme Court. He also served as a litigator in the U.S. Office of the Solicitor General during the first Bush administration and the Clinton administration. The law firm received $892,273 from the recount committee for the services of a legal team that reportedly included Estrada and Ted Olson, now solicitor general. Eugene Scalia, who served as acting solicitor for the Department of Labor but was never confirmed by the Senate, is a partner in the firm as well.

But while the appointments of Scalia, son of Supreme Court Justice Antonin Scalia, and Olson, the respected conservative attorney who argued Bush's case in front of the Supreme Court, could have been expected from any Republican administration, they are not the end of the firm's representation on the Bush team. Rob Bonner, a former corporate lawyer who was a partner at Gibson, Dunn & Crutcher's Los Angeles office, is now the commissioner of U.S. Customs. Bonner himself has a past record of public service in the first Bush administration. M. Sean Royall, a former Gibson, Dunn lawyer, is now deputy director of one of the nation's most important antitrust watchdog agencies, the Federal Trade Commission Bureau of Competition.

Other recount law firms whose lawyers later landed high government positions included the third largest recipient of funds from the Bush-Cheney recount fund, White & Case ($619,713 in legal bills), which sent international law partner Tim Flanigan to serve as deputy assistant to the president and deputy White House counsel. Bush also tapped Marcos Daniel Jimenez, from the Miami offices of White & Case, as U.S. attorney for the Southern District of Florida. Attorney General John Ashcroft later named Jimenez to the Attorney General's Advisory Committee for U.S. Attorneys, where he has a hand in national policy.

Bush found two major nominees at the number five recount firm, Greenberg Traurig ($485,636). A major national law practice with important ties to both parties, the firm provided two of the Pentagon's top civilian lawyers: Alberto Mora, general counsel of the Navy, and Michael P. Socarras, general counsel of the Air Force.

But most noteworthy for sheer numbers is Baker Botts, LLP, the venerable firm of former secretary of state Jim Baker with ties to the Bush family going back at least three generations. Fourth in terms of billing ($561,461), Baker Botts sent Baker to lead Bush's Florida effort. Appointees with ties to Baker Botts include Kirk Van Tine, general counsel of the Department of Transportation; Claude Allen, deputy secretary of the Department of Health and Human Services; Angela Styles, administrator of the Office of Federal Procurement Policy (she worked at Baker Botts in the mid-1990s before going to Miller & Chevalier); Robert Jordan, the ambassador to Saudi Arabia; Patrick Wood, chairman of the Federal Energy Regulatory Commission; and John P. Elwood, counselor to the assistant attorney general for the Department of Justice, Criminal Division.

MOVING THROUGH THE COURTS

While Americans have seen a parade of partisanship from Republican and Democratic members of Congress and presidents, during the post-election maneuvering many citizens were startled by the extent to which our judicial system itself seemed infected by political influences. Before the U.S. Supreme Court essentially decided who would become the next president of the United States, the Florida Supreme Court—with all seven of the justices appointed by Democratic governors—handed down several crucial decisions in favor of Gore. The court was immediately and continually criticized for making decisions that ignored Florida election law.

On November 16, the Florida Supreme Court ruled that the manual recounts should proceed in the three Democratic counties where Gore had asked for such counts. Five days later, after Katherine Harris ruled that hand recounts from those three counties could not be included in the statewide total, the Florida Supreme Court, in a unanimous decision, ruled that the recounted ballots, which gave Gore additional votes, be included. The Florida court also threw out the statutory deadline for certifying the votes, substituting its own instead.

Gore had petitioned for recounts in only four heavily Democratic counties, and Bush had petitioned for no recounts. Still, the Florida judges, in a surprising 4-3 decision on December 8, 2000, ordered a statewide recount of all ballots on which no vote had been recorded for president, a move that some believed favored Gore.

Republicans argued that the Florida Supreme Court had overstepped its bounds on a number of occasions, first by extending the deadline for recounting and then by authorizing a recount of the entire state, in an effort to ensure that Gore was elected. Former Republican National Committee chairman Haley Barbour said of the latter decision, "This goes to show that if a majority of judges is partisan enough there is no limit to how far they will go in abusing their authority."

Jack Kemp, former Republican vice presidential nominee and Bush advisor, went as far as to accuse the four judges of attempting "a judicial coup d'état." "The public is experiencing a lesson in the danger of judicial tyranny as exemplified in the Florida Supreme Court," Kemp said.

But looking back at the electoral madness of the 2000 presidential election—which was so close that "the margin of error exceeded the margin of victory"—nothing about the electioneering or the overcaffeinated legaleering is as historically stunning as what happened with the U.S. Supreme Court. Never in our lifetimes has the High Court decided who would occupy the White House. Besides halting a statewide manual recount in Florida by a 5-4 vote on December 9, 2000, at the request of Republican candidate George W. Bush, five Republican justices pulled the plug on the 2000 presidential election on December 12, effectively making him the next president of the United States.

The U.S. Supreme Court's breathtaking decision will be debated and discussed for years to come; millions of words and a few books already have been published about the decision and the state and federal court decisions that preceded it.

Five Republican Supreme Court justices awarding the White House to the Republican presidential candidate is controversial enough, but in legal circles there were other striking anomalies about *Bush v. Gore*. For example, when on December 9 the Court granted a stay in response to the petition from Bush's lawyers, voting 5 to 4 along partisan lines to halt the statewide manual recount mandated by the Florida Supreme Court, the reasoning struck many observers as a bit thin. Justice Scalia stated the ostensible rationale in his opinion: "The counting of votes that are of questionable legality does in my view threaten irreparable harm to petitioner, and to the country, by casting a cloud upon what he claims to be the legitimacy of his election. Count first, and rule upon legality afterwards, is not a recipe for producing election results that have the public acceptance democratic stability requires."

> **"This goes to show that if a majority of judges is partisan enough there is no limit to how far they will go in abusing their authority."**

A stay is an exceptionally rare judicial maneuver, as it requires approval of five justices, and the petitioner seeking the stay must show he or she will suffer "irreparable harm" if it is not granted. However, even if the U.S. Supreme Court allowed the recounting to continue, it still could have decided later to throw out the recounted ballots. In his dissent to the stay, Justice Stevens emphasized that "counting every legally cast vote cannot constitute irreparable harm." In language similar to Scalia's, but drawing the opposite conclusion, Stevens said, "Preventing the recount from being completed will inevitably cast a cloud on the legitimacy of the election." Terrance Sandalow, former dean of the University of Michigan Law School and a judicial conservative who opposes *Roe v. Wade*, was much blunter. He reportedly said, "The balance of harms so unmistakably were on the side of Gore" that granting the stay was "incomprehensible." He further denounced the stay as "an unmistakably partisan decision without any foundation in law."

The Court's decision at 10 P.M. on December 12 came under heavy criticism. For one thing, the opinion was issued *per curiam*, meaning "by the court" (making it hard to determine precisely who wrote the final judgment)—a peculiar choice because *per curiam* Supreme Court opinions are generally used in uncontroversial, unanimous decisions. But hiding its parentage was only the beginning of the crisis of confidence it caused. The elder statesman of legal journalism in the United

States, Anthony Lewis, who wrote the classic, widely acclaimed *Gideon's Trumpet* in 1964 and retired a few years ago from the *New York Times*, said, "The problem is not so much that the court intervened in politics. It is that the majority's stated reasons for its decision were so unconvincing." He quoted one law professor whose opinion he said was emblematic of law teachers he'd spoken to generally: "How can I convince my students now that the integrity of legal reasoning matters?"

Another columnist, E. J. Dionne Jr., writing in the *Washington Post*, was troubled that "the five most conservative appointees on the court . . . chose to intrude in Florida's election process having always claimed to be champions of the rights of states and foes of 'judicial activism' and 'judicial overreach.'" That was a common complaint, as echoed by Harvard professor Michael Sandel: "Not only did the court fail to produce any compelling argument of principle to justify its ruling. But, on top of that, the conservative majority contradicted its long-held insistence on protecting states' rights against federal interference. That's why this ruling looks more like partisanship than principle."

The five Supreme Court justices chose the equal protection clause of the Fourteenth Amendment as the constitutional grounds for the majority opinion. This clause, passed after the Civil War to prevent racial discrimination, became a popular tool of the judicial activists on the Warren Court as a means to strike down unfair state action.

A majority of the U.S. Supreme Court declared that the manual recount prescribed by the Florida Supreme Court violated the equal protection clause of the Fourteenth Amendment because ballots were subjected to arbitrary and disparate treatment, and "the standards for accepting or rejecting contested ballots might vary not only from county to county but indeed within a single county from one recount team to another." The

Court explained that a state cannot use varying standards to "value one person's vote over that of another" in such a way that dilutes "the weight of a citizen's vote."

But Florida was not unique. Best-selling author and lawyer Vincent Bugliosi, who wrote *The Betrayal of America: How the Supreme Court Undermined the Constitution and Chose Our President*, wrote that 44 of the 50 states have varying voting methods, equipment, and standards. Therefore, he argued, "to apply the equal protection ruling of *Bush v. Gore* would necessarily invalidate virtually all elections throughout the country."

The Court's noble concern for "the weight of a citizen's vote" will always have a decidedly hollow ring to many people. As William H. Chafe, dean of the faculty of arts and sciences at Duke University, wrote, "Dilapidated voting machines—those whose age and condition are most often associated with malfunction and large numbers of 'undercounted' ballots—were three times as likely to be located in Black precincts as in White precincts." Blacks voted 90 percent Democratic in the 2000 presidential election nationwide.

The great irony of the Florida election debacle was that in citing the equal protection clause as a justification to halt the recount and the election, the Court was effectively disenfranchising thousands of minority voters. As the *New York Times* stated in an editorial five days after the historic decision, "Our citizenship is devalued and our historical progress as a nation is negated if we passively accept that a poor, inner-city African-American's voice in selecting the next president is not accorded the same attention as that of an affluent suburban voter."

The more sunlight on this decision, the worse it looks. Harvard Law School professor Alan Dershowitz found in his book *Supreme Injustice*, "In virtually every equal-protection case, it is easy to identify the victim." He explained that in a 1995 equal protection case, the same five justices ruled that the defendant had to show "individualized harm." In *Bush v. Gore*, however, both Bush's legendary team of competent attorneys and the justices on the Supreme Court failed to identify a specific victim or group of victims who were actually harmed by the 2000 Florida recount.

Indeed, presumably not believing that this was the strongest constitutional argument in their case, Bush's team buried the equal protection issue, addressing it for fewer than 5 pages of a 50-page brief. And during the oral argument, Bush's lawyer made only one quick, unelaborated reference to the equal protection issue in his presentation to the court. Weeks earlier, when Governor Bush initially sought redress from the Supreme Court, the justices sent the case back to Florida, and didn't mention the equal protection clause.

Newsweek reported that Justice Sandra Day O'Connor, after hearing CBS anchor Dan Rather declare incorrectly that Al Gore had won Florida, gasped, "This is terrible."

Many scholars were astonished by this unusual use of the equal protection clause. Even conservative constitutional law professor John C. Yoo of the University of California at Berkeley School of Law said he was "surprised" by the equal protection rationale employed by the court, though he agreed with the outcome of the decision. Others strongly disagreed with the justices' reasoning. Indeed, there are no prior cases in which the equal protection clause has been applied in this manner. Of the mere four cases that the justices do cite in their opinion, not one of the cases "on its facts, comes close to supporting its analysis and result," according to Yale law professor Akhil Reed Amar. Few things seem to matter more to lawyers, and especially judges, than legal precedent, and it was unusual to cite so few previous cases when making such an important ruling.

The justices themselves were aware of the door they were opening with judicial activism and unusual application of the equal protection clause, claiming, "Our consideration is limited to the present circumstances, for the problem of equal protection in election processes generally presents many complexities." In yet another unusual statement, the Court made it clear that this historic decision is not to be applied to any other case. Rarely are opinions drafted for use in only one court decision. David D. Cole, a Georgetown University law professor, noted that the conservative justices effectively "created a new right out of whole cloth and made sure it ultimately protected only one person—George Bush."

Thomas Friedman, a three-time Pulitzer Prize winner, said what many people perceived: "You don't need an inside source to realize that the five conservative justices were acting as the last in a team of Republican Party elders who helped drag Governor Bush across the finish line. You just needed to read the withering dissents of Justices Breyer, Ginsburg, Souter, and Stevens, who told the country exactly what their five colleagues were up to—acting without legal principle or logic."

The unabashed political partisanship of the five justices came under attack as well. Justice Clarence Thomas was a long-serving official in the Reagan administration, Chief Justice Rehnquist was in President Nixon's Justice Department, and Justice Sandra Day O'Connor had once served as the Republican majority leader of the Arizona State Senate. *Newsweek* reported that Justice O'Connor, after hearing CBS anchor Dan Rather declare incorrectly that Al Gore had won Florida, gasped, "This is terrible." Her husband, John O'Connor, elaborated on her comment by saying that he and his wife were hoping to retire to Arizona soon, but she did not want to retire if her replacement would be appointed by a Democrat. O'Connor later denied the story.

And then there were the justices' family ties to Bush himself.

Justice Thomas's wife was a member of Bush's transition team, helping to collect money for his inauguration. Both of Justice Scalia's sons, Eugene and John, were lawyers working for firms that represented George W. Bush in Florida or before the Supreme Court.

But perhaps no anecdote of partisanship is more disturbing than the one reported in the *Washington Post*, which leaves readers with a chilling *Seven Days in May* feeling. Only days after deciding the 2000 presidential election, Justices Antonin Scalia and Anthony M. Kennedy celebrated the holiday season by attending the annual Christmas party held at the home of President Ronald Reagan's favorite Republican senator, now a Washington lobbyist, Paul Laxalt, and his wife Carol. Scalia and Kennedy clinked glasses with Dick Cheney, newly elected vice president of the United States. Guests at the party thanked the justices for their decision, congratulated Cheney on his success, and at one point in the evening, went downstairs to watch and cheer Al Gore's long-awaited concession speech.

Not surprisingly, the credibility of the U.S. Supreme Court suffered after *Bush v. Gore*. In a Gallup poll taken on December 11, 2000, more than half of the respondents thought that "the Justices on the U.S. Supreme Court are being influenced by their personal political views when deciding this case." Even among Bush supporters, 36 percent believed that the justices were influenced by partisanship. In a similar poll taken by *Newsweek*, almost two-thirds of Americans, 65 percent, believed that politics and partisanship played a role in the Supreme Court decision. Meanwhile, every major decision by the Florida Supreme Court, of which a majority of the justices were Democrats, favored Democratic Party presidential nominee Gore. Suddenly, for the first time for many Americans, those black robes in courtrooms had developed newly discernible partisan stripes.

Justice Stevens—appointed to the Court by Republican president Gerald Ford months after the Watergate scandal ended in 1975, second in seniority only to Chief Justice William Rehnquist—offered an ominous warning about the negative impact of the court's decision on the judiciary. One thing is certain, he said in his dissent. "Although we may never know with complete certainty the identity of the winner of this year's Presidential election, the identity of the loser is perfectly clear. It is the Nation's confidence in the judge as an impartial guardian of the rule of law."

Indeed, after the 2000 presidential election, no American will ever look at voting, elections, judges, or the political process in quite the same way again.

Private Parties

L et me now . . . warn you in the most solemn manner against the baneful effects of the spirit of party," President George Washington said in his farewell address in 1796. Political parties, he said prophetically, "are likely in the course of time and things, to become potent engines, by which cunning, ambitious, and unprincipled men will be enabled to subvert the Power of the People and to usurp for themselves the reins of Government."

Washington's prophetic fears may be truer and more real than any of us would like to admit. The two major parties are powerful private corporations with outsized public responsibilities and little public transparency or accountability. Their chairmen, functionaries, and spokespeople, of course, all vociferously assert that they *are* the people, and anything they say or do is honestly and sincerely on behalf, and in the best interests, of Americans. Nonetheless, getting past the bombast, it is the ideas, constituencies, organizations, and money surrounding the parties that substantially define what each public official actually stands for today. And we cannot begin to understand our national politics or presidential candidates if we do not fully comprehend the milieu in which they function. Each party has an informal working alliance of vested economic, ideological, or other interests, as major backers directly and indirectly but also as eminently effective, discreet policymaking partners. The candidates function inside of—indeed, must be active creatures of—these power networks that substantially control the political governance of our Republic.

"Strategic industrial coordination" and "corporate coordination" certainly are not new concepts in business—look at the Japanese *keiretsu* or the South Korean *chaebol* systems of collaboration. And in the United States, for decades, entire distinctive industry sectors, each composed of company competitors in the marketplace or hundreds of labor unions, have frequently worked together as needed on specific legislative issues. What is less publicly acknowledged is the loose but unmistakable network that exists between these economic interests, all of whom want something from government and the access to power that the major political parties possess. The tobacco companies or the National Rifle Association or the Christian Coalition rarely attack the Republican Party or its leading public officeholders, because they are all partners in a strategic and financial power network. Similarly, the trial lawyers or the labor unions or the Sierra Club will rarely publicly challenge the Democratic Party, because they are unofficial, traditional allies. And beyond the balloons and placards we see every four years at convention time, a central, unpublicized purpose of each political party is to assist and further the public policy agendas of its principal patrons.

When one political party controls all three elected branches of the federal government, as the Republicans do for the first time in half a century, there is an obvious power "surge" that alters the network alignments in many ways, something we will later explore. Not surprisingly, one of the manifestations of these new circumstances is financial—money has always been drawn to power like flies to honey. For example, in 1992, when George H. W. Bush was president but the Democrats controlled Congress, the pharmaceutical companies gave $2.5 million to Republican campaigns and party committees and $2.4 million to the Democrats, according to the Center for Responsive Politics. But in the 2002 election cycle, with both the White House and Congress in Republican control, the most profitable industry in the United States gave $16.3 million to the Republicans, but only $4.4 million to the Democrats. In 1990, the controversial tobacco industry gave 51 percent of its campaign cash to Republicans, but in 2002, with that party in control, it gave 78 percent of its political contributions, or nearly $7 million, to Republicans.

Actually, the Republican Party has been dominating the Democratic Party financially in the post-Watergate, Federal Election Commission era, although the gap narrowed somewhat in the 1990s. In the 2002 election cycle, the Republican Party's three national committees (national, senatorial, and congressional) raised $652 million—$186 million more than the Democratic national committees. In the previous midterm election cycle, 1997–1998, when the Democrats controlled the White House, the Republicans still outraised the Democrats (hard and soft money combined) $405 million to $245 million, a difference of $160 million.

Indeed, in the last *six* election cycles, starting with 1991–1992, the Republicans collected more total (hard and soft) campaign contributions than the Democrats each time, with an average GOP advantage of $162 million for each election. Considering that incumbent President George W. Bush is expected to break the $200 million fundraising barrier and outspend his Democratic opponent by as much as four times, the campaign finance landscape looks rather bleak for the Democrats, to put it charitably.

Despite George Washington's warning and the serious implications of their powerful position in society, we all have an understandable tendency to make fun of or belittle our political parties, the same way we have incessantly derided politics and our politicians since the Republic began. It was Mark Twain who famously said, "It could probably be shown by facts and figures that there is no distinctly native American criminal class except Congress." But humor and a healthy spleen aside, to fully comprehend the uses and abuses of power in Congress and in the White House and entire executive branch, and how it all relates to the intersection of democracy and capitalism in this country, we must not forget one very salient fact of political life: no one has been elected to the White House since the Civil War who is not either a Republican or a Democrat.

> **No one has been elected to the White House since the Civil War who is not either a Republican or a Democrat.**

Over more than two centuries, we have had different party permutations and historic eras—there is a long body of work chronicling the political evolution, ebb, and flow of our two-party system. The United States of America actually began without political parties, and as two-time Pulitzer Prize–winning historian Arthur M. Schlesinger Jr. has observed, neither the Articles of Confederation nor the Constitution provided for them. But factions and parties inevitably began to coalesce, which worried Washington. Years later, in 1835, French political scientist and diplomat Alexis de Tocqueville wrote in his classic work, *Democracy in America*, that "Parties are a necessary evil in free governments; but they have not at all times the same character and the same propensities. . . . America has had great parties, but has them no longer."

Party organizations were created in the mid-nineteenth century, principally to conduct national conventions. The Democratic National Committee was created in 1848. The new Republican Party established the Republican National Committee in 1856. Eventually both parties developed campaign committees for Senate and House candidates as well. But the national parties didn't actually hire professional staffs or set up permanent headquarters until after World War I. Now, of course, both have slick, multimillion-dollar bureaucracies with a full bevy of fundraisers, lawyers, accountants, communications operatives, opposition researchers, and political consultants.

Not coincidentally, our politics have become more partisan, more sharply divided, and more ideological. As political scientists William J. Keefe and Marc J. Hetherington have noted in *Parties, Politics, and Public Policy in America*, in 2000 Americans voted the straight party ticket more often than any time in the previous 30 years. And notwithstanding the assertions of Green Party presidential candidate Ralph Nader, 64 percent of Americans said they perceive major differences between the two political parties, the highest margin since that question was first asked by the National Election Study back in 1960. Over the past two decades, the American people have increasingly characterized the Republican Party as "conservative" and the Democratic Party as "liberal."

ENTICEMENTS OF APATHY

Before we get more deeply enmeshed in whom the political parties represent or to whom they appeal, we need to recognize the significance of the no-shows today. Democracy is not a spectator sport, but in every federal election, 100 million Americans choose to stand on the sidelines and watch, largely regarding the entire political process as so much hot air, not sufficiently relevant to their lives to merit the act of voting itself. From 1960 through 2000, from presidential, nonpresidential, and primary voting statistics, there has been a significant decline in voter participation, which, as Thomas E. Patterson, in *The Vanishing Voter*, put it, "could be a danger to democracy." Our youngest and poorest adult citizens participate less; overall, Americans have declining interest in contributing to political campaigns or parties, to attending campaign rallies, or even to paying attention to election-related news.

By not voting, such people not only foreclose the possibility that their ballot will be counted (or, perhaps it should be said, miscounted, uncounted, recounted); they also help to ensure that their public policy preferences won't count. Their concerns are—no surprise here—substantially ignored because there is no pressing imperative for politicians or their parties to be responsive to nonvoters. Or as Plato put it differently, "One of the penalties for refusing to participate in politics is that you end up being governed by your inferiors." Of course, even if citizens exercise their right to vote but do not possess millions of dollars to organize themselves politically along with other kindred souls, or to support and persuade like-minded politicians or their political party of the extraordinary wisdom of their issues, one could argue that they probably don't matter all that much either in the public policy power grid of Washington.

Voting or not, 40 percent of Americans in 2000 identified themselves as "independents," greater than the identification with either major political party. There is no single political party that has gained the sustained allegiance or support of the independents, which, as we will discuss, is not entirely coincidental. And the highest-polling third party in the 2000 presidential election was the Green Party, which garnered almost 2.9 million votes out of 105 million cast, or 2.7 percent. Partly because so many Americans say they are "independent," politicians generally do not use overtly partisan language in their public utterances. Indeed, one enterprising communications scholar at the University of Texas, Roderick Hart, actually tallied and analyzed the total number of words and found that between 1948 and 1996, presidential candidates talked more about themselves and less about their parties.

Down in the trenches of actual voting combatants—those independents, Republicans, and Democrats who make their choices at the polls—it is possible, using the detailed, nationwide Bush-Gore election night returns and exit polling, to ascertain telling differences between the ultimate supporters of the two parties. These distinctions in fact have been gradually evident in several recent congressional and presidential elections. Indeed, as Michael Barone and others have noted, the returns and polling reveal a tale of two nations, separated by geography, gender, race, religiosity, and class.

Recalling those TV network, red-and-blue graphic maps of the United States, so indelibly etched into our national consciousness, major metropolitan areas are, generally speaking, heavily Democratic; rural and newer metropolitan areas are overwhelmingly Republican. More women voted Democratic (54 to 43 percent), but beneath the much ballyhooed gender gap, married women actually were pretty evenly divided between Bush and Gore (49 to 48 percent), suggesting that it is unmarried women who lean unmistakably Democratic. Whites supported Bush (54 to 42 percent); Blacks (90 to 9 percent), Hispanics (62 to 35 percent), and Asians (55 to 41 percent) backed Gore.

The breakdown of religious demographics is by itself starkly illuminating. White voters identifying themselves as members of the "religious right," who comprise 14 percent of the national electorate, overwhelmingly supported Bush over Gore (80 to 18 percent). White Protestants, more broadly beyond just the "religious right"—altogether a majority of Americans at 56 percent—backed Bush (63 to 34 percent). Jewish voters—4 percent of the nation—sided with Gore (79 to 18 percent). But most stunning are the polling data surrounding the extent of involvement in organized religion. Churchgoers attending religious services at least weekly—42 percent of the electorate—supported Bush (59 to 39 percent). Those who don't regularly attend religious services, "seldom or never"— which happens also to comprise 42 percent of the electorate— voted for Gore (56 to 39 percent).

> **Whites supported Bush (54 to 42 percent); Blacks (90 to 9 percent), Hispanics (62 to 35 percent), and Asians (55 to 41 percent) backed Gore.**

In terms of income and class, most people with annual incomes over $100,000 voted for Bush over Gore (54 to 43 percent). And most people with annual incomes under $15,000 supported Gore (57 to 37 percent), who exhorted a populist, "the people versus the powerful," campaign message.

DOWN AND DIRTY WITH THE TWO PARTIES

Beyond the particulars about who gravitates to which party on Election Day, the fact is that Americans are enormously unimpressed with our two major political parties. In 1996, according to an ABC News–*Washington Post* survey, two-thirds of Americans agreed with the statement that "both political parties are pretty much out of touch with the American people." Worse, in more recent polling by Democrat Mark Mellman and former

Reagan strategist and pollster Richard Wirthlin, more than three in four Americans believe that large contributions to political parties have a great deal of impact on public policy decisions made by the federal government. An overwhelming majority of citizens, 84 percent, said that members of Congress will be more likely to "listen to those who give money to their political party in response to their solicitation for large donations." On the other hand, only one in four Americans (24 percent) believes that a member of Congress is likely to give "the opinion of someone like them special consideration."

Sad to say, these dim views of the two parties and their soul-searing money chase were underscored by some of the sworn depositions in the Bipartisan Campaign Reform Act litigation.

Indeed, however effective or historically meaningful the hard-won McCain-Feingold legislation proves to be, the litigation in response to it has spawned considerable candor and glimpses of raw truth—under oath—from dozens of players from all sides about politics in America. For example, in October 2002, lawyers for the National Rifle Association and the Federal Election Commission journeyed out to Cody, Wyoming, to question former Republican U.S. senator Alan Simpson, who was blunt and often funny when in office—traits that have only become magnified in retirement. At one point after several specific questions, he barked at the NRA's attorney, Hamish Hume of the Washington law firm of Cooper and Kirk: "I'm 71 years old, and I get tired of this kind of nitpicking crap. What is it you are after from me? What is—ask the goddamn question! What is it you want from me? Ask me something, not just whatever, whatever, whatever. What is it? What do you want?"

But in the FEC deposition, Simpson cut through it in a way rarely heard anywhere today. "The campaign fundraising system of America has a corruptive and corrosive effect on government. . . . It makes people look at the system and say, what are they doing now?"

Under oath, Simpson admitted he never liked raising money for the Republican Party, but apparently liberated in retirement after decades of dependency, he saved his strongest reaction for the donors. Simpson received thousands and thousands of dollars from the NRA and its individual members over the years, which is not surprising because he represented a rural Western state and the NRA has been the seventeenth most generous patron to the Republican Party since 1978, sending millions of dollars to the three national committees and hundreds of GOP candidates. Although Simpson referred to Charlton Heston, the former actor and until recently president of the NRA, as "a very close friend of mine," he had less kind words for what the NRA does. "It's called whoring," he said. "And that's where you all are right now. . . . It's not giving according to your deep-held philosophy. It's giving so you can get access and kiss butt and do all the rest of the things so you won't get knocked off the perch."

(Is it remarkable that the "whoring," in Simpson's mind, is restricted only to donors? Welcome to the warped Washington world of compartmentalized reality and situational ethics.)

He scorched those powerful single-interest organizations with hundreds of thousands of members nationwide, to whom they send detailed "scorecards" about lawmakers' legislative "performance." Besides trashing the NRA to their lawyer's face, Simpson said, "NEA, National Education Association, tough, mean sons of bitches. AARP [American Association of Retired Persons], tough, mean sons of bitches. These guys smile a lot and carry a dirk up their sleeve."

Simpson talked about how these groups shamelessly play on the most basic instincts of fear and survival to raise a buck. "You can raise a hell of a lot more money—every group I'm connected with, a member of the VFW [Veterans of Foreign Wars] or the American Legion or the NRA or the AARP—I joined them just so I could find out how wretched their advertising is—that the more money they can get is to say, now we're in the political system. Take part or get taken apart. Do you realize as a veteran that you're going to get screwed until your eyeballs fall out unless you get active in lobbying this Congress?"

Finally, he complained about the "disruptive" and inordinate amount of time legislators must devote to fundraising. "I was assistant majority leader of the Senate under Bob Dole. And I can't tell you how many times in the course of a day that we'd have something scheduled, and they'd say, 'Bob and Al, I won't be there tonight. I got to be in Detroit for a fundraiser.' 'Got to be in New York.' And I used to say to them, 'You know, you get paid 133,600 bucks. Why don't you show up here and vote and stick with us so we can get the nation's business done?' 'Well, I'd like to, but I can't, because I'm on the phone all afternoon. I have to go to another building. And I'll be on the phone all day over there, doing the calls.'"

It is a violation of federal law to solicit campaign funds from U.S. government property, so members of Congress slink off down the street to their respective party headquarters and dial for dollars there.

Under oath, other senators echoed Simpson's sentiments. Former Republican senator Warren Rudman, in a written statement submitted into evidence, said the access and influence accorded to major donors "is inherently, endemically, and hopelessly corrupting. You can't swim in the ocean without getting wet; you can't be part of this system without getting dirty."

And parties have a way of ensuring their members get dirty. Internal, secret, tally sheets are kept by the House and Senate Republican and Democratic Party campaign committees, not unlike local capos marking down weekly protection payments up and down the block. As a made public official, you pony up for the party. You don't have to talk like Marlon Brando in *The Godfather*, and you're not likely to wake up with a bloody horse head next to you, but it is clearly understood that you either raise cash for the party or you don't move up the political hierarchy in either house of Congress.

Congresswoman Marcy Kaptur, Democrat of Ohio, worked in the Carter White House before serving as a member of the U.S. House of Representatives for the past two decades. "You're now expected to produce dollars, dialing for dollars, to help your colleagues, to the tune of hundreds of thousands of dollars if you are going to move forward. . . . When you go to a [party] caucus meeting, you are now graded and publicly embarrassed about how much money you've raised compared to the rest of your colleagues," she told the Center for Public Integrity. "And it's that way on both sides of the aisle. . . . People bid on both sides of the aisle for committee positions based on how much money they've raised."

> **"Do you realize as a veteran that you're going to get screwed until your eyeballs fall out unless you get active in lobbying this Congress?"**

One person who knows as much about political parties, devastating scandal, and fundraising as just about anyone in the nation is Bill Brock, who served as congressman and senator from Tennessee for 14 years. Brock was the U.S. trade representative and later secretary of labor in the Reagan administration and from 1977 to 1981 served as chairman of the Republican National Committee. When last interviewed by the Center for Public Integrity in 1992, he candidly acknowledged the nightmare he faced trying to lead the GOP out of the dark wilderness of Watergate. "The party was in awesome disarray," he told the Center. "We'd been decimated from two consecutive elections. . . . The Watergate damage was pervasive. There were questions about whether the party should still exist. We had a lot of discussion about whether we should change our name."

Brock, a lobbyist for years in Washington since leaving the Reagan cabinet, ran unsuccessfully for the U.S. Senate in heavily Democratic Maryland in 1994. During the campaign he was astonished by the large soft-money contributions that had flooded the political zone. He declared in a recent sworn statement as part of the McCain-Feingold litigation, that in his opinion—contrary to the current Republican Party's position— "political parties, the essential 'connection' between citizens and their government, were weakened. In effect the parties increasingly became conduits for single-interest influence rather than for the development of broadly based representative government. . . .

"These contributions compromise our elected officials. When elected officials solicit these contributions from interests who almost always have matters pending before the Congress, [they] become at least psychologically beholden to those who contribute. It is inevitable and unavoidable. The contributors, for their part, feel they have a 'call' on these officials. Corporations, unions and wealthy individuals give these large amounts of money to political parties so they can improve their access to and influence over elected party members. Elected officials who raise soft money [for the party] know this. The appearance of corruption is corrosive and is undermining our democracy."

A MERCENARY MILIEU

Nothing focuses a politician's mind better than hard, cold campaign cash. Consider the under-oath insights of former congressman Pat Williams, a Democrat from Montana who represented his district from 1979 to 1997.

"Throughout the West, the past 25 years of polls . . . have indicated a strong desire for Westerners to protect the land and water and air with strict environmental laws and regulations. However, they vote for federal candidates who are on the other side of those very issues. And I believe that that division, that gap, that dichotomy is caused by money, and the portraying of some candidates in very bad light and other candidates in very good light. Thus, confusing voters to such a degree that they end up voting for people who don't actually do what the majority of voters want."

The top five mining contributors to the political parties in the 2000 and 2002 election cycles—Peabody Energy, Addington Enterprises, Freeport-McMoRan, Boich Group, and the National Mining Association—gave more than $2.4 million, 89 percent of their party donations, to the Republican national committees and just $309,000 to the Democrats.

The mining industry is feeling rejuvenated after its frustrations with the previous administration and its "extreme ideology that drove extreme solutions," as Jack Gerard, president of the National Mining Association, told the *New York Times*. Nine months into the Bush administration, Interior Secretary Gale Norton rewrote Clinton-era regulations, thereby preventing the Bureau of Land Management from vetoing mining operations that could cause irreparable harm to the environment or Native American cultural sites. She also systematically permitted mining on sites that her predecessor, Bruce Babbitt, had vetoed because he determined they had endangered species or would impact sacred Native American sites. In addition, Norton bowed to industry pressure when a federal judge threw out regulations that once required mining companies to report a low concentration of toxic release pollutants that are said to be extremely dangerous if leaked into the water supply. The administration chose not to appeal the decision. The Bush administration rolled back the disclosure requirements of the Environmental Protection Agency's annual Toxic Release Inventory, a publicly available database that allows citizens to know what hazardous chemicals are in their area. The mining industry has been the largest worldwide industry polluter since 1997. More than half of the mining industry's 3 billion pounds of annual waste may now go unreported.

On the influence front, Peabody Energy, the world's largest coal production company, and largest mining contributor to the Republican Party, sent two executives to Vice President Cheney's Energy Task Force in 2001 to promote the use of coal. The task force report ultimately recommended increases in coal production.

But not in their wildest dreams did the industry imagine that a kindred soul—hell, one of their lobbyists—would become chairman of the Republican Party.

One of Governor Bush's campaign confidantes and public spokesmen during the 2000 Florida recount was Montana Governor Marc Racicot (pronounced ROS-coe); the two men had met years earlier and become friends. For eight years as governor, Racicot was a deft and popular politician whom local critics regarded as too close to the mining and logging industries, and not just because he took thousands of dollars in campaign contributions from them.

One of his major embarrassments as governor occurred when the national news media broke the story that asbestos poisoning at W. R. Grace & Co.'s vermiculite mine in Libby, Montana—Racicot's hometown—had killed or sickened hundreds of residents. Racicot, who missed the first open meeting in Libby over the issue because he was in New Hampshire campaigning with

Bush, claimed total ignorance about the mine being a major health hazard. Former congressman Pat Williams found that assertion preposterous and disingenuous, noting that it had been well known for decades, even prompting Williams to introduce legislation in 1985 to help workers get compensation for occupational diseases such as the kind afflicting Libby.

Racicot signed a new law in 1999, weakening Montana's Superfund statutes by protecting polluters from responsibility for cleanup costs. In 2000, he signed a bill changing existing state law so that mining companies needn't always refill open pits once mining had ended, resulting in "weaker reclamation standards, more unreclaimed land and toxic, polluted water in Montana," the Montana Conservation Voters, an environmental group, claimed. During his tenure as governor, he opposed Montana voter Initiative 137 banning cyanide use in new and expanded Montana gold mines. A *New York Times* editorial decried his poor environmental record: "Mr. Racicot endorsed an easing of Montana's clean water laws, supported drilling for natural gas on the Rocky Mountain Front, criticized Mr. Clinton's plan to protect roadless areas in the national forests and resisted reasonable solutions aimed at stopping the slaughter of bison that migrate each year from Yellowstone National Park."

> **But not in their wildest dreams did the mining industry imagine that a kindred soul—hell, one of their lobbyists—would become chairman of the Republican Party.**

After his national television exposure in the Florida recount and his highly publicized role as an articulate Republican governor close to the new President—and shortly after leaving public office—Racicot and his wife moved to the nation's capital, where he quickly became a rich man as a Washington lobbyist, cashing in on his new fame and proximity to power. Bracewell & Patterson, a Houston-based firm with 350 lawyers and 11 offices worldwide, hired him as a partner in its Washington office in February 2001. It has proven to be a bonanza for all concerned. According to federal lobbying records, in 2000 Bracewell & Patterson earned $2.8 million in lobbying income from clients. In 2001, the firm's lobbying income jumped to $4.6 million.

Racicot became a registered lobbyist working Washington and the new administration on behalf of Enron, the American Forest and Paper Association, Burlington Northern Santa Fe, the National Energy Coordinating Council, the Recording Industry Association of America, and Quintana Minerals. They paid Racicot's firm $710,000 in lobbying fees in just the first half of 2001. The *Los Angeles Times* reported that on behalf of the National Electric Reliability Council, Racicot had personally lobbied Vice President Dick Cheney on the Environmental Protection Agency's attempts to require old plants to update their clean-air equipment. The Cheney task force later recommended that the Justice Department consider dropping lawsuits it had filed against certain companies for alleged environmental violations. The Bush administration continues to stonewall requests for public information about the secret energy task force.

Racicot also went on the corporate boards of Burlington Northern Santa Fe, the Mass Mutual Financial Group, and Siebel Systems. BNSF, best known as the second largest railroad in the country, is the largest transporter of low-sulfur coal in the United States, generating revenues of more than $2 billion from it in 2001. The railroad hauls 90 percent of the traffic from the Powder River Basin of Wyoming and Montana to coal-fired electric generating stations in Midwest and Mountain states.

From the BNSF's own annual report, we are informed that "deregulation in the electric utility industry is causing power generators to seek lower cost fuel sources and this increases demand for Powder River Basin coal." Besides employing Racicot as a board member and lobbyist, the company has also added Republican former House member J. C. Watts. BNSF was a campaign contributor to Racicot when he ran for governor.

Siebel Systems, with 5,000 employees operating in 33 countries, was the first software company to reach $1 billion in sales—ahead of Microsoft. In 1999, the company began selling electronic government software, and by early 2001 it had come to understand how the influence game is played in Washington. Siebel created from scratch one of the largest political action committees in the software industry. As the *San Jose Mercury News* reported, in a 12-month period, the company raised $2.1 million from 373 employees, all but 18 of them giving the maximum annual contribution, $5,000. Billionaire company founder Thomas Siebel is a major Republican donor, giving $500,000 to the National Republican Congressional Committee in 2000, the largest single donation ever to that national GOP committee.

Why the sudden interest in politics and Washington? Well, to paraphrase that famous philosopher Willie Sutton, that's where the money is. Thomas Gann, the Siebel Systems "vice president of government affairs"—a Washington euphemism for lobbyist—reportedly acknowledged that the company sees government as "a good commercial opportunity." That was the understatement of the year, especially after September 11, 2001. Just weeks later, in November, with a 40-foot American flag draped on its San Mateo headquarters, Siebel Systems also unfurled its new homeland security software. According to the *San Jose Mercury News*, that same month board member Marc Racicot touted the Siebel software directly to White House homeland security director Tom Ridge. His eyes firmly on those tens of billions of dollars in homeland security contract prizes, Siebel also found time to personally meet with Ridge. His company officials have "demoed" the software to several Bush administration officials, in a full dog-and-pony show that included mug shots of the September 11 hijackers.

At the same time, the company launched a multimillion-dollar public relations campaign, including radio ads, and got out the trumpets on its Web site. "Siebel Solutions for Homeland Security provide a comprehensive multi-agency, multi-channel suite of applications software to enable governments to anticipate, track, prevent, and respond to national security threats," the company declared.

In February 2002, Siebel testified before the House Committee on Government Reform's Subcommittee on Technology and Procurement Policy, essentially offering a public Washington advertisement for Siebel Systems. "Chairman [Tom] Davis, Ranking Member [Jim] Turner, and distinguished Members of the Committee," he began. "It is my privilege to speak to you today about the homeland security challenges facing our nation and possible solutions offered by private sector technology." The committee's chair, Representative Tom Davis, also chairs the National Republican Congressional Committee, which Siebel had seeded with half a million dollars a year and a half earlier, $80,000 in November 2001, and $100,000 roughly two weeks after the hearing. Davis's own reelection campaign received $10,000 from the Siebel Systems PAC in the 2002 election cycle.

It's too soon to tell how Siebel's investment will pay off, but given the amount of campaign cash it had donated, and given that its board includes presidential pal and party leader Marc Racicot, what company could possibly be *ahead* of Siebel Systems in the long line for major federal contracts from the

Department of Homeland Security? One securities analyst, Sameer Bhasin with Okumus Capital Corporation in New York, told CBS.MarketWatch.com, "There's no other company competing in the homeland security area as aggressively." Government contracting business could not come at a more crucial time for Siebel Systems. The company is battling a serious sales slump that has plagued the software industry since the tech bubble burst in May 2000. For Siebel, which has also fired hundreds of employees as corporate demand for its products has dropped, the federal government is potentially a growth market.

Meanwhile, sometime after September 11, 2001, Racicot's firm also had begun to move into the homeland security contracting area, even though they don't actually make anything. With a bald eagle and American flag on its Web site, Bracewell & Patterson announced: "We feel a duty to our clients and our country to help resolve these uncertainties in a way that strengthens our nation and preserves the freedoms that define it." The Washington office of the firm hosted or participated in two seminars in 2003 for its corporate clients: The National Homeland Security Law Conference and "Selling in the Homeland Security Marketplace" before the National Contract Management Association, an organization for government and private sector procurement officers. It touted two of Racicot's areas of expertise: "Homeland Security" and "Government Relations, Advocacy and Strategy."

> "There's been ample history on both the Democratic and
> Republican side of chairmen being involved
> in either lobbying or having outside sources
> of income."

Who better to become chairman of the Republican National Committee?

The White House announced that Racicot—an active, registered lobbyist who would be allowed to continue his corporate lobbying—was the President's choice to chair the RNC in December 2001. It was a stunning metaphor for how power, money, and hubris in Washington can dull the ethical judgment of an administration that vowed to "restore honor and dignity" to the White House. It also provides another glimpse of the seamy side of our major political parties.

A party chairman whose party controls both ends of Pennsylvania Avenue necessarily is in regular, face-to-face contact with the president, the vice president, cabinet secretaries, and the senior White House staff, as well as the Speaker of the House and other GOP congressional leaders. He knows the precise vote counts of all major pending legislation before the roll is called and exactly what legislation the White House plans to introduce on Capitol Hill—pure gold for any lobbyist competing in today's mercenary milieu. He has infinitely more power and access than other lobbyists, but without the accountability, financial sacrifice, or ethics laws of government officials. Although political parties are major public institutions in our society, top party officials are not regulated by conflict-of-interest laws and are not even required by law to reveal their sources of annual income. Nor does the Freedom of Information Act apply to them, so whom they telephone, meet, or correspond with is elusive and generally unknown.

Racicot, as Republican Party chairman, said he would not accept his $150,000 annual salary, but instead earn much more as an active partner in the law firm. The president, said Racicot, has no problem with his wish to "continue on with my occupation." But critics, including Senator John McCain and conservative columnists Robert Novak and William Safire, found it offensive. The *New York Times* reported that before the firestorm of criticism, party officials had offered Racicot as much as $500,000 a year—more than three times the customary salary for the RNC chairman position—if he would stop lobbying, but Racicot had refused. Ultimately, Racicot made a minor concession to the public furor and vowed to cease all corporate lobbying. He continued to work at Bracewell & Patterson, reportedly getting paid $700,000 a year by the firm while *also* chairing the Republican Party. At the end of his 18-month tenure at the RNC, he became chairman of the Bush-Cheney reelection campaign.

Racicot was paid $1 a year as an RNC "volunteer." Under this Orwellian construct, thousands of well-heeled corporate lobbyists are all political volunteers in Washington, and Americans apparently should be grateful for their civic participation. The Bush White House similarly didn't see anything wrong with this picture. Former White House press secretary Ari Fleischer said, "There's been ample history on both the Democratic and Republican side of chairmen being involved in either lobbying or having outside sources of income."

Unfortunately, Fleischer was correct—conflicts of interest are a way of life for political party chairmen. The Center for Public Integrity found in an earlier study that between 1977 and 1993, *half* of the national party chairmen received outside income from corporations and law firms—despite party charters expressly stipulating that the chairman's position is full-time.

Republicans, among others, expressed outrage at revelations in 1992 by the Center for Public Integrity and others about the late Ron Brown's conduct as chairman of the Democratic Party in the early 1990s, when he simultaneously maintained a corner office at the lobbying firm of Patton, Boggs as a full partner and maintained business relationships with at least three of its clients. He solicited government contracts for both his law firm and a company he headed, while heading the party.

Because of the Brown controversy, when Washington lobby-ist Haley Barbour became GOP chairman in late 1992, he publicly pledged to party leaders and on CNN that he would completely sever his ties to Barbour, Griffith & Rogers. But in fact he never sold his interest in the firm, deriving income from its tobacco, pharmaceutical, and other clients. The subterfuge only became known to reporters in the final days of his four-year term, when Barbour's firm landed a contract representing the Swiss government and had to register ownership and other information with the Justice Department under the Foreign Agents Registration Act.

Barbour admitted, in an interview for *The Buying of the President 2000*, that he kept his equity share in the firm, but insisted that he has always operated in a carefully correct manner. "When I ran for chairman, I said I would not actively lobby because I didn't want a member [of Congress] to wonder whether I was coming down there for the Republican Party or for some business deal that is in Haley's interest."

Barbour's counterpart, Democratic National Committee chairman Don Fowler, worked simultaneously as a lobbyist for various corporate interests, including Chem-Nuclear Systems Inc., registered in South Carolina and Illinois. When later asked about this apparent, though not widely known, conflict of interest during his DNC chairmanship, Fowler said: "My private business concerns never became an issue while I was there, and really haven't since." Recall that when mysterious soft-money donors gave millions of dollars to the Democratic Party in the 1996 presidential election, one of them, Johnny Chung (later convicted for bank fraud, tax evasion, and conspiracy), said: "The White House is like a subway. You have to put in coins to open the gates." Fowler and his staff set up Chung's White House meetings, and Fowler later defended "servicing" the donors in his testimony to the Senate Governmental Affairs Committee. "I have long believed that one of the principal functions of a political party is to provide a link between the people and government," he said. "I thus believe it fully appropriate for the head of a national party to secure a meeting for a supporter with an administration official and to advocate a worthy cause."

Racicot's unabashed public declaration at the onset of his tenure as national party chairman that he would simultaneously actively lobby for major corporate clients with business before the federal government—with the public assent of the President—was another "first," even in ethically challenged Washington.

THE RNC'S GREAT ENABLER

Forget those quaint notions that political parties exist almost entirely to elect candidates. Parties and their chairmen raise hundreds of millions of dollars each election cycle from various special interests that often want something from government. They are the enablers in this ongoing addictive process, helping their elected officials to keep drinking in the campaign cash and helping their patrons to feel good about giving it. Besides being lobbyists in chief, chairmen help to deliver access and other favors to the most generous party patrons. If you think about it unsentimentally, being a corporate schmoozer in our nation's capital is perfect preparation and experience for the chairman of a political party, needing to keep the far-flung *keiretsu* functioning, with its officeholder party members and fundraisers, the friendly outside groups running their "independent" expenditure issue ad campaigns, and all of those myriad vested interests desperately seeking access and influence and willing to pay substantially for it.

So whom did the White House and Republican National Committee choose to replace Marc Racicot as chairman? Why, another lobbyist, of course. In June 2003, Ed Gillespie was named to succeed Racicot. And in light of the earlier controversies surrounding the former Montana governor, Gillespie said he would retain partial ownership in his Washington lobbying firm but neither work for nor draw any salary from it while serving as party chairman.

Gillespie is a fixture in recent national GOP politics, a Zelig-like character with an instinct for power. He helped his party take control of Congress in 1994 and draw up the "Contract with America." He worked for Republican House leader Dick Armey for a decade before becoming RNC communications director under party chairman Haley Barbour during the 1996 elections. He helped secure the White House for George W. Bush by helping Andy Card (now White House chief of staff) run the party convention in Philadelphia and by playing key roles for the campaign from both Austin and Miami during the recount. In 1995, the *National Journal* called him one of the "chief power wielders in the new House." In 2001, *The New Republic* dubbed him "The Insider: the most powerful Bushie you've never heard of."

Gillespie had begun raking in serious corporate dough while he worked with former RNC chairman Barbour in 1997. He became president of Policy Impact Communications, which Barbour chaired and which was associated with Barbour's high-profile firm, Barbour, Griffith & Rogers. Recognizing that Bush might indeed become the next president of the United States, in January 2000, Gillespie—like Racicot, only sooner—cashed in on his new access to the Bush administration, teaming up with former Clinton White House counsel Jack Quinn to form a new lobbying shop, Quinn Gillespie & Associates.

Gillespie practices a time-honored Washington inside game

as an enormously talented political consultant who also works as a highly paid lobbyist for corporate clients needing political access and favors, the same kind of in-and-out influence-peddling role that Charles Black and James Lake played for Bush's father. Lake functioned as an unpaid deputy campaign manager of the 1992 presidential reelection campaign while *simultaneously* working as a registered foreign agent for a major investor in the Bank of Credit and Commerce International, BCCI, better known as the Bank of Crooks and Criminals International, at the time the corrupt bank was being investigated by numerous federal grand juries.

> Gillespie practices a time-honored Washington inside game as a political consultant who also works as a highly paid lobbyist for corporate clients needing political access and favors.

Gillespie helped the President-elect as spokesman for the Presidential Inaugural Committee and by assisting close Bush friend Don Evans set up the Commerce Department. He has also earned the loyalty and trust of White House political advisor Karl Rove and the Bush inner circle by doing some of the sensitive political work they can't be seen doing themselves. Gillespie reportedly helped to plant and "spin" some negative news stories about Gore in the crucial weeks before the 2000 election, including accounts of pollution at Gore's Tennessee farm and an endorsement Gore received from a group of pornographers. He is believed to have helped to orchestrate the infamous "penny-loafer protesters" riot of Republican Capitol Hill aides flown in by Representative Tom DeLay in Miami during the Florida recount. He has also helped the party as a fundraiser; for instance, he was involved in a GOP power and fundraising project called

ROMP ("Retain Our Majority Program") run by GOP House leader Tom DeLay to funnel campaign cash to vulnerable Republican candidates, in Gillespie's case squeezing major bucks out of Washington's K Street corridor of lobbyists and lawyers.

From January 2000 through 2002, the Quinn Gillespie firm took in $27.4 million in lobbying fees from such clients as Microsoft, PriceWaterhouseCoopers, the Chamber of Commerce, Tyson Foods, and the National Association of Realtors, according to a report by Public Citizen.

Gillespie's firm received $700,000 from Enron in 2001 to, essentially, put a happy face on the California energy crisis and block any potential federal regulatory efforts to institute such things as price controls in the troubled Western electricity market. Gillespie also launched the 21st Century Energy Project—one of those corporate-funded "independent advocacy groups" so much in abundance in Washington—reportedly moving money from Enron and DaimlerChrysler to conservative organizations like Americans for Tax Reform and Citizens for a Sound Economy as a way of advancing the Bush administration's energy plan while preventing any new regulation.

The top five electric utility contributors to the political parties in the 2000 and 2002 election cycles—Dominion Resources Inc., Southern Company, Exelon Corporation, Texas Utilities Company, and the National Rural Electric Cooperative Association—gave nearly three-quarters (74 percent) of their party donations, $5.1 million, to the Republican national committees and just $1.8 million to the Democrats. Back in 1994, when Democrats controlled the White House and the Congress, the industry was more "bipartisan" in its giving, donating $3.3 million to the Democrats and $2.7 million to the Republicans, according to the Center for Responsive Politics.

The electric utility industry has gotten excellent returns on its political access fees. It was, for example, successful in changing—with the leadership of the Bush administration, of course—a provision known as "New Source Review" in the 1977 Clean Air Act, thereby enabling electric generating and other companies to forego putting new, expensive pollution controls in their facilities. Another "independent" organization, the Electric Reliability Coordinating Council, funded by Southern Company and five other energy companies, was formed to work with the Bush administration in getting this law changed, and Racicot and his firm were paid more than $150,000 to lobby in 2001 solely on this issue. The ERCC, the Edison Electric Institute led by Bush Pioneer and George W. Bush's former Yale roommate Thomas Kuhn, and other energy interests were fired up over Clinton administration EPA-initiated litigation, including indictments, against seven power companies for violating this provision of the Clean Air Act.

Two of Quinn Gillespie's major telecom clients have been Verizon (formerly Bell Atlantic) and SBC Communications, who just happen to be the seventh and twelfth most generous Republican Party patrons, giving more than $4.5 million and $3.7 million, respectively, to the three national committees since 1978. Verizon and Verizon Wireless paid the firm $1.4 million from 2000 through 2002 to lobby on telecom spectrum issues. SBC, which in 2002 had 67 lobbyists in Washington, retained the firm for $1.2 million to lobby on broadband policy issues.

The top five telephone company contributors to the political parties in the 2000 and 2002 election cycles—AT&T, Verizon, SBC, BellSouth Corporation, and MCI (formerly WorldCom)—gave 58 percent of their party donations, more than $9.9 million, to the Republican national committees; 42 percent, $7.1 million, went to the Democrats.

Since their creation in 1984 when the government broke up AT&T's nationwide telephone monopoly, some of the "Baby Bells" have chafed under a rule that they must, in the spirit of competition, lease parts of their local networks to competitors at discounted rates. Complaining that the regulation essentially compels them to finance the success of their competitors, they have long tried to persuade the FCC and Congress to rescind the law.

In the wake of the 2002 elections and Republican control across the board, SBC and Verizon had reason to believe that the tide in Washington had turned in their favor. Particularly with a Republican majority on the Federal Communications Commission, including a new chairman, Michael Powell, a tech-savvy, free-market advocate of deregulation who happens to be the son of Secretary of State Colin Powell. And in fact in February 2003 he came extremely close to eliminating the phone regulations that obligate the companies to lease their networks to competitors. But he was foiled when a Republican commissioner, Kevin Martin, unexpectedly voted with the Democrats—prompting Republican House Commerce chairman Billy Tauzin to dub him a "Renegade Republican." Nonetheless, Powell and major party patrons SBC and Verizon did win an important consolation prize: the commission voted to free them from having to share new high-speed data lines with competitors.

As we noted earlier, the most profitable U.S. industry has become increasingly aligned with the Republican Party. The top five pharmaceutical contributors to the political parties in the 2000 and 2002 election cycles—Pharmaceutical Research & Manufacturers of America (known as PhRMA), Bristol-Myers Squibb, Pfizer, Pharmacia Corporation (since merged into Pfizer), and Eli Lilly—gave 87 percent of their party donations, nearly $11.2 million, to the Republican national committees and just $1.7 million to the Democrats. Moreover, Pfizer, PhRMA, and Bristol-Myers Squibb are, respectively, the fourth, fourteenth and sixteenth most generous Republican party patrons overall.

The discovery documents from the BCRA (McCain-Feingold) litigation reveal the recent increased coziness between the industry and the GOP. In an internal briefing memorandum dated February 8, 1999, and addressed to Alan Holmer, the president of PhRMA, a staff lobbyist wrote, "We are scheduled to meet with Senator [Mitch] McConnell tomorrow.... You are meeting with the Senator principally in his leadership role as chair of the NRSC [National Republican Senatorial Committee]. In that regard, industry has been a solid supporter (see attached correspondence [based on FEC records] reflecting industry support for the Republican Party during the 1997–98 election cycle)." The stated objectives of the meeting include apprising McConnell "of industry's concern with attention on pharmaceutical costs and efforts by Democrats to demagogue the issue at Republican expense, e.g. Sen. Kennedy prepared to force Republicans to choose between a tax cut for the rich and a drug benefit for seniors." The final objective: "expressing PhRMA's willingness to be a resource, substantively and politically, to assist in maintaining a Republican majority in 2000."

> The top five pharmaceutical contributors to the
> political parties in the 2000 and 2002 election
> cycles gave 87 percent of their party donations
> to the Republican national committees.

PhRMA attorney Judith Bello, in a sworn deposition in 2002, acknowledged the shift to one party. "We have more heavily made contributions to Republicans than Democrats because they more often favor market-oriented approaches," she said. According to the *Washington Post*, over the past decade, PhRMA and its member companies have spent more than $1 billion to influence the public policy process in Washington, easily more than anyone else, hiring in that time more than 600 lobbyists, including numerous former lawmakers.

In mid-2003, the *New York Times* obtained confidential budget and other documents from inside PhRMA, revealing that the lobbying organization planned to spend $150 million at the state, federal, and international level, an increase of 23 percent over the preceding year. One document noting the "demonization of the industry," worried that "unless we achieve enactment this year of market-based Medicare drug coverage for seniors, the industry's vulnerability will increase in the remainder of 2003 and in the 2004 election year."

Just weeks after those documents surfaced, Congress passed historic market-based Medicare drug coverage for seniors, supported by the White House, the legislation moving to the conference stage. "We applaud the Senate and House for their action," said Holmer, the PhRMA president.

THE DNC's TEFLON CHAIRMAN

Meanwhile, for the Democratic Party, there is no aspirin strong enough for the migraine it faces. Since Election Day 2000, the Democratic National Committee and its colorful chairman Terry McAuliffe have been out of luck, out of power, and short on money, at least when compared to the Republicans. For example, when McAuliffe took over as chairman, he discovered the party only had e-mail addresses for 70,000 voters nationwide, compared to 1 million for the GOP. "The Democratic Party has 21st century ideas, but we had Stone Age technology," he told *Business Week*. McAuliffe immediately set about to update the DNC's technological capacity.

The stampede to the GOP covers a wide array of industries. In addition to the ones we've briefly discussed—tobacco, mining, and pharmaceuticals—in the 10 years since the 1992 election cycle, such industries as beer, wine, and liquor; accounting; health service/HMOs; commercial banking; defense; insurance; and automotive manufacturing significantly cut back the percentage of money that they gave to the Democratic Party. That amounts to millions of dollars not available for Democratic Party campaign activities. What's worse for the Democrats, in this zero-sum game the money actually flowed to the Republican Party, which already had a long history of financial superiority.

Ironically, the most successful and prolific fundraiser in Democratic Party history is the current chairman of the Democratic National Committee. Like Gillespie, Terry McAuliffe seems to know and have worked with everyone in his party. But while Gillespie excels in strategic consulting and communication, McAuliffe has made his name in national politics as a marathon money man. He has raised hundreds of millions of dollars over more than two decades for the Democratic Party and its leading candidates, starting out in the finance department of President Jimmy Carter's reelection campaign in 1980 and ending as the finance chairman of the DNC.

McAuliffe was the finance director for the 1996 Clinton reelection campaign, amidst some of the most controversial campaign finance decisions and scandals of that period. President Bill Clinton became the first chief executive to spend tens of millions of soft-money party dollars for nationwide television commercials about, well, Bill Clinton. It was actually Terry McAuliffe's idea—expressed in a formal memo to the president, with which Clinton enthusiastically agreed—to reward major Democratic Party donors with overnight stays in the Lincoln Bedroom and elsewhere in the Clinton White House: McAuliffe was cochair of the Presidential Inaugural Committee and first friend to Bill Clinton when it came to raising greenbacks for the

Clinton Legal Defense Fund, the Clinton Presidential Library, and even the Clintons' home in Westchester County, New York. The wealthy McAuliffe even offered to lend the Clintons the $1.35 million they needed to buy the home, but the public furor made the notion untenable.

Like his Republican counterpart, McAuliffe worked at a lobbying firm in Washington in the 1990s. Unlike Gillespie, though, McAuliffe has also been a successful businessman outside Washington and the world of politics, an entrepreneur as well as a lawyer. He takes no salary as DNC chairman. But McAuliffe also has brushed up against potentially serious public scandals over the years, remarkably without ever being ensnared.

Despite the hundreds of hours of congressional hearings over the Clinton campaign finance scandals of 1996 and 1997, plus a subsequent, multiyear Justice Department investigation that netted many small fish; despite two different Independent Counsel preliminary investigations focused on either Vice President Al Gore or White House aide Harold Ickes, in which the Democratic Party had to return millions of dollars in illicit campaign contributions from Asia and more than 45 people took the Fifth Amendment or fled the country—somehow the Democratic Party's former finance chairman and finance director for the president's reelection campaign emerged from the tawdry debacle with barely a scratch.

A federal investigation in the late 1990s involving McAuliffe's real estate business deals resulted in no charges or fines against him, but the companies or labor unions involved with him either settled out of court or were fined by the government. McAuliffe was also implicated in a series of money swaps between Teamsters president Ron Carey and the Democratic Party in 1996. Through a complicated—and, it turned out, illegal—scheme, the Teamsters had poured significant sums of money into the Clinton-Gore campaign and Democratic Party committees with the understanding that the Democrats would help Carey finance his own campaign that year. Following the investigation, three aides to Carey's campaign—Martin Davis, a consultant; Jere Nash, his campaign manager; and Michael Ansara, a telemarketer—pled guilty to embezzlement, mail fraud, and conspiracy. The three were sentenced to probation, fined, and had to pay restitution to the union. A fourth, Teamsters political director William Hamilton, was convicted on six counts of corrupt practices related to the illegal diversion of union funds.

In February 2001, Carey himself was indicted for seven counts of perjury for lying during the investigation (he was later cleared of the charges). According to media reports, former DNC finance director Richard Sullivan testified that Hamilton and McAuliffe hatched a plan in which $500,000 of Teamsters' money would flow to the Democratic Party. But the money would be given in return for a $50,000 contribution to Carey from a donor recruited by the DNC. However, the plan failed to materialize because the first proposed donor was rejected by Carey's aides as unsuitable and no replacement was found. Presumably because McAuliffe—who has always denied any wrongdoing—never conducted the illegal trade, he was never prosecuted.

More recently, McAuliffe's name was brought up in the Global Crossing affair. The chairman of the now-bankrupt telecommunications company, Gary Winnick, gave McAuliffe an opportunity to invest $100,000 in the private concern. Two years later, McAuliffe sold his interest for $18 million after the company went public. In 1997, around the time McAuliffe was given this exclusive offering, Global Crossing was dealing with federal regulators in Washington. And McAuliffe reportedly got Winnick a golf outing with President Clinton. Was Global Crossing seeking political influence with the president's money man? Was McAuliffe peddling his access to power? "You invest in stock, it goes up, it goes down," McAuliffe, said on the Fox News Channel. "If you don't like capitalism, you don't like making money with stock, move to Cuba or China."

Clearly, like his Republican counterparts, this political party chairman understands how intertwined the private sector is in the daily business of the political parties and knows how to weave and mesh multiple agendas seamlessly. For McAuliffe, the art of the deal, whether personally as an entrepreneur, politically as a legislative and public relations tactician, or professionally as premier fundraiser, is intoxicating. So what if sometimes personal and professional deals are with the same people who happen to be donors to the Democratic Party?

> **Democratic candidates have long been compelled to showcase the more liberal strains of their respective agendas and tout union-friendly initiatives.**

Such has been the attitude and culture of the DNC in recent years. In 1996, for example, when the Center for Public Integrity first published *The Buying of the President*, we wrote about a vice chair of the DNC named Lottie Shackelford, a former mayor of Little Rock, Arkansas, and a friend of Clinton's who was simultaneously registered as a lobbyist for a firm called Global USA. Shackleford is still at both places. At Global USA she has been the executive vice president of the government relations and international consulting firm since April 1994. According to its Web site, Global USA "assists its clients in understanding and addressing the complexities of U.S. Government regulations and legislation" through lobbying and government relations. It claims to have expertise in a myriad of issues ranging from international trade to telecommunications and grassroots lobbying. Shackelford represents a number of clients for Global, which works with Miami-Dade County Florida, FM Watch, Psychemedics Corporation, Quest Software, and United to Secure America.

Linda Chavez-Thompson is another DNC vice chair with an interesting day job, simultaneously serving as executive vice president of the AFL-CIO.

UNION SUPPORT

Unions certainly are the single most important constituency for any Democratic presidential candidate. Indeed, they have been without question the most consistent and generous supporters of Democratic candidates in modern American history. For the past quarter century, 6 of the Democratic Party's top 10 patrons are unions: American Federation of State, County and Municipal Employees; Service Employees International Union; Communications Workers of America; Carpenters Union; American Federation of Teachers; and the United Food & Commercial Workers. AFSCME is the top patron of the Democratic Party, contributing more than $16.4 million—the highest total given by a single organization to *either* political party. In the 2000 and 2002 election cycles alone, labor groups transferred nearly $175 million to Democratic campaigns; Republicans received less than 1 out of every 10 union dollars.

These substantial numbers don't even take into account the extensive national grassroots networks composed of thousands of unionized American workers who are at the disposal of a candidate who wins labor's endorsement. The decades-old debate between the two parties, which we have addressed in the past, rages on. Whenever Republicans are asked about their substantial fundraising advantage over the Democrats, they respond by citing research by a Rutgers University economics professor named Leo Troy, who estimates that the "in-kind contributions" provided by unions in every presidential election amount to hundreds of millions of dollars. Union leaders scoff at such assertions, but there is no denying that it is worth millions of dollars to the Democratic Party. And unlike in-kind company contributions, there is no public disclosure requirement for the unions to report the value of such efforts.

In order to maintain this essential support, Democratic candidates have long been compelled to showcase the more liberal strains of their respective agendas and tout union-friendly initiatives that range from minimum wage legislation, industry protection, and heath care reform. But in addition to these traditional concerns, unions have new worries about the new president and his party's control of Congress—along with policies diametrically opposed to organized labor and its agenda. On one front, Bush's Labor Department, complaining of perennial union corruption, is pushing for increased disclosure of union finances. Union bosses naturally protest on the grounds that more stringent accounting would cost millions of dollars. In *The Buying of the President 2000*, we wrote extensively about union corruption. (Ironically, although in nearly eight years Clinton and Gore never once publicly uttered the phrase "union corruption," the Clinton Justice Department was more aggressive in identifying union crimes than the Ashcroft Justice Department has been, according to Syracuse University's Transactional Records Access Clearinghouse data on federal prosecutions.)

Of course, there's been no ebb in union scandals, and none is more interesting than the ULLICO affair. Robert Georgine typified, more than most international union presidents, the well-paid, well-fed life. He earned two annual salaries plus bonuses plus a private jet. He was the president of the AFL-CIO

Building and Construction Trades Department, earning $264,331, and chairman and chief executive officer of the Union Labor Life Insurance Company, where insiders put his salary in 2002 at $1 million. ULLICO is a 1,400-employee health and life insurance company. In 1997, ULLICO invested $7.6 million in Terry McAuliffe's favorite company, Global Crossing, which appreciated in value—to some $486 million. ULLICO then sold 40 percent of the stock, holding the rest right up to the time Global Crossing declared bankruptcy.

An outside, independent investigator, former Illinois governor Jim Thompson, found that 18 ULLICO board directors and officers should return more than $5.5 million in "not appropriate" profits from the sales of ULLICO stock, including Georgine, who had pocketed $837,760. He and three other executives with similarly lavish compensation "were already receiving a bonus, separate from their regular annual bonus, under the Global Incentive Program and significant earnings under the Deferred Compensation Plan. . . . these officers may not have been entitled to another 'bonus.'"

Georgine and much of the ULLICO board are gone, and, to his credit, AFL-CIO president John Sweeney, who sat on the board, took no inappropriate compensation and actually quit the board when Georgine refused to publicly release the damning Thompson report. In this particular case, the unions—sensitive to corporate governance issues, even counseling and financially assisting Enron employees at the time—ultimately put their own house in order.

Understandably, unions feel threatened by Bush's plans to privatize as many as 800,000 government jobs—most of them unionized public employees—and to forbid new Homeland Security Department employees from unionizing. This is a significant issue to the dwindling labor movement, which now represents just 14 percent of the workforce, because a majority of the newest members are white-collar workers from government and service sectors. "I think that [Bush] is the most anti-worker, anti-union of all the presidents [in the past three decades]," Sweeney told us. "Sure, we had some tough times with his father, but you didn't see the same kind of blatant attack on workers that you see today. In the Nixon years, with all the problems there were, he was one of the presidents that was focused on issues of welfare and health care reform."

The heady Clinton administration days of rides on Air Force One and shared agendas and actual, enacted legislation are long gone for Sweeney and the union presidents on the AFL-CIO executive council.

TRAVAILS OF THE TRIAL LAWYERS

Another important part of the Democratic Party's funding base—with links to consumer, environmental, civil rights, and other public interest groups—are the trial lawyers. Between 1999 and 2002, the Association of Trial Lawyers of America made $8.4 million in political contributions to political parties, PACs, and candidates, with $7.5 million—89 percent—going to Democrats. ATLA is the nineteenth largest Democratic Party patron, contributing more than $3.7 million to the national committees since 1978. The most generous trial lawyer firm supporting the Democratic Party is Williams & Bailey LLP, which has given $4.7 million over the same time frame.

This disproportionate giving reflects the fact that Democrats have been sympathetic to the trial lawyers' agenda. As an industry, trial lawyers became rich and influential through the substantial fees they received from multimillion-dollar settlements. For a long time, businesses, hospitals, and insurance companies, the groups that usually pay out these enormous settlements, have complained that the awards are outlandish and urged "tort reform"—legislative limits on liability, punitive damages, and lawyer fees. While tort reform passed in some states over the last decade, it did not really catch on nationally in the 1990s. In the course of the eight years of the Clinton administration, almost no proposals on the issue were advanced by Democrats; Clinton, a former law professor, vetoed two reform bills that made it to his desk.

But the trial lawyers' charmed existence ended after the 2000 election. Unlike his predecessor, President Bush has an infamous reputation among trial lawyers. While governor in Texas he championed tort reform and pushed a sweeping legal reform package that was a trial lawyer's worst nightmare: the institution of liability limits, raising taxes on law firms, and measures to curb "frivolous lawsuits." In his presidential campaign, Bush promised to make tort reform a part of his legislative agenda; he has come through on that pledge. The Republicans in control of Washington are working with their allies in the business sector to curb trial lawyers' ability to sue corporate America. Their primary initiatives include moving multimillion-dollar class action lawsuits to federal courts from state courts, where trial lawyers tend to win bigger settlements, and capping a slew of economic punitive awards in medical malpractice cases and asbestos reform—ending costly lawsuits against companies that used asbestos by setting up a trust to pay victims.

> **The Democrats blocked a terrorism insurance bill for more than a year after the September 11 attacks because Republicans wanted to limit punitive damages that victims could seek.**

Though they're backed into a corner, trial lawyers are fighting back. With the support of its 60,000 members, ATLA spent

$3.5 million lobbying Congress in 2002; their Democratic backers responded. In an effort to forestall any attempt at tort reform, the Democrats blocked a terrorism insurance bill for more than a year after the September 11 attacks because Republicans wanted to limit punitive damages that victims could seek. In the waning days of the 107th Congress the Republicans abandoned the liability provision and the bill passed. Then in July 2003, Senate Democrats again blocked a bill, this time on medical malpractice reform, because it would have capped jury awards for pain and suffering at $250,000.

BUYING INFLUENCE: THE EMERGING POWERS

Both the Democratic and Republican parties have had to adapt to the new campaign finance landscape nationwide in recent years, and not just because of the historic passage of, and subsequent litigation opposing, the Bipartisan Campaign Reform Act ban on soft money to the national party committees and on "issue ads" within 60 days of the election.

As part of that legislation, the doubling of hard-money limits has clearly given the Republican Party, particularly George W. Bush, a major additional fundraising advantage. The Republicans have always had more maximum-allowance contributors, and moving from $1,000 to $2,000 is hardly difficult for most of them, especially with such astonishingly effective bundling systems as the Bush Pioneers, and now Rangers.

Meanwhile, the proliferation of outside groups and the use of 527 groups and 501(c)(3) "educational" organizations that don't have to disclose their funding sources are radically changing the campaign dynamic for the parties. The Democratic and Republican parties have created such mechanisms themselves essentially to keep raising big six-figure and seven-figure soft-money checks, under organizations with new names. Realistically, who is going to stop them? The President, who went to a fundraising event just hours after signing the McCain-Feingold law with no White House speech or ceremony and allowed his own political party to challenge the constitutionality of that same law? The Congress, which has demonstrated similar ambivalence about "reform" for years, and is equally addicted to hundreds of millions of dollars from vested interests every two years? The Federal Election Commission, which eviscerated McCain's new law in a loophole-ridden rule-making process?

Most candidates cannot win today without an informal alliance of outside groups, major party support, and their campaign committee. A coalition of interests working together is the new politics of the twenty-first century for those few districts that are even contested.

What is not well understood by the American people is the substantially lawless extent to which the political parties launder hundreds of millions of dollars throughout their labyrinth of state and local party committees. There are certain "Cayman Island" states that have no limits on contributions and no public disclosure, and dubious donors can easily slide their big checks into those states, knowing a transfer can be made to another place. The FEC has even "interpreted" the recent campaign finance legislation to mean that members of Congress can raise soft money for state parties. *Voilà!*

The Center for Public Integrity, working with two other organizations, tracked the expenditures and contributions of 225 party committees in the 50 states—analyzing 340,000 database records. We found that in the 2000 elections, Democratic and Republican state party committees raised $570 million, with 46 percent of it coming as soft-money transfers from national party organizations. Donors we thought had given hundreds of thousands of dollars to a political party had actually written *millions* of dollars in checks to state party committees nationwide, especially in the last week of the presidential election, strategically directed by the national party headquarters to close "battleground" states.

Campaign finance anarchy reigns, and the two major political parties thrive in the chaos. They can cavort and collude with powerful vested interests that want something from government, with very little if any accountability. The amounts of money will increase, and accessibility by ordinary, well-intended, serious folks will become even more limited.

A neutered Federal Election Commission ruled recently that the party organizers for the 2004 Republican Convention in New York and the Democratic Convention in Boston can raise as much money as they want from whomever they wish. The post-Watergate system established that each party convention would get public funding and could augment the costs from private sources. In 1980, for the two party conventions in Detroit and New York, private special-interest money accounted for 13 percent of the total available cash. In 2000, for the conventions in Philadelphia and Los Angeles, private organizations gave 208 percent more than the government provided. In other words, as an analysis by the Campaign Finance Institute found, U.S. taxpayers gave a total of $27 million to the two political parties for their lavish conventions, but they went out and raised another $56 million from private vested interests. How much will the parties raise for the 2004 conventions? The institute estimates the orgies this time will run up an $89 million tab, not counting the $30 million total from taxpayers.

The conventions themselves have become extravaganzas. In Los Angeles in 2000, there were 130 "invitation only" star-studded parties, receptions, lunches and dinners, and 300 fundraisers and opportunities for vested interests to get "face time" with elected officials, from discreet Beverly Hills estates to the Santa Monica pier. In Philadelphia there were hundreds of parties and fundraising and donor-maintenance events. There were golf tournaments, rock concerts, and large yacht parties. Cars and drivers were made available to every GOP member of Congress.

So the cash will keep flowing and parties will keep selling access and influence. As we leave the mercenary culture of the political parties and turn towards specific investigative profiles of the major 2004 presidential candidates, let us not forget, then, that they seek to win the nomination of their parties, with all the unstated encumbrances and financial alliances that go with them. Every president, upon election, rewards specific vested interests and thousands of campaign workers for their past loyalty, and the organizing principle for all of this is his political party.

As citizens and voters, we are not just electing a president, but by extension his family, his closest aides and advisors, and his national political party. It is a package deal. And that means *caveat suffragator*, voter beware. Remember James Madison's warning in the *Federalist Papers*. The danger in any republic, he said, is when "men of factious tempers, of local prejudices, or of sinister designs, may by intrigue, by corruption or by other means, first obtain the suffrages, and then betray the interests of the people."

The Republican Party

Top Fifty Donors

1. **PHILIP MORRIS, NEW YORK** $10,335,170

2. **AMERICAN FINANCIAL GROUP INC./LINDNER FAMILY BUSINESSES, CINCINNATI** $6,566,758

3. **ALTICOR INC., ADA, MICHIGAN** $6,019,447

4. **PFIZER INC., NEW YORK** $5,587,933

5. **AT&T CORPORATION, NEW YORK** $5,549,326

6. **FREDDIE MAC, MCLEAN, VIRGINIA** $4,605,106

7. **VERIZON COMMUNICATIONS CORPORATION (FORMERLY BELL ATLANTIC), NEW YORK** $4,580,252

8. **MICROSOFT CORPORATION, REDMOND, WASHINGTON** $4,175,966

9. BP PLC, WARRENVILLE, ILLINOIS (NORTH AMERICAN HEADQUARTERS) $4,136,810

10. R.J. REYNOLDS TOBACCO HOLDINGS INC., WINSTON-SALEM, NORTH CAROLINA $3,785,815

11. CITIGROUP INC., NEW YORK $3,735,876

12. SBC COMMUNICATIONS INC., SAN ANTONIO, TEXAS $3,724,155

13. UST INC., GREENWICH, CONNECTICUT $3,494,041

14. PHARMACEUTICAL RESEARCH & MANUFACTURERS OF AMERICA, WASHINGTON, D.C. $3,427,344

15. CHEVRONTEXACO CORPORATION, SAN RAMON, CALIFORNIA $3,302,135

16. BRISTOL-MYERS SQUIBB COMPANY, NEW YORK $3,294,608

17. NATIONAL RIFLE ASSOCIATION, WASHINGTON, D.C. $3,251,750

18. FDX CORPORATION, MEMPHIS $3,013,422

19. ARCHER-DANIELS-MIDLAND COMPANY, DECATUR, ILLINOIS $2,981,754

20. UNION PACIFIC CORPORATION, OMAHA, NEBRASKA $2,959,608

21. **CINTAS CORPORATION, CINCINNATI** $2,756,200

22. **LIMITED BRANDS INC., COLUMBUS, OHIO**
$2,737,277

23. **UNITED PARCEL SERVICE OF AMERICA INC., CHICAGO**
$2,704,218

24. **BLUE CROSS AND BLUE SHIELD, CHICAGO**
$2,665,872

25. **ENRON CORPORATION, HOUSTON** $2,598,533

26. **GLAXOSMITHKLINE, BRENTFORD, MIDDLESEX, UNITED KINGDOM** $2,543,228

27. **BROWN & WILLIAMSON TOBACCO, LOUISVILLE, KENTUCKY**
$2,513,687

28. **BELLSOUTH CORPORATION, ATLANTA** $2,512,291

29. **ELI LILLY AND COMPANY, INDIANAPOLIS**
$2,498,684

30. **ANHEUSER-BUSCH INC., ST. LOUIS** $2,457,615

31. **VIVENDI UNIVERSAL, PARIS, FRANCE** $2,439,227

32. **GOLDMAN SACHS GROUP INC., NEW YORK**
$2,409,779

33. **KOCH INDUSTRIES, WICHITA, KANSAS** $2,398,086

34. **MERRILL LYNCH & COMPANY INC., NEW YORK**
$2,390,599

35. **MORGAN STANLEY, NEW YORK** $2,381,834

36. **MBNA CORPORATION, WILMINGTON, DELAWARE**
$2,367,260

37. **CSX CORPORATION, JACKSONVILLE, FLORIDA**
$2,326,315

38. **NORTHROP GRUMMAN CORPORATION, LOS ANGELES**
$2,274,382

39. **MCI (FORMERLY WORLDCOM INC.), ASHBURN, VIRGINIA** $2,247,028

40. **AFLAC INC., COLUMBUS, GEORGIA** $2,211,211

41. **AOL TIME WARNER INC., NEW YORK** $2,200,120

42. **WELSH, CARSON, ANDERSON & STOWE, NEW YORK**
$2,157,750

43. **BANK OF AMERICA CORPORATION, CHARLOTTE, NORTH CAROLINA** $2,125,384

44. **AMERICAN INTERNATIONAL GROUP INC., NEW YORK**
$2,104,577

45. **UBS PAINE WEBBER INC., NEW YORK** $2,071,151

46. **COCA-COLA COMPANY, ATLANTA** $2,067,628

47. **ERNST & YOUNG LLP, NEW YORK** $2,041,240

48. **BOEING COMPANY, CHICAGO** $2,037,604

49. **MGM MIRAGE, LAS VEGAS** $2,025,900

50. **WASTE MANAGEMENT INC., HOUSTON** $2,024,340

This list is based on individual, corporate, and PAC hard- and soft-money contributions to the Republican National Committee, National Republican Congressional Committee, National Republican Senatorial Committee, and affiliated committees between January 1, 1978, and June 30, 2003.

The Democratic Party

Top Fifty Donors

1. AMERICAN FEDERATION OF STATE, COUNTY AND MUNICIPAL EMPLOYEES, WASHINGTON, D.C. $16,491,501

2. SABAN ENTERTAINMENT INC., LOS ANGELES
$12,703,582

3. SERVICE EMPLOYEES INTERNATIONAL UNION, WASHINGTON, D.C. $12,549,102

4. COMMUNICATIONS WORKERS OF AMERICA, WASHINGTON, D.C. $10,008,890

5. NEWSWEB CORPORATION, CHICAGO $9,032,500

6. CARPENTERS UNION, WASHINGTON, D.C.
$7,790,904

7. AMERICAN FEDERATION OF TEACHERS, WASHINGTON, D.C.
$7,490,494

8. **STEPHEN BING/SHANGRI-LA ENTERTAINMENT,
LOS ANGELES** $7,438,000

9. **UNITED FOOD AND COMMERCIAL WORKERS,
WASHINGTON, D.C.** $6,293,492

10. **LORAL SPACE & COMMUNICATIONS LTD., NEW YORK**
$5,313,800

11. **LABORERS' UNION INTERNATIONAL OF NORTH AMERICA,
WASHINGTON, D.C.** $5,139,475

12. **INTERNATIONAL BROTHERHOOD OF ELECTRICAL WORKERS,
WASHINGTON, D.C.** $5,091,721

13. **NATIONAL EDUCATION ASSOCIATION, WASHINGTON, D.C.**
$4,900,621

14. **WILLIAMS & BAILEY LLP, HOUSTON** $4,717,400

15. **S. DANIEL ABRAHAM/SLIM-FAST FOODS CORPORATION,
WEST PALM BEACH, FLORIDA** $4,178,430

16. **AT&T CORPORATION, NEW YORK** $4,134,669

17. **STEVEN KIRSCH/PROPEL SOFTWARE CORPORATION,
SAN JOSE, CALIFORNIA** $3,936,286

18. **GOLDMAN SACHS GROUP, NEW YORK** $3,902,333

19. **ASSOCIATION OF TRIAL LAWYERS OF AMERICA,
WASHINGTON, D.C.** $3,776,600

20. SBC COMMUNICATIONS INC., HOUSTON $3,632,128

21. ANGELOS LAW OFFICES, CUMBERLAND, MARYLAND
$3,577,500

22. AMERICAN FEDERATION OF LABOR-CONGRESS OF
INDUSTRIAL ORGANIZATIONS, WASHINGTON, D.C.
$3,382,445

23. SIMON PROPERTY GROUP INC., INDIANAPOLIS
$3,313,873

24. BUTTENWIESER & ASSOCIATES, PHILADELPHIA
$3,310,000

25. SHEET METAL WORKERS INTERNATIONAL ASSOCIATION,
WASHINGTON, D.C. $3,260,154

26. MILBERG WEISS BERSHAD HYNES & LERACH, NEW YORK
$3,222,650

27. FREDDIE MAC, MCLEAN, VIRGINIA $3,208,020

28. VIVENDI UNIVERSAL, PARIS, FRANCE $3,188,423

29. AOL TIME WARNER INC., NEW YORK $3,150,335

30. CITIGROUP INC., NEW YORK $3,125,015

31. INTERNATIONAL ASSOCIATION OF MACHINISTS AND
AEROSPACE WORKERS, WASHINGTON, D.C. $3,123,250

32. O'QUINN, LAMINACK & PIRTLE, HOUSTON
$2,894,000

33. NIX, PATTERSON & ROACH, DAINGERFIELD, TEXAS
$2,868,500

34. VERIZON COMMUNICATIONS CORPORATION (FORMERLY BELL ATLANTIC), NEW YORK $2,798,104

35. UNITED AUTO WORKERS, DETROIT $2,735,295

36. SHORENSTEIN COMPANY, SAN FRANCISCO
$2,638,028

37. NEWS CORPORATION LTD., NEW YORK (U.S. HEADQUARTERS)
$2,609,537

38. PHILIP MORRIS, NEW YORK $2,524,583

39. CONNELL COMPANY, BERKELEY HEIGHTS, NEW JERSEY
$2,384,679

40. INTERNATIONAL ASSOCIATION OF FIRE FIGHTERS, WASHINGTON, D.C. $2,276,758

41. NATIONAL ASSOCIATION OF LETTER CARRIERS, WASHINGTON, D.C. $2,232,451

42. FDX CORPORATION, MEMPHIS $2,214,228

43. PLUMBERS AND PIPEFITTERS UNION, WASHINGTON, D.C.
$2,195,430

44. **AMERIQUEST CAPITAL CORPORATION, ORANGE, CALIFORNIA** $2,170,000

45. **ANHEUSER-BUSCH INC., ST. LOUIS** $2,168,289

46. **MICROSOFT CORPORATION, REDMOND, WASHINGTON** $2,141,977

47. **DREAMWORKS SKG, GLENDALE, CALIFORNIA** $2,118,529

48. **BELLSOUTH CORPORATION, ATLANTA** $2,056,633

49. **MCI (FORMERLY WORLDCOM INC.), ASHBURN, VIRGINIA** $2,013,962

50. **PALOMA PARTNERS MANAGEMENT, GREENWICH, CONNECTICUT** $1,976,500

This list is based on individual, corporate, and PAC hard- and soft-money contributions to the Democratic National Committee, Democratic Congressional Campaign Committee, Democratic Senatorial Campaign Committee, and affiliated committees between January 1, 1978, and June 30, 2003.

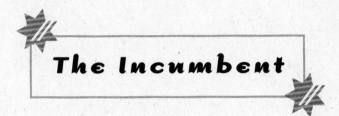

The Incumbent

George W. Bush
The Texas Years

The curious, the converts, and, of course, the faithful all turned out for President George W. Bush's visit to Pinellas County, Florida, on March 8, 2002. This was Bush's eighth trip to the Sunshine State since taking the oath of office some thirteen and a half months earlier, and over his four-hour visit that Friday he again demonstrated the acumen that had been a boon to both his personal approval ratings, which hovered near 80 percent, and ever-swelling Republican campaign coffers.

The day's itinerary in and around St. Petersburg included a $25,000-a-plate fundraiser, the primary beneficiary of which was Bush's younger brother, Jeb, who was gearing up for what would ultimately be a successful gubernatorial reelection bid. Raising money on behalf of GOP candidates, some of them his handpicked challengers to Democratic incumbents, was a mission that the nation's forty-third president embraced with unprecedented zeal and success: an analysis by *USA Today* revealed that Bush raised more than $100 million during his first 19 months in office, a total unmatched by any of his predecessors. By comparison, Bill Clinton—dubbed "fundraiser in chief" by Republican detractors—raised $38.7 million during this same time in office.

But the trip to the Tampa Bay area wasn't just about hobnobbing with the party faithful. Earlier that day, during a visit to
America II Electronics, Inc., a distributor of semiconductors,
Bush wowed those assembled with a 26-minute speech that
focused in large measure on patriotism and the war on terrorism. With the six-month anniversary of September 11 just three
days away, and the nation still very much fixated on the deadly
attacks and their aftermath, an emotional Bush brushed away a
tear as he mourned two Army Rangers from Florida killed in
Afghanistan. "I know your heart aches, and we ache for you,"
Bush told the soldiers' survivors, who looked on from the front
row. "But your son and your brother died for a noble and just
cause. May God bless you. May God bless you." And the crowd of
500, who would interrupt their commander in chief some two
dozen times with enthusiastic applause, rose in unison for a 30-
second tribute.

Bush would soon switch gears, first touting his economic
policies and then addressing corporate responsibility—an
increasingly menacing political issue spawned by Enron, Global
Crossing, and a seemingly interminable series of other high-
profile scandals. With insider trading, corporate malfeasance,
overstated earnings, unreported loans, and decimated 401(k)
accounts a staple of daily news coverage, Bush had weighed in a
day earlier with a plan for restoring investor confidence. In a
speech some two miles from the White House, the president
listed this among his prescriptions for reform: "Corporate officers should not be allowed to secretly trade their company's
stock. Every time they buy or sell, they should be required to tell
the public within two days."

That proposal, roundly approved by the Washington audience, was similarly well received by the America II employees.
Bush further argued for corporate openness and transparency,

and then, before finally imploring the crowd to also embrace a new era of personal responsibility, he declared: "In order to usher in a period of responsibility in America, a culture of responsibility, corporate America must be responsible, must make sure that there are no shenanigans or sleight of hands, must make sure there is an openness and disclosure about true liabilities and true assets, and if they don't," Bush said to more applause, "they must be held to account."

> **Throughout Bush's public and private careers, including, most recently, his tenure as the nation's chief executive, he has displayed an obsession with secrecy.**

But a dozen years earlier, as a director of a publicly traded corporation, citizen Bush engaged in the very behavior that, as U.S. president, he held up to bully pulpit ridicule. In fact, throughout Bush's private and then public sector careers, including, most recently, his tenure as the nation's chief executive, he has displayed an obsession with secrecy and a disdain for making information public. And while stiff-arming entirely reasonable requests for information, whether from legislators or journalists, has only stoked the fires of suspicion in some quarters, Bush has resisted disclosure, and has done so without apology.

GO WEST, YOUNG MAN

As governor of Texas, George Walker Bush made a lot of his West Texas childhood. He proudly boasted of his tenure at San Jacinto Junior High School in Midland, where his first foray into politics earned him the title of class president.

But his birthplace—absent from his biography on the White House Web site for the first two years of his presidency—was New Haven, Connecticut, where the family's next-door neighbor was the president of Yale University. The storied Ivy League college was like a second home to the Bushes of Greenwich: Bush's grandfather, Senator Prescott Bush, graduated from Yale in 1917. Uncles Prescott Jr. and Jonathan were alumni. At the time of George W.'s birth—July 6, 1946—his father, George H. W. Bush, was pursuing his undergraduate degree in economics there.

Bush returned to New Haven in 1964, this time as a member of the freshman class at Yale. He wasn't the all-around scholar-athlete his father had been (the elder Bush was a member of Phi Beta Kappa and captain of the varsity baseball team, while George W. hung up the baseball spikes after freshman year), but he nevertheless was elected president of the sports-minded Delta Kappa Epsilon fraternity. What's more, like his father and grandfather before him, he was inducted into the exclusive and secretive Skull & Bones Society.

Upon graduating in 1968, Bush faced the prospect of military service in Vietnam. With American casualties escalating and anxieties building about prolonged U.S. military involvement in Southeast Asia, many draft-age men sought to avoid combat via stateside service in the National Guard; in fact, in late May of that year, when Bush signed up for pilot training with the Texas Air National Guard, the guard maintained a nationwide waiting list of some 100,000 applicants. But immediately after applying, Bush was sworn in as a member of the 147th Fighter Group. Ben Barnes, then speaker of the Texas House of Representatives, said in a sworn deposition in September 1999 that he secured that coveted spot for Bush at the urging of Simon Adger, a Houston businessman and close friend of Bush's father, at the time a U.S. representative from Houston. Bush wasn't the only son of a prominent Texan in his unit, however. Others included the sons of former U.S. representative (and future U.S. senator) Lloyd Bentsen and Senator John Tower, and at least seven members of the Dallas Cowboys football team.

The only battles Bush fought during those post-college years were on the home front. He says he struggled to establish an identity separate from that of his father, who went on to become U.S. ambassador to the United Nations, chairman of the Republican National Committee, chief of the U.S. Liaison Office in the People's Republic of China, and, in 1976, director of the Central Intelligence Agency. When he finished his active-duty service with the National Guard, for example, George W. Bush considered running for the Texas legislature, but his inexperience kept him on the sidelines. Young George's identity crisis reportedly reached its climax one night in Washington when he was confronted by his father for taking his 15-year-old brother, Marvin, out drinking. Bush, the story goes, rebuffed his father with the challenge: "I hear you're looking for me. You want to go *mano a mano* right here?"

But if there was any doubt that a sometimes rebellious Bush would hew to the family path, it was soon laid to rest. After being rejected by the University of Texas School of Law, he enrolled in Harvard Business School. Two years later, with an M.B.A. and a grubstake left over from an educational trust fund (media reports put the amount between $13,000 and $20,000), he returned to Midland to find his fortune in the oil fields, just as his father had done more than a quarter century earlier.

His first venture, Arbusto Energy Inc. (*arbusto* is Spanish for bush), was launched in 1977, but the would-be entrepreneur took a quick detour into politics before actually commencing operations. In 1978, Bush ran for a seat in the U.S. House of Representatives after assembling the trappings of a candidate: In addition to starting his business he married Laura Welch, a public school teacher and librarian who was born and raised in Midland. His best friend, Texas oil man Don Evans, ran the campaign.

Bush lost the election to state senator Kent Hance, a conservative Democrat who years later would become a major fundraiser for Bush's first presidential bid. His performance on the campaign trail also earned him the respect of relatives and family friends, who agreed to gamble on Arbusto. Starting in 1979, some fifty individuals pumped nearly $4.7 million into the company and its successor, Bush Exploration. Among them were some of the elder Bush's most durable political supporters, who guaranteed that George W.'s shaky company stayed afloat.

John Macomber, the chief executive officer of Celanese Corporation, invested $79,500; William H. Draper III, a venture capitalist, put up $93,000. Draper went on to serve as president of the Export-Import Bank of the United States under President Ronald Reagan, while Macomber, a friend of Bush's uncle Jonathan Bush, would land the same job under the elder President Bush.

George Ohrstrom and his wife invested $100,000 in Arbusto. Ohrstrom had attended Greenwich Country Day School, in Connecticut, at the same time as Bush's father. Ohrstrom was a business partner of New York investor Philip Uzielli, whose investment management company, Executive Resources Corporation, was based first in the Dutch West Indies and later in Panama. Uzielli put $50,000 into an early Arbusto partnership, and then in January 1982, with Arbusto facing a cash-flow crisis, Executive Resources paid an additional $1 million for 10 percent of the oil company's stock. That made Uzielli Arbusto's largest investor, a privilege he paid handsomely for: at the time, the company's total assets were valued on its balance sheet at less than half a million dollars. Uzielli, incidentally, had another connection to the Bush clan—he'd been a close friend of James Baker III since they were classmates at Princeton University. Baker, who was intimately involved in the elder Bush's political career, managed or chaired his presidential campaigns in 1980, 1988, and 1992 (and the Reagan-Bush campaign in 1984) and was secretary of state during Bush's sole term as president.

Russell E. Reynolds Jr., founder of the international executive search firm Russell Reynolds Associates, put up $23,250; H. Leland Getz, the firm's cofounder, invested $46,500. "These are all the Bushes' pals," Reynolds once told the *Dallas Morning News*, speaking of Arbusto's backers. "This is the A team."

Reynolds, in fact, had attended Yale with George W.'s uncle Jonathan Bush, an investment manager and New York Republican Party official who lined up many of Arbusto's backers from his firm's client list. Reynolds also served as chairman of the George Bush Finance Committee in Connecticut; he raised $4 million for Vice President Bush's 1988 presidential campaign.

Investing in Arbusto was a poor financial decision. By April of 1984, according to the *Dallas Morning News*, Arbusto had drilled 95 holes, with 47 yielding oil, 3 yielding natural gas, and 45 proving to be nothing but pipe dreams. The venture had returned only $1.5 million to its investors. "I think we got maybe twenty cents on the dollar," Reynolds recalled.

Philip Uzielli tried to shore things up by buying another 10 percent stake for $150,000, to no avail. "We lost a lot of money in the oil business," Uzielli told the *Wall Street Journal* in 1991. "We had a lot of dry wells. . . . Things were terrible. It was dreadful."

"We wrote the money off the minute we invested," added Stephen Kass, a Bush classmate at Harvard Business School. But the A team was willing to take a bath to help out a Bush, and in 1982—in hopes of capitalizing on that loyalty—the struggling entrepreneur renamed his company Bush Exploration.

At the time, George H. W. Bush had been vice president for more than a year. But replacing Arbusto (Ar-BUST-o to detractors) with the famous family name proved to be of no help. As the world price of oil collapsed, only the savviest independent oil companies managed to stave off bankruptcy, and by 1984 the survival of Bush's business hinged on finding well-heeled partners.

> **Bush spent much of 1987 and 1988 working on his father's presidential campaign—an arrangement that was just fine with Harken's management.**

Thanks to an introduction by a mutual acquaintance, William DeWitt Jr. and Mercer Reynolds III proved to be those white knights. Steeped in professional sports (his father had owned the Cincinnati Reds baseball team), DeWitt, like Bush, had graduated from both Yale and Harvard Business School. He and Reynolds, his investment firm partner, founded a Texas-based oil-and-gas exploration outfit called Spectrum 7 Energy Corporation. What the Cincinnati businessmen lacked was someone to run the privately held firm.

Enter Bush, the son of the sitting—and soon to be re-elected—vice president. The would-be oil tycoon may have been looking for the means to prop up his ailing enterprise, but DeWitt and Reynolds, who later became donors to both the elder Bush's 1988 presidential campaign and George W.'s run for the White House, crafted an altogether different arrangement. They bought Bush Exploration outright and merged it with Spectrum 7. As part of the deal, Bush was given 1.1 million shares of Spectrum 7 stock and the title of chairman and chief executive officer, at an annual salary of $75,000.

But Bush's latest venture fared no better. Two years after the merger, in 1986, ever-declining oil prices pushed Spectrum 7 to the brink of bankruptcy. Bush and his partners needed a bailout, and fast. This time, the savior was Harken Energy Corporation, a small Dallas-based oil exploration company that proposed a merger.

Even though Spectrum 7 carried $3 million in debt and was posting sizable operating losses (over a six-month period not long before, it racked up some $400,000 in red ink), the firm's partners received about $2 million worth of Harken stock (at the time, Bush's cut was worth about $320,000). As part of the deal, Bush was named a member of Harken's board of directors and was also granted warrants to buy Harken stock at a potentially steep discount. What's more, he was paid annual consulting fees that one year reached $120,000, and he was also the beneficiary of lucrative stock options.

Despite his consultant status, Bush spent much of 1987 and 1988 working on his father's presidential campaign—an arrangement that was just fine with Harken's management. "His name was George Bush," Phil Kendrick, Harken's founder, told *Time* magazine. "That was worth the money they paid him."

E. Stuart Watson, who was a Harken board member at the time of the Spectrum 7 deal, echoed that view in a 1994 interview with the *Dallas Morning News.* "George was very useful to Harken," Watson said. "He could have been more so if he had had funds, but as far as contacts were concerned, he was terrific."

IVY LEAGUE CONTACTS AND CONTRACTS

Indeed, once Bush signed on, Harken's fortunes took a turn for the better.

As the talks with Spectrum 7 progressed, Harken officials were trying to line up a major new financial backer: Harvard

Management Company Inc., which manages the multibillion-dollar endowment of its only client, Harvard University.

A month after Bush came on board, Harvard Management—via a subsidiary called Aeneas Venture Corporation—agreed to invest $20 million in Harken and buy another $2 million worth of newly issued Harken stock.

The Bush name may have helped seal the deal.

Michael Eisenson, a Harvard Management Company partner who sat on Harken's board of directors after the investment was made, said that he and other Harvard officials picked Harken after reviewing proposals from several energy companies. "Harken management seemed capable and honest, and has proven to be so," Eisenson told the *Dallas Business Journal* in 1991.

But the Bush name certainly would have made an impression on Robert Stone Jr., who was one of Harvard Management's directors and one of the seven members of Harvard University's senior governing board. Stone was "the driving force" behind Harvard's Southwest oil and gas investments, according to Scott Sperling, who worked with Eisenson at Harvard. Stone was no oil industry neophyte; at the time, he was the chairman of Kirby Exploration Company, a diversified Houston-based firm whose businesses included oil and natural gas exploration and production. A long-time resident of Greenwich, Connecticut, Stone contributed to the elder Bush's presidential campaigns in both 1980 and 1988. And like George W.'s Uncle Jonathan, Stone would later join the board of directors of Russell Reynolds Associates, the executive search firm whose founders had thrown money at Arbusto Energy.

In an interview with the Center for Public Integrity, Scott Sperling said he didn't recall Harken as "an investment that had come specifically recommended by any board member." But according to Bing Sung, chief equity trader at Harvard

Management Company until 1986, "You just don't knock on the door of a major endowment, which Harvard certainly was, and say, 'Listen, I've got a great idea and I want to present it to the board,' . . . unless you have an in."

Harvard Management's commitment to Harken Energy Corporation—its first major foray into Texas wildcat operations—was surprising, given the oil firm's condition. In October 1986, when Aeneas announced its agreement to invest, Harken had no refineries or, for that matter, any other significant assets, and revenues that year would total a paltry $4 million.

But flush with cash from Harvard and two other institutional investors, Harken went on a buying spree that, by 1989, pushed annual revenues beyond the $1 billion mark. The jump in revenues by no means told the whole story, however. Harken's finances were far from transparent. "I took some time and looked at it and I went, God, I don't want to be anywhere near this," a prospective Harken investor from the late 1980s told the Center for Public Integrity. "This thing looks like a train wreck."

In fact, even company insiders characterized Harken's operations as not quite on the up-and-up. "It's been a fast-numbers game," company founder Phil Kendrick Jr., who sold out in 1983 but remained a shareholder, told *Time* magazine in an interview. Board director E. Stuart Watson characterized the company's deals as "convoluted," while Mikel Faulkner, Harken's longtime chief executive officer, described the firm's financial statements as "a mess."

Insiders insist, however, that Harvard's money managers wouldn't have kept pumping money into Harken Energy (they would eventually come to own some 10.1 million shares) if they didn't think it would become profitable. And on the cusp of the go-go '90s, they had reason to believe.

Their hopes were no doubt bolstered on January 30, 1990,

when Harken issued a press release announcing that its newly formed, wholly owned subsidiary had just inked an agreement with the government of Bahrain. Harken Bahrain Oil Company, the release proclaimed, signed a production-sharing deal that gave the company "the exclusive right to carry out exploration, development, production, transportation, and marketing of petroleum throughout most of Bahrain's Arabian Gulf offshore territories."

That the government of Bahrain and its state-owned petroleum franchise, Bahrain National Oil Company, or BANOCO, should choose Harken Energy to explore for oil off its coast came as a surprise to industry experts. After all, among those also interested in the contract was the global oil giant Amoco, which had been in negotiations with the Bahrainis for more than two years.

Harken, by contrast, had virtually no experience in either international or offshore oil production. What's more, while revenues may have been rising, Harken was so cash-poor that it lacked the funding required to finance phase one of the overseas drilling. Even more surprising, Harken hadn't even actively sought the deal.

"It was not our intention to seek out international opportunities," Monte Swetnam, the president of Harken subsidiary Harken Exploration Company, told the industry trade publication *World Oil*. "However, we were introduced to officials in Bahrain and were able to present our credentials to them. And from that, a relationship developed . . . that has evolved into one of mutual respect, ultimately resulting in signing the production-sharing contract."

Of course, the relationship held the promise of more than just respect. The fields to be explored were situated between the world's largest known single reserve of oil, in Saudi Arabia, and

Qatar's North Dome Field, the largest known offshore gas field. The Bahraini offshore reserves—and the profits they would yield—had the potential to be enormous.

But as a handful of press reports noted months later, George W. Bush's affiliation with Harken raised questions about whether the government of Bahrain, in choosing such an unlikely business partner, was merely looking to cozy up to a presidential son. For example, in December 1991, the *Wall Street Journal* noted in a front-page story that while its reporting had not revealed evidence of wrongdoing or influence peddling by the younger Bush or others connected to Harken, questions remained. "Yet what does emerge," *Journal* reporters added, "is a complex pattern of personal and financial relationships behind Harken's sudden good fortune in the Middle East, raising the question of whether the Bahrainis or others in the Middle East may have hoped to ingratiate themselves with the White House."

Bush has always maintained that he pulled no strings to win the contract, that he in fact argued against the deal—a claim corroborated by Harken officials. His mere presence, however, may have been enough. According to Monte Swetnam, the Bahrainis knew that Bush was on the company's board of directors and "were clearly aware he was the president's son."

But if Bush had no active role in securing the deal, it was his wealthy patrons who ensured that cash-strapped Harken could pull it off. First in line were the Bass brothers of Fort Worth, a quartet of Yale-educated billionaires whose Bass Enterprises Production Company put up millions to finance the initial exploratory drilling. Yet another infusion came from Harvard Management's Aeneas Venture Corporation, whose stake in Harken's common stock grew to nearly 30 percent.

Alas for Harken and its investors, the Bush name wasn't

magical enough to ensure a strike deep beneath the Persian Gulf. In fact, in October 1991, Aeneas took a reported $92 million write-down from its highly speculative commodity investments, Harken among them. And the Bass brothers, who one day would be among George W. Bush's most generous political patrons, also struck out: after the first two Bahrain wells proved to be dry holes, Bass Enterprises paid Harken $2 million to be released from its obligations to drill a third time.

STOCK ANSWERS

Bush himself fared better, although in doing so he became entangled in a controversy that, to this day, still begs for answers.

> At issue was whether Bush was guilty of illegal insider trading—that is, whether he sold the shares in question while in possession of material, nonpublic information.

Consider the sequence of events. On August 20, 1990, while the media were still fawning over the ill-fated Bahrain deal, Harken reported a quarterly loss of $23.2 million—a precipitous drop in earnings compared with results of a year earlier, when net income totaled $3.6 million. Wall Street's reaction was swift and punishing: the share price of Harken common stock, which at the time traded on the New York Stock Exchange, tumbled 21 percent, from $3 to $2.375. Although the price quickly rebounded, another earnings disappointment followed in November, and by year's end a 74.4 percent decline in the company's stock would earn Harken the number five spot on the *Dallas Times Herald*'s list of worst-performing local businesses.

While the August 20 earnings announcement dealt a financial

blow to Harken shareholders, at least one managed to narrowly avoid the downturn in company fortunes. Two months earlier, on June 22, 1990, George W. Bush had unloaded 212,140 shares (about two-thirds of his holdings) at $4 per share. Bush had become managing general partner of a group that, in April 1989, had finalized a deal to buy the Texas Rangers, and some of the $848,560 in proceeds from his stock sale were used to repay a loan he'd taken to invest in the Major League Baseball team.

As an outside director of Harken, Bush was required to promptly report the stock sale to the Securities and Exchange Commission. But the SEC received the paperwork some eight months later—a delay that, at the time, Bush blamed on the commission's mishandling of his documents. Whatever the case, the filing delay attracted the attention of SEC investigators, who decided that the timing of the transaction seemed too good to be true. So on April 5, 1991, the commission opened an informal inquiry into Bush's sale of Harken stock—a fact-finding procedure that included interviewing witnesses and examining records, but stopped short of compelling testimony or the production of records by subpoena.

At issue was whether Bush was guilty of illegal insider trading—that is, whether he sold the shares in question while in possession of material, nonpublic information about the security. As a member of the Harken board's audit committee, Bush was familiar with the company's finances and was aware that it was about to restructure its debt. In addition, he may have been alerted that the company was about to post a huge loss.

After all, internal Harken Energy Corporation documents, which the Center for Public Integrity first made public in 2002, demonstrate that the oil and gas exploration firm was gingerly walking a fiscal tightrope. For example, on April 20, 1990, company president Mikel Faulkner sent a confidential memorandum to Bush and other Harken directors detailing an impending cash-flow crisis, which the firm's executive committee would address three days hence. On May 11, following approval by the board of directors, Bruce Huff assumed the role of Harken Energy's chief financial officer. Seven days later, Huff dispatched a memo to Bush, Faulkner, and board member E. Stuart Watson about a proposed common stock rights offering—that is, the sale of shares (in this case, shares of two Harken subsidiaries) to existing stockholders. In addressing details of the offering, which was anticipated to raise more than $40 million, Huff included a dire warning: "No other source of immediate financing is available to the Company." Two days later, in a memo to other Harken officials, Huff raised the warning flag even higher: by June 15, he predicted, Harken "will deplete all available cash to pay payroll and other basic needs" unless money was forthcoming from royalty payments or the Bass brothers.

It was against this backdrop that on June 22 Bush unloaded the 212,140 shares of Harken stock. It would be another nine and a half months before the SEC would consider the stock sale—and Harken's subsequent earnings shortfall announcement—and begin connecting the dots.

When the investigation began, in April 1991, the chairman of the SEC was Richard Breeden, who had been appointed by President George H. W. Bush. Before joining the commission, Breeden had for several years been the president's assistant for issues analysis, focusing on such matters as problems with the savings-and-loan industry. From 1985 to 1989, when he joined the Bush administration, Breeden was a partner in the Washington office of Baker Botts LLP, a powerhouse Texas law firm whose pioneers included the great-grandfather of James A. Baker III, President Bush's secretary of state. Among Breeden's other credentials: fundraiser for and advisor to the presidential campaign of the man who later appointed him SEC chairman.

The SEC's general counsel, who would be ultimately responsible for any litigation initiated by the commission, was James Doty. Like Breeden and Secretary of State Baker, Doty was also a veteran of Baker Botts, where he represented George W. Bush in contract negotiations related to the purchase of the Texas Rangers. Coincidentally, Bush was represented during the SEC inquiry by Robert Jordan, at the time a senior partner at Baker Botts.

Along with vacuuming up boxes full of documents and correspondence, SEC investigators interviewed both Harken's in-house and outside counsels; the company's auditing team from the accounting firm of Arthur Andersen; as well as Ralph Smith, the institutional trader with Sutro & Company who'd sold Bush's stock. SEC staff did not, however, talk to Bush or other Harken directors or officials.

Following its investigation, the SEC Division of Enforcement sent the commission an action memorandum concluding it would be difficult to establish that Bush possessed material nonpublic information when he sold his stock. Harken may have had profound cash-flow problems, but SEC investigators concluded that Bush "was not aware of the majority of the items that comprised the loss Harken announced on August 20." What's more, it would be difficult to establish that Harken's August 20 earnings announcement was material, the memo noted, given the rapid rebound of the stock price. The SEC would also have had difficulty proving that Bush's violation was deliberate, since he obtained approval for the sale from Harken's attorneys. No enforcement action in this matter is appropriate, the staff concluded, and on October 18, 1993, the matter was dropped. But Bruce Hiler, associate director of the

SEC's Division of Enforcement, wrote to Bush's attorney that the end of the probe "must in no way be construed as indicating that the party has been exonerated or that no action may ultimately result" from the staff's investigation.

The confidential investigation may have died an unceremonious death, but when word of it leaked out a year later, Governor Ann Richards made it an issue during Bush's challenge to take away her job. Bush, who had left Harken's board in late 1993, had a campaign-trail response: "My sale of Harken stock was entirely legal and proper."

> By the time George W. Bush was installed as managing partner of the Texas Rangers, in 1989, he already had his eye on the governor's mansion in Austin.

The SEC of course turned up no evidence to the contrary, and all those questioned, from Breeden on down, later insisted that everything was done by the book, that Bush received no favorable treatment. (In 1994, James Doty told the *Houston Chronicle* that he hadn't even known about the investigation until after he left the SEC, in December 1992.) But while the SEC found no grounds for further action, the commission's inquiry nevertheless failed to answer some still-nagging questions, most notably, Who bought Bush's stock?

Under questioning by SEC investigators, Ralph Smith said that he solicited the shares at the behest of an unnamed institutional investor—a mystery that has fueled much speculation, since Bush parlayed those sale proceeds into multimillion-dollar gains and, as was his intention at the time, a career in politics now left with no more rungs to climb. Why the continuing secrecy, it's been asked. Was the buyer looking to bail out Bush, whose career in oil was being swapped for one around major-league diamonds? And if so, was there ever any quid pro quo?

Or are the conspiracy theories nothing but baseless speculation, as Smith suggested in an interview in the summer of 2002. "It's nobody's business," the retired stock trader told the *Los Angeles Times*. "There isn't anything there. And nothing was done wrong."

"Bush didn't even know who the buyer was at the time," Smith added. "He still doesn't know. No one but me ever knew who the buyer was. And no one ever will know."

PLAYING HARDBALL

By the time George W. Bush was installed as managing partner of the Texas Rangers, in 1989, he already had his eye on the governor's mansion in Austin. But the political long shot knew that he'd need better credentials than a not-so-illustrious career as an oilman and a failed bid for a seat in the U.S. House of Representatives. "My biggest liability in Texas," he told *Time* magazine three months after the Rangers deal was finalized, "is the question, 'What's the boy ever done?' So he's got a famous father and ran a small oil company. He could be riding on Daddy's name if he ran for office. Now I can say, 'I've done something—here it is.'"

But if Bush had something new to call his own, he also had some trusty old family connections to help him plan for the political arena. Back in 1973, when "Poppy" was chairman of the Republican National Committee, George W. befriended one of his assistants—a young political upstart named Karl Rove, whose credentials included the top leadership post with the College Republicans. Rove cut his teeth alongside Lee Atwater, who would catapult through the ranks to become the elder Bush's chief political strategist and his 1988 presidential campaign manager. As for Rove, he would one day emerge as George W.'s own Atwater.

Rove helped in Bush's unsuccessful 1978 run for the U.S. Congress and later served Texas governor William Clements before starting his own political-consulting business. As the Rangers deal was being hatched, Rove joined a chorus of Bush allies who counseled that running a baseball team was his ticket to the big time. Bush's foray into baseball, Rove told reporters, "anchors him clearly as a Texas businessman." What's more, Rove predicted, it's the sort of high-profile position that voters would remember.

Indeed they would.

The segue to America's pastime got underway in the fall of 1988, when William DeWitt Jr., who helped bring Bush to the Spectrum 7 oil firm, set out to buy the Texas Rangers. In addition to DeWitt, a line of would-be suitors—Bush among them— also later expressed interest in the franchise. As a long-time friend of the Bushes, Rangers owner Eddie Chiles, whose health and finances were failing in tandem, wanted George W. to follow him into the owner's box. Bush's access to capital couldn't quite match his connections, however, so he and DeWitt teamed up yet again. But the deal hit a snag when Peter Ueberroth, the commissioner of Major League Baseball, balked at the partners' dearth of local ownership; without it, Ueberroth feared, the new owners might relocate the team. The commissioner wanted the deal approved before his term expired at the end of 1989, so he and American League president Bobby Brown sought out Fort Worth financier Richard Rainwater.

Rainwater and Bush weren't exactly strangers. Rainwater was a contributor to the elder Bush's presidential campaigns. Until 1986, when he left to manage his own fortune, Rainwater was the wildly successful chief money manager for the Bass brothers, the Fort Worth millionaires-turned-billionaires who financed Harken Energy's initial drilling in Bahrain. What's more, Bush had already solicited Rainwater's participation in the Rangers deal, to no avail. But Ueberroth's sales pitch was apparently more convincing: Rainwater agreed to ante up, although only if his trusted associate, Edward "Rusty" Rose III, was installed as a general managing partner along with Bush.

So on April 21, 1989, Bush and his partners bought Eddie Chiles's majority share of the Rangers. Using his Harken stock as collateral, Bush borrowed $500,000 from a bank in Midland, where he was once a director. He later invested an additional $106,302, giving him a 1.8 percent share of the team.

Bush made up for his minor stake by taking a major share of the credit for bringing together the investors—a claim pooh-poohed by Ueberroth, for one, who in 1999 told the *New York Times* that credit actually belonged to him, Rainwater, Rusty Rose, and Bobby Brown, the league president. Whatever the truth, Bush's partners rewarded him with a $200,000 salary and, if the venture proved profitable, an additional 10 percent ownership stake.

> **Bush made up for his minor stake in the Texas Rangers by taking a major share of the credit for bringing together the investors.**

Parked in a box seat by the dugout, his feet up and a bag of peanuts in his lap, Bush became a popular, high-profile franchise leader who helped turn a perennial basement-dweller into a true contender. But the rumored heir-apparent to the baseball commissioner's post was sometimes flashing decoy signs: Bush put a congenial face, for example, on a stadium pact involving a questionable land deal.

When Bush's group inked its purchase agreement, the Rangers were playing in a former minor-league stadium that, despite a series of facelifts, had few sky boxes or other lucrative amenities. Coupled with a proportionally large number of lower-priced general admission seats, the franchise lacked the required revenue to compete for baseball's increasingly high-priced talent.

As plans advanced for the much-lauded retro-parks in cities like Cleveland and Baltimore, rekindling fading fan memories of natural grass and irregularly shaped outfields, Bush and his partners envisioned their own field of lucrative dreams. But there was a hitch: they didn't want to finance its construction. Instead, they wanted taxpayers to foot the Texas-sized bill.

No politician wants to preside over the loss of a professional ball club, so officials in Arlington, Texas, paid attention when the Rangers front office played their own brand of hardball: without a likeable stadium deal, they hinted, they might have to move home plate to another locale in the Dallas–Fort Worth area. So city fathers crafted an agreement stipulating that a half-cent hike in the city's sales tax would raise $135 million of the $191 million cost of the new stadium and nearby family entertainment complex. Arlington mayor Richard Greene, a major backer of the deal, said team owners would make an up-front, $48 million payment out of their own pockets. It was, the parties agreed, the perfect public-private arrangement, of benefit to one and all.

It didn't quite work out that way, however: the owners actually raised a hefty portion of their down payment from fans, through a $1 surcharge on tickets. But the city spent mightily on an advertising and telemarketing campaign to persuade voters of the deal's virtues, its high-gloss brochures featuring the likes of legendary Rangers pitcher Nolan Ryan. Charges of welfare for the rich were drowned out by the civic boosterism, and on January 19, 1991, Arlington voters overwhelmingly approved the referendum to raise the sales tax and build the new park.

Between the sales tax revenue, state tax exemptions, and other financial incentives, Texas taxpayers handed the privately owned Rangers more than $200 million in public subsidies. Taxpayers didn't get a return from the stadium's surging new revenues, either. The profits went almost exclusively to the team's already wealthy owners.

But Bush and his partners still weren't satisfied. They wanted adjacent property to further boost the value of the stadium, and to that end they orchestrated a land grab that short-changed local landowners by several million dollars.

As part of the deal, the city created the Arlington Sports Facilities Development Authority to manage stadium construction. Using the power of eminent domain granted by the city, ASFDA condemned about a dozen acres of nearby land for future development.

While on paper ASFDA was a public entity, in practice it was merely a puppet for Bush and his partners. According to documents obtained by the Center, Bush's partners would identify the tracts they wanted to acquire. Then one of those limited partners, realtor Mike Reilly, would offer to buy the parcels for the prices he set, which in several cases were well below what the landowners believed their property was worth. If they refused to sell at the offered price, ASFDA could take possession of their land and leave the price to be determined in court.

Several landowners sued ASFDA over the seizures and won settlements totaling $11.1 million. But in a final insult to taxpayers, the Rangers resisted paying the settlements, trying to pass off yet another cost to Arlington residents. (In early 1999 the ball club, under new ownership, finally agreed to reimburse

ASFDA for the settlements, to be paid out—along with interest—
over 26 years.)

When confronted with the seamy details of the land grab,
Bush professed ignorance. But Tom Schieffer, the team's president, testified in a deposition that he kept Bush aware of the
land transfers. And in October 1990, Bush also let slip to a
reporter for the *Fort Worth Star-Telegram*, "The idea of making
a land play, absolutely, to plunk the field down in the middle of a
big piece of land, that's kind of always been the strategy."

It was a strategy that would have an enormous payoff for
Bush personally.

After becoming governor of Texas, in 1995, Bush put all of
his assets into a blind trust, with one notable exception: his
stake in the Rangers. Schieffer kept Bush apprised of efforts to
sell the team to Thomas Hicks, chairman of Hicks, Muse, Tate &
Furst, a private investment firm that specializes in leveraged
buyouts.

Hicks and the firm's employees rank ninteenth as Bush's
career patrons, having given him at least $233,000. But in 1998,
Hicks helped provide Bush with an even greater windfall: he
bought the Texas Rangers for $250 million, three times what
Bush and his partners had paid 10 years earlier. The new stadium
and the real estate around it greatly boosted the final sale price.
And since his partners had upped Bush's stake in the team from
1.8 percent to 11.8 percent, his cut from the proceeds of the sale
was $14.9 million, nearly a 25-fold return on his investment.

Just as important as the cash, however, was the cachet that
came with the deal's success. The Ballpark at Arlington finally
opened in April 1994, just as Bush was running for governor.
While his critics labeled the stadium deal corporate socialism,
Bush touted it as a winning proposition for taxpayers, the team,
and, most certainly, himself. As Bush proclaimed the day after

the sale, "When it is all said and done, I will have made more money than I ever dreamed I would make."

THE LAY OF THE POLITICAL LANDSCAPE

The congratulatory letter from Kenneth Lay, dated November 11, 1998, was unabashed in its praise and enthusiasm for George W. Bush. "What a fabulous victory for you and the entire Republican slate in Texas," the five-paragraph note proclaimed of the previous week's elections. "While the rest of the Republican ticket was clearly strong in its own merit, your leadership and ability no doubt had much to do with the unprecedented sweep of statewide offices that the Republican party enjoyed."

Unprecedented indeed. Running as a "compassionate conservative," his campaign focused from start to finish on lower taxes and increased funding for education, the 52-year-old Bush had become the first Texan elected to consecutive four-year terms as governor, carrying all but 14 of the Lone Star State's 254 counties and winning nearly 70 percent of the vote. His popularity extended clear across the landscape—even a quarter of liberals voted for him—helping Republicans complete a historic sweep of all seven top statewide offices. And as icing on the inaugural cake, the landslide appeared to make Bush an immediate contender for the 2000 presidential race.

> Enron CEO Kenneth Lay had written Bush more than twenty times since February 1995, on the heels of the former baseball executive's first gubernatorial victory.

But first things first. The November 11 letter from the chairman and CEO of Enron, one of Texas's—in fact, one of the nation's—largest companies, quickly segued from post-election kudos to political realities. "Your focus on opportunity and responsibility was one that I believe resonates around the country as well as in Texas," it noted. "As one of those opportunities, we hope that you will again actively support efforts to pass a bill restructuring the electric industry in Texas." And prior to a second round of congratulations, topped off by a warm, handwritten postscript that testified to a relationship characterized by more than mere business, the letter concluded with a most generous offer: "Please have your team let me know what Enron can do to be helpful in not only passing electricity restructuring legislation but also in pursuing the rest of your legislative agenda."

This was not the first time that Lay had privately lobbied Bush on issues important to the Houston-based energy company, which three years hence would go belly up in the nation's then largest-ever bankruptcy filing and become the very symbol of corporate malfeasance. Lay had written Bush more than 20 times since February 1995, on the heels of the former baseball executive's first gubernatorial victory. Among the topics covered were a pending meeting between Bush and the ambassador of Uzbekistan, which Lay hoped would advance Enron's negotiations to develop and transport that country's natural gas reserves, and a note thanking Bush for his call to Governor Tom Ridge of Pennsylvania touting Enron's proposal to provide energy to Philadelphia consumers.

Lay's contact with Bush was augmented by his role as chairman of the Governor's Business Council, a nonprofit organization created in 1994 by Democratic governor Ann Richards. The stated function of the GBC was to assist the governor in creating business opportunities and economic growth. At the time of its founding, however, it was seen by some as a mere political ploy by Richards to gain the support of the business community, which might otherwise throw its support to her Republican challenger.

Under Governor Bush, who defeated Richards with 53.5 percent of the vote, the GBC was anything but an insubstantial and politically expedient partnership; instead, it became an important part of Bush's policy efforts, and its members, whose ranks reached about one hundred by the time Bush left for Washington, were rewarded with access to the governor's ear. The GBC was supported primarily with dues paid by members, who made up a virtual who's who of the Texas business elite: CEOs from the energy industry, bank chairmen, and presidents of insurance companies, among others. Council committees included Welfare and Workforce Development, International Trade, Tax Policy, Telecommunications, Electric Utilities and Regulatory, Legal Reform, and Education.

Education, in fact, was at the forefront of the GBC's agenda, a politically savvy move that kept the group in sync with the architect of what would come to be touted as the "Texas Miracle." Throughout his first gubernatorial campaign, Bush harped on the need to reform the state's public school system, to raise reading test scores, and, most controversially, to exempt school districts from state mandates. "Education is to a state government what defense is to the national government—its number one responsibility," the aspiring politician said on the campaign trail.

The public agreed: six months before the November election, a poll of likely voters conducted by Texas A&M University found that education was far and away the most important issue in the governor's race. And once Bush was installed as the state's chief executive, the GBC ratcheted up its assistance around this high-profile issue. For example, the group secured assistance from one of Enron's law firms, the global powerhouse Akin, Gump, Strauss, Hauer & Feld, which helped successfully lobby state legislators to adopt Bush's first education reform proposals. The GBC's education committee chairman subsequently met with Bush's commissioner of education, and then with Bush himself, who formally approved of the GBC's ongoing assistance. "Essentially, I think we should work as an informal extension of the Governor's and the Commissioner's staff, providing advice, information and political support wherever needed," Charles Miller later wrote in a June 1995 memo to Ken Lay.

"I was especially pleased with the Commissioner's initial plans and with his willingness to use our help," Miller added. "He needs it, probably more than he realizes, and it would have been a very poor signal if he had chosen another direction."

But if Commissioner Mike Moses didn't at first recognize the value of Miller, Lay, and their business-council cohorts, he would soon enough. With school systems increasingly relying on computers, for instance, the GBC—with voluntary support from top-tier corporate strategist McKinsey & Company—agreed to sponsor a review of the state's plan for the use of technology in education. When Bush expressed interest in charter schools, the GBC helped facilitate a charter school loan fund set up by Bank of America. When Bush unveiled a plan to raise scores on reading proficiency tests, the GBC, in support of this effort, raised contributions of money and services from such financial powerhouses as Capital One and NationsBank, insurance giant Aetna, and energy companies Houston Lighting & Power and Diamond Shamrock. And when Bush spoke to Lay about providing some "outside" momentum for the Governor's Reading Initiative, whose goal, in part, was for all students to read on grade level by the end of third grade, the GBC quickly authorized an additional $25,000 in funding for promotional efforts to sell the plan statewide.

As Bush's first term progressed, his personal and professional relationships with Lay were well cemented, documents show. ("One of the sad things about old friends is that they seem to be getting older—just like you!" Bush jokingly wrote to Lay on his fifty-fifth birthday. "Laura and I value our friendship with you.") So in June 1998, when legislative caps on state-agency payrolls threatened an internship program with the governor's office, Bush sought financial aid from the GBC chairman. "I believe this is a good opportunity for the public and private sectors to join together and continue the tradition of such a valuable and educational program," Bush wrote to Lay. "The Governor's Business Council's participation and assistance in establishing such a program will serve as a legacy to the state of Texas and future Governors.

"The Council's consideration of establishing a program is appreciated."

> **Members of the boards of the two largest business-backed tort reform organizations donated $4.5 million to Bush's gubernatorial campaigns.**

The GBC, whose members contributed more than $2.3 million to Bush's campaign efforts during his six years as governor, was all too happy to comply. Five months later, Bush wrote a short note to Lay that began: "Thank you and the Governor's Business Council for the successful implementation of the Governor's Fellowship Program."

THE BUSINESS OF GOVERNMENT

If education was the issue that the GBC used to raise its good-citizen profile, it was tort reform that, for many members, topped the list of priorities. Weeks before Bush's first swearing-in ceremony, in January 1995, Ken Lay wrote to remind him of the urgency attached to civil justice reform. And once Bush's name graced the governor's office, Lay was at it again, this time including a GBC report with 17 "essential" recommendations for "restoring common sense and fairness to our judicial system."

Bush hardly needed arm-twisting. While Texas may be thought of as home to cowboys and oil tycoons, in the 1990s, the state's business community rechristened it the land of frivolous lawsuits and out-of-control juries. Real or imagined, this perception led Bush to make tort reform one of his top campaign promises. And once in office, he wasted little time before pushing to restrict the ability to sue and reduce damage awards stemming from civil litigation.

In fact, only four days after his inauguration, Bush declared tort reform an "emergency issue," claiming that "ending lawsuit abuse will encourage new jobs and ensure that the truly injured get prompt access to the courts."

This clarion call brought Bush millions in campaign donations from insurers like Farmers Insurance Group of Companies, based in Los Angeles, and others hell-bent on reducing their exposure to compensatory and punitive damages. The *Los Angeles Times* reported in 1999 that members of the boards of the two largest business-backed tort reform organizations donated $4.5 million to Bush's gubernatorial campaigns. One of them, Texans for Lawsuit Reform, became the largest contributor to the legislature in the entire state of Texas, according to the *Dallas Morning News*. The group's founder and driving force is Governor's Business Council member (and Bush contributor) Richard Weekley, who personally gave Bush $25,000. Weekley runs two Houston companies—a real estate brokerage and a shopping center development firm. In addition, he's part owner of his brother's home-building outfit, which has been sued dozens of times for such alleged practices as knowingly building inadequate foundations. The result, plaintiffs claimed, was that their homes literally cracked.

Despite opposition from trial lawyers and consumer groups, the legislature lined up behind Bush and rapidly pushed through seven major tort reform bills. The first lowered the cap on punitive damages and also raised the standard of proof needed to award such damages. Other changes placed limitations on where suits may be filed (to prevent plaintiffs from seeking out compliant judges), made it harder for consumers to sue real estate agents and other professionals, and empowered judges to sanction those who bring frivolous actions.

Tort reformers insisted that such changes would benefit the average Texan by lowering insurance claims, leading to lower prices for consumers. Of course, businesses may have been the real beneficiaries, thanks to provisions that reduced large damage awards. In 1999, for example, a woman who sued Diamond Shamrock Refinery Company after her husband died in an explosion saw a $42.5 million jury award reduced to a mere $200,000 by a judge complying with the new laws. (On appeal, however, the case was remanded to the lower court, allowing the possibility of a higher award.)

Although endowed with millions in donations, Texans for Lawsuit Reform was unable to flex enough political muscle to sustain momentum after its 1995 string of legislative victories. But the Governor's Business Council, whose ranks included corporate chieftains terrified of high-dollar civil suits, and whose Legal Reform Committee chair was none other than tort reform crusader Richard Weekley, was not about to let the trial lawyers regain the upper hand.

So in a December 21, 1998, letter on GBC stationery, Ken Lay listed for Bush the council's recommendations for tort reform, specifically advocating changes that would make it more difficult to bring class action suits, afford legal protection to the high-tech industry for problems resulting from the Y2K bug, and change the rules for proportionate responsibility among defendants. A month later, the governor offered to collaborate: "I look forward to working with you during the upcoming legislative session to address these issues," he wrote to Lay.

Bush held true to his word. In his State of the State speech less than a week later, Bush framed Y2K protection as a tort reform issue and endorsed legislation that would restrict lawsuits over potential damage done by the much-dreaded millennium bug. The legislature eventually passed this bill and considered class action lawsuits and other tort reforms. In the end, the 1999 session did not quite produce the sweeping changes that advocates helped enact in 1995, but Richard Weekley nevertheless labeled it "a very positive session for civil justice reform."

Noxious Politics

The hundreds of electric power, oil refining, chemical manufacturing, and industrial production plants that spew toxic particles into the air over Texas have levied a heavy toll on the state's environment. According to recent data from the Environmental Protection Agency, Texas ranks first in the nation in the emission of so-called criteria air pollutants—a half-dozen potentially injurious, environmentally ruinous substances whose ranks include lead, carbon monoxide, and ground-level ozone, which is the major component of smog. When EPA ranked states by the health risks associated with the release of these same pollutants, Texas earned the runner-up spot to California.

There's a ready explanation for this unenviable status. When the Texas legislature amended the Texas Clean Air Act in 1971, facilities already built or under construction were "grandfathered"—that is, they were exempted from complying with the new rules, which mandated more stringent pollution-control permitting requirements. At the time, the prevailing wisdom held that these older plants would eventually be modernized or shuttered. As it turned out, however, many of them kept right on running, and with dire consequences: in early 1997, the *Houston Post* reported that these 800-plus grandfathered plants accounted for 900,000 tons of pollution annually, or 36 percent of the statewide total.

In December 1996, staff members of the Texas Natural Resources Conservation Commission (the TNRCC, which was renamed the Texas Commission on Environmental Quality in September 2002) began talks with representatives of 11 companies and trade associations about reducing the emissions of these grandfathered plants. But six weeks later, following the working group's second meeting, John Howard, Bush's environmental director, realized that tinkering with the quarter-century-old exemption faced the lobbying equivalent of a Texas twister. "Industry has expressed concern that the TNRCC is moving too quickly and may rashly seek legislation this session," he wrote in a memo to his boss.

The governor took note. In early March, Bush tapped two members of the Governor's Business Council—Victor G. Beghini, the president of Marathon Oil Company, and Ansel L. Condray, the president of Exxon USA—to craft a plan allowing grandfathered facilities to voluntarily comply with the state's clean-air regulations, rather than be forced, by law, to eventually meet the standards of the Texas Clean Air Act. According to documents obtained by the Sustainable Energy and Economic Development Coalition, a public interest group based in Austin,

Beghini and Condray presented their proposal at a June 19, 1997, meeting of about 40 people, most from the oil and gas industry, and other companies like Alcoa and Texas Utilities. In his notes of the meeting, which included presentations by representatives of Exxon, Amoco, and Marathon Oil, James E. Kennedy, of chemical manufacturing giant E. I. du Pont de Nemours and Company, wrote, "It was a very strange meeting to me in that the approach of the presenters was pretty much like, 'This is the way it's going to be—do you want to get on board or not?'"

If Kennedy felt left out of the process, the plan drafted by Beghini and Condray, and backed by Governor Bush, would consider even less of the public's sentiments. "The concept put forward," Kennedy added, "was that the industry group and the Governor's Office would develop the program, then take it to some broad-based group, including public representatives, who would then tweak it a little bit and approve it."

Given the controversial nature of the matter, Kennedy considered it a long shot that the industry could craft a detailed program and get the public to buy in. "If support from the 'public' is a goal, they will have to be involved much earlier in the process," he e-mailed his colleagues. "This thought was pretty much dismissed—I believe mainly because the leadership doesn't have any real value for public involvement."

Indeed they didn't. On September 10, 1997, the TNRCC announced the appointment of 11 Texans to help develop the Clean Air Responsibility Enterprise, which would be charged with crafting a voluntary program to reduce emissions from grandfathered facilities. As it turned out, however, CARE simply rubber-stamped the proposal that Exxon, Amoco, and Bush had already signed off on.

Two months later, at the Port of Houston, Bush announced

that 10 companies had pledged to voluntarily reduce emissions at their grandfathered facilities. And then on March 31, 1998, Bush appeared at a press conference flanked by executives from Exxon, Amoco, and Texas Utilities, among others, to proclaim that another 26 companies—representing 60 of the hundreds of grandfathered plants around the state—had pledged to reduce emissions by a total of 15,000 tons per year. "You finally had a governor who stood up and got Texas industry to respond," Bush later proclaimed. "They didn't have to respond, and I led, and I said, 'Respond,' and they did." And by all appearances, his leadership soon paid dividends: in October, the governor's office told the Associated Press that the voluntary effort had "already resulted in dozens of plants reducing emissions the equivalent to the smog of 500,000 vehicles."

Well, not exactly. In early December, the Environmental Defense Fund (since renamed Environmental Defense) published a study showing that the true reduction in emissions was only about one-sixth of what the governor's office had reported two months earlier. What's more, EDF disclosed that just 3 of the 36 volunteers had made cuts in pollution, and just 10 more had pledged further reductions. As Jim Marston, in the group's Texas office, told the Center, "The grandfather program did nothing to reduce emissions. All it did was buy political cover for Governor Bush."

> "The grandfather program did nothing to reduce emissions. All it did was buy political cover for Governor Bush," Jim Marston told the Center.

Bush nonetheless hailed his voluntary compliance plan as a rousing success, a model of public-private partnership good enough to take on the road to the presidential primaries. In fact, the *San Antonio Express-News* reported that three weeks after Bush announced the formation of a presidential exploratory committee, his spokesman, Scott McClellan, boasted: "Governor Bush was the first governor in Texas to tell grandfathered industries, 'It's time to clean up.' Voluntary programs are working in Texas."

However, as Bush himself acknowledged that year, they weren't working all that well. Under increasing public pressure, Bush finally signed a bill that forced power plants to cut their emissions in half by 2003.

But if Bush was finally forced to cave to public pressure, the energy industry was still grateful for his efforts on their behalf. According to a study by Public Research Works, Bush raised $566,000 from just 43 grandfathered polluters for his two gubernatorial campaigns. And from March 4, 1999, to March 31, 1999, he raised another $316,300 from PACs, employees, lobbyists, and lawyers for grandfathered companies for his presidential campaign. Their ranks included large donors to Bush, including Vinson & Elkins, a law firm that represented Alcoa, whose Milam County plant produced the most grandfathered emissions; companies owned by the Bass family; and Enron, Bush's top career patron.

While energy giants like Chevron and Exxon each claimed at least a dozen grandfathered facilities, Enron had but one: a methanol operation in Pasadena, just miles from Houston.

Also known as wood alcohol, methanol is a clear and colorless liquid used most frequently in the United States for the production of methyl tertiary-butyl ether, or MTBE, which is added to reformulated and premium grades of unleaded gasoline. Because it's a suspected carcinogen, the EPA has included it on a list of contaminants for which health standards may be set. Soil and groundwater contamination are among the greatest risks posed by MTBE. When MTBE contaminated the drinking water of Santa Monica, in 1996, California officials later banned it entirely from their state.

Enron's methanol operation, which it bought from Tenneco in late-1991, went a long way toward scuttling company attempts to portray itself as environmentally sensitive. The state, for example, cited the facility for air pollution violations. Neil Carman, director of the Houston Sierra Club's clean-air program, told the Center that the violation record meant the facility ranked as one of the dirtier sources in Harris County, where the nation's largest petrochemical complex stretches along the Houston Ship Channel. In 1999, when Enron officials pledged to obtain one of the pollution reduction permits offered under Governor Bush's highly touted voluntary program, the company's methanol plant ranked seventh in the Houston area in grandfathered emissions of all air pollutants.

But Enron's pledge proved to be hollow. In June 2001, Bush's successor, Governor Rick Perry, signed into law a bill that finally killed the controversial grandfather loophole. At the time, Enron still had not obtained its pollution reduction permit. It had, however, racked up substantial fines for increases in emissions from the plant and other indiscretions.

THE ROUTE BACK EAST

On the evening of April 7, 2000, the toughest ticket in Houston was for the Astros' home opener—the formal christening of the city's new Major League Baseball ballpark. After 35 seasons in the much-maligned Astrodome, which saddled the sport with the likes of painted roof panels and artificial turf, the Astros moved downtown to their new $250 million home, Enron Field, which was built, in part, on the promise of $100 million to be paid over 30 years by the local energy giant for naming rights and a package of financial and promotional incentives.

There was plenty of pomp and circumstance on that opening day. The Houston Symphony performed the National Anthem; a quartet from the U.S. Army's Golden Knights Parachute Team leapt from a helicopter and delivered the American flag to center field; and among the dignitaries who graced the Diamond Club—the 250-seat lounge area behind home plate—were the Lone Star State's most notable political luminaries: former president George Bush and wife, Barbara, and Texas governor George W. Bush, whose own year-old quest for the White House was rapidly gaining momentum.

That momentum was fueled in large part by money, and plenty of it. Tapping into a network of donors who had helped fund his father's presidential campaigns and later his own gubernatorial bids, George W. and his advisors created a fundraising juggernaut that left would-be competitors playing a futile game of catch-up.

At the heart of this effort were more than 500 Pioneers, each of whom pledged to raise at least $100,000 from individuals and PACs (and in many cases chipped in with large contributions of their own). Bush tried to keep the Pioneers roster secret, but in July 1999, under pressure from public interest groups, he finally made part of the lineup public. (A fuller list of Pioneers was not revealed until May 2003, when documents stemming from the McCain-Feingold campaign finance legislation disclosed another 312 names the Bush camp had withheld.) Its ranks included such familiar names as Lee Bass, whose family financed Harken Energy's initial drilling in Bahrain; William DeWitt and Mercer Reynolds, who bought out Bush's failing oil-exploration company; Rusty Rose, who was general managing partner of the Texas Rangers along with Bush; R. Steven Hicks, whose brother (and business partner) Thomas Hicks bought the Texas Rangers and, in the process, brought Bush a $15 million windfall; and Kenneth Lay, of Enron.

Lay's inclusion on this list was hardly unexpected. After all, Enron's chairman would personally donate at least $400,000 in soft money to the Republican Party, while his company's unmatched largesse included $50,000 to help fund the governor's second inaugural bash. Just three weeks after the opening-day game at Enron Field, Lay cochaired a fundraising dinner in Washington that raised a record $21.3 million for the Republican National Committee's swollen election year coffers. And with Republican loyalists migrating in increasingly large numbers to Bush's camp, a note from Lay the previous December—a Christmas present thank-you from the Enron chief and his wife—suddenly looked prescient rather than pie-in-the-sky: "George and Laura—Linda and I are so proud of both of you and look forward to seeing both of you in the White House."

Following the historic election of 2000, Lay would get his wish.

George W. Bush

Top Ten Career Patrons

Ranking	Patron	Total
1	Enron Corporation, Houston	$597,625
2	Merrill Lynch & Company Inc., New York	$441,550
3	Vinson & Elkins LLP, Houston	$399,150
4	Bass Brothers Enterprises Inc., Fort Worth, Texas	$378,427*
5	Crédit Suisse First Boston, New York	$373,200
6	MBNA Corporation, Wilmington, Delaware	$358,791
7	International Bank of Commerce/Sanchez Companies, Laredo, Texas	$343,250†
8	Goldman Sachs Group, New York	$274,049
9	Haynes and Boone LLP, Dallas	$271,850
10	Sterling Chemicals Inc., Houston	$260,000

This list is based on individual, corporate, and PAC contributions to Bush's gubernatorial campaigns and inaugural committees through December 31, 1998, and the Bush-Cheney 2000, Inc-Recount Fund through December 31, 2002, and on individual and PAC contributions to Bush's congressional campaign from 1977 to 1978, Bush's 2000 presidential campaign, and Bush's 2004 presidential campaign through June 30, 2003.

Sources: Federal Election Commission, Internal Revenue Service, Texas Ethics Commission.

*Includes contributions from Charlie and Lee Bass, their families, employees of their various businesses, and associated political action committees.

†Includes bank employees, bank founder Tony Sanchez, and employees of related companies, including Sanchez Oil and Gas, of which Sanchez is chairman.

George W. Bush
The War President

A weary nation turned its collective attention to the U.S. Capitol on the evening of September 20, 2001, in hopes of finding at least some measure of solace in a world suddenly turned upside down. Nine days after the terrorist attacks on the Pentagon and twin towers of the World Trade Center, the American psyche appeared to be irreparably damaged. And so it was against this backdrop of anxiety and fear that the forty-third president of the United States approached the podium in the packed House chamber.

Before the attacks, many Americans would have found it hard to imagine that George W. Bush could rise to such a challenge. Throughout the maiden spring of his presidency, Bush had been dogged by the residue of an electoral trauma that had polarized the nation like perhaps no other. For 36 days, as all eyes remained on the Florida vote recount and the legal wrangling that accompanied it, party line divisions only deepened. The ill-will was further inflamed by media reports chronicling ballot shortages, inaccurate voter lists, and presidential ballots in the November 7 election invalidated at higher rates in Black neighborhoods than in White neighborhoods—irregularities that systematically disenfranchised large numbers of voters and presumably tipped the election in favor of Bush. By the evening of December 12, when the Supreme Court of the United States stayed the Florida recount and, in the process, sent to the White House a one-and-a-half-term governor who had lost the popular vote, the electorate remained steadfastly, and grudgingly, divided. To shell-shocked Democrats, the Bush presidency would always lack legitimacy. The election, they argued, had been stolen from Al Gore.

But running as a "compassionate conservative," and endowed with much-touted people skills, Bush managed to move the electorate beyond the hanging chads and Electoral College scrutiny that had helped carve such a deep divide. By August, with his approval ratings rising by about 10 points to near 60 percent, Bush acted as if the controversy surrounding his ascendancy to the nation's highest elective office had never happened. He heartily pursued his conservative agenda, rejecting a global warming treaty, for example, and ramming past obstinate Democrats a 10-year, $1.35 trillion tax cut. And if a 30-day vacation at his ranch in Crawford, Texas, seemed overly long to the public and the White House press corps, Bush was unrepentant. "I know a lot of you wish you were in the East Coast, lounging on the beaches, sucking in the salt air," he told reporters. "But I'm getting a lot done and it's good to be on my ranch. It's good to be home."

There was trouble in paradise, however. While Bush's approval ratings were respectable on the home front, a Pew Research Center poll found that they were downright dismal overseas: 29 percent in Italy, for example, 23 percent in Germany, and just 16 percent in France. Polls showed that voters may have liked Bush personally, that his ethical standards were viewed as a welcome Oval Office change, but these polls also revealed that a majority of the nation believed his priorities were wrong. Add in his lack of diplomatic experience, the frequent malapropisms that called into question his intellect, and such controversial policy edicts as proposing to dump standards to restrict arsenic in drinking water, and Bush still remained something of a divisive figure.

But on that Thursday night in September, as Bush stood before a Joint Session of Congress and addressed an uneasy nation, his political fortunes did an immediate about-face. In a 34-minute speech that would redefine his presidency, George W. Bush assured the United States—and the world—of the government's resolve to both retaliate for the attacks and step up its commitment to homeland security. "Our war on terror begins with al Qaeda, but it does not end there," Bush proclaimed, foreshadowing a war in Iraq that would be launched a year and a half later. "It will not end until every terrorist group of global reach has been found, stopped, and defeated."

In an address punctuated by the applause of legislators, who would line up in lock step behind the commander in chief, Bush grieved for the fallen, thanked the world for its support, and identified the "enemies of freedom" who, he promised, would incur America's wrath. And halfway through his speech, Bush prepared the nation for the realities of what would follow: "Our response involves far more than instant retaliation and isolated strikes," he said. "Americans should not expect one battle, but a lengthy campaign, unlike any other we have ever seen. It may include dramatic strikes, visible on TV, and covert actions, secret even in success."

In many ways, that brief passage symbolized the way the Bush administration has conducted its business, whether near or far from the theaters of war. For in addition to the high-profile fights, be they on judicial nominations, tax-cut policy, or affirmative action, Bush's term in office has been characterized by stealth and a zeal for secrecy, even at the cost of undermining the historically free flow of information to which citizens have always enjoyed, and expected, access.

EMPOWERING BIG BROTHER

The Defense Advanced Research Projects Agency, which serves as the central research and development organization for the U.S. Department of Defense, oversees eight technical offices whose missions have run the gamut from developing a precursor to the Internet to crafting the means of defending against the likes of biological weapons. For DARPA's Information Awareness Office, which was founded as a response to the September 11 attacks, the mandate is somewhat more esoteric: creating the means to counter "asymmetric threats"—that is, threats posed by less-powerful adversaries, against whom conventional defenses may prove ineffective. "The most serious asymmetric threat facing the United States is terrorism," the office notes on its Web site, "a threat characterized by collections of people loosely organized in shadowy networks that are difficult to identify and define. IAO plans to develop technology that will allow understanding of the intent of these networks, their plans, and potentially define opportunities for disrupting or eliminating the threats."

To that end, IAO has hatched 13 programs focused on the likes of automatic speech-to-text transcription, which would detect foreign-language phone conversations or broadcasts, for example, and translate them into written English; a multilingual translation device, which would permit battlefield soldiers involved in activities like refugee processing or medical triage to easily translate such "high-terrorist-risk" languages as Arabic,

Mandarin, and Pashto; and a program to develop automated biometric identification technologies—including face recognition, gait recognition, and iris recognition—that would make it possible to identify suspicious people from long distances. If successful, the Human Identification at a Distance program would accurately distinguish terrorists, criminals, and other "human-based threats" from afar, thereby affording the intelligence to head off a suicide bomber, for instance, who had targeted a government facility.

> Bush's term in office has been characterized by stealth and a zeal for secrecy, even at the cost of undermining the historically free flow of information to citizens.

The Terrorism Information Awareness Program, however, has earned DARPA's Information Awareness Office the most attention—much of it unwelcome. (Until May 20, 2003, when the name was abruptly changed, the program was known as Total Information Awareness System, and hence was familiarly known by that same three-letter abbreviation.) At its heart, TIA boasts a notable goal: "Revolutionize the ability of the United States to detect, classify, and identify foreign terrorists—and decipher their plans—and thereby enable the U.S. to take timely action to successfully preempt and defeat terrorist acts." In a post–September 11 world, with the government's attention focused everywhere from the Middle East to the domestic infrastructure, counterterrorism obviously commands increasingly large resources and assets.

But TIA, which serves as a sort of umbrella for the Information Awareness Office's other 12 programs, and which has become more or less synonymous with IAO's overarching mission, has proved to be a lightning rod for criticism from across the political spectrum. Take, for example, the original logo, which was revealed on IAO's Web site in late 2002 and banished from public view soon thereafter. The emblem sported the familiar eye-over-the-pyramid icon that graces the back of the dollar bill, the all-seeing orb casting beams of light across the globe, and beneath the graphics the Latin motto *Scientia est potentia* ("Knowledge is power"). To critics, that logo smacked of an intrusive Big Brother, and as such offered more proof of what they'd been saying for months—that IAO and its Total Information Awareness program had cooked up a kind of Orwellian plot to ensnare guilty-until-proven-innocent citizens, thereby usurping their civil liberties.

The controversy first flared months earlier, with the revelation that the Information Awareness Office would be headed by John Poindexter, who as President Ronald Reagan's national security advisor had played a key role in the Iran-Contra operations. The arms-for-hostages scandal forced Poindexter's resignation from the White House, and three and a half years later, in April 1990, the retired U.S. Navy vice admiral was convicted of five felonies related to the illegal U.S. government operations and their cover-up—specifically, destroying the only government document authorizing the secret arms deals and then lying about the matter to Congress. U.S. District Judge Harold Greene sentenced Poindexter to a six-month prison term, but a year and a half later a three-judge appeals court panel overturned his convictions on a legal technicality by a 2-to-1 vote. Both judges voting to exonerate Poindexter were Reagan appointees.

Despite his previous troubles, Poindexter earned the unflinching support of George W. Bush. "Admiral Poindexter is somebody who this administration thinks is an outstanding

American and an outstanding citizen who has done a very good job in what he has done for our country, serving in the military," presidential press secretary Ari Fleischer told reporters after news of Poindexter's appointment surfaced. When pressed about Bush's sentiments, Fleischer added: "The president thinks that Admiral Poindexter has served our nation very well."

As the months passed and details of the Total Information Awareness project were unveiled, the criticism of Poindexter got increasingly acerbic. From the *Fort Worth Star-Telegram*, for example: "But in all the land, surely the Pentagon could have found an information systems specialist who did not resign an influential government post amid scandal." From the *Guardian*, of London: "Poindexter is frighteningly smart and very unscrupulous." From Senator Charles Schumer, Democrat of New York: "If we need a big brother, John Poindexter is the last guy on the list that I would choose." And from *New York Times* columnist William Safire, whose barbs raised the public profile of Poindexter's mission and, in the process, spawned the most excoriating and widespread condemnation: "This ring-knocking master of deceit is back again with a plan even more scandalous than Iran-Contra." Ultimately, the criticisms became too much for Poindexter. On August 12, 2003, after word of another initiative of his office became public—a plan to create a "futures market" in which players would bid on when and where the next attack was most likely to occur—the controversial head of IAO resigned from his post.

Poindexter's detractors were particularly roiled by IAO's Total Information Awareness project and its intended use of "data mining," a common marketing tool that in this incarnation, they charged, promised to obliterate the traditional boundaries of personal privacy. But Edward "Pete" Aldridge, the undersecretary of defense for acquisition, logistics, and technology, tried to dampen the trepidation by insisting that this data-mining component of TIA would merely facilitate the search for connections between transactions—a strategy, he asserted, designed to "determine links and patterns indicative of terrorists activities." To accomplish that, TIA computers will trawl virtually everywhere for digital bits of presumably useful information: they'll examine passport and visa records, work permits, drivers' licenses, credit card transactions, e-mails, airline ticket purchases, telephone call records, rental car agreements, college transcripts, court documents, gun license information, book purchases, mortgage payments, chemical purchases, arrest records, prescription drug records, insurance records, and banking transactions, among others. In addition, TIA could use images from surveillance cameras, whether placed at interstate toll booths or along inner-city street corners, and also incorporate the technologies being developed by the likes of IAO's Human Identification at a Distance program—fishing expeditions that would match real faces to the endless agglomeration of monitored digital data. The unprecedented repository of global information is envisioned as being so enormous it could fill the Library of Congress, which houses some 18 million books, more than fifty times over.

> **The largest information technology professional association warned that TIA threatened identify theft and other security problems, such as exploitation and attack by hackers, criminals, and terrorists.**

Aldridge maintained that the Department of Defense would not actually collect this information about individuals. Instead,

Poindexter's troops, who rely almost exclusively on outside contractors, would merely develop an experimental prototype that others could then deploy. "It is absurd to think that DARPA is somehow trying to become another police agency," Aldridge said at a Pentagon press briefing. "DARPA's purpose is to demonstrate the feasibility of this technology. If it proves useful, TIA will then be turned over to the intelligence, counterintelligence, and law enforcement communities as a tool to help them in their battle against domestic terrorism."

This hardly mollified civil libertarians, politicians, and computer security professionals, who feared that TIA would create a system of national surveillance, that the data collected might be misused and innocent Americans would be unwittingly victimized in the process. For some of these critics, TIA represented an entirely unwelcome sea change in the way that the government sought to treat U.S. citizens: "It has always been the distinction of American society that citizens are left alone unless there is some probable cause to believe that they are involved in criminal activity," David Sobel, general counsel of the Electronic Privacy Information Center, told the *Austin American-Statesman* in an interview. "This system would really turn that tradition on its head, and basically say that everyone is potentially suspect and that all of our transactions and all our communications should be monitored by the government."

Senator Ron Wyden, Democrat of Oregon, called TIA "the most far-reaching snooping program ever proposed against law-abiding Americans." Former U.S. representative Bob Barr, an outspoken Georgia Republican and avowed conservative, noted that many had mistakenly likened TIA to the Bush administration's much-maligned Terrorism Information and Prevention System (Operation TIPS), which sought to turn a million letter carriers, utility workers, and others with access to private homes into government informants. "In fact," Barr insisted, "the danger of Total Information Awareness to our basic freedom is far worse than Operation TIPS. Whereas TIPS would have actively recruited government-sanctioned peeping toms, Total Information Awareness will establish just the high-tech infrastructure necessary to make such voyeurism easy, cheap, and universal."

The U.S. Public Policy Committee of the Association for Computing Machinery, an organization that claims the world's largest membership of information technology students and professionals, laid out its many concerns in a letter to key members of the Senate Committee on Armed Services. For starters, the group warned that TIA threatened identity theft and other security problems, such as exploitation and attack by hackers, criminals, and terrorists. There are also privacy risks, the organization contended: citizens, for instance, could not verify that information collected about them is accurate. "Worse yet would be the resulting lack of protection against harassment or blackmail by individuals who have inappropriately obtained access to an individual's information, or by government agencies that misuse their authority." What's more, the group contended, TIA would also pose both economic liabilities and, perhaps most disconcertingly, personal risks: "Any type of statistical analysis inevitably results in some number of false positives—in this case incorrectly labeling someone as a potential terrorist. As the entire population would be subjected to TIA surveillance, even a small percentage of false positives would result in a large number of law-abiding Americans being mistakenly labeled."

An increasingly wary Congress, concerned that TIA's datamining routines might indeed quash civil liberties and compromise constitutional guarantees, approved legislation placing restrictions on the program. On February 20, 2003, President Bush signed the measure into law. Exactly three months later, with the storm over TIA still unabated, it was officially renamed the Terrorism Information Awareness program. In a report to Congress, DARPA lamented that the old name "created in some minds the impression that TIA was a system to be used for developing dossiers on U.S. citizens. That is not DoD's intent," the agency reiterated, "in pursuing this program."

BEYOND THE BUREAUCRACY

Lost in the debate about TIA were details of its genesis and operational methods, which in many ways reflect the Bush administration's preferred methods of conducting government business.

TIA was actually the brainchild of John Poindexter, who had the right connections to help fulfill his vision. Syntek, the technical and engineering services firm for which he worked, was a DARPA contractor, and when Pentagon brass bought Poindexter's terrorist-fighting pitch they in turn tapped him to be director of the new Information Awareness Office. Poindexter's recruits included IAO Deputy Director Robert Popp, who came to the government from defense contractor ALPHATECH Inc., where he served as program manager for several DARPA-sponsored efforts. Although the men's biographies—along with those of other IAO staff—once graced the office's Web site, they were removed from public view in November 2002, thereby limiting disclosure about this government research effort.

IAO's list of contracts with private industry is similarly not disclosed. But thanks to a successful Freedom of Information Act lawsuit against the Defense Department, the Electronic Privacy

Information Center unearthed documents that reveal nearly two dozen companies and universities that were selected to receive funding for work on the Total Information Awareness System. Among those listed: ALPHATECH Inc., IAO Deputy Director Robert Popp's former employer. Other documents show that in September 2002, the Defense Department also awarded a contract for a research project called Technical Support of Wargaming the Asymmetric Environment, one of the 13 programs under exploration by Poindexter's Information Awareness Office. According to the defense department, the $5 million-plus contract was competitively procured, although just one offer was received—from Syntek Technologies, Poindexter's former employer.

IAO's reliance on private contractors is hardly surprising; DARPA, its parent agency, doesn't conduct any research in-house, but rather farms it all out. What's more, DARPA doesn't require contractors to share their research solely with the agency. "The government benefits when there are commercial applications [from DARPA research] because it keeps the cost down," Jan Walker, a spokesperson for the agency, told the Center for Public Integrity. In fact, Anthony Tether, the director of DARPA, once likened his operation in an interview to a venture capital firm, although with a twist: government-funded inventors get to keep the rights to their intellectual property, he said, and the military will pay to use it.

This approach could, theoretically, make sensitive snooping technology developed for Poindexter's Total Information Awareness System commercially available to the sort of sophisticated terrorist in the United States that it was meant to foil. But it's nonetheless a modus operandi that jibes neatly with the Bush administration's big-picture views on the role and functioning of government. In fact, candidate Bush, in a campaign-trail speech in June 2000, was very clear about his plans to reform the federal bureaucracy: "I will open government to the discipline of competition," he told a Philadelphia audience. "If the private sector can do the better job the private sector can get the contract."

> "I will open government to the discipline of competition," Bush announced. "If the private sector can do the better job, the private sector can get the contract."

In August 2001, with the publication of "The President's Management Agenda," Bush indeed nudged the government toward his preferred market-based approach. The 60-plus-page document, which the president dispatched to Congress, laid out a blueprint for reform that identified 14 areas for improvement, including one that would strike fear throughout the federal workforce: "competitive sourcing," a controversial plan designed to ultimately force hundreds of thousands of government employees to compete for their jobs with the private sector. To the administration's way of thinking, the problem was unmistakable: nearly half of all federal employees perform commercially available tasks like data collection and administrative support, but competition between government and private sector providers to perform those functions—a process that has supposedly yielded cost savings of as much as 50 percent—is the exception rather than the rule. "For many activities," the management agenda proclaimed, "citizens do not care whether the private or public sector provides the service or administers the program. The process of competition provides an imperative for the public sector to focus on continuous improvement and removing roadblocks to greater efficiency."

The administration official designated to sell this reform to members of Congress was Angela Styles, administrator for federal procurement policy at the Office of Management and Budget. Styles was formerly counsel to the government contracts group of a Washington, D.C., law firm, and from 1994 to 1996 she served with the Government Contracts Group at Baker Botts, the high-profile Texas firm that is George W. Bush's seventeenth-largest career patron.

In media interviews and Capitol Hill testimony, Styles dutifully repeated the administration's message: competitive sourcing isn't about outsourcing or downsizing, but rather about creating opportunities for efficiency and innovation through competition. To fend off critics worried about gutting the federal bureaucracy, the reform plan was slated for a gradual phase-in: for fiscal year 2002, the proposal decreed, not less than 5 percent of full-time employees should be subjected to "public-private or direct conversion competition." This was slated to rise by 10 percent in fiscal year 2003, and, according to Styles, eventually affect perhaps 425,000 full-time employees—about half of the federal workforce employed in food service, landscaping, eyeglass production, and other positions not considered "inherently governmental."

For the Bush administration, competitive sourcing promised everything from increased private sector employment and a bump in contracts for U.S. small businesses to decreased costs of conducting government affairs. But opponents attacked the initiative as a blueprint for privatization at the expense of government unions—a plan that would outsource jobs ranging from health care providers in Veterans Administration hospitals to mine safety inspectors. David Holway, president of the National Association of Government Employees, charged that Bush's proposal would entice "private profiteers" to unfairly take jobs from federal employees. "These profiteers will initially come in at a substandard rate and after a period of time will increase their contract price which will inevitably be more costly for taxpayers," Holway wrote in comments to the Office of Management and Budget. Bobby L. Harnage Sr., president of the American Federation of Government Employees, labeled the administration's plan an "attempt to use privatization to pay off its contractor cronies with taxpayer dollars."

As the push to privatize went forward, naysayers voiced other reservations about competitive sourcing. In June 2002, for example, the Bush administration quietly amended a Clinton-era order that classified air traffic control as an inherently governmental function. The White House portrayed the change as a mere technicality, although members of the National Air Traffic Controllers Association were not quite so sanguine: the following winter, alarmed that the administration's action produced a "slippery slope" toward privatization, they took to leafleting at airports in hopes of generating a public outcry. Shortly thereafter, 26 U.S. senators wrote the president to express their concern that air traffic control had been reclassified as a "commercial activity"—a move, they feared, that might indeed one day lead to privatization. "In our view, from a homeland security and safety perspective, air traffic control is a quintessentially governmental function and should be so designated," they wrote Bush.

The stepped-up privatization of federal prisons—a trend that started during the Clinton presidency—has generated warnings from the nation's corrections officials. They point to studies by bureau of prisons research organizations which concluded that privatized correctional facilities cost more to operate and have higher staff turnover rates and more rampant drug use among prisoners. On December 13, 2002, Bush turned his attention to the future of the nation's mail service by establishing the President's Commission on the United States Postal Service. Among the commission's tasks: examining whether parts of the Postal Service should be privatized—an idea that critics contend would spell certain doom for guaranteed universal service.

There have also been charges that competitive sourcing will take an unwelcome toll on the nation's Armed Services. In the spring of 2001, for example, the Department of Defense noted in a report to Congress that the military's contract workforce had, for the first time, exceeded its civilian payrolls. So in late 2002, when the Army announced its intention to privatize an additional 200,000-plus military and civilian jobs, dozens of federal lawmakers expressed apprehension that such a wholesale transfer of personnel could have the unintended effect of threatening national security. The American Federation of Government Employees, already at odds with the administration over the push for increased privatization, weighed in with additional concerns: the Army and other agencies, the union contended, planned to privatize large numbers of jobs "without any public-private competition, using a corporate welfare—style method called 'divestiture,' which turns out to be nothing less than the transfer to politically well-connected contractors of services performed by federal employees, the actual federal employees who perform those services, and the equipment used by the federal employees who perform those services."

And privatization will likely create other systemic problems. For example, private-sector workers taking over government jobs might not be entitled to the protections afforded government whistleblowers, leaving them vulnerable to retaliation and dismissal. As a result, reports of waste and fraud could be suppressed. What's more, the push to privatize so many federal jobs may sabotage the Freedom of Information Act by restricting citizen access to data about government agencies and projects. Charles N. Davis, executive director of the Freedom of Information Center at the Missouri School of Journalism, warns that contracting out government functions leaves an unmistakable void: the scrutiny that comes with being part of the government.

Some states, he says, have in fact amended their open-records laws to include private contractors. Following a scandal at a privately operated prison, for example, Texas amended its statutes in order to keep prison records public, whether a facility is operated by government employees or private contractors. But the bottom line, Davis told the Center for Public Integrity in an interview, is that it's hard to make open-records laws applicable to contractors. And unless the Freedom of Information Act is amended to specifically include such private workers, prying free facts about government programs will inevitably be harder.

Davis was pessimistic, however, about the likelihood of such reforms. Asked whether there had been efforts to amend the federal Freedom of Information Act to keep pace with the Bush administration's outsourcing, he said none had so far materialized. "That would be no small effort," he added. "I can hardly even imagine what the lobbying war would be like."

TINKERING WITH THE SAFETY NET

On June 18, 2001, Secretary of the Treasury Paul O'Neill served up a high-profile broadside in George W. Bush's nascent campaign to dramatically reform Social Security, the government-administered program that provides financial benefits to retired and disabled workers. The blunt-spoken O'Neill, who once described stock traders as "not the sort of people you would want to help you think about complex questions," was invited to join some four dozen securities industry executives at the organizational luncheon of their new political lobbying group, the Coalition for American Financial Security. In a small dining room at Windows on the World, the posh eatery on the 107th floor of the north tower of the World Trade Center, O'Neill minced no words for those assembled: Social Security was a revolutionary idea for its time, he said in a brief address, but the current-day program was on a collision course with insolvency. In fact, the system would likely be so strained by those millions of retiring baby boomers that the trust fund's coffers were projected to be empty by 2038. Without reform, O'Neill warned, the government might not be able to meet its obligations to future retirees.

> Private-sector workers taking over government jobs might not be entitled to the protections afforded government whistle-blowers, leaving them vulnerable to retaliation and dismissal.

But the treasury secretary had a solution—a much-ballyhooed plan that Bush had unveiled on the campaign trail some 13 months earlier: the partial privatization of Social Security. Under the president's scheme, those paying into the Social Security system would be permitted to shift some of their contributions to private accounts and to invest that money in the stock and bond markets. "Every American should have behind them, and in front of them, the prospect of wealth accumulation so when they retire they can live with dignity and respect more than they do now," O'Neill told the lunchtime gathering.

On the street below, however, roughly 150 protesters decried the idea of subjecting their fiscal safety net to the gyrations of the equity and credit markets. "Last year Social Security sent out a half-billion checks and not one of them was late or worth less because the stock market went down. That's security, not risk," Dan Schulder, assistant director of the Alliance for Retired Persons, told a reporter. Others among the crowd of union and elderly activists complained that the proposal was yet another way to enrich those investment bankers and mutual fund managers who had helped send Bush to Washington.

O'Neill dismissed the plan's skeptics with a concise jab: "Those who are against it," he said, "just don't understand the facts." Of course, members of the Coalition for American Financial Security, who welcomed the treasury secretary into their midst, certainly understood one compelling fact: by some estimates, the Bush administration reforms could spawn more than 100 million investment accounts—a windfall that could generate untold billions of dollars in annual fees and commissions for Wall Street firms.

The coalition, it turns out, was a political advocacy group founded by executives of the Frank Russell Company investment firm, best known for having created the Russell 2000 stock index. The group's roster boasted executives of leading Wall Street firms, who fervently shared the Bush administration's goal of partially privatizing Social Security. In fact, as candidate Bush touted his privatization plan, these and other financial giants poured enough money into the campaign to make them among his biggest financial backers for the 2000 election. According to an analysis by the Center for Public Integrity, Merrill Lynch, Crédit Suisse First Boston, Goldman Sachs, UBS PaineWebber, and Morgan Stanley ranked second, fifth, eighth, fourteenth, and twenty-eighth, respectively, among those giving to Bush's campaigns, with combined contributions exceeding $1.5 million. For good measure, they collectively donated $327,500 to Bush's inaugural committee.

In May 2001, Bush stoked the coalition's hopes for reform by establishing the President's Commission to Strengthen Social Security. The bipartisan group, whose members were recruited from politics, academia, and business, was tasked with producing a report that adhered to a strict set of principles: "Modernization must include individually controlled, voluntary personal retirement accounts, which will augment the Social Security safety net." To insure against potentially embarrassing dissenting opinions, all 16 of Bush's appointees pledged their support for partially privatizing the retirement benefits program. So it was hardly surprising that the commission's final report, released in December 2001, offered as its central finding an endorsement of Bush's position: "Social Security will be strengthened," the report decreed, "if modernized to include a system of voluntary personal accounts."

But while there was unanimity on that point, commission members couldn't agree on a privatization proposal; instead, they took the unusual step of recommending consideration of three different plans, and further raised eyebrows by suggesting that rescuing Social Security from insolvency might very well require a cut in benefits for retirees and disabled Americans. And with Bush's blessing, the commission further recommended that legislative action on its proposals be postponed for a year—that is, until after the 2002 elections, thereby giving antsy Republicans political cover should they choose to endorse this dramatic change in the Social Security system.

Critics of the proposals were unrelenting in their condemnation. Representative Robert Matsui of California, ranking Democrat on the Subcommittee on Social Security of the Committee on

Ways and Means, insisted that privatization had no relevance to fixing Social Security. "Privatization is a gimmick for some on Wall Street to feather their own nest," he said.

Matsui—joined by other prominent Democrats—kept up the criticism. The following March, he challenged Representative Dick Armey of Texas, the House majority leader, to bring GOP privatization plans to the House floor for a vote. "We keep hearing about these privatization plans—how they won't cut benefits and how they will solve the problem," Matsui said during a hearing on a privatization bill championed by Armey. "If these plans are credible, why can't we debate them, mark them up in Committee, and vote on them? The simple fact is that none of these plans is credible, and nobody has the intention of bringing any of them to the floor in any form." Four months later, with the major stock market indices hovering at five-year lows, Matsui joined Democratic leaders in their call for Republicans to justify their privatization plans. "The president and his Republican colleagues are determined to privatize Social Security, but they refuse to talk about it until after the election," he said. "It makes sense that they would try to hide their plans. Look at the stock market and the crisis in corporate America. Who would feel comfortable taking the guaranteed benefits of Social Security and gambling it on Wall Street?"

Despite the rebukes, and despite tepid public support for partial privatization, Bush remained committed to these Social Security reforms. In February 2002, for instance, at a national summit on retirement savings, the president beat the drum for personal retirement accounts. Five months later, in his daily press briefing, presidential press secretary Ari Fleischer reaffirmed his boss's enthusiasm for the idea. And in his 2003 State of the Union speech, Bush declared: "As we continue to work together to keep Social Security sound and reliable, we must offer younger workers a chance to invest in retirement accounts that they will control and they will own." In doing so, he kept alive the privatization hopes of his Wall Street patrons.

Finance and accounting executives also put their faith in Bush. And like those thirsting for lucrative retirement accounts, these donors have found reason to cheer the administration's other initiatives.

> **"Privatization is a gimmick for some on Wall Street to feather their own nest," said California's Robert Matsui.**

For example, MBNA, the top donor to Bush's 2000 presidential committees, and his number six career patron overall, gave $358,000 to the future president, according to a Center analysis. The self-described "world's largest independent credit card issuer," MBNA devoted much of its $5.58 million lobbying budget for 2000 and 2001 toward securing reforms that would have made it harder for individuals to declare bankruptcy without having to repay debt. A bill that would have done just that passed Congress by a wide margin in 2000, only to be vetoed by President Bill Clinton.

MBNA's political contributions seemed likely to pay off when Bush moved into the White House. In early 2001, both Houses of Congress again passed legislation designed to curb abuse, this time creating a means test for bankruptcy filers that would force more people to pay off their debts. Critics contended that the new laws would be a boon for banks, credit card companies, and predatory lenders but would bring financial ruin for those honestly unable to pay their bills, including many beset by illness, unemployment, or divorce. "In all my years in and out of the Senate, I've never seen a bill that was so one-sided," said former senator Howard Metzenbaum, chairman of the Consumer Federation of America. "The cries, claims and concerns of vulnerable Americans who have suffered a financial emergency have been drowned out by the political might of the credit card industry."

But as the bankruptcy legislation headed for a House-Senate conference committee, Bush nonetheless made clear that he supported the bill's "commonsense reforms," and that he looked forward to a final version of it reaching his desk. Unfortunately for MBNA, millions in campaign contributions and lobbying fees were unable to overcome a partisan tiff over an obscure provision applying to anti-abortion protestors, and the bill never emerged from conference. Bush's payback to this credit card company would have to wait.

THE UNDERSTUDY

There would, however, be no such delays for Halliburton Company, the Texas-based energy services behemoth whose chairman and CEO had resigned to pursue a second-in-command spot in the nation's capital.

It was a natural career move for Richard Bruce Cheney, who was born in Lincoln, Nebraska, on January 30, 1941. When he was 13, his family moved to Casper, Wyoming, where his father, Richard Herbert Cheney, toiled as a soil conservation agent for the U.S. Department of Agriculture. At Natrona County High School, Cheney's credentials included senior class president and captain of the "Mustangs" football team. A scholarship brought him to Yale University, but unlike George W. Bush, who stuck around New Haven for his diploma, Cheney dropped out during sophomore year and returned to the Cowboy State. Resuming his studies, he earned two political science degrees at the University of Wyoming: a B.A. in 1965 and an M.A. in 1966.

Cheney again left home, this time for doctoral studies at the University of Wisconsin and then a stint in the office of Wisconsin's governor. In 1968 he won a fellowship that landed him in the Washington office of U.S. Representative William Steiger, a young Republican who, a decade later, would adroitly engineer a dramatic cut in capital gains rates, thereby setting the stage for the Ronald Reagan–led tax-cutting revolution. Cheney subsequently headed for the executive branch, where he served in the Office of Economic Opportunity. The agency's director at the time was Donald Rumsfeld, who had resigned from a fourth term in the House of Representatives to join the cabinet of President Richard Nixon.

In 1971, Nixon tapped Rumsfeld to be White House counsellor, and Cheney was recruited to be his deputy. In the summer of 1974, when the Watergate scandal forced Nixon to resign the presidency, President Gerald Ford tapped Rumsfeld to serve as chairman of his transition team and then chief of staff. Rumsfeld, in turn, brought in Cheney as his assistant. Cheney's ascendancy up the political ladder accelerated in November of 1975: when Rumsfeld was named secretary of defense, the 34-year-old Cheney was appointed White House chief of staff, a post he served in through the remainder of the Ford administration.

Cheney returned to Wyoming in 1977, and the following year, running as a Republican, he was elected to the U.S. House of Representatives. He was reelected five times, finally leaving Congress in 1989 to serve as George H. W. Bush's secretary of defense. During his four-year tenure at the Pentagon, Cheney oversaw Operation Desert Storm, which expelled invading Iraqi troops from neighboring Kuwait. For his efforts, George

Bush awarded him the Presidential Medal of Freedom on July 3, 1991.

When Cheney took the Halliburton reins in 1995, he had no energy-industry experience. He did, however, possess a high political profile and a Rolodex overflowing with enviable global contacts, most notably in the oil-rich Persian Gulf region. In fact, his instantaneous rise to CEO was purely serendipitous: after leaving government service, Cheney's partners on a weeklong fishing trip to Canada included Halliburton CEO Thomas Cruikshank, who was apparently considering retirement. Cheney so impressed Cruikshank with his grasp of world politics, the story goes, that Cruikshank pressed his board of directors to make Cheney his successor. "Here's a guy who knew people all over the world," former U.S. representative (and Bush political patron) Kent Hance, who served with Cheney in Congress, and who later spoke with Cruikshank about the matter, told the *Austin American-Statesman*. "He could get an audience with them and get Halliburton's foot in the door. . . . If the former secretary of defense wants to meet with the CEO and president of Shell Oil in Amsterdam, they're going to see him. If he wants to meet with King Fahd in Saudi Arabia, they're going to see him."

> Halliburton landed some $2.3 billion in U.S. government contracts during Cheney's five-year tenure—nearly double the $1.2 billion it earned from the government in the five years before he arrived.

Of course, as Cheney well knew, having access to American politicians and key agency personnel also has its rewards, and he took steps to insure that Halliburton had a prominent seat at the table. For example, a Center for Public Integrity analysis reveals that in the three election cycles prior to Cheney's arrival,

Halliburton's PAC and employees donated about $740,000 in hard and soft money to candidates and committees, with 73 percent going to Republicans and 22 percent to Democrats (the remainder went to minor parties and nonpartisan committees). Then, in the three election cycles during Cheney's chairmanship, donations more than doubled to $1.6 million, although only one party actually shared in the spoils: Republicans received 86 percent of those funds, records show, while Democrats received just 4 percent. And for good measure, Cheney continually upped Halliburton's lobbying efforts. From 1996 to 1999, annual expenditures climbed from $280,000 to $360,000 and then $540,000, finally topping out at $600,000. The firm's government relations squad included Dave Gribbin, who worked for Cheney both on Capitol Hill and then as his assistant secretary of defense for legislative affairs. (Cheney later brought Gribbin along to work on the presidential transition, as well.)

It was money well spent. According to Center for Public Integrity calculations, Halliburton landed some $2.3 billion in U.S. government contracts during Cheney's five-year tenure—nearly double the $1.2 billion it earned from the government in the five years before he arrived. In addition, in the five years before Cheney joined Halliburton, the company managed to secure about $100 million worth of loans and loan guarantees by the U.S. Export-Import Bank and the Overseas Private Investment Corporation. During Cheney's tenure, that figure jumped to about $1.5 billion.

And Cheney did indeed exploit those overseas connections that made him so appealing to Halliburton's board. Just months after landing in his new job, for example, Cheney joined the elder George Bush and former national security advisor Brent Scowcroft on a tour of Persian Gulf states that included private audiences with members of the ruling families. This was the sort of pull that paid rich dividends. There was, for instance, the story of Halliburton officials striking out in their repeated attempts to get a meeting with the oil minister of Qatar, in hopes of cooking up a deal. As the *Los Angeles Times* reported, the cold shoulder ended with Cheney's involvement: " 'Within an hour, the meeting was facilitated and set up,' said Halliburton's chief financial officer, Gary V. Morris, a tone of wonder in his voice. 'Having access is a great thing.' "

Cheney also joined Scowcroft and a group of political heavyweights that included James A. Baker III, secretary of state under the elder George Bush and, more recently, senior partner in the Texas law firm of Baker Botts, in working to open Central Asia's oil-rich Caspian Sea region to American oil interests. This effort, intended to produce some green-ink gushers for Halliburton and its peers, was fraught with controversy for a number of reasons. For starters, Cheney sought partial repeal of the Freedom Support Act, which was signed into law in October 1992 by the elder George Bush. Section 907 of the law, from which Cheney sought a waiver, banned direct U.S. assistance to the former Soviet republic of Azerbaijan because of that government's blockade and "offensive uses of force"— its campaign of ethnic cleansing—against Armenia and the people of Nagorno-Karabagh, an autonomous mountain region that declared its independence in January 1992. The blockade of food, medicine, and other vital necessities spawned a calamitous humanitarian crisis in Armenia and Nagorno-Karabagh, thus precipitating reprisals by the U.S. Congress, which aimed to pressure the Azerbaijan government to lift the blockade. Cheney's interests were a bit more mercenary than those of Congress: he wanted to ensure that Halliburton shared in the huge oil and gas riches that the Caspian region offered, and a foothold in Azerbaijan—endowed with much of that coveted hydrocarbon—was one sure path to profit. As Halliburton's CEO publicly proclaimed: "The good Lord didn't see fit to put oil and gas only where there are democratic regimes friendly to the United States."

Equally problematic, the good Lord also landlocked the Caspian Sea, making the transport of its oil—by some estimates, the near-equivalent of Persian Gulf reserves—an overland necessity. And therein lay another problem for Cheney: while Russia wanted the crude piped across its borders to the Black Sea, American oil interests preferred that it be moved to the Persian Gulf—a southerly route straight across Iran. But traversing Iran was just a maddening pipe dream, thanks to a 1995 executive order prohibiting American businesses from dealing with this rogue nation. Cheney was similarly frustrated by a trade embargo against Libya—another major oil producer—imposed by President Reagan in 1986. So he lobbied for a change in U.S. policy, arguing that these unilateral sanctions—as opposed to U.N.-imposed sanctions, for example—froze American businesses out of potentially lucrative contracts. "They don't work," he once told an audience at the Cato Institute, the Washington, D.C.–based libertarian think tank. "I think it is important for us to recognize as a nation the enormous value of having American businesses engaged around the world."

But if U.S. law forbade American companies from doing business with these sponsors of terrorism (Libya, for example, was accused of harboring two men indicted for the bombing of Pan Am Flight 103 over Lockerbie, Scotland), Halliburton still managed to profit there via foreign subsidiaries—a strategy that, technically speaking, did not break U.S. law. In Iran, for instance, a Halliburton subsidiary worked on various offshore-drilling contracts. In Libya, Halliburton subsidiary Brown & Root began working on the Great Man-Made River Project—officially, a massive desert irrigation project—in 1984. (Unofficially, the *New York Times* reported, the massive network of underground tunnels was rumored to be for clandestine military purposes, such as moving around troops or storing weapons of mass destruction.) When the sanctions went into effect, the company simply switched the project to its British office, thereby doing an end-run on U.S. policy—a ruse that earned it $3.8 million in fines.

Brown & Root, which Halliburton acquired in 1962, and which is today known as Kellogg Brown & Root, Inc. has an enviable record of winning domestic contracts, as well. The company can trace those good fortunes to its longstanding—and unusually generous—support for Lyndon Johnson's political career, patronage that was rewarded with a steady stream of lucrative government business. These deals, which gradually helped make the firm a major global player in construction and engineering, included Vietnam War–era assignments building the likes of landing strips and military bases.

> From 1994 to 2002, the Center found, Brown & Root was awarded more than six hundred contracts by the Defense Department.

Brown & Root's military-related fortunes further brightened during Dick Cheney's tenure as secretary of defense, beginning with a particularly fortuitous 1992 contract: the Pentagon chief hired the company to prepare a confidential report determining the feasibility of privatizing certain functions of the Defense Department. By year's end, those managing the Logistics Civil Augmentation Program decided to henceforth designate a single firm to provide the Army with worldwide logistical support, and they awarded Brown & Root a one-year contract that promised to pay costs, additional fees, and sizable incentives for work deemed well done. And along with four additional option years, the deal proved to be a huge, ongoing windfall for the Texas firm.

Brown & Root's initial contract with LOGCAP, first used in Somalia in 1992, later sent the company's crews to provide contingency support in such nations as Albania, Croatia, Haiti, Kosovo, Kuwait, Saudi Arabia, and Zaire, among others, where the tasks included everything from base camp construction and maintenance to providing mail delivery, laundry service, and sewage removal. Some of these projects earned Brown & Root just a few million dollars, while the 1994 Operation Uphold Democracy, launched to support the return of democracy in Haiti, was worth $133 million to the Halliburton subsidiary. But it was Brown & Root's peacekeeping support work in the Balkans—the largest contract for services to U.S. forces, according to the General Accounting Office—that really proved to be pay dirt. Dubbed "the mother of all service contracts" by the Contract Services Association of America, a Washington-area trade group, the deal has been valued at $2.2 billion over five years. So ubiquitous were Brown & Root employees that the company sometimes counted nearly three of its contractors for every two soldiers stationed in Bosnia, Kosovo, and other Balkan countries, according to *Government Executive* magazine. In the former Yugoslavia alone, Brown & Root has had as many as 20,000 contractors on the ground, the magazine reported.

From 1994 to 2002, the Center found, Brown & Root was awarded more than 600 contracts by the Defense Department. Endowed with such contracts, Brown & Root proved to be a boon to Dick Cheney's Halliburton—a steady source of revenues to temper the cyclical gyrations of the world oil markets. And whether it was the result of happenstance or shrewd management (the financial community couldn't quite agree), by the time Cheney signed on as aspiring presidential understudy the company had expanded its global reach, profits had surged, and the stock price was tracking straight north. At the same time, however, Cheney's 1998 acquisition of Dresser Industries, to help Halliburton increase its share of the oil-services business, would later saddle the firm with costly (some claimed potentially ruinous) asbestos litigation—a revelation that would remain buried until after Cheney's departure, when it would contribute to a precipitous decline in the company's stock price.

That return to politics was as unforeseen as his instantaneous rise to CEO: After George W. Bush tapped Cheney to be his one-man vice presidential search committee, he decided that the Halliburton chief—rather than such contenders as Tom Ridge, Elizabeth Dole, and Christine Todd Whitman—would, in fact, be the best choice. Cheney at first declined, but in July 2000, following a meeting at Bush's Texas ranch, he added his name to the ticket.

The Halliburton board, whose members included Cheney recruit Lawrence Eagleburger, the elder George Bush's secretary of state, gave their 59-year-old chairman and CEO a memorable sendoff: an early-retirement package of stock, stock options, and benefits that, by some estimates, topped $20 million. But that windfall was just part of the generous exit package. A financial disclosure form filed with the Office of Government Ethics shows that in the year he left Halliburton, Cheney's salary, stock option sales, and various other compensations earned him more than $35.1 million. And a subsequent disclosure form shows that, even after assuming the vice presidency, Cheney received from Halliburton an "elective deferred salary payout" of $162,392. Ultimately, Cheney's deferred compensation is expected to total at least $2.1 million, Halliburton records show.

Not surprisingly, Cheney's relocation to Washington hardly doomed his firm's relationship with the federal government. In April 2001, for example, the U.S. Navy awarded Halliburton subsidiary Kellogg, Brown & Root (or KBR, as it came to be known), a five-year construction and support contract—an arrangement that let the military service craft deals with the company without first having to seek competitive bids. The following December, as the war on terrorism was ratcheted up, the Army awarded another LOGCAP contract to KBR, this one a 10-year pact for worldwide combat support that also obviated the need for competitive bids. As the *New York Times* reported, the contract put no lid on spending by the Halliburton subsidiary—the Army's only logistical arrangement without an estimated cost.

The Navy contract was awarded to KBR over the protests of the General Accounting Office, which questioned the criteria used to evaluate bidders. What's more, both the Army and Navy contracts were awarded at a time when KBR was fighting allegations of fraud for improperly billing the U.S. government for services provided at Fort Ord, California. In February 2002 Halliburton paid the government $2 million to settle the 1997 lawsuit. Under terms of the settlement, the company denied any wrongdoing.

But the greatest controversy to swirl around Halliburton involved a contract to aid in the post-war reconstruction of Iraq. Events began unfolding in November 2002, when Kellogg, Brown & Root, in its capacity as LOGCAP contractor for the Army, was called on to create a contingency plan to deal with war-related damage to Iraqi oil production facilities. On February 14, 2003, KBR began prepositioning equipment and personnel to deal with the possibility of such mishaps. Then, on

March 8, about a week and a half before coalition forces initiated action against Saddam Hussein's regime, KBR was awarded
another Army contract—this one separate from its LOGCAP
deal—to actually implement the contingency plan. No other
companies were notified about the contract or allowed to bid on
it. Congress, likewise, was kept in the dark.

In fact, the mere existence of the arrangement was only
revealed on March 24, in news releases issued by both Halliburton and the Department of Defense. But scant details and syn-
tactical sleights of hand led the nation's news media to believe
that the contract had been awarded that very day, and that its
scope of work would be limited to extinguishing oil well fires,
cleaning up related environmental damage, and, if necessary,
repairing Iraq's petroleum-producing infrastructure.

On April 8, however, in reply to an inquiry by Representative
Henry Waxman, Democrat of California, Lieutenant General
Robert B. Flowers noted: "The total estimated cost [ceiling cost] of
the contract is $7 billion, and the term of the contract is two years."

The criticism that followed this revelation was unrestrained.
The *New York Times*, for example, complained in an editorial:
"This looks like naked favoritism and undermines the Bush
administration's portrayal of the war as a campaign for disarmament and democracy, not lucre." For his part, Waxman
called on the General Accounting Office to investigate allegations that Cheney's former employer had received "special
treatment" from the Bush administration in the awarding of
lucrative defense department contracts.

As it happened, Iraqi oil fields suffered far less damage than
anticipated, earning KBR about $50 million for its efforts. And
with an estimated $600 million worth of related work to complete,
including the operation of Iraqi oil fields and the distribution of
the country's oil, the Army Corps of Engineers—aware, no doubt,

of the swirling political winds—decided to open the remainder of the work to competitive bids.

Of course, Halliburton need not have worried about losing out to competitors. Indeed, with Cheney in the White House, thereby assuring the firm a friend in high places, company executives cut lobbying expenses in half.

VENTURING OFFSHORE

In July 2002, as Congress hastily prepared to authorize creation of the Department of Homeland Security, Democratic Connecticut Representative Rosa DeLauro offered an amendment designed to bar the new department—formed as part of the largest government reorganization in more than half a century—from granting contracts to American companies that incorporate overseas to dodge U.S. taxes. "Corporate expatriates should not continue to benefit from government largesse, but they do, billing $2 billion a year in government contracts," DeLauro said in House floor debate. "Not only have these companies abandoned their responsibilities to our country, they put responsible corporate citizens at a disadvantage."

> With Cheney in the White House, thereby assuring the firm a friend in high places, company executives cut lobbying expenses in half.

The amendment was denounced by the Republican leadership, who argued that it would cost American jobs, but a rebellion among the rank and file ultimately precipitated a lopsided vote: 318 yeas to 110 nays. Six weeks later, the Senate approved a similar amendment introduced by Senator Paul Wellstone, Democrat of Minnesota.

But expatriates targeted by the amendments, including a trio singled out for scorn during congressional debate, retaliated by unleashing a brigade of lobbyists. The aggrieved included Ingersoll-Rand, the manufacturer of such products as Kryptonite locks and Thermo King refrigeration units, which on December 31, 2001, deserted New Jersey (legally, but not physically) and reincorporated in Bermuda—a corporate makeover that saved the company an estimated $55 million in taxes during 2002 alone. Tyco International, the diversified global giant whose top three executives—including CEO L. Dennis Kozlowski—were accused of unlawfully enriching themselves at the expense of the company, in 1997 merged into a Bermuda corporation (a gimmick called an "inversion"), thereby generating single-year tax savings of more than $400 million. And then there was Accenture, the global management and technology consulting firm hatched from Andersen Consulting, which had been spun off from the disgraced Big Five accounting firm Arthur Andersen. Although its corporate headquarters are in New York, Accenture, like Tyco and Ingersoll-Rand, did the Bermuda shuffle in 2001. Mysteriously, the familial ties to Arthur Andersen have been entirely purged from the firm's official history, and officials insist they're in fact a Swiss firm, and therefore not actually American expatriates.

The DeLauro-Wellstone amendments held foreboding consequences for this troika, as well as other publicly traded contractors feeding off the federal government. For example, an Associated Press investigation revealed that over a one-year period beginning October 1, 2001, Accenture received nearly $441 million in federal contracts, much of it from the Internal Revenue Service and the Transportation Security Administration, which is part of the new Department of Homeland Security. In October 2002, a General Accounting Office study of

U.S. companies either incorporating or reincorporating in Bermuda, the Cayman Islands, and other favored "tax haven" countries revealed that during fiscal year 2001, Tyco was awarded federal contracts worth nearly $206.4 million.

With so much to lose, the companies shored up their lobbying efforts with some well-connected Washington muscle. Tyco, for instance, retained three lobbying firms, including the legal powerhouse of Wilmer, Cutler & Pickering and a pair of veteran Capitol Hill insiders affiliated with former Senate majority leader Bob Dole. Ingersoll-Rand spent $720,000 on its lobbying campaign. And Accenture retained a gaggle of lobbyists that included Kenneth Duberstein, chief of staff in the Reagan White House, and former U.S. representative Robert Livingston, Republican of Louisiana, who served as chairman of the House Appropriations Committee. Both men—along with Duberstein colleague Michael Berman, who was also recruited for this task— were named among Washington's top lobbyists in 2002 by *The Hill*, the Capitol Hill newspaper.

It proved to be money well spent: the Republican leadership, in consultation with the White House, abruptly introduced a revised homeland security bill that effectively gutted the offshore-contracting prohibition via a generous list of waivers. For example, one such dispensation allowed the secretary of the Department of Homeland Security to ignore the provision in order to "prevent the loss of any jobs in the United States"—a condition that would likely apply to any U.S. company in jeopardy of losing a contract. What's more, Republicans sidestepped committees and quietly buried a number of other eleventh-hour provisions in the 500-page bill. Representative Dick Armey inserted language designed to protect pharmaceutical manufacturer Eli Lilly and Company from lawsuits over a vaccine preservative that purportedly had been linked to autism in children.

Lilly was not only a major donor to the Republican Party (having given almost $2.5 million since 1978), but it had a friend in high places: Mitchell Daniels Jr., at the time the director of the Office of Management and Budget, was previously the drug company's senior vice president of corporate strategy and policy.

As the issue gained visibility, George W. Bush deftly played both sides of the fence. On July 31, 2002, when asked whether the practice of moving corporate headquarters to foreign tax havens should be outlawed, Bush replied: "I think we ought to look at people who are trying to avoid U.S. taxes as a problem. I think American companies ought to pay taxes here, and be good citizens." But Bush never pressed the issue, and his administration's preferred line, courtesy of the Treasury Department and presidential spokesman Ari Fleischer, was that the convoluted American tax code—rather than the questionable behavior of American corporations—was the real culprit. Democratic outrage notwithstanding (Senator Robert Byrd, for instance, dubbed the homeland security bill "a monstrosity"), Republicans argued that a few "extraneous" provisions shouldn't stand in the way of defeating terrorism, and on November 25, 2002, Bush signed the bill into law.

The exodus offshore, be it for the tax advantages or other reasons, has at times resembled a stampede. The roll call includes Halliburton, which under the leadership of Dick Cheney dramatically increased its subsidiaries located in offshore tax havens (the firm, which has defended such behavior as both legal and ethical, claimed at least 20 subsidiaries in the Cayman Islands alone). The private banking divisions of Citibank, Merrill Lynch, and other financial titans, which profit handsomely by managing hundreds of billions of dollars for so-called high-net-worth individuals, stash much of this client wealth offshore—a tax-advantage strategy for some and, for others, a way to shelter assets from real and anticipated lawsuit judgments. And others taking advantage of lax offshore regulations and favorable tax rates include more obscure companies like the Carlyle Group, a private global investment firm based in Washington, D.C. Carlyle, which oversees $16 billion in investments for more than 550 individuals and institutions from 55 countries, invests in defense, energy, telecommunications, and a hodgepodge of other industries. Until May 2003, when Carlyle unveiled a new Web site, the firm kept its activities under wraps. But details nonetheless trickled out. In August 2001, for example, it filed paperwork with the Securities and Exchange Commission that revealed an interest in U.S. Technologies Inc., a venture capital firm based in Washington, D.C. The filing listed eight limited partnerships that collectively owned 9 percent of U.S. Technologies. All of the partnerships were based in the Cayman Islands, yet all listed their "principal business office" as c/o the Carlyle Group at its Washington headquarters, six blocks from the White House.

> Halliburton, which under the leadership of Dick Cheney dramatically increased its subsidiaries located in offshore tax havens, has defended such behavior as both legal and ethical.

So far, the Bush administration has been loath to spoil the party for those venturing offshore as a means to avoid taxes. And those interests are in a position to press their case about maintaining the status quo, thereby keeping details of their clients' investments and financial transactions away from state and federal regulators. A number of the nation's largest banks and brokers, for example, are among the top contributors to Bush, a Center analysis shows. The list includes Crédit Suisse

First Boston ($373,200 in contributions), UBS Paine Webber ($238,100), Morgan Stanley Dean Witter ($191,550), Merrill Lynch ($441,550), Goldman Sachs Group ($274,049), and Bank of America ($235,800). As for Carlyle, its access may be unmatched. The chairman emeritus is Frank Carlucci, secretary of defense under Ronald Reagan and former college wrestling teammate of Donald Rumsfeld, the current secretary of defense. James A. Baker III, who was secretary of state for the elder George Bush and oversaw George W.'s recount effort in Florida, is Carlyle senior counselor. Other one-time government officials working for the firm include John Major, former U.K. prime minister; Arthur Levitt, former chairman of the Securities and Exchange Commission; Fidel Ramos, former president of the Philippines; William E. Kennard, former chairman of the Federal Communications Commission; Richard G. Darman, former director of the Office of Management and Budget; and Charles O. Rossotti, who served as commissioner of the Internal Revenue Service from 1997 until 2002. And if Carlyle really wants the president's ear, it counts George H. W. Bush as a senior advisor.

STATE SECRETS

If history is any guide, George W. Bush will not seek to undo the regulations that help hide so many financial transactions from view. After all, his presidency has been characterized by a zeal for secrecy, an unrelenting push to stem the free flow of information.

One particularly notable example has been the administration's effort to undermine the Freedom of Information Act, the 1966 law that grants citizens access—although with some exceptions—to federal agency records. By statute, government FOIA officers may withhold records dealing with classified national security information, trade secrets, personnel or medical issues, and a handful of other matters—decisions that in each case are left to an official's own discretion (although those denied the requested information may appeal). In October 1993, to better standardize the process and create more openness in government, Attorney General Janet Reno dispatched a memorandum revamping the way the act would be administered; from now on, the memo directed, FOIA officers should "apply a presumption of disclosure." To drive home the point, Reno decreed that, in the event of FOIA-related litigation, the Justice Department would no longer defend an agency's withholding of information merely because there was a "substantial legal basis" for doing so. "Where an item of information might technically or arguably fall within an exemption," she added, "it ought not to be withheld from a FOIA requester unless it need be."

But eight years later, in the aftermath of the September 11 terrorist attacks, Reno's successor renounced that presumption of disclosure. In a memo to the heads of federal departments and agencies, Attorney General John Ashcroft decreed that a well-informed citizenry may be vital to government oversight, but not at the expense of undermining national security. "Any discretionary decision by your agency to disclose information protected under the FOIA should be made only after full and deliberate consideration of the institutional, commercial, and personal privacy interests that could be implicated by disclosure of the information," he wrote. And unlike Reno, whose policies engendered more government in the sunshine, Ashcroft promised legal cover for agencies coming down on the side of nondisclosure. "When you carefully consider FOIA requests and decide to withhold records, in whole or in part, you can be

assured that the Department of Justice will defend your decisions unless they lack a sound legal basis or present an unwar-
ranted risk of adverse impact on the ability of other agencies to
protect other important records," his memo added. In other
words, Justice would bow out of litigation only if its participation might subsequently imperil the government's ability to
withhold other information.

While September 11 was the presumed catalyst for the
revamped FOIA guidelines, the policy change was actually in
keeping with Bush's historical aversion to the release of government papers. In 1997, for example, Bush successfully championed legislation that allowed the governor of Texas to designate
an in-state university or alternate institution, in lieu of the
Texas State Library and Archives, as the repository for his or her
papers. And he later exploited the law by ordering that his own
gubernatorial papers be deposited in the George Bush Presidential Library and Museum, at Texas A&M University, which is
home to his father's executive records.

At the time, the shipment of Bush's documents received
scant attention. But the relocation effort later generated con-
sternation among reporters, historians, researchers, and others seeking access to the 1,800 boxes of not-yet-cataloged
papers. The reason? Because records at the presidential library
are under the jurisdiction of the National Archives and Records
Administration, which is a federal agency, there was confusion
about whether release of the younger Bush's papers was bound
by the federal Freedom of Information Act or the Texas Public
Information Act, which mandates a much speedier response
time for requested records.

Bush's attorney denied that the move reflected a desire to
restrict public access to the papers. And in an interview with the
Center, Chris LaPlante, the state archivist, also dismissed the

conspiratorial claims of open-government activists. He and his colleagues, he said, knew that the governor's papers were destined for an alternate repository, and they assumed that the Bush library staff were equipped to deal with the documents. But Bush's action nonetheless imposed weeks-long—even months-long—delays on the release of documents. And it left consumer advocacy organizations such as Public Citizen grumbling that the departed Texas governor lacked the legal authority to give away state records or place them beyond the reach of the state's open-records law. In May 2002, following protracted legal wrangling, Texas attorney general John Cornyn agreed. He ruled that the disputed papers were indeed state property and therefore subject to the Texas open-records law.

But while Texans earned easier access to some historical records, the public at large was being saddled with a variety of new impediments to an open federal government. To wit:

- On November 1, 2001, President Bush signed Executive Order 13,233, not-so-aptly titled Further Implementation of the Presidential Records Act. In truth, the executive order actually overrides the 1978 Presidential Records Act, the Watergate-inspired edict which stipulated that the papers of presidents and vice presidents would be made available to the public 12 years after they leave office. Under Bush's plan, however, former presidents or their heirs may veto the release of their presidential papers, as may the sitting president—a decision that vested George W. Bush with the authority to block release of his father's papers, for example, or even those of Bill Clinton. Bush's order drew fervent bipartisan condemnation on Capitol Hill (although not enough to force reinstatement of the 1978 act), and it particularly rankled librarians and historians.

The comments of Steven Hensen, president of the Society of American Archivists, were typical. Writing in the *Washington Post*, he asked: "How can a democratic people have confidence in elected officials who hide the records of their actions from public view?"

- Following the September 11 terrorist attacks, the Bush administration encouraged federal agencies to purge a wide array of potentially sensitive data from their Web sites—a decree that, for a time, removed the entire online presence of the Nuclear Regulatory Commission, and which ultimately resulted in hundreds of thousands of pages being deleted from sites maintained by the Department of Energy, the Environmental Protection Agency, the National Archives and Records Administration, and other federal entities. "It is no longer possible for families and communities to get data critical to protecting themselves—information such as pipeline maps (that show where they are and whether they have been inspected), airport safety data, environmental data, and even documents that are widely available on private sites today were removed from government sites and have not reappeared," OMB Watch, which for two decades has been chronicling the activities of the Office of Management and Budget, noted in a paper released in October 2002.

- On March 25, 2003, President Bush signed an order that postponed, by three years, the release of millions of 25-year-old documents slated for automatic declassification the following month. What's more, Executive Order 13,292, which amended a Clinton administration order, granted FOIA officers wider latitude to reclassify information that had already been declassified, and further eliminated a provision that instructed them not to classify information if there was "significant doubt" about the need to do so. While President Bush maintained that the order balanced national security with open government, some were not convinced. For example, the *Washington Post* quoted Thomas Blanton, executive director of the nonprofit National Security Archive, as saying that the order sends "one more signal from on high to the bureaucracy to slow down, stall, withhold, stonewall."

· When the Reporters Committee for Freedom of the Press surveyed the post–September 11 landscape, the First Amendment watchdog concluded that the government had embarked on "an unprecedented path of secrecy" that stifled the press's and the public's right to know. Among the reporters ensnared by the government's flight from the traditional culture of openness is John Solomon, deputy bureau chief of the Associated Press. Solomon, who works out of the Washington, D.C., bureau, was twice victimized. In one incident, a package sent by Federal Express to Solomon from another AP bureau was intercepted by the U.S. Customs Service and forwarded to the FBI, where its contents—an eight-year-old, unclassified bureau lab report previously made public in a court case— were seized and withheld for seven months. In a previous incident, the Justice Department subpoenaed Solomon's home phone records in an attempt to unearth his confidential source for a wire service story. Solomon, who only learned about the subpoena months later, told the Center that it is his understanding that the traditional practice of subpoenaing reporters as an absolute last resort in a "leaks" investigation is no longer the department's modus operandi. "I'm not quite sure it's gotten the public attention it deserves," Solomon told the Center. "I don't think

the profession has realized the importance of the change
of standards that has occurred as a result of my case."

> **The Patriot Act decreased the ability of
> American citizens to obtain information
> about their government and, at the same
> time, gave the government the means to pry
> into the personal lives of those same citizens.**

These incidents were part of a much larger pattern. For
example, on November 13, 2001, President Bush signed an order
decreeing that suspected terrorists may be tried in military tri-
bunals instead of regular courts—a policy that kept secret the
identities of more than 700 detainees. (In June 2003, a federal
appeals court sided with the Justice Department and ruled that
the government did not have to disclose the names of the
detainees.) One month later, Bush invoked executive privilege
to block a congressional subpoena related to the FBI's use of informants in Boston-area criminal investigations—an action that
so enraged Republican Representative Dan Burton, chairman of
the House Committee on Government Reform, that he labeled
Bush a "dictatorial president" at a congressional hearing exploring the matter. In March 2002, White House Chief of Staff
Andrew Card Jr. instructed government agencies to safeguard
"sensitive but unclassified information," an overly vague direc-
tive that led to untold thousands of documents being pulled
from government Web sites and library shelves. In September
2002, a General Accounting Office report revealed that backlogs
of pending FOIA requests were rising at many executive branch
agencies, despite the fact that FOIA requests were decreasing.
When Vice President Dick Cheney repeatedly refused to provide
the General Accounting Office with records related to his

national energy task force, including the names of lobbyists and corporate executives with whom he met, the GAO took the unprecedented step of filing suit to get the records.

And there was the Uniting and Strengthening America by Providing Appropriate Tools Required to Intercept and Obstruct Terrorism Act of 2001, better known by its acronym, USA PATRIOT. First introduced in the House on October 2, 2001, and signed into law just three and a half weeks later, the measure decreased the ability of American citizens to obtain information about their government and, at the same time, gave the government the means to pry into the personal lives of those same citizens.

In essence, the Patriot Act authorized a host of new law enforcement and intelligence-gathering provisions sought by Attorney General John Ashcroft and the Bush administration. For example, the act includes changes to the laws regulating surveillance, making it easier for the government to surreptitiously gather information about individuals. It permits greater use of "roving" wiretaps, making it possible to intercept all of a person's phone conversations (no matter what equipment they use) or Internet communications (although not necessarily the actual content of e-mail messages). It allows for "sneak and peek" searches of homes without notifying residents until well after the fact. And it makes it easier for federal investigators to obtain court orders for domestic surveillance.

On the day Bush signed the act into law, Ashcroft praised its terrorism-fighting capabilities and, in a nod to the unfolding controversy, tried to soothe a skittish public. "The American people," he said, "can be assured law enforcement will use these new tools to protect our nation while upholding the sacred liberties expressed in the Constitution." Such promises hardly pacified civil libertarians, however, who charged that the law—rammed through Congress with minimal debate—greatly expanded the government's authority to spy on Americans and codified end-runs on traditional checks and balances. A year and a half later, those detractors were stunned to learn of a proposed sequel.

The details were first revealed in February 2003, when the Center for Public Integrity published a leaked Department of Justice draft of legislation designed to strengthen and extend provisions of the Patriot Act. The Domestic Security Enhancement Act of 2003, dated January 9, 2003, included provisions that would further inflate government powers of surveillance and punishment, while at the same time decrease judicial review and public access to official information.

Rumors of the proposed act, known informally on Capitol Hill as Patriot Act II, had swirled for months, but the advanced state of the January 9 draft took many by surprise. "We haven't heard anything from the Justice Department on updating the Patriot Act," Jeff Lungren, spokesman for the House Judiciary Committee, told the Center. Senior members of the Senate Judiciary Committee minority staff inquired repeatedly about updates to the law, but were rebuffed at every turn. In fact, in the very week the Center posted the confidential draft on its Web site, these Democratic staffers were still being assured that no such legislation was in the works.

Like its predecessor, Patriot II proposed some dramatic and sweeping changes to the law. For example, the government would be able to sentence people to death for various terrorist actions not currently covered by the death penalty and strip citizenship from Americans who provided material support to groups designated as "terrorist" organizations, even if those individuals didn't break the law or consider that group to be terrorist.

What's more, the draft legislation would further impinge on

privacy rights, giving federal investigators the ability to secretly request credit reports, authorize surveillance under certain circumstances without court approval, and sanction the creation of a DNA database for suspected terrorists—a long leap from current law, which permits the FBI to create such databases only from those actually convicted of certain crimes. The draft also sought to decrease public access to government information. Most notably, it proposed to modify the Freedom of Information Act to specifically bar the release of information about those detained on suspicion of terrorism—an end run to a lawsuit that sought information about those detained in the months following the September 11 attacks. But the legislative flimflam proved unnecessary, as a federal appeals court struck down the lawsuit in June 2003.

On the heels of the Center's disclosure, Barbara Comstock, director of public affairs at the Department of Justice, issued a statement insisting that no conclusions should be drawn from what was, after all, one of many "discussions drafts." "Department staff have not presented any final proposals to either the Attorney General or the White House," her statement said. "It would be premature to speculate on any future decisions, particularly ideas or proposals that are still being discussed at staff levels."

But in the months that followed, Attorney General John Ashcroft left no doubt about his wishes for Patriot Act revisions. For example, on June 5, 2003, in testimony before the House Committee on the Judiciary, Ashcroft maintained that it would be difficult, if not impossible, to prevent another catastrophic attack on American soil without the Patriot Act. "Unfortunately," he added, "the law has several weaknesses which terrorists could exploit, undermining our defenses." And with that, Ashcroft ticked off a series of weaknesses in the law that, coincidentally, were remedied in the confidential draft made public by the Center.

As for George W. Bush, he stayed silent on the need for the Patriot Act upgrade. But four days after Ashcroft's remarks, presidential press secretary Ari Fleischer left open the possibility that Bush might one day press Ashcroft's case. Fleischer, who just weeks earlier had announced that he would soon resign his post, labeled the war on terrorism an ongoing issue that demanded continual review. "And this is something that I think will be with us for quite some time," he told reporters. "And this will also be, of course, done with an eye toward maintaining civil liberties and constitutional protections."

George W. Bush
The Administration

Three weeks after President Bill Clinton was reelected, in November 1996, the U.S. Environmental Protection Agency raised a ruckus by proposing more stringent national air quality standards for particulate matter and ground-level ozone—two of the six so-called criteria air pollutants for which EPA develops standards, as mandated by the 1970 Clean Air Act. At the time, the agency decreed that the proposal was based on "evidence of harm to human health and the environment"; along with clean-air programs already planned, the EPA predicted, the proposed standards would reduce premature deaths by 40,000 per year and reduce serious respiratory problems in children by 250,000 cases per year. "We are now hoping to hear from a wide range of the American people," EPA administrator Carol M. Browner declared upon announcing the proposal, "from scientists and environmentalists to industry experts, small business owners, doctors and parents, to receive the broadest possible public comment and input on this important issue."

Browner got her wish, and then some: the EPA and Vice President Al Gore were besieged with comments, with environmentalists and health care advocates generally lending their support to the proposal and business interests, worried about increased costs for compliance, lining up against it.

The critics also contended that the EPA proposal was based on flawed assumptions and questionable science. They argued, for instance, that the agency had relied on a biased set of air quality studies. They maintained that the proposed standards offered uncertain health benefits. And in some cases, those petitioning Gore complained that the harm done by EPA's proposed actions would ripple throughout society.

For example, there was an anxious letter to the vice president from Dick Cheney, then chairman and chief executive officer of Halliburton Company, the global oil field services firm. "Implementation of these standards," Cheney wrote to Gore, "would cause great harm to consumers, my own industry, and the U.S. economy and will still not deliver the promised significant enhancement of health protection to the American public."

Cheney's five-paragraph letter, dispatched from Halliburton's Dallas headquarters on May 30, 1997, went on to take issue with the EPA's scientific methodology, finally concluding with a plea for Gore: "I urge you to counsel EPA to issue final rules which maintain the existing ozone and particulate matter standards so that unanswered questions regarding the scientific justification, benefits, costs, feasibility and alternatives to new air quality standards are addressed in full and open debate."

Four years later, as Gore's vice presidential replacement, it was Cheney's turn to field the suggestions of America's energy service firms, trade associations, public interest groups, and others interested in matters with profound environmental implications. But as point man for the development of a national energy policy, the vice president was no longer interested in full and open discourse. Instead, he was only intent on chairing off-the-record skull sessions, the substance of which, along with the identities of those who attended, was forever deemed of no interest to the public, the Congress, historians or, for that matter, anyone else outside the Bush-Cheney administration.

FELLING UNFAVORABLE COVERAGE

On November 27, 2002, the nation's airports, highways, and train stations had a welcome look of congested normalcy throughout much of the nation. A year earlier, with the terrorist attacks on the Pentagon and World Trade Center still casting long and unnerving shadows, many Americans decided to forgo their traditional Thanksgiving travel plans for celebrations close to home. But the passage of time, augmented by more stringent security measures, helped make this preholiday Wednesday again look like one of the busiest travel days of the year.

The throngs of out-of-town travelers included President Bush, who retreated to his 1,600-acre ranch in Crawford, Texas, for the five-day holiday. Given his schedule over the previous week, Bush's reprise at his beloved Prairie Chapel Ranch must have seemed particularly welcome. A NATO Summit trip had taken Bush to Romania, Lithuania, the Czech Republic, and Russia, where he spoke with President Vladimir Putin about an increasingly likely war against Iraq. Upon his return to Washington, Bush presided over three major bill-signing ceremonies: legislation that created the Department of Homeland Security, provided insurance coverage for catastrophic losses from potential terrorist attacks, and established an independent commission to investigate the September 11 attacks. And in between, in a nod to White House tradition, Bush publicly granted a Thanksgiving pardon to a white-feathered gobbler named Katie—the first female turkey to have ever received the time-honored Rose Garden reprieve.

But not all of the President's actions during that holiday-shortened week received such high-profile treatment. For example, as the pre-Thanksgiving exodus got underway in earnest, the Bush administration unceremoniously unveiled a proposal to revamp quarter-century-old forest management policies—changes, environmentalists charged, that could significantly increase logging in the country's 155 national forests, thereby threatening the health of the lands and the many species of wildlife that inhabit them.

> **Releasing controversial environmental proposals during holidays, when the media and the public are not likely to be paying close attention, is a tactic the Bush administration turned into standard operating procedure.**

In essence, the administration proposed to grant local managers of national forests greater leeway to approve logging, drilling, mining, and recreational activities on the 192 million acres they collectively manage without first conducting scientific or environmental reviews. Forest Service officials portrayed the proposal—which sought to overturn Clinton administration regulations—as a way to eliminate red tape and free regional managers from unnecessarily seeking out scientific data. Congressional critics of the plan countered that it failed to establish procedures for ecological studies and offered no solid, long-term protections for wildlife and the environment.

Conservationists, who had been at odds with the administration from the get-go, faulted the rules change for similar reasons. "This proposal eliminates the most meaningful requirements and substitutes agency discretion, reduces public involvement, all but eliminates scientific oversight, and is a

clear abuse of the regulatory process for the benefit of the timber industry," Rodger Schlickeisen, president of Defenders of
Wildlife, charged shortly after the draft rule was made public.
And Schlickeisen added another complaint: "After months of
waiting, the administration has timed this environmental attack
to come out quietly on the week of Thanksgiving in a transparent
attempt to sneak it past the media and the public."

In fact, releasing controversial proposals late on Friday or
during holidays, when the media and the public are not likely to
be paying close attention, is a time-tested strategy that politicians have often used to their advantage. But it's a tactic the
Bush administration turned into standard operating procedure,
particularly when environmental issues have been involved.
Consider some of the administration's other late-2002 actions:

- August 30: On this Friday before the three-day Labor Day
  weekend, Secretary of the Interior Gale Norton announces
  the appointment of Allan Fitzsimmons to oversee the
  president's recently unveiled Healthy Forests Initiative,
  whose stated purpose is to reduce wildfire danger on public lands. The appointment of Fitzsimmons, a free-market
  policy analyst who also toiled for the Reagan and elder
  Bush administrations, draws the ire of environmentalists fearful of increased logging in national forests, as
  well as editorial writers, who have their own concerns:
  "As a policy analyst for libertarian and ultraconservative
  think tanks," the *Atlanta Journal-Constitution* later notes,
  "Fitzsimmons has criticized not just environmentalists
  but the Catholic Church and other religious groups that
  have embraced the importance of biodiversity. He argues
  that it would be no crisis if all endangered and threatened
  species became extinct."

- November 11: As the nation celebrates Veterans Day, the seismic search firm WesternGeco—a joint venture of oil-field services giants Schlumberger and Baker Hughes—is busily drilling hundreds of 60-foot-deep holes in two eastern Utah counties, as part of an oil and gas survey that will later include the use of explosives. The Bureau of Land Management gave the green light for the drilling late Saturday. But because federal courts are closed for the holiday, no legal challenges to the project are possible until the land has already been pockmarked.

- December 24: On Christmas Eve, the Bush administration announces that, two days hence, it will publish a rule in the *Federal Register* designed to resolve property-title disputes involving thousands of roads, trails, and paths that cross national forests and other federal lands. The administration says the change to Bureau of Land Management regulations are designed to give state and local governments more control over these rights-of-way, but environmentalists charge that the policy will only open up more wilderness to mining, oil and gas drilling, and other development. Congressional critics include Senator Joseph Lieberman, a Connecticut Democrat, who complains: "Once again the administration is using stealth tactics to pay off special interests and do tangible damages to public resources."

- December 31: As Americans prepare for their New Year celebrations, the administration issues changes to the New Source Review regulations that effectively make it easier for refineries and other plants to modernize without having to install costly pollution controls—an action that spawns an immediate lawsuit by nine Northeastern states, whose officials maintain that the new regulations

would exempt major polluters from clean-air requirements and, in the process, jeopardize public health. And
on that same day, the administration also makes public its
controversial decision (later delayed by a court pending
the outcome of a lawsuit) to allow tuna caught by deliberately chasing, harassing, and encircling dolphins to be
sold under the "dolphin-safe" label.

A year earlier, the New Year's Eve announcement involved
another logging issue. The U.S. Department of Agriculture Forest Service disclosed that it might seek to amend a management
plan for 11.5 million acres of national forests in the Sierra
Nevada that would allow more logging and off-road recreation.
One local environment group estimated that the stepped-up
"fuel reduction" strategy in the Sierra Nevada—the largest roadless area in the lower 48 states—could increase the harvesting of
lumber by an additional 350 million board feet each year. Forest
protection groups feared the proposed change would be devastating. Logging advocates concurred, although for a different
reason: the increase in allowable harvests, they complained,
wasn't large enough.

But timber-related industries have had relatively little else
to complain about during George W. Bush's White House
tenure, their notable victories including the Healthy Forests
Initiative that the president formally announced on August 22,
2002. Bush unveiled the plan near the Oregon-California border, where the so-called Biscuit fire would eventually burn half
a million acres, in the largest fire in Oregon history. As
explained by the administration, the new initiative was predicated on a two-pronged strategy: "thinning" forests and reducing "unnecessary regulatory obstacles that hinder active forest
management."

To that end, the administration sought to exempt this and other forest management projects from the National Environmental Policy Act, a Nixon-era law that, among other things, sets national environmental policy and establishes a basis for environmental impact statements. In essence, NEPA seeks to ensure that federal agencies consider the environmental effects of their actions and that the public has a voice in those matters.

The administration claimed that its three-month-old review of NEPA—spearheaded by the White House Council on Environmental Quality—was an attempt to update and improve the law, not to gut it. But neither that claim nor the Healthy Forests Initiative, which proposed curtailing public input, resonated with the public or the media. For example, some of the nation's editorial and op-ed writers labeled the actions mere back-door ploys to allow more commercial logging in national forests, and thereby reward loyal political patrons. The comments of the Nashville *Tennessean* were typical: "The President claims the move is designed to protect against fires, but what it really does is help the logging industry." An assistant editorial-page editor of the *Kansas City Star* was even more blunt about motive: "He wants Americans to buy into saving the forests from fires by giving the forests over to the lumberjacks."

"Bush's proposal," she added, "would make it more difficult for environmental groups to appeal decisions of the Forest Service to allow logging in previously protected areas. The timber companies, among the President's biggest backers, must have been snickering to think that Mother Nature gave their side this handy issue."

The timber industry has indeed been a generous benefactor of the Bush-Cheney administration. Ditto the mining industry, coal-burning utilities, chemical companies, and other manufacturers routinely singled out for their environmentally unfriendly practices. A September 2002 report by Public Campaign and the public interest law firm Earthjustice revealed that these corporate interests have collectively donated more than $44 million to the administration and the Republican National Committee. The financial analysis, which included political action committee contributions to the 2000 Bush-Cheney campaign and individual contributions of at least $200, contributions to inaugural and vote recount funds, and hard- and soft-money contributions to the RNC for the 2000–2002 election cycles, calculated that the timber industry's contributions totaled $3.39 million. Chemical and other manufacturers led the pack with $18.6 million, while the oil and gas industries, which have successfully lobbied for the right to drill in and near national parks, contributed some $17 million, the report noted.

> **The oil and gas industries, which won the right to drill in national parks, contributed some $17 million to Bush and the RNC.**

Like the chemical manufacturers, the mining firms, and the oil and gas drillers, the timber industry has received an enviable return on its campaign-spending investment. For example, in early March 2003, 14 months after the Forest Service floated the idea of stepping up logging in the 11 national forests in the Sierra Nevada, the agency released recommendations calling for a threefold increase in timber harvests there over the next decade. What's more, the proposed rules also called for limiting the amount of time for public comment and related litigation. And to the chagrin of environmentalists, the proposed rule changes included a controversial provision known as "stewardship contracting": in return for clearing small trees and brush from these national forests, thereby easing the threat of forest fires, timber companies would be permitted to harvest the large and profitable old-growth trees they so covet.

Critics argued that profit-minded logging companies hardly seemed like the best stewards of the national forests along California's eastern border. But their protests were more or less pointless, because the authority for stewardship plans, which offer logging companies 10-year contracts, had been signed into law just two weeks earlier. Unlike other controversial environmental provisions, however, this one wasn't introduced in the midst of a holiday weekend. Instead, the Bush administration buried it deep within a $397.4 billion federal-agency spending bill that received only cursory congressional review. In fact, neither public interest groups nor many members of Congress had any idea that the provision had been slipped in to the 3,000-page bill until the president had signed it into law.

POLITICAL PAYBACKS

Among those designated to help sell Bush's Healthy Forests Initiative to the American public was James L. Connaughton, chairman of the Council on Environmental Quality. Bush appointed Connaughton on May 1, 2001, and the Senate confirmed him six weeks later. In his position as chairman of the CEQ, Connaughton was tapped to serve as the president's main policy advisor on environmental issues, helping to coordinate federal-agency efforts in this arena and develop executive branch policies and initiatives.

The Yale University graduate was certainly no environmental policy novice. He came to the White House from the Washington, D.C., office of Sidley & Austin, a Chicago-based global law firm, where he was a member of the high-profile environmental practice group. (The month Connaughton was nominated, Sidley &

Austin merged with the Wall Street law firm of Brown & Wood.)
For more than seven years, Connaughton was also a lead U.S.
negotiator on an international committee that develops voluntary environmental standards.

It was at Sidley & Austin that Connaughton became well
acquainted with the inner workings of the Council on Environmental Quality. Reports filed with the clerk of the U.S. House of
Representatives show that he lobbied the CEQ on behalf of
industrial behemoths ARCO (Atlantic Richfield Company),
Alcoa, and General Electric Company, as well as Asarco Inc., a
producer of copper and other metals. Connaughton also represented the Chemical Manufacturers Association.

Most of Connaughton's lobbying—whether before the CEQ,
federal regulatory agencies, or the U.S. House and Senate—dealt
with business-friendly reforms to the Superfund Program,
which was established by Congress in 1980 to clean up the
nation's worst uncontrolled or abandoned landfills and other
hazardous-waste sites. Connaughton's clients were some of the
most egregious Superfund polluters. In 1977, for example,
ARCO bought a 22-year-old open-pit mining operation, in
Butte, Montana, from the Anaconda Copper Mining Company.
By the time ARCO sold Berkeley Pit and the associated property
in 1985, mining there had been discontinued, the city of Butte
and nearby areas had been declared a Superfund site, and,
thanks to ARCO's decision to turn off the pumps that kept some
3,000 miles of mine tunnels from flooding, the 675-acre pit
began filling with contaminated water. More than 2 million gallons a day now flow into the 1,780-foot-deep pit, which threat-
ens the area's supply of fresh water and which has taken a
particular toll on migrating waterfowl: for instance, an estimated 350 to 400 snow geese that set down in the pit one year
died after the acidic water, which is currently rising at the rate of

about 1 foot per month, damaged the birds' organs and ate away the lining of their esophagi.

When Connaughton lobbied on behalf of Alcoa, the aluminum producer was involved in environmental cleanups at a number of Superfund and other waste sites, including two that remain high on its list of priorities: a New York State plant that generated a massive cleanup of PCBs from the adjacent Grasse River and a facility in southern Texas that has allegedly released mercury into an adjacent bay, forcing the company to undertake a substantial dredging operation of contaminated soil. Asarco, another of Connaughton's clients, currently bears some responsibility for environmental cleanup at more than three dozen sites across the United States, including at least 10 Superfund projects. And then there's one-time client General Electric, which holds responsibility for what may be the nation's largest Superfund site—a 200-mile stretch of the Hudson River that's contaminated with PCBs. Cleanup costs are estimated at half a billion dollars.

> **Dozens of key posts throughout the Bush-Cheney administration—from cabinet-level appointees on down—went to people working either for or on behalf of industries they would now be regulating.**

Connaughton wasn't the only one who came to the administration by way of General Electric, a conglomerate whose $1.4 million worth of campaign contributions during 1999 and 2000 favored Republicans by nearly two to one, and whose largess included a $5,000 donation to the Bush campaign and another $100,000 for the presidential inaugural. Francis Blake, GE's senior vice president for corporate business development, was appointed deputy secretary of the Department of Energy. In addition to the Superfund, the regulation of nuclear power is among GE's environmental concerns.

GE's lobbyists have plenty of company: dozens of key posts throughout the Bush-Cheney administration—from cabinet-level appointees on down—went to people working for or on behalf of industries they would now be regulating. And while the appointments were spread from the White House, to regulatory agencies, to Justice, Labor, and other governmental departments, many of these political appointees shared two traits: they had been recruited for posts that would place them in charge of matters with enormous environmental implications, and their résumés boasted credentials that left no doubt about their close ties to industries with questionable environmental records.

- Take the Interior Department, for example. Secretary Gale Norton is a former fellow at a free-market environmental think tank, funded in part with grants from companies such as Amoco, ARCO, and Conoco, that has argued against the constitutionality of the Endangered Species Act. Deputy Secretary J. Steven Griles is a former coal industry executive and lobbyist, whose lengthy client list included the American Petroleum Institute, the National Mining Association, oil giant Sunoco, and the Edison Electric Institute, which is the electric utility trade association. General counsel William Geary Myers III represented timber companies, while the Idaho-based law firm he worked for has represented oil and gas companies on such matters as exploration on public and Indian lands.
- At the Environmental Protection Agency, Deputy Administrator Linda Fisher, the agency's second in command, previously served as vice president of government and public affairs in the Washington, D.C., office of Monsanto

Company, the giant herbicide manufacturer. Jeffrey Holmstead, assistant administrator for the Office of Air and Radiation, represented the chemical industry before the agency following a stint in the elder Bush's administration, where he helped draft regulations designed to weaken the Clean Air Act.

- At the Department of Justice, Tomas Sansonetti, assistant attorney general for environment and natural resources, lobbied on behalf of Peabody Coal and other mining interests.

- At the Department of Labor, David Lauriski, assistant secretary for mine safety and health, joined the department after three decades in the coal mining industry, including stints as a board member of the Utah Mining Association and, just prior to his appointment, general manager of Energy West Mining Company, one of the nation's largest underground coal producers.

- At the Department of Agriculture, Mark Rey, who as undersecretary for natural resources and environment oversees the U.S. Forest Service, spent nearly two decades toiling for timber industry trade groups, including the American Forest and Paper Association and the National Forest Products Association.

- And at the White House, Chief of Staff Andrew Card, as former president and CEO of the American Automobile Manufacturers Association, led a $25 million lobbying campaign on behalf of the "Big Three" U.S. automakers, often fighting against more stringent environmental standards. Among Card's private sector missions on behalf of the automakers, who heaped more than 70 percent of their federal campaign contributions on Republicans during the 2000 election cycle: lobbying against the Kyoto Protocol, an international agreement targeting global warming that called for a 7 percent reduction in U.S. emissions by 2008. Two months after Bush took office, he announced that the United States would withdraw from the treaty.

The list goes on, and it's augmented by a coterie of political appointees whose ranks include the likes of Mercer Reynolds, who served as U.S. ambassador to Switzerland and Liechtenstein until April 2003. Although he boasts impressive business acumen, having moved between such diverse worlds as banking, real estate development, oil and gas exploration, and professional sports, Reynolds came to his overseas posting lacking hands-on experience with international affairs. But his credentials included a close personal relationship with the man who appointed him, which clearly trumped his inexperience. "The best thing about my time in the oil business," Reynolds admitted in his maiden speech as ambassador, "is that it brought me together with George W. Bush."

The president might very well have said the same thing about Reynolds. After all, when his company, Bush Exploration, was teetering on insolvency, Reynolds and investment firm partner William DeWitt Jr. bought the failing enterprise and merged it with their oil-and-gas-exploration firm—a deal that earned Bush the title of chairman and chief executive officer of Spectrum 7 Energy Corporation, at an annual salary of $75,000, along with 1.1 million shares of Spectrum 7 stock. In 1988, it was DeWitt and Reynolds who asked Bush to serve as the managing partner of the group that bought the Texas Rangers. This foray into Major League Baseball not only earned Bush a 25-fold return on his investment, but it also proved to be his ticket to the political arena, where Reynolds was again at the ready: he served on the Executive Finance Committee of the Bush-Cheney campaign

and later toiled as cochairman of the Presidential Inauguration Committee, which raised $42 million in just 30 days. He
also signed on as one of the Bush team's Pioneers, the peri-
patetic supporters who pledged to raise at least $100,000 for
the cause. Federal Election Commission records show that
Reynolds personally gave more than $200,000 to Bush and
the Republican Party from 1999 to 2001, along with another
$100,000 donation to the Presidential Inauguration Commit-
tee. And after leaving his ambassadorial post, Reynolds signed
on as chief fundraiser for the Bush-Cheney reelection bid.

Reynolds's posting to the historic city of Bern, which is in
close proximity to the spectacular Swiss Alps, might appear to
some like repayment for his loyal service. But in February 2001
a White House spokeswoman told *National Journal* that quid pro
quo is by no means part of the ambassadorial selection process:
"We're looking for people with high ethical standards," she
said, "who are good communicators and who don't think about
an appointment as if it was a reward, but as an opportunity to
serve enthusiastically."

> **Robert Jordan, who defended Bush during the probe into
> his Harken stock sale, and whose law firm,
> Baker Botts LLP, is among Bush's top patrons,
> was appointed ambassador to Saudi Arabia.**

As it turns out, many of the Pioneers who have served enthusiastically in the Bush administration have done so in particularly
choice locations, including Austria, Belgium, Belize, France, Ireland, Norway, and Portugal. (By contrast, ambassadors appointed
to the likes of Angola, Cambodia, Mongolia, Nicaragua, and
Turkmenistan are all State Department or Foreign Service veterans; the practice of awarding the ambassadorships in the most

desirable locations to campaign supporters has been a Washington practice for decades.) They included John Price, a corporate CEO whose Pioneer outreach netted more than $335,000 for the Bush-Cheney ticket, according to a tally by the nonprofit research organization Texans for Public Justice. Price was named ambassador to a group of tropical island nations off the east coast of Africa, including Mauritius and the Seychelles, renowned for their unspoiled Indian Ocean beaches. Robert Jordan, who defended Bush during the Securities and Exchange Commission probe into the sale of his Harken energy stock, and whose law firm, Baker Botts, is among Bush's top 20 career patrons, was appointed ambassador to Saudi Arabia. Clifford Sobel, chairman of a publicly traded Internet telephone service who raised nearly $331,000 for the campaign, was later given the plum ambassadorial post in the Netherlands. Sobel, along with the ambassadors to France, Belgium, and Ireland, donated $100,000 apiece to the presidential inaugural. Yet another Pioneer who donated $100,000 to the inaugural (along with $125,000 in soft money to the RNC at about the same time) is George Argyros Sr., former owner of the Seattle Mariners Major League Baseball club. He is now ambassador to Spain and Andorra.

Membership in the Pioneers was by no means a prerequisite for winning a coveted diplomatic post. For example, Bush appointed longtime family friend (and $100,000 inaugural contributor) William S. Farish to be ambassador to the Court of Saint James's, a post whose perks include a stately residence that sits on 12.5 acres of prime London parkland.

By contrast, some Pioneers chose to serve their country at home. Their ranks include Tom Ridge, secretary of homeland security; Elaine Chao, secretary of labor; Donald E. Powell, chairman of the Federal Deposit Insurance Corporation; and

Ned Siegel, a member of the board of directors of the Overseas Private Investment Corporation (and $100,000 contributor to the Bush inaugural). The president and managing partner of a South Florida real estate development company, Siegel was sworn in for his government post by another Florida developer, Melvin Sembler, a prominent fundraiser for the Republican National Committee who served as U.S. ambassador to Australia and Nauru under President George H. W. Bush. Sembler returned to public service in November 2001, this time as ambassador to Italy. Records show that his shopping center development firm, the Sembler Company, also contributed $100,000 to the George W. Bush inaugural.

But if membership in the Pioneers offered a no-fuss short-cut from private sector to plenipotentiary, unusually high dollar donations weren't the only path to a government salary. For example, Samuel Bodman, the deputy secretary of the Department of Commerce, chose to forgo inaugural tithing, giving the Bush-Cheney campaign a mere $1,000, and, along with his wife, donating a respectable $20,000 to the RNC. But the former chairman and CEO of Cabot Corporation, a Boston-based manufacturer of specialty chemicals, may have endeared himself to the president for reasons other than middle-of-the-pack giving: in the spring of 1999, when Governor Bush unveiled his ill-fated plan for "grandfathered" polluters to voluntarily reduce discharges, Bodman put Cabot's carbon black plant in Pampa, Texas—the state's fourth worst offender—on the original short list of facilities willing to take the pledge. In doing so, Bodman helped Bush stave off the public's demands that egregious polluters actually comply with the state's Clean Air Act.

On the other hand, many earned key government posts by virtue of their viewpoints, track records, or longstanding commitments to initiatives that jibed with the administration's regulatory playbook, no matter what the potential for real or perceived conflicts of interest. Mark Rey, for instance, who oversees the USDA's Forest Service, spent 1976 to 1994 working for a quartet of timber industry trade associations—an employment history that, as Rey himself has noted, hasn't been overlooked by the media: "Most reporters who cover this beat," he once complained, "think that my full, given, Christian name is Mark Rey Former Timber Industry Lobbyist." In 1995, when Rey joined a Senate subcommittee as a professional staff member, Congress passed a rider to a budget bill that authorized renewed logging in long-protected national forests. Two years later, *National Journal* included the congressional aide on its list of the federal government's one hundred most influential decision makers, noting that the controversial logging amendment "had Rey's fingerprints all over it." What's more, the magazine noted, Rey was "a key architect" of a legislative package that would change how the federal government manages national forests—landmark legislation, industry officials gushed, that "comes close to hitting a bull's-eye."

Yet another of the many former lobbyists who passed Bush administration muster is J. Steven Griles, deputy secretary of the interior. Prior to his appointment, Griles wore two professional hats: he was president of his own lobbying outfit, J. Steven Griles & Associates, and a principal of National Environmental Strategies, a consulting operation cofounded by Haley Barbour, former chairman of the Republican National Committee. Both firms helped a wide array of companies and trade associations navigate the complexities of energy and environmental policies, whether on the state or federal level. In fact, Griles lobbied for some four dozen clients, from Sunoco, Devon Energy, and Pittston Coal Company to the Chlorine Institute and the American Chemistry Council—a roster so expansive that

Senate Democrats, concerned about the potential for unending conflicts of interest, delayed his confirmation vote for four months. "He has placed the interests of powerful special interests above the public," Senator Ron Wyden, Democrat of Oregon, charged before the floor vote. To assuage such fears, Griles later signed an agreement pledging to sever professional and financial ties with his eponymous consulting firm and recuse himself, for one year, from official matters involving former employers and clients.

That was on August 1, 2001. Documents unearthed by Friends of the Earth and the Citizens Coal Council revealed that, two weeks later, Griles held the first of three meetings with senior officials of the National Mining Association, a former client that at the time was lobbying the Interior Department to relax mining regulations. Then, in September, Griles met a group of utility officials affiliated with another former client, the Edison Electric Institute, which was also actively lobbying the department.

The following April, Griles was at the center of a higher-profile ethical dustup. At issue was his memo to Linda Fisher, deputy administrator of the Environmental Protection Agency, about EPA's analysis of a proposal for the extraction of coalbed methane from tens of thousands of wells in Wyoming's Powder River Basin. Before the methane—a natural gas—could be extracted, the EPA had to evaluate an environmental impact statement estimating the proposed harm from the process, which pumps massive amounts of water onto nearby lands. In a draft letter, an acting regional director of the EPA—soon to be replaced by a Bush administration appointee—had declared the federal government's review of the drilling project to be "environmentally unsatisfactory," potentially putting it in jeopardy.

In his memo to Fisher, Griles complained that EPA's staff had repeatedly ignored his agency's requests for information detailing their concerns about the coalbed methane project. He therefore urged a meeting to address such matters, "versus sending a letter that will create, at best, misimpressions and possibly impede the ability to move forward in a constructive manner."

> J. Steven Griles, Bush's nominee for deputy secretary of Interior, "has placed the interests of powerful special interests above the public," charged Senator Ron Wyden, Democrat of Oregon.

Griles may have been worried about more than just misimpressions. Before arriving at Interior, he had lobbied on behalf of Devon Energy Corporation, Redstone Gas Partners, Western Gas Resources, Inc., and Yates Petroleum Corporation—companies with a direct stake in the EPA evaluation of coalbed methane drilling in the Powder River Basin. What's more, Griles was tethered to the issue via a monetary stake: to make good on his divestiture pledge, Griles sold his consulting firm to National Environmental Strategies—a deal that promised him an annual payout of $284,000 over four years. As it turned out, National Environmental Strategies also represented firms that were developing coalbed methane deposits in the Powder River Basin.

Environmental groups complained that the memo to Fisher, along with Griles's ongoing lobbying firm payouts, offered proof positive that he had violated his conflict-of-interest agreement. But Interior Department lawyers cleared the agency's second-in-command of ethical misconduct, ruling that his memo to Fisher, along with associated phone contact, was merely "procedural in nature" and did not address specific issues of the proposed environmental impact statements. In the end, an agency solicitor suggested that Griles sign another recusal statement that specifically disqualified him from deliberations involving the environmental impact statements for coalbed methane drilling. Within days, Griles complied.

When it came to voluntarily withdrawing from official matters, Griles was hardly alone: in September 2002, the *Washington Post* reported there were at least 10 other high-ranking Interior Department officials who had recused themselves from government activities that might affect their former clients or industries. But by violating the spirit—if not the actual letter—of his conflict-of-interest agreement, the department's deputy secretary raised eyebrows both on Capitol Hill and in the media. In West Virginia, for example, where coal is a potent economic engine, the *Charleston Gazette* dubbed Griles's behavior "an outrage" and called for his resignation. "Federal regulators are supposed to represent the interest of the general public, not a specific industry," the newspaper said in an editorial. "Griles' case clearly represents not only the appearance of a conflict, but an undeniable and unconscionable sellout of the American people." Senator Wyden, who had remained opposed to Griles's confirmation, called for an investigation into allegations that he had in fact violated both his recusal agreements and federal government conflict-of-interest rules. "I think that it's critical to get to the bottom of this situation," Wyden told the *Washington Post*, "and not have the public wondering if powerful special interests get dealt a winning hand, with Mr. Griles doing the dealing."

In his defense, Griles told the paper that the meetings with industry officials, for instance, were merely social or informational, and that he had first sought clearance from the department's ethics lawyers for those sessions that might be construed as improper. "The president said he wanted this administration to be held to the highest ethical standards," he said, "and I don't want it ever to be said that I didn't."

THE POWER ELITE'S LEGISLATIVE CLOUT

As the U.S. Senate prepared to adjourn on March 19, 2003, partisan politics gave way to a sober acknowledgment that the nation was most likely on the brink of another war. Two days earlier, in a televised address to the nation, George W. Bush issued a stern ultimatum to Iraqi president Saddam Hussein and his sons: leave their country within 48 hours or the U.S. would commence military action there at a time of its choosing. With the clock having technically run out just an hour earlier, Nevada senator Harry Reid, the assistant Democratic leader, took to the floor and somberly closed out the day's business on a bipartisan note. "As we retire tonight," Reid said, "I think I speak for the entire Senate when I say our thoughts and prayers are with those who have to make this momentous decision, especially the president."

Earlier that afternoon there was far less unanimity among what's familiarly known as the world's greatest deliberative body, as routine parliamentary arm-twisting turned into a full-scale verbal scuffle. At issue was an amendment designed to quash a key component of the president's energy plan: drilling in the Artic National Wildlife Refuge (known as ANWR), the magnificent home to dozens of species of birds and 45 species of marine and land mammals, including wolves, caribou, muskoxen, and polar bears. The previous year, the White House had come up short in its bid to convince lawmakers to authorize drilling in a remote area of the 19-million-acre refuge; this time around, fearing a repeat, administration lobbyists were out in force. The heaviest pro-drilling muscle, however, was provided by Alaska Republican Ted Stevens, whose behavior preceding the vote hardly typified the gentlemanly demeanor for which the U.S. Senate is so well known: "I make this commitment," Stevens said.

"People who vote against this today are voting against me, and I will not forget it."

In 2002, the White House had come up short in its bid to convince lawmakers to authorize drilling in the Arctic National Wildlife Refuge; fearing a repeat, administration lobbyists were out in force.

Legislative bluster notwithstanding, opponents of the administration's plan—both in and out of Congress—took issue with more than just the idea of encroaching on this pristine land, whose actual oil reserves have remained an ongoing source of speculation and debate. The previous day, for example, a *Washington Post* editorial had castigated the Bush administration and its congressional allies for including the Arctic-drilling provision in a budget bill rather than letting it run its normal legislative course—that is, debating its merits in committees concerned with the environment. "It is inexcusable for powerful members of Congress to continue to shove legislation affecting Alaska wildlife into unrelated bills simply because it would be impossible to get enough votes any other way," the *Post* proclaimed. Senator John Kerry, who two years earlier had threatened to filibuster any legislation opening "America's Serengeti" to drilling, echoed that view during floor debate. The Massachusetts Democrat, who had formally declared his own presidential aspirations three and a half months earlier, not only objected to the potential for wilderness destruction, but he had another complaint: the oil-drilling provision, he said, had been "slipped into the budget for the specific purpose of trying to bypass the normal rules of the Senate."

This legislative gambit may have angered drilling opponents, but the Bush administration was determined to eke out a victory any way it could get one. Its sights, after all, had been on

ANWR and its incalculable energy treasures since the nascent days of this presidency—a position that George W. Bush had unflinchingly articulated during the 2000 campaign. "It will produce a million barrels a day," he argued during a debate with Democratic rival Al Gore. "Today we import a million barrels from Saddam Hussein."

Bush's arrival at the White House, it turned out, had coincided with the California power crisis, which sent electricity rates soaring, pushed the state's two largest utilities to the verge of bankruptcy, shuttered businesses, and, thanks to rolling blackouts, left angry consumers in the dark—hard times, the new administration warned, that might be relived elsewhere without the imposition of nationwide energy reforms. But the California situation notwithstanding, Bush had already placed this issue near the top of his domestic agenda. In fact, just nine days after taking office, he established a task force—with Vice President Dick Cheney at the helm—charged with devising the administration's energy policies. The National Energy Policy Development Group counted among its members the secretaries of energy, interior, and transportation. Its mission was to "develop a national energy policy designed to help the private sector, and as necessary and appropriate federal, state, and local governments, promote dependable, affordable, and environmentally sound production and distribution of energy."

Skeptics had no doubt that whatever emerged from the months-long exercise would include recommendations to extract ANWR's subterranean riches. But some, like the *New York Times*, also aimed their barbs elsewhere: "It hardly signals a balanced approach to put Vice President Dick Cheney, also an oil man, in charge of a task force aimed at developing an energy strategy to reduce America's 'reliance on foreign oil' and 'bring more energy into the marketplace,'" the paper said in an editorial.

When the task force report was finally made public, on May 17, 2001, it highlighted a host of recommendations urging the increased use of renewable and alternative energy, from wind and solar power to hydrogen fuel cells. If conservationists weren't exactly jubilant, however, it was because of the report's other recommendations, which, to no one's surprise, included exploring ANWR for oil.

This was welcome news for BP, ChevronTexaco, and Exxon-Mobil, which eagerly sought the rights to drill there. All three, it turns out, have been generous benefactors of George W. Bush's political career: ExxonMobil contributed $117,075 to his campaigns, while BP has given him $96,093 and ChevronTexaco has contributed $82,350, according to figures compiled by the Center for Public Integrity. And the trio share another distinction: each donated $100,000 to the Bush-Cheney inaugural, BP via the corporation and the oil giant's two peers via top company officials.

The task force report also held the promise of lucrative prizes for other oil and gas firms, including more development offshore and on public lands. Records compiled by the Center show that Bush's list of career patrons includes energy industry stalwarts Shell Oil Company ($82,412), El Paso Corporation ($68,634), Phillips Petroleum Company ($55,861), and Occidental Petroleum Corporation ($38,179); also included on the roster are such lower-profile—yet nonetheless generous—players as Hunt Oil Company ($152,250), Alkek Oil Corporation ($126,000), and Koch Industries ($79,950), whose core businesses include petroleum and natural gas. Top officials of El Paso, Hunt, and Shell, records show, were members of the Governor's Business Council, the group of industry bigwigs who advised Bush during his tenure as Texas's chief executive. At the time, the GBC's elite ranks also included the president of Halliburton Company, Richard B. Cheney.

The administration's energy blueprint was similarly kind to the electric utility industry: recommendations included legislation that would repeal the Public Utility Holding Company Act, which bars the use of profits from regulated utility businesses to fund unrelated enterprises, and reform the Public Utility Regulatory Policies Act of 1978, which was designed, in part, to both augment electric utility generation with more efficiently produced power and ensure fair rates for consumers. The industry's push to reform these laws boasted some notable lobbying clout with the new administration; the presidents of the Edison Electric Institute and FirstEnergy Corporation were among George W. Bush's fundraising Pioneers. So was Erle Nye, the chairman and chief executive of TXU Corporation (formerly knows as Texas Utilities), who was also a member of the Governor's Business Council during Bush's tenure. Edison, FirstEnergy, and TXU have all given thousands to Bush's campaigns (the latter ranks thirty-sixth on the list of career patrons, with contributions of $159,299, according to calculations by the Center). What's more, Anthony J. Alexander, the president and chair of FirstEnergy, and Erle Nye, of TXU Energy, contributed $100,000 to the Bush-Cheney inaugural. And if Nye's clout wasn't quite sufficient, his company's lobbying roster included Diane Allbaugh, whose husband, Joe Allbaugh, was Bush's campaign manager during the 2000 election.

> **The utility industry's push to reform these laws boasted lobbying clout with the new administration: the presidents of the Edison Electric Institute and FirstEnergy Corporation were among Bush's Pioneers.**

Across the board, in fact, energy producers found reason to cheer the recommendations of Dick Cheney's task force. The coal industry, for example, which in recent years has been something of an energy-sector pariah, received a wholehearted endorsement from the task force report: "If rising U.S. electricity demand is to be met," the document noted, "then coal must play a significant role." To that end, the task force suggested that the Department of Energy invest $2 billion over 10 years to fund research in clean coal technologies, and that current research-and-development tax credits be made permanent. Among those who stand to benefit from the migration back to coal is James "Buck" Harless, a West Virginia coal and timber baron who served as a Bush Pioneer, and who later donated $100,000 to the presidential inaugural. Harless, one of more than thirty energy industry officials who served on the Bush Transition Energy Advisory Team (Erle Nye, of TXU, served as well), seems to have maintained his connections within the White House: according to the *Charleston Gazette*, Harless was apparently behind the appointment of Michael Castle to a position created specially for him in the Philadelphia office of the Environmental Protection Agency—the regional office whose territory includes West Virginia. Castle, formerly West Virginia's top environmental official, worked as a consultant to the coal industry following his departure from state government. He has also been an engineer and once even ran his own small coal company.

The nuclear energy industry, which for years lived under a cloud spewed by Three Mile Island, saw would-be allies in Bush and Cheney, and as such gave them more than a quarter of a million dollars during the 2000 campaign. It was money well spent: the task force report included a recommendation that the President "support the expansion of nuclear energy in the United States as a major component of our national energy policy." And much to the industry's relief, the report also urged extension of the Price-Anderson Act, which both limits the amount of insurance that nuclear operators must carry and caps their liability in case of catastrophic accident.

But the industry's greatest favor came in the form of administration support for a legislative end-game to a twenty-year battle for an unlikely prize: Yucca Mountain, located in a desolate, federally protected tract of desert about 100 miles northwest of Las Vegas. While the industry has long considered Yucca Mountain a suitable place to store its radioactive spent nuclear fuel—the Energy Department first explored the idea in 1978—Nevada legislators joined environmentalists in condemning the notion, citing potential health and safety risks. And legislators elsewhere later joined the opponents, their fears stoked by the possibility that cross-country nuclear waste shipments, whether by train or truck, would make alluring targets for terrorists. Prior to a vote on the matter, then Senate majority leader Thomas Daschle, Democrat of South Dakota, voiced another concern: "We are being forced to decide this issue prematurely, without sufficient scientific information, because this administration is doing the bidding of special interests that simply want to make the deadly waste they have generated someone else's problem," he said.

The nuclear power industry tied its very survival to congressional approval of this plan: with storage space for spent nuclear fuel dwindling, lobbyists and industry officials argued, some utilities faced the prospect of soon shuttering their reactors. To ensure that the industry got its way, President Bush played a deft game of political hardball. Utah's senators, for instance, were given an ultimatum: if the storage facility isn't built in Nevada, it would be relocated to their home state.

In the end, Bush and Cheney—and the industry that supported them—got their way, but the plan still has to survive court challenges. Although the president has used bill-signing ceremonies to tout his environmental credentials, no reporters were permitted to witness the signing of this legislation, on July 23, 2002. But a top industry spokesman was not so low-key: "This is a great day for U.S. energy security and commonsense environmentalism," Joe Colvin, president and CEO of the Nuclear Energy Institute, the industry's lobbying arm, proclaimed. Among Colvin's other credentials: a place on the Bush administration's Transition Energy Advisory Team.

LEGAL FISTICUFFS

While Dick Cheney's national energy policy task force report received considerable scrutiny, many of its conclusions proved to be less controversial than the process by which the document was created—a closed-door series of off-the-record meetings whose participant roster was guarded like a list of Skull & Bones Society recruits. In fact, the administration's insistence that details of task force meetings were unfit for public—even congressional— consumption provoked an unprecedented legal melee that, for some historians, politicians, and legal scholars, ended with what they deemed the subversion of open government.

The battle was first joined on April 19, 2001, when two veteran Democratic U.S. representatives—John Dingell of Michigan and Henry Waxman of California—asked the General Accounting Office to immediately undertake an investigation of the energy task force, which, they noted, had been meeting for at least a month. Underlying their request, the lawmakers wrote, were apparent efforts to shield the task force's membership and deliberations from public scrutiny.

"The process of energy policy development needs sunshine," the duo added in their letter to David Walker, who as comptroller general of the United States heads the GAO. "At a minimum, the public has the right to know who serves on this task force; what information is being presented to the task force and by whom it is being given; and to learn of the costs involved in the gathering of the facts."

> While Dick Cheney's national energy policy task force report received considerable scrutiny, many of its conclusions proved to be less controversial than the process by which the document was created.

Concurrent with their request to the GAO, which serves as the audit and investigative arm of Congress, Dingell and Waxman presented Andrew Lundquist, the executive director of the task force, with a series of detailed questions about the group's operation. Of particular concern, they wrote, was the decision to meet behind closed doors and exclude "certain parties" from participation in discussions—a possible violation, they contended, of the Federal Advisory Committee Act, which mandates openness and public participation for those boards, commissions, and similar entities that advise the executive branch of the federal government. Three days earlier, in an article about the task force's penchant for secrecy, the *Washington Post* had publicly identified those excluded parties: "Environmental groups complain that Cheney won't meet with their leaders," the paper reported, "while the vice president sits down with a parade of industry officials."

On May 10, the GAO informed Dingell and Waxman that it had deemed their request to be within its scope of authority and would therefore proceed with a study of the energy task force. But the congressmen already knew that GAO investigators would no doubt face imposing hurdles. A week earlier, the counsel to Vice President Cheney had informed the two House members that, to his way of thinking, FACA did not apply to the energy task force. As a result, attorney David Addington labeled their request legally specious and rebuffed their demands for information, thereby laying the groundwork for a challenge that might presumably cast Cheney as an overly secretive obstructionist.

But if the White House was at all concerned about the legal jousting, it wasn't apparent. Following a two-week campaign to engender support for his energy policies, Bush released the task force report and set about to convince both the public and wary party loyalists of its virtues. He faced a formidable task: a CNN/*USA Today*/Gallup poll revealed only a tepid response to the energy blueprint, with the nation more or less evenly split over its potential merits. What's more, the advantage of Dick Cheney's tie-breaking vote in the 50-50 Senate was suddenly erased by the defection of Vermont Republican James Jeffords, who abandoned his party and became an independent. Among the reasons Jeffords cited for firing his political torpedo: disagreements with the president's positions on energy policy and the environment.

As the pundits debated whether Jeffords had left the GOP's hopes of wide-ranging energy reform DOA, the General Accounting Office pressed ahead on its task force study. On June 1, 2001, Comptroller General Walker asked task force attorney David Addington to provide details about the group's meetings, including the names and titles of attendees. Addington refused. Walker asked again three weeks later, but the vice president's counsel only demurred. On July 18, Walker wrote Cheney directly to demand "full and complete access" to the pertinent records, as mandated by the U.S. Code. On August 2, Cheney in turn dispatched memos to the Senate and House of Representatives claiming that Walker's requests exceeded his lawful authority, and that acquiescing to them would "unconstitutionally interfere with the functioning of the Executive Branch."

Cheney never wavered from this position, entrenching him-self in a high-profile bout of legal fisticuffs that would drag on for another 18 months. But if he remained convinced of his statutory footing, his resoluteness was undermined by a growing public perception that withholding the list of task force partici-pants was tantamount to an admission of wrongdoing. "Two reasons may help explain why Cheney is stonewalling," the *Los Angeles Times* said in an editorial that typified the criticism. "The first is that the administration wants to run future, controversial policies through the vice president's office to shield them from scrutiny and accountability, and it is trying to use this as a model. The other reason is that handing over the list would probably confirm what an embarrassment President Bush's energy plan is."

There was another reason: the CNN/*USA Today*/Gallup poll that revealed indifference about the president's new energy plan also found that 61 percent of respondents believed energy com-panies had too much influence over the administration's energy policies. By contrast, only 32 percent of those asked said the energy companies did not wield too much sway. As the *Los Ange-les Times* went on to say in its editorial: "Cheney can't be thrilled about letting Americans see the depth of influence that the oil and gas industry has on the energy plan and in the White House."

While Bush and Cheney fought mightily to squelch all details of the task force meetings, a window into its operations was later provided courtesy of a federal judge. In response to a lawsuit by the Natural Resources Defense Council and Judicial Watch, a nonprofit government watchdog that had previously harangued President Bill Clinton over such matters as his "eleventh-hour pardons," the Department of Energy was ordered to produce thousands of pages of documents that, in some cases, proved to be particularly illuminating. Although heavily edited by the government, with pages missing and large blocks of text deleted, the e-mails, phone logs, and other paperwork nevertheless showed, for example, that over the course of its operation, which stretched from January 2001 to September 2001, the energy task force solicited the views of industry officials and lobbyists while all but ignoring the input of public interest organizations and consumer groups. According to an analysis released in May 2002, the NRDC concluded that industry representatives had 714 direct contacts with task force members while nonindustry representatives had only 29. Another 105 direct contacts could not be definitively categorized, the NRDC reported.

> **None of Energy Secretary Spencer Abraham's task force meetings, documents show, included representatives of environmental or consumer groups.**

From mid-February to late-July, for instance, Secretary of Energy Spencer Abraham attended 11 task force meetings, one of which was called to release the group's long-awaited report, "Reliable, Affordable, and Environmentally Sound Energy for America's Future." The secretary's calendar entries include:

- February 14, 2001: meeting with the president and two other top officials of the National Association of Manufacturers (which has favored drilling in ANWR and has opposed the Kyoto Protocol global-warming treaty)
- March 14: meeting with oil and gas industry officials, including the chairman and president of the Independent Petroleum Association of America
- March 28: meeting with municipal and public power authorities

- April 3: Meeting with the CEO of UtiliCorp United (a Missouri-based distributor of electricity and natural gas, since renamed Aquila, Inc., that is one of 37 companies later accused by the Federal Energy Regulatory Commission of manipulating western U.S. markets during the California energy crisis of 2000–2001)
- April 3: meeting with two officials of the American Coal Company
- April 25: meeting with coal producers at the White House

None of Abraham's meetings, documents show, included representatives of environmental or consumer groups.

And there were two other threads that wound their way across the lists of coal, electricity, natural gas, and nuclear power executives and lobbyists who attended task force meetings: many had contributed mightily to Bush and the Republican Party, and their points of view were sometimes included—almost verbatim—in the final energy blueprint. Language in the final report, for instance, was altered from previous drafts to favor Halliburton, Cheney's former employer.

There was also the matter of Enron, George W. Bush's number one career patron, according to a Center for Public Integrity analysis. In January 2002, a month after the once high-flying energy firm had filed for bankruptcy, the White House told Henry Waxman that Cheney or his aides had met with officials of the company six times during the previous year. One such meeting, which lasted a half-hour, involved the vice president and Kenneth Lay, Enron's chairman. Following the meeting, the White House added a provision to the final energy report potentially favorable to Enron.

On January 30, 2002, the General Accounting Office announced that it would soon proceed with its lawsuit against

Cheney—a planned action it had shelved following the terrorist attacks of the previous September 11. In a letter to the White House and congressional leaders, Comptroller General Walker was at the same time both resolute and rueful about his decision: "In our view, failure to pursue this matter could lead to a pattern of records access denials that would significantly undercut GAO's ability to assist Congress in exercising its legislative and oversight authorities. . . . This will be the first time that GAO has filed suit to enforce our access rights against a federal official," he wrote. "We hope it is the last time that we will have to do so."

In the end, this maiden attempt proved fruitless. On December 9, 2002, U.S. District Judge John D. Bates, a George W. Bush appointee, ruled that the GAO has no legal standing to sue the vice president. Two months later, the GAO—its annual budget dependent on the Republican-controlled Congress—grudgingly decided against appealing the ruling, thereby granting the White House the wish to which it had so steadfastly and adamantly clung: to forever keep secret the details of Cheney's private meetings with industry. (Judicial Watch and the Sierra Club sued to make public certain task force details, and their lawsuit, which in July 2003 survived a key federal appeals court challenge, may ultimately reveal those documents the GAO had sought.)

With all eyes on Iraq, however, Judge Bates's noteworthy decision received little attention. In fact, as the buildup to the invasion proceeded, otherwise controversial proposals like drilling in ANWR went forth without the usual scrutiny of the press and public. But if Bush and Cheney hoped to quietly win approval for this coveted piece of their energy scheme, they were to be disappointed: on March 19, 2003, by a margin of 52 to 48, the Senate voted to prevent consideration of drilling in the Alaskan wildlife refuge. The fight was over—for now. As Alaskan

Republican senator Ted Stevens warned: "It's never decided until we win."

If Bush and Cheney have their way, they'll have another chance to record that victory. In early March, while an increasing number of U.S. troops prepared for an assault on Iraq, and while a fractured nation debated the wisdom and efficacy of the intended military action, the president authorized his advisors to quietly begin planning his reelection strategy. Details of the embryonic effort were characteristically hard to come by, although strategists did let on that the game plan called for raising some $200 million (twice what he raised during the 2000 elections), and perhaps as much as $250 million. By mid-April, when the conventional warfare in Iraq had more or less ended, sources made it known that, a month hence, Bush would resume his political fundraising activities at a $2,500-a-plate "President's Dinner," cosponsored by the Republican House and Senate campaign committees. And in May, as Bush prepared for his return to the campaign trail, his aides unveiled yet another fundraising wrinkle: those raising $100,000 would again earn the coveted Pioneer title, but only those raising $200,000 would be included in the new, more elite club known as the Rangers. Soliciting so much money may have seemed like an overly ambitious goal, but by early July, just six weeks after Bush's first campaign outing, the Rangers roster already included at least a half-dozen names. And there was apparently a large contingent on their way to joining those fundraising virtuosos: during those same six weeks, the Bush-Cheney reelection committee registered more than $34 million in donations, more than all nine announced Democratic challengers combined.

Dick Cheney

Top Ten Career Patrons

RANKING	PATRON	TOTAL
1	Morgan Stanley, New York	$49,500*
2	National Association of Realtors, Chicago	$38,430
3	American Medical Association, Chicago	$31,750
4	FMC Corporation, Philadelphia	$23,800
5	Association of Trial Lawyers of America, Washington, D.C.	$19,250
6	J. P. Morgan Chase Company, New York	$18,500
7	Goldman Sachs Group Inc., New York	$16,500
8	Westar Energy, Topeka, Kansas	$15,750
9	Brown Brothers Harriman & Co., New York	$15,000
10	National PAC, Washington, D.C.	$15,000†

This list is based on individual and PAC contributions to Cheney's congressional campaign committee from 1979 to 1995.

Source: Federal Election Commission.

*Includes contributions from employees of Morgan Stanley, its predecessors Morgan Stanley and Dean Witter (including the Reynolds & Co.), and its subsidiary Van Kampen Industries. From 1981 to 1993 Dean Witter was a subsidiary of Sears Roebuck & Co. Individuals who identified themselves as employees of Dean Witter are included. Individuals who identified themselves as employees of Sears are not.

†An independent, pro-Israel political action committee based in Washington, D.C.

The Challengers

Wesley Clark

In 2004, the Democratic challenger to President Bush will be chosen, in all likelihood, no later than the first week of March. By then, nearly 30 states—including the three largest, California, Texas, and New York—will have held their primaries and divided their delegates among the candidates vying for the Democratic nomination. The front-loaded schedule—agreed upon by the Democratic National Committee in January 2002—made the pre-primary jockeying for money, endorsements, media attention, consultants, and organization all the more important for the presidential hopefuls.

As early as January 2002, news stories assumed that House Minority Leader Richard Gephardt and Senators John Kerry and John Edwards were in the running. Howard Dean, then the little-known governor of the state of Vermont, spent a good portion of that year—his last as the Green Mountain State's chief executive—traveling the country, wooing potential supporters while developing his message. Though the event did not make national news, on May 31, 2002, Dean filed papers with the Federal Election Commission, allowing his campaign committee to begin accepting contributions. Al Sharpton, the controversial civil rights figure, appeared on NBC's news and public affairs program *Meet the Press* in August 2002 to make clear his interest in running for the White House. Joe Lieberman, who had promised not to run if his running mate in the 2000 election, Al Gore, threw his hat into the ring, wasted no time in making his intentions official when Gore chose not to run in December 2002.

As 2003 wore on, the candidates appeared at debates, and verbally flayed the incumbent they hoped to replace. Polls showed who was up and who was down. The emergence of Howard Dean, who had trailed better-known figures like Kerry, Gephardt, and Lieberman early in the year, became the story of the summer for political junkies. Dean topped polls in Iowa and New Hampshire and built a formidable fundraising operation. *Time* and *Newsweek* both devoted cover stories to his insurgent campaign. Still, much of the nation showed little interest in the nomination contest—a poll released in August 2003 found that two-thirds of likely voters could not name a single Democratic candidate for the White House.

That same month, television ads began airing in Iowa, New Hampshire, Arkansas, and Washington, D.C., calling for an alternative to the nine Democrats already in the field. "Unafraid to speak his mind," the announcer intoned. "Unwilling to put politics ahead of duty, he has never failed to answer our country's call to preserve, protect, and defend our nation—and all for which it stands." The ad was paid for by DraftWesleyClark.com, which billed itself as a grassroots movement. "We're fighting a two-front war," John Hlinko, the group's cofounder, explained to the *Des Moines Register*. "We want Democrats to keep from making up their minds at the same time we're trying to get General Clark to run."

Wesley Clark didn't disappoint. On September 17, 2003— about 21 months after his more experienced rivals had begun the arduous task of assembling their campaigns—the military man who had never run for elective office announced his intention to seek the presidency. While many state party officials and outside observers questioned whether Clark could be a credible candidate after entering the race so late, he quickly confounded expectations. Within a week of his announcement, polls showed him leading the Democratic pack and even with or slightly ahead of President George W. Bush.

> "You're not old enough, you're not big enough, and you're not smart enough," one senator told the 16-year-old.

Even more impressive, a group of high-powered advisers and supporters lined up behind Clark for his bid. Jumping onto the general's bandwagon were Mickey Kantor, the former commerce secretary and chair of the 1992 Clinton-Gore campaign, and Donnie Fowler, national field director of Al Gore's 2000 campaign and the son of former DNC chairman Don Fowler. Mark Fabiani, who served as Clinton's point man on Whitewater for the 1996 campaign and as Gore's deputy campaign manager in 2000, also signed on, as did Ron Klain, a Washington attorney who worked on Clinton's 1992 campaign, his transition team, and later as former attorney general Janet Reno's chief of staff.

Political neophytes generally can't count on assembling seasoned campaign hands, but then Clark isn't exactly a political neophyte. Unlike the legendary Cincinnatus, the Roman citizen-soldier who, after winning a war, retired quietly to his farm, Clark raised his profile as a television analyst, landed a job at a politically powerful Arkansas investment bank, and plied the age-old game of trading on his military contacts as a corporate lobbyist. The former supreme allied commander in Europe, four-star general, and Rhodes scholar is a very savvy Washington insider.

THE MAKING OF A GENERAL

Wesley Kanne Clark was born in Chicago on December 23, 1944, to Vannete and Benjamin Kanne. Four years later his father suffered a fatal heart attack, and his mother returned with her son to her hometown of Little Rock, Arkansas. There she met and married a banker by the name of Victor Clark.

Given his stepson's small wiry frame, Victor informed Wesley that he was not destined to play basketball. So in the eighth grade, Clark channeled his competitive drive in another direction and started swimming at the Little Rock Boys Club. He attended Joseph Pfeifer Kiwanis Camp, where, under the tutelage of swimming director Jimmy Miller, he developed into a strong swimmer. The Boys Club also taught the youth about leadership, and awakened in Clark an interest in public service.

When he entered Hall High in the 1950s, opposition to a Supreme Court order to desegregate schools forced the Little Rock school system to temporarily shut down. Fearing that the schools might not reopen for Clark's sophomore year, his parents sent him away to Castle Heights Military Academy in Lebanon, Tennessee, where he stuck it out for a year before returning home. He reenrolled at Hall High and helped the school's swim team win the state championship by swimming two legs of the four-man individual medley relay. He graduated in 1962.

Despite being offered scholarships to Ivy League schools, Clark had decided during his junior year that the United States Military Academy at West Point and a career in the military best suited his desire to be a public servant. Only one obstacle stood in his way—a congressional appointment. Every cadet entering the academy must receive a nomination from a member of Congress or the Department of the Army.

> **In his rise to the top, Clark had relied on the top brass to advance him at the expense of his fellow officers, earning him their enmity.**

Clark got no response from his letter to Arkansas senator J. William Fulbright, but the 16-year-old was undeterred and went to Capitol Hill in search of a sponsor. First, he visited Arkansas senator John L. McClellan, who gruffly informed Clark, "You're not old enough, you're not big enough, and you're not smart enough." Failing with the senators, Clark turned to Arkansas representative Dale Alford, then serving his only term in Congress. Alford decided to select his nominee by administering the potential cadets a civil service exam. Clark received the highest score on the test and won the appointment.

At West Point, Clark continued to excel. He finished first in his class as a plebe and went on to graduate first among the class of 1966. After graduation, Clark attended Oxford University as a Rhodes Scholar, where he earned a masters degree in philosophy, politics, and economics. While there, he went on a speaking tour to explain the U.S. policy in Vietnam, though he was one of the first members of his West Point class to question the war.

Shortly thereafter he found himself in Vietnam, where he served with the 1st Infantry Division staff in Lai Kae before being transferred to a field command. Soon after, Clark was shot four times while out on patrol, but managed to direct a counterattack and successfully lead the platoon to safety. For his injuries he received a Purple Heart, and for his valor, a Silver Star.

The severity of the injuries landed Clark an extended stay in the hospital and a ticket out of Vietnam; he needed months of care and a year of rehabilitation to recover from his wounds. When he had recovered, Clark accepted a teaching position at West Point; he was soon promoted to major and assigned to the staff of the supreme allied commander of NATO forces in Europe, then Alexander Haig, who went on to become Ronald Reagan's first secretary of state.

Clark quickly ascended through the military ranks, taking command of a tank battalion at Fort Carson, then the Army's National Training Center at Fort Irwin, California, in the late 1980s. In 1994 he accepted a position with the Joint Chiefs of Staff as director of strategic plans and policy, an appointment that garnered the general his third star and further contacts necessary to finish his ascent.

As military aid to Chief Negotiator Richard Holbrooke, Clark helped plan and implement the military side of the Dayton Peace talks that brokered an end to the war in Bosnia. This feat earned the general his fourth star, and helped position him for his next assignment—commander in chief of U.S. Southern Command, Panama, where he assumed responsibility for all U.S. forces in the region. Just over a year later, Clark reached the pinnacle of his military career when President Clinton nominated him as NATO's senior military officer, as supreme allied commander of Europe. His prowess would soon be tested.

> **Two weeks after declaring, Clark was still registered to represent a high-tech contractor, giving him the rare distinction of seeking the White House while registered as a lobbyist.**

Throughout much of 1998, Slobodan Milosevic and his Serbian supporters led a sporadic, though bloody campaign against the ethnic Albanian population of Kosovo. The United Nations passed a series of resolutions aimed at stopping the carnage, but Milosevic continued the incursions. Clark offered a "carrot and stick" approach to the negotiations—threatening the use of air attacks to force Milosevic to make concessions. While the Clinton administration signed-off on the strategy, General Joseph Ralston of the U.S. Air Force questioned its wisdom. As Clark related in his account of the Kosovo conflict, *Waging Modern War*, Ralston asked, "Wes, what are we going to do if the air threat doesn't deter him?" Clark answered that they would have to bomb, and, if that didn't work, escalate the conflict further.

"I think you have to work at the front end of the policy, on how to make it effective," Clark added. "Besides, I know Milosevic; he doesn't want to get bombed."

On March 23, 1999, Milosevic proved that Clark didn't know him as well as the general thought he did. Instead of quaking at the threat of allied air power, Milosevic refused to come to terms during a last-ditch negotiating effort led by Richard Holbrooke in Belgrade. Holbrooke left the capital of the rump Yugoslavian state that day, and NATO Secretary-General Javier Solana ordered Clark to begin what would be a 78-day air campaign. In the following weeks, Milosevic intensified the ethnic cleansing, leading to a refugee crisis and mass graves. The Yugoslavian army used heavy weaponry, including tanks, against unarmed Kosovars; because NATO pilots bombed from high altitudes, they could have little effect on the situation on the ground. Clark tried to follow through on his intention to escalate the attacks, arguing for a ground campaign and the deployment of Apache helicopters, which are highly effective against tanks, to the Balkans. Ivo Daalder and Michael O'Hanlon found, in *Winning Ugly: NATO's War to Save Kosovo*, that the total cost of shipping the Apaches and their crews to Albania, building a base for them, and practicing maneuvers came to some $500 million, or about 20 to 25 percent of the total U.S. budget for the war. Because of logistical difficulties presented by the mountainous terrain and the fear of heavy losses, the Apaches were never deployed in the fighting.

Ultimately, on June 3, 1999, Milosevic and his parliament agreed to NATO's terms for a peace plan; the capitulation led to the Serbian leader's downfall. Ironically, Clark's success also cost him his job at the top of NATO, although not before he almost caused an international incident in the closing days of the Kosovo war.

When a detachment of peacekeepers from Russia, a traditional ally of the Serbs that had opposed the war, were en route to Kosovo's largest airport in Pristina, Clark ordered British General Mike Jackson to block the runways. Jackson, according to Clark's book, refused, and replied, "Sir, I'm not starting World War III for you." Clark explained his reasons for wanting to stop the Russian deployment:

I saw the problem in strategic terms. This could be a defining moment for the future of NATO. Would we or would we not be able to conduct our own peacekeeping missions? Would Russia be coequal with NATO in this operation? Would Russia get its way by deception and bluff or by negotiation and compromise? Would we have an effective operation or another weak U.N.-type force?

Jackson prevailed. Six months later, Clark was replaced as supreme allied commander of Europe by Joe Ralston, the general who had asked what would happen if the "carrot and stick" approach failed. There are conflicting accounts of the reasons for Clark's dismissal; in his book, he blamed it on Defense Secretary William Cohen and General Hugh Shelton, then the chairman of the Joint Chiefs of Staff, adding that Bill Clinton said he had nothing to do with the early departure.

Clark's competitive nature—a State Department official once told the *New York Times* that "He's competitive drinking coffee with you"—might have had something to do with his dismissal. In his rise to the top, the commander had relied on the top brass to advance him at the expense of his fellow officers, earning him their enmity. "There are an awful lot of people who believe Wes will tell anybody what they want to hear and tell somebody the exact opposite five minutes later," one retired four-star general, who requested anonymity, told the *Washington Post*. "The people who have worked closely with him are the least complimentary, because he can be very abrasive, very domineering. And part of what you saw when he was relieved of command was all of the broken glass and broken china within the European alliance and the [U.S.] European Command." Clark's conduct in Kosovo also landed him on the wrong side of Cohen and Shelton, particularly his incessant demand for ground troops and Apache helicopters, and his public questioning of his superior's judgment. In January 2000, Clark left his job at NATO; that summer, the four-star general retired from the military.

THE GENERAL BECOMES A LOBBYIST

After more than three decades of military service, the general transitioned to civilian life, accepting a consulting position with Arkansas-based Stephens Inc., one of the largest investment banking companies off Wall Street. The Stephens firm, which has underwritten common stock issues and invested in everything from real estate to hazardous waste incineration, serves what its Web site calls "a world-wide base of high net-worth clients including corporations, state and local governments, institutions and individuals." The Stephens firm has long been a player in Arkansas politics—Jackson Stephens, the brother of the firm's founder and its CEO from 1956 to 1986, was a friend of and fundraiser for Bill Clinton. In the 1970s, Stephens Inc. engineered a deal with Bert Lance, the head of Jimmy Carter's Office of Management and Budget who was forced to resign over personal improprieties, allowing the Bank of Credit and Commerce International, better known as BCCI, to penetrate the U.S. banking market. At the time, the comptroller of the currency had barred the bank from doing business in the United States. Stephens admitted no wrongdoing in the affair, but agreed never to do business with BCCI again.

Clark, who studied economics at West Point and Oxford, is a licensed investment banker; he joined Stephens as a consultant in July 2000 and became managing director of merchant banking, a post he held until February 2003. The firm's merchant banking arm invests in oil and gas, media properties, healthcare, agriculture, and high-tech businesses, according to its Web site.

Politics were soon on the general's mind. Democrats in Arkansas hoped he'd run for governor against Republican incumbent Mike Huckabee. Soon, a "Draft Clark" movement emerged, with supporters hoping to persuade Clark to challenge Arkansas Republican senator Tim Hutchinson in the 2002 midterm elections.

Neither opportunity proved alluring enough to draw Clark into politics, but he was soon back in the public eye. After the September 11, 2001, terrorist attacks, his views were sought out by newspapers, magazines, and especially CNN, which hired him as its military analyst. In a September 2002 commentary in *Washington Monthly*, the general who had wanted to use force to prevent the Russians from turning the occupation of Kosovo into "another weak U.N.-type force," found new respect for the international organization. "Soon after September 11, without surrendering our right of self-defense, we should have helped the United Nations create an International Criminal Tribunal on International Terrorism," Clark wrote. "We could have taken advantage of the outpourings of shock, grief, and sympathy to forge a legal definition of terrorism and obtain the indictment of Osama bin Laden and the Taliban as war criminals charged with crimes against humanity."

On February 5, 2003, he told a CNN audience about the impending war in Iraq, "The credibility of the United States is on the line, and Saddam Hussein has these weapons and so, you know, we're going to go ahead and do this and the rest of the world's got to get with us." He added that, "The U.N. has got to come in and belly up to the bar on this. But the president of the United States has put his credibility on the line, too. And so this is the time that these nations around the world, and the United Nations, are going to have to look at this evidence and decide who they line up with."

While Clark's numerous statements on CNN and other venues might come back to haunt him—he lavishly praised the leadership of George W. Bush in the aftermath of the war in Iraq, for example—he never disclosed that, while he was offering his expert commentary on the War on Terror, he was also representing, as a paid lobbyist, a firm seeking terrorism-related contracts with federal agencies.

Two weeks after declaring his intention to run for president, Clark was still registered to represent a high-tech contractor, Acxiom Corporation, giving him the rare distinction of seeking the White House while registered as a lobbyist. Shortly after Clark announced his candidacy, a company spokesman said the general no longer lobbied for Acxiom, but, according to the

Senate Office of Public Records, Clark had not filed any termi-
nation papers.

Clark has been lobbying for the firm since January 2, 2002,
and has received more than $830,000 to advance Acxiom's
agenda and meet with government officials. Clark also served on
the company's board of directors. In a 2003 proxy statement
filed with the Securities and Exchange Commission, Acxiom
spelled out its agreement with Clark.

> During the past fiscal year we had an agreement with an
> affiliate of Stephens Group Inc. ("Stephens"), whereby
> we retained the consulting services of a former Stephens
> employee who is also one of our board members, General
> Wesley K. Clark, in connection with our pursuit of
> contracts with various government agencies. Under the
> agreement, commissions were payable to the Stephens
> affiliate on revenue from government contracts attribut-
> able to Clark's efforts, which commissions were to be off-
> set against an annual consulting fee of $300,000. As of
> March 1, 2003, General Wesley K. Clark resigned from
> Stephens and founded Wesley K. Clark & Associates, a
> business services and development firm. As of that date
> we replaced the agreement with the Stephens affiliate
> with an agreement with Wesley K. Clark & Associates for
> the consulting services of General Clark. Under the terms
> of the new agreement, Acxiom will pay Clark an annual
> retainer of $150,000 plus commissions for new business
> obtained through Clark's efforts, which commissions will
> be offset against the retainer.

According to federal disclosure records, Clark lobbied
directly on "information transfers, airline security and home-

land security issues," for Acxiom, which sought funding to do controversial informational background checks on passengers for airlines. Privacy advocates have criticized the program, called the Computer Assisted Passenger Pre-Screening System II, because of concerns that the data collected would be an overly invasive violation of individuals' rights to privacy. The public outcry has been so strong that there is a bipartisan effort to create more oversight for the program to protect privacy interests if CAPPS II is implemented.

Clark lobbied the Department of Justice, the Central Intelligence Agency, and the Department of Transportation for the company. Clark also reported, on his lobbyist disclosure forms, that he promoted Acxiom to the Senate and the executive office of the president. According to an *Arkansas Democrat-Gazette* report, he even met personally with Vice President Richard Cheney.

He also made a pitch for the kind of tracking that the company's wares can perform while acting as a commentator on CNN. On January 6, 2002, four days after filing as a lobbyist for Acxiom, Clark told an interviewer, in response to worries that private planes could be used for terrorist attacks, "We've been worried about general aviation security for some time. The aircraft need to be secured, the airfields need to be secured, and obviously we're going to also have to go through and do a better job of screening who could fly aircraft, who the private pilots are, who owns these aircraft. So it's going to be another major effort." He did not reveal to CNN's viewers that the company he lobbied for had a substantial stake in this issue.

FINDING THE INSIDE TRACK

On September 24, 2003, one week into his campaign, the man who had upset the conventional wisdom about the Democratic nomination battle gave a speech at East River Park in New York City. Clark chose to talk not about his sterling résumé or his expertise in foreign affairs or even his newly appointed status as front-runner but rather his economic program.

How long he'd stay atop the pack was anyone's guess. Because he entered the race so late, his campaign had yet to file a financial report with the Federal Election Commission, making it impossible to gauge whether he had the money to sustain a run for the White House. In the park in New York, Clark alluded to his recent entry into the race: "One week ago today, I stood up in my hometown of Little Rock, Arkansas, and said 'yes' to thousands of people across the country who have spent their time and energy and money urging me to run for president."

Clark referenced all those who set up personal Web sites, or volunteered for the larger efforts like DraftWesleyClark.com, which ran the ads calling for the general to enter the race. In one of the commercials, an announcer extolled his virtues, drawing attention to the fact that the Rhodes Scholar with the graduate degree in economics from Oxford "chose duty and country over a business career." And he thanked those who contributed money to those independent efforts.

But Clark had been doing some fundraising of his own—through a nonprofit he set up before he joined the race. On October 3, 2002, Clark created an advocacy-based nonprofit called Leadership for America, which collected contributions during the months that followed. The nonprofit's Web site described Clark as the group's founder; District of Columbia corporation records list him as a director. Five days after he announced his intention to run for the presidency, Leadership for America's Web site, which featured a large picture of Clark, and said it was "dedicated to fostering the national dialogue about America's future" was taken offline and replaced with a disclaimer stating "Leadership for America is not affiliated or connected with General Clark's presidential campaign."

However, there are striking similarities between the Leadership for America and Clark '04. For instance, the same picture and background anchors both Web sites; they both use the same biography word-for-word, and two of the three directors—including Clark—on Leadership for America's articles of incorporation work on the Clark for President campaign.

Many other presidential candidates have raised millions through various soft-money committees through the IRS's 527 system. But Clark's nonprofit may be more nebulous. Under law, Leadership for America is not required to disclose information about its donors or the contributions it has received.

"Much of what I know about the United States, I learned in the United States Army," Clark told the crowd that day in New York.

It is understandable, of course, that Clark chose not to highlight his own lucrative career as a lobbyist seeking taxpayer dollars for homeland security. After all, much of what the general knows of political organization shows the touch of a shrewd insider.

Howard Dean

On a picture-perfect New England day, thronged by his supporters in a square in Burlington, Vermont, Howard Dean announced his candidacy for president. "I speak for a new American century and a new generation of Americans—both young people and the young at heart," the newly minted candidate said. "We seek the great restoration of American values and the restoration of our nation's traditional purpose in the world."

Dean spoke to the cheering crowd, and the estimated 80 reporters there to capture his words, of the strength of the country, invoking one of its darkest moments to emphasize his faith in his fellow citizens. "If September 11, 2001, taught America anything it is that we are stronger when we are beholden to each other as a national community, and weaker when we act only as individuals."

He talked of his plans and policies—universal health care, fiscal responsibility, a focus on the needs of children. He obliquely criticized his fellow Democrats. "I have wanted my party to stand up for what we believe in again," he said. He castigated the president for his foreign policy, the falling stock market, and rising unemployment.

On that June day, cheered on by the crowd, Dean announced what everyone already knew, that the former governor of Vermont was a candidate for president. The first time around, the response he got was a little more muted. Dean had not made much headway with the public in 2002, when his campaign actually began. As late as January 2003, the medical doctor, self-proclaimed outsider, and underdog remained virtually unknown to voters outside of his home state. A *Newsweek* poll of registered Democrats and independents taken that month, after most candidates were already in the race, showed 4 percent of respondents backed Dean, behind other long-shot candidates, Al Sharpton, Carol Moseley Braun, and Dennis Kucinich. Even the people who knew him best seemed doubtful their former governor would be up to the task of running the nation. A March 2002 poll of Vermont registered voters found that only 23 percent would back him for the White House.

But on June 23, 2003, Dean was riding high and challenged for the position of front-runner in the campaign. He had raised his stature by picking fights with his Democratic rivals who had supported war in Iraq. He blasted George W. Bush at every turn. Some in the press began to compare his campaign to that of Senator John McCain, who told it like it was on the "Straight-Talk Express."

Dean can certainly be blunt, but not necessarily candid. In the most contentious issue he faced as governor—a state supreme court ruling that same-sex couples could not be denied the legal benefits of marriage—he chose not to answer the question that was being asked around the country: should gays have full and equal access to the altar that heterosexuals enjoy? Dean favored a bill that created a different legal category, civil unions, for same-sex couples, which some gay and lesbian advocates denounced as a form of "separate but equal" rights.

"I think it's not 'separate but equal.' It's 'different but equal,'" Dean said. He declined to spell out where he stood on gay marriage, and would not say whether he would veto a bill that conferred full marriage rights on homosexual couples. "I think [a gay marriage bill] is inadvisable for a variety of reasons, which I'm not going to go into," he told reporters a few days after the historic ruling. When asked why he wouldn't elaborate, he displayed some of his characteristic temper. "Because it's my personal business and I don't feel like I need to share it with anybody."

Dean is an accomplished, if sometimes thin-skinned, practitioner of the art of politics. While he supported civil unions, and did a masterful job fending off activists who thought the measure went too far or not far enough, he chose to sign the historic bill behind closed doors. He backed a stringent campaign finance law, then opted out of the system in his 2000 reelection bid. His administration was blithely indifferent to concerns about a hospital renovation that ended up more than doubling in cost, for which he denied having any responsibility. He demanded that the Bush administration answer questions about how it used sensitive intelligence reports, but he fought reporters in court who wanted him to disclose the trips he took to campaign for president while he served his final year as governor.

Like his staged presidential announcement, made over a year after he had formed his campaign, the would-be straight-talker has reinvented himself to ride a wave of liberal discontent. But history tells a different story about the politics of Howard Brush Dean III.

To the Manor Born

Dean was born to wealth, on November 17, 1948, in New York City. He is the son, grandson, and great-grandson of Wall Street financiers. His father, the late Howard B. Dean Jr., was a stock-broker who dabbled in Republican politics before his death in 2001. Dean's mother, Andree Maitland Dean, is an art appraiser. When the campaign trail takes Dean back to New York City, he usually stays with his mother at the family home-stead, a Park Avenue apartment described by *New York* magazine as "serenely decorated with small African sculptures, and mod-ernist paintings and prints."

Howard was the oldest of four boys. His brothers are James, a market researcher in Fairfield, Connecticut; William, a bond trader in Boston; and Charlie, who died in 1974. Dean rarely speaks of his younger brother's untimely death. In 1974, Charlie, 24, and a friend were traveling by boat along the Mekong River, in Laos, taking pictures. The pair were abducted by local Com-munist guerrillas and executed as alleged U.S. spies. Their bod-ies have never been recovered. Andree Dean said in a February 2003 *New York* magazine interview that the Dean family believed their son indeed might have worked for the Central Intelligence Agency, but their suspicions have never been confirmed.

Dean went to Laos in 2002 to see what was believed to be his brother's burial spot. *New York* magazine reported that he spoke with an eyewitness who claimed to have seen Charlie's body put into a foxhole. "It gave me closure," Dean said of the trip.

The Dean boys grew up on Park Avenue, were educated at the city's elite preparatory schools, and spent their summers in the Hamptons, the playground of New York's moneyed class. The elder Howard Dean and his wife were members of the famously exclusive Maidstone Club, whose membership over the years consisted of titans of capitalism: Julian S. Myrick, who founded the Mutual of New York insurance company; Juan Terry Trippe, founder of Pan American Airlines; John A. Dix, presi-dent of the Union Pacific Railroad during the late 1800s; and

William Clay Ford, of the Ford Motor Company's founding family.

Despite his background, Dean doesn't project an air of wealth. He's been described as "frugal" and prone to "plain, well-worn suits." He was not opposed to flying coach early in the campaign and avoids high-priced hotel suites in favor of modestly priced rooms or the homes of supporters. "Howard never has acted like a rich, to-the-manor-born type," Peter Freyne, a columnist for *Seven Days*, an alternative weekly newspaper in Burlington, Vermont, told the *Los Angeles Times*.

> **Despite his well-to-do background, Dean doesn't project an air of wealth.**

In 1967, Dean left Manhattan and headed off to Yale University, where he majored in political science. According to friends, he showed no interest in anything as ambitious as running for president of the United States. In fact, he was preparing to take up the family profession, a career in high finance. After graduation, Dean took a job as a stockbroker, but that lasted only two years. He then enrolled at the Albert Einstein College of Medicine in New York.

At medical school, Dean met Judith Steinberg, a Princeton-educated daughter of two physicians. After graduation, Dean and Steinberg married. In 1978, he began a residency at the University of Vermont Medical Center. He later moved to Shelburne, Vermont, where the couple established a medical practice. Until he became governor, they worked together.

Dean's first foray into the public arena came when he helped clean up the Lake Champlain waterfront around Burlington. The waterfront had become an eyesore and, worse, a hazard. Old barges and rusting railroad boxcars littered the area. Meanwhile, residents wanted to create a bicycle path in town. The Citizens'

Waterfront Committee was born. It was a perfect vehicle for Dean to get involved in local politics. He helped the group raise money, fend off developers, and, ultimately, organize the volunteers that turned the Lake Champlain waterfront into a 9-mile-long recreation area meandering by the foothills of the Adirondack Mountains. "If you get a chance to see it, it's an extraordinary thing," Dean told one interviewer. "If you go down to the waterfront you can walk all the way to the Winooski River. In fact, I finished it off as governor; we're going to build a bridge across that river."

The waterfront project whet Dean's appetite for public service. In 1982, he ran for and won a seat in the House of Representatives in Vermont's part-time legislature. In 1986 he successfully ran for lieutenant governor and won three consecutive terms. Five years later, Vermont was mired in recession and facing a $60 million budget deficit. The administration of Governor Richard Snelling, a Republican, was pushing for a tax increase. Democrats in the Vermont legislature wanted more spending on social programs; Republicans fought higher taxes, which, they argued, would slow economic growth in already difficult economic times. Tempers flared. Friendships were strained. A political train wreck of major proportions was waiting to happen.

Then, on August 14, 1991, Governor Snelling died at age 64. Dean, the liberal Democratic lieutenant governor, was treating a patient at his office when he heard the news. He rushed to the statehouse in Montpelier and was hastily sworn in. Snelling's death churned the political waters when the state was in a financial crisis. The governor's mansion shifted suddenly from Republican to Democrat. No one knew quite what to expect. Dean, however, reassured the citizens of Vermont that he would continue Snelling's policies. "I intend to do my very best to continue his program of responsibility in fiscal matters," Dean told reporters at the time.

Dean, who wasn't known for fiscal conservatism when he took over Snelling's job, inherited three problems from the moderate Republican: a deficit, tax increases, and budget cuts. He also took on a new image. He kept Snelling's cabinet and wrung his hands about the need to follow Snelling's fiscal policies in the tough economy and fought members of his own party who wanted to increase spending. "The most important part of transition is a sense of stability, an assurance that there is still a firm hand on the tiller," Dean said two months after taking office.

Within six months, he did offer an olive branch to members of his own party, who had proposed a plan for universal health care. Though he opposed their plan, he did order state agencies to cut 3 percent from Snelling's $672 million budget so he could have money to pay for his own policy preferences, including a health reform bill that created a commission to design his own plan for universal coverage. Just as the Clinton administration saw its own health care plan collapse in 1994, Dean's first effort was also a failure. That year, his commission released two plans to provide greater access to health care for Vermonters; neither one passed the legislature.

But he continued to stress spending cuts over tax increases whenever the budget was tight. Indeed, when deficits struck at the end of his administration, Dean again trimmed spending rather than run deficits or raise taxes. In fact, during the boom of the go-go 1990s, with soaring stock markets and booming revenues for state governments, Dean pushed for and got income tax cuts. Dean assumed more than an office when his predecessor died: he remade himself in the image of arguably the state's most successful politician.

He served 11 years as governor of Vermont, longer than anyone in the twentieth century. During that time, he served terms as head of both the National Governors Association and the Democratic Governors' Association. During his administration, Vermont pulled back from the verge of fiscal disaster and went on to achieve the highest credit ratings in New England.

"WHAT WE DID IN VERMONT"

On March 7, 2003, Dean appeared on a local public television program called *Iowa Press* in one of a series of interviews conducted with the Democratic presidential primary candidates. Asked about farm issues, Dean told the interviewer, "I've got an agricultural plan that I think will work. It has a lot to do with what we did in Vermont in terms of the dairy compact."

On May 13, 2003, Dean appeared on CNN's program *Inside Politics* to discuss the health care plans of his rivals for the Democratic nomination. "Ours is much easier to understand," he told interviewer Candy Crowley. "It's much cheaper. It's based on what we did in Vermont."

On June 26, 2003, in Los Angeles, Dean participated in a debate on the environment sponsored by the California League of Conservation Voters. Asked how he would persuade Americans to stop buying the large, gas-guzzling sport utility vehicles, Dean replied, "Let me talk a little about that, in terms of what we did in Vermont."

Yet Vermont's laws allow for little public scrutiny of the workings of government. The Center for Public Integrity's States Project has examined ethics and disclosure laws in all 50 states. Vermont is one of four states that lacks an ethics statute covering the conduct of legislators. It is one of three states that does not require legislators or executive branch officials to file financial disclosure forms. With fewer than 617,000 residents, Vermont ranks forty-ninth in population out of 50 states, but it ranks twenty-second for the total amount of money spent by lobbyists. There were more registered lobbyists in Vermont than in New Jersey, Kentucky, Tennessee, Colorado, or Oregon. And because of the state's weak lobby-disclosure laws, what those lobbyists are up to is a matter of conjecture; Vermont ranked thirty-fifth in terms of the amount of information its lobbyists must disclose.

> **Dean assumed more than an office when his Republican predecessor died: he remade himself in the image of arguably the state's most successful politician.**

During his 11 years as governor, Dean did not propose a law requiring financial disclosures for legislatures or executive branch officials. In fact, Vermonters got their first look at their governor's personal financial holdings only when he decided to run for president and filed a federal personal financial disclosure form. Dean's disclosure pegged the value of his assets and income at almost $4 million, with a significant portion invested in the stock market. Dean also has a Salomon Smith Barney cash account worth more than $910,000, Treasury bonds worth $441,000, and stocks in companies like Intel, General Electric, and Merck. According to Dean's 2001 tax returns—which he provided to the Center for Public Integrity—he and his wife reported a combined annual income of $170,000.

The lack of transparency extended to some of Dean's closest supporters. David Coates was a KPMG partner in Burlington, Vermont, and had been a longtime advisor to Dean. In 1995, the governor appointed his friend to the board of directors of the Vermont Municipal Bond Bank, which manages tens of millions of dollars a year in bonds issued by the state's cities.

Coates also served as chairman of the Vermont Economic Progress Council, a quasi-public panel created to lure businesses to relocate or expand in the state through the use of tax credits and incentives. In 2000, the council had issued roughly $900,000 in credits to businesses and said it expected to dole out another $65 million in coming years. But there was a problem. Some Vermont lawmakers had raised questions about whether the council had ensured that businesses receiving tax credits were living up to their commitments to create new jobs. Lawmakers asked state auditor Edward Flanagan to investigate.

During the inquiry, Coates and Christopher D'Elia, the council's executive director, told investigators that no notes had been taken during the council's closed-door executive session meetings. The council's administrative staff person later contradicted their sworn testimony about note-keeping. State attorney general William Sorrell recused himself from the case; a subsequent investigation into Coates and D'Elia cleared them of any wrongdoing and did not pursue criminal charges.

Sorrell's wife, Mary Alice McKenzie, was a business associate of Coates. McKenzie was president of a Burlington-based food products company; Coates served as an investor and member of the company's board of directors. Of course, ordinary Vermonters would have no way of knowing about the connection—neither official had to publicly disclose their business interests or those of their spouses.

While Vermont has little in the way of disclosure requirements and no state ethics agency to oversee the conduct of legislators or executive branch officials, it's not completely the wild, wild Northeast. Dean issued executive orders, the last on June 13, 2000, that set ethical standards for government appointees and employees. It included a provision barring them from being "an advocate for any private entity before any public body or before the state legislature" for one year after they left their state job. The provision did little to keep the revolving door from turning in Dean's Vermont.

The deputy manager of Dean's presidential campaign is Robert Rogan, whom Dean met over a decade ago when the Texas native was working as a staff advisor to Lawton Chiles, the former governor of Florida. Dean had just taken over as chairman of the National Governors Association and needed a staff person with political experience. Rogan was his man. Rogan had not only worked for Chiles when Chiles served in Congress, but he also put in time with Senator Bob Graham, the Florida Democrat who was also seeking the party nomination in 2004.

In 1994, Rogan moved up to Vermont to work as Dean's deputy chief of staff. He kept the post through 1998, when he left the administration to become vice president of public affairs and lobbyist for the Central Vermont Public Service Corporation, the largest of the state's 22 electric utility providers. He advised Dean during the most trying times of the administration when it came to public utilities, and, particularly, electric utilities. In 1998, a state commission appointed by Dean was considering how to deregulate Vermont's utilities.

Even after Rogan went to work for CVPS, he continued to act as an advisor to Dean, according to the Vermont *Rutland Herald*. But then, Dean and Vermont's electric utility executives have had a close relationship. Dean backed the agenda of the utility, sometimes seemingly at odds with financial interests of residential utility customers. He pushed for utility contract provisions that saved the power companies but cost Vermont families millions of dollars in substantially higher rates.

Robert Young, chief executive at Central Vermont Public Service Corporation and chairman of the Vermont Yankee Nuclear Power Corporation, and his wife, Victoria, have donated the maximum $5,000 to Dean's Fund for a Healthy America PAC. Young told the Associated Press they gave because he and his wife "agree with many of the things the fund is talking about—fiscal conservatism, education, health care." Dean agreed with Young and CVPS about a lot more than education and health care, though.

Vermont has some of the highest utility rates in the Northeast (and sixth highest in the country), due in part to a series of long-term contracts between its major power companies, including CVPS and Green Mountain Power Corporation, and Canada's Hydro-Quebec power generation plant. In the early 1990s, Dean pushed the Vermont Department of Public Service, the state's utility regulatory authority, to approve the contracts, which proved to be a bad deal for consumers when electricity prices around the country plummeted. Vermonters were contractually obligated to pay rates negotiated at a time when power prices were high.

> **Dean claimed that two documents analyzing Vermont power purchases from the Canadian utility were covered by "executive privilege" and that his staff's recommendations should not be released to the public.**

In 1992, when environmentalists and overcharged citizens wanted to know why Dean supported allowing Vermont's 17 electric companies to buy their power from Hydro-Quebec, their governor resisted. Dean claimed that documents analyzing Vermont power purchases from the Canadian utility were covered by "executive privilege" and that his staff's recommendations should not be released to the public. Environmentalists were also rebuffed when they asked for communications from Dean's office that led to the 25-year Hydro-Quebec's deal.

"Where there's a big company with a lot of economic impact

confronting a regulatory obstacle, Howard would go to bat for the company," John McClaughry, a Republican who challenged Dean for the governor's post and heads the Ethan Allen Institute, a public policy think tank in Concord, Vermont, told the Center for Public Integrity.

Under Dean, the Department of Public Service gave up on its attempt to force CVPS and its subsidiaries to bear the high costs of buying power from Hydro-Quebec, shifting the burden to ratepayers, who would pick up 90 percent of the tab for the expensive power from north of the border in the coming years, which could amount to hundreds of millions of dollars.

The connections to the utility industry have not escaped the notice of public interest groups in Vermont. "Administration actions going back some years betray an inappropriate coziness with the utilities," Paul Burns, executive director of the Vermont Public Service Research Group, told the Associated Press. "I am not prepared to say it's a result of contributions given. But these contributions present the appearance of impropriety or appearance of influence that it probably would have been better to avoid."

A Dean aide told the Associated Press that Dean had never let campaign contributions influence policy. But Dean himself bluntly suggested that donations buy a certain access. "People who think they're going to buy a contract or buy some influence are mistaken," Dean said during a debate over a Vermont campaign finance reform bill in 1996. "But they do get access—there's no question about that. . . . They get me to return their phone calls."

PHYSICIAN, AUDIT THYSELF

On the stump, Dean is fond of comparing himself and his views to that of the late Senator Paul Wellstone. When speaking before progressive audiences and party activists, one of Dean's favorite applause lines was coined by Wellstone, that he "represents the democratic wing of the Democratic Party." He boasts that he persuaded Vermont lawmakers to conserve thousands of acres of farm and forestland and that he pushed for balanced budgets and sought to maintain school funding reforms. And the state did become an attractive, business friendly environment for investors, which, Dean says helped create more than 50,000 new jobs under his watch.

He tells the story of Vermont's success under his steward-ship. When he took office as governor, the state was drowning in red ink; when he left, the state was in the black, with the highest bond rating ever. It was a fiscal and political trifecta when Ver-mont emerged from the financial brink, improved its bond ratings, and became one of the first states to guarantee health care coverage for all children under the age of 18.

Dr. Dean made much of the issue early on. He was an ardent supporter of universal access to health care and complained of out-of-control costs and what he saw as the irrational allocation of resources by the country's health care system. "Fifty percent of Medicare is spent on patients in [intensive care units], only half of whom will emerge alive," he told the *Boston Globe* in 1991. "Fifty percent of our total spending is on patients in the last six months of their lives. I question how much improvement there is in the quality of life."

In 1992, Dean told *American Health Line* how he'd pay for his ambitious plans. "My own preference is to move to a broad-based tax system, but I have no illusions about ramming that through the legislature over the objections of the business com-munity." He did mention one levy he'd favor instituting. After noting that excise taxes on cigarettes and alcohol were the only way to get smokers and drinkers to pay their fair share of health

costs, Dean targeted Twinkies, potato chips, and burritos.
"Well, I'm perfectly happy to have a junk-food tax as well. I've
long believed we ought to do that."

The Vermont health care plan, which covers adults and children, is a centerpiece of Dean's campaign. "Nearly 92 percent of
adults now have coverage. Most importantly, 99 percent of all
Vermont children are eligible for health insurance and 96 percent have it," his campaign Web site proclaims. But it's come at
a price. Vermont faced a health care crisis in 2001 that has yet to
be fully resolved. The state and federal government payments
for health care services don't cover the actual costs, meaning
that private insurers—and those that pay the premiums for it—
must cover the difference. Employers saw their health care costs
rise 20 percent or more.

> **Dean formed a bipartisan commission to study problems
> with the state's medical insurance plans, which
> concluded in 2001, "Health care in Vermont
> is near a state of crisis."**

Dean formed a bipartisan commission to study the problem, which concluded in 2001, "Health care in Vermont is near
a state of crisis—some of us would say it is already in crisis."
The panel, headed by former Vermont Human Services secretary Cornelius Hogan, issued a dire warning: "We are rapidly
approaching the point at which these costs will directly conflict
with our ability to do such things as to maintain roads and
bridges, for example, or to provide cost-effective services to
our infants and children, to promote agriculture and tourism,
or to provide any other services our citizens have come to
expect."

Dean placed the blame on the high price of pharmaceuticals

and on hospitals for providing costly services like magnetic resonance imaging when cheaper ones, like x-rays, would do. His commission concluded that more precise diagnostic tools find serious problems earlier, allowing doctors to treat problems before they become serious.

Though Dean complained about hospital costs, his administration didn't do much to contain them. In 2001, the state's largest hospital, Burlington-based Fletcher Allen Health Care, launched a huge construction and renovation project. The hospital sought state approval for an ambitious $173 million upgrade of its facilities, dubbed the Renaissance Project. It also sought a $150 million bond issue, backed by Vermont taxpayers, to pay for the project. It got approval for both.

Within two years, state and federal authorities had launched probes of Fletcher Allen, its top management had resigned, its board of trustees was under fire, and the state was left with a project whose costs had skyrocketed, by one state-sponsored estimate, to $370 million. The primary fault lay with hospital management, which arranged off-the-books loans for part of the project and hid $88 million in additional costs in the facility's operating budget, a report by John P. Crowley, commissioner of the Department of Banking, Insurance, Securities and Health Care Administration, found.

Though a number of citizens complained to the Department of Banking, Insurance, Securities and Health Care Administration, the state agency that oversaw the project, Fletcher Allen's mishandling of the Renaissance Project wasn't revealed until the summer of 2002. The hospital's former chief financial officer, David Cox, gave a five-and-a-half-hour deposition to state authorities, laying out the actual costs of the project and the means by which Fletcher Allen had hidden them. In August 2002, while Dean was still governor, the *Burlington Free Press* reported that the state's attorney general, William Sorrell, and federal prosecutors were investigating the deal. Dean was less than enthusiastic about the probe. "It is a very difficult case because we have to make sure that the institution stays healthy," he told the paper, adding, "We also have to make sure that this kind of stuff isn't allowed."

Other state officials took a more negative tone. Bernie Sanders, Vermont's lone House representative, told WVNY-TV, "I can't go back to Washington and say increase Medicare and Medicaid at a time when a hospital may be wasting substantial sums of that money or using it in an illegal way." While critical of hospital management, Sanders also noted the lack of oversight. "The governor's role should have been a very strong role," he told the *Burlington Free Press*.

Dean, for his part, blamed hospital management for the cost overruns, eventually labeling them "crooks" and suggesting they could be prosecuted for wrongdoing. He denied that his administration had dropped the ball in overseeing the Renaissance Project. Crowley, who was appointed by Dean's successor as commissioner of the Department of Banking, Insurance, Securities and Health Care Administration, concluded otherwise. "The department should have realized earlier that Fletcher Allen was misrepresenting the facts," he wrote. "Questions posed by individual critics of Fletcher Allen should have alerted the Department earlier to Fletcher Allen's regulatory violations."

NOMINATION SUPERHIGHWAY

In the closing days of the second fiscal quarter of fundraising in 2003, the Dean campaign announced that it would raise at least $7.5 million in the reporting period, doubling the amount

Dean had raised in the first quarter. It was a stunning feat, financially. Dean had collected more cash than every other Democrat, including well-known figures like Senator Joseph Lieberman, who had been Al Gore's running mate in 2000, and former House Democratic leader Richard Gephardt. Dean raised at least $1.5 million more than Senator Kerry, his nearest rival.

Suddenly, improbably, Howard Dean—who walked away from sure reelection as governor of Vermont to launch what many observers assumed, given his low presidential polling numbers in his home state, a quixotic campaign for president— was a challenger for the title of Democratic front-runner. And his success may very well have marked a watershed moment in the use of the Internet in elective politics.

The Gallup poll found in 2002 that 15 percent of Americans go online everyday for news (22 percent listen to talk radio). A study by the commercial ratings service Arbitron found that three-fourths of Americans have access to the Internet, and nearly two-thirds can surf the Web at home.

For a candidate as low-tech as Dean (he reportedly does not carry a laptop computer or e-mail pager device), he has assembled a remarkably tech-savvy campaign that was able to close the gap between retail politics and the Internet. There was the Howard Dean Internet Web site. There was the Dean "blog," or Web log, a sort of running narrative from the campaign trail, updated daily by the candidate and his staff. The "Blog for America," as it's called, links to flattering news accounts, instructs other Web site operators on how to link to the Dean Web page, and toots its own horn, on occasion: "Okay, so it's not quite the same as the news this morning that Dean is now leading in California. But here it is: Blog for America is now ranked number 19 of the Top 100 weblogs, according to the Daypop score." Daypop, incidentally, measures "the probability that a blog reader randomly hopping from blog to blog will hit that weblog."

There's Howard Dean TV for the real enthusiast, which, using streaming video software, delivers coverage of Dean's appearances and campaign commercials directly to visitors to the Dean Web site 24 hours a day, 7 days a week. The campaign also mounted an online "adopting Iowans" program to induce his supporters across the country to write letters to Iowans touting Dean. "It's a chance to get everybody else in the country who is supporting us involved in Iowa," Campaign Manager Joe Trippi told the Associated Press.

The Internet strategy paid off in the second fiscal quarter of 2003. Tens of thousands of new supporters joined online at Meetup.com, a free Web site that facilitates group meetings on just about any subject, anywhere. They used computers and modems to arrange rallies drawing dozens or even hundreds. And perhaps most importantly, of the $7.5 million Dean raised, at least $3 million poured in from Internet donors who logged on to Dean's Web site or the Web sites of his supporters.

> For a candidate as low-tech as Dean, he has assembled a remarkably tech-savvy campaign that was able to close the gap between retail politics and the Internet.

Dean's online prowess is a function of his campaign message, which dovetails nicely with the priorities of an online activist site, MoveOn.org, whose "Internet primary" Dean won handily. A pair of Silicon Valley entrepreneurs, Wes Boyd and Joan Blades, launched MoveOn.org in 1998 to lobby against the impeachment of President Bill Clinton. The message to

Congress was to "Censure and move on," and the site collected online signatures to add heft to its petition. The couple expanded MoveOn.org into a successful advocacy PAC that, among other things, opposed President Bush's war with Iraq. It reportedly added some 100,000 activists to its ranks in the spring of 2003, organized in opposition to issues such as the Federal Communications Commission's decision to relax ownership rules on media companies, a ruling that is widely believed to lead to further concentration of the media.

MoveOn.org has raised huge sums of money over the Internet for various causes and candidates, without the conventional costs of running a political organization. In 2000, the group raised $3.2 million for candidates; in 2002, it raised $4.1 million. The group is credited with using the Internet to organize peace activists during some of the largest antiwar demonstrations in the United States, France, Germany, and Russia in the months prior to the beginning of the U.S. invasion of Iraq.

On its Web site, MoveOn.org solicits donations to run issue ads, the political commercials that can attack a candidate but must stop short of specifically encouraging citizens to vote for a particular candidate. The group funded a provocative, 30-second antiwar commercial that mimicked the so-called Daisy ad aired during the 1964 presidential race. The original ad depicted a 6-year-old girl plucking petals from a daisy, along with a missile launch countdown, then a nuclear mushroom cloud. The 2003 version, which ran in January, showed the same images, with added scenes of burning oil wells, tanks, wounded soldiers, and street protests. It closed with a mushroom cloud and the warning: "War with Iraq. Maybe it will end quickly. Maybe not. Maybe it will spread. Maybe extremists will take over countries with nuclear weapons. Maybe the unthinkable."

Though the ad's dire warning of extremists getting a nuclear bomb as a result of U.S. military action proved as chimerical as the claims made in forged intelligence documents that Saddam Hussein had sought uranium in Niger, MoveOn.org was back at it again in July 2003. The group solicited contributions to run an ad, titled "Misleader," that took the Bush administration to task over the intelligence assessments it used, and those it ignored, in making the case for war. "We're launching a series of newspaper ads around the country that call on Members of Congress who haven't pledged to support a commission to place truth over politics," the solicitation ran. "We'll need to raise about $225,000 to make a real impact. We can do that if we all contribute—$5 or $500." The group provided a handy link allowing donors to view the ads.

Perhaps the group's most memorable political stunt was hyping an Internet poll as an "online primary." The organization's antiwar, anti-Bush message was tailor-made for Dean, who was among the most vocal of the Democratic candidates opposing war in Iraq. So perhaps it is not surprising that when the results of the "MoveOn.org PAC primary" were announced, Dean was the runaway winner, with 44 percent. Dennis Kucinich, a House member from Ohio and another antiwar candidate, was runner-up, with 24 percent of the vote.

By contrast, a scientific, national poll conducted by Quinnipiac University of Democratic voters over six days starting July 17 had Dean coming in fourth, trailing rivals Joe Lieberman, Richard Gephardt, and John Kerry, with Kucinich the choice of a mere 2 percent of those polls. Internet polls are inaccurate measures, since the sample isn't scientifically sampled. Those who regularly visit a site with a particular viewpoint will be more likely to share that view than the public at large, and choose their candidate accordingly.

Nevertheless, MoveOn.org's Internet poll drew a great deal of media coverage for Dean, adding to his momentum. The group noted that the 317,000 votes cast in the digital poll were more than the Iowa caucuses and New Hampshire primary combined. Some of Dean's opponents complained that MoveOn.org dispatched one of its top staffers to Dean headquarters in the weeks prior to its primary, but that information was lost in the headlines that Dean had won the group's poll. The media attention helped, but was not as important as the money that poured in from the crowd that surfed their Internet Web sites.

But Dean didn't just take the money of the Internet sector. He took their advice and their consulting services. His campaign paid $8,500 for Web-related services to Meetup Inc. in May and June 2003. He also paid MoveOn.org more than $2,700 for Web consulting at the end of June, just three days after the group announced that Dean had won its Internet poll. Of course, that's a drop in the bucket for a group that raised $4.1 million as recently as 2002.

The Internet did for Dean almost overnight what a year on the stump could not: It made him a serious contender. With all the speed of the online "instant messages" that keep the high-tech world in touch, Dean had money and an apparent groundswell of support. And he was willing to plug the Web site whose Internet poll brought him so much attention. In his June 23, 2003, "announcement," Dean mentioned it by name. "Like MoveOn.org we seek to build a community of millions and strengthen the voice of the people," he said.

OPEN GOVERNMENT?

Perhaps it's just as well for Dean that $3 million of his campaign cash has come from faceless transactions over the Internet.

At a fundraiser at which Dean reportedly raised $35,000 from well-heeled supporters, held at an "inconceivably regal" New York City brownstone, Dean had an uncomfortable moment. He repeated his proclamation that evening that "I'm for the ordinary person," to which one guest, a *New Yorker* magazine editor, replied, "All very fine, but I'm struck by the fact that there are no African Americans in this room." In fact there was at least one African American in the crowded room. "We're just stuck in the back of the bus," he piped in. Dean left not long afterward, according to the *New York* magazine Web site.

> He also paid MoveOn.org more than $2,700 for Web consulting at the end of June, just three days after the group announced that Dean had won its Internet poll.

As uncomfortable as the contretemps might have been for Dean, he handled it well, which was no slight feat. Dean is hot-tempered. The less-than-charitable critics have put it bluntly: he sometimes speaks before his brain is fully engaged. As a result, Dean has been forced to apologize on more than one occasion for off-the-cuff remarks, which, at times, reflect an insensitivity unusual in a big-time politician. In 1993, in the midst of a national public debate over welfare reforms in the states, Governor Dean was quoted as saying that people who received welfare "don't have any self-esteem. If they did, they'd be working." The uproar was swift, and so was the apology.

Despite his seeming openness with his views, Dean has never expressed much enthusiasm for greater transparency in government. In fact, when the Vermont legislature passed land-mark campaign finance reforms into law in 1997 and thereby became a national leader in efforts to reduce the influence of big

money in politics, the governor could offer only lukewarm support for the new, stricter regulations.

Publicly financed campaigns for qualified candidates for
lieutenant governor and governor, spending caps, and contribution limits were the main components of the new law. But when
the 2000 elections rolled around, neither Dean nor his Republican opponent accepted state political campaign money because it
would have limited their campaign spending to $300,000 each.

By January 2002, in one of his last major moves as governor,
Dean pushed to eliminate $1.3 million in funding for public
financing of political campaigns. It was a reversal of his earlier
position, justified by his desire to redirect the money to the state's
general fund to plug a hole in the operating budget. His proposal
angered legislators and clean government groups alike. "The
actions he is suggesting, if taken, totally gut the campaign finance
fund," Republican state representative Richard Westman said at
the time.

Just before leaving the governor's office, Dean decided to
seal his government records for 10 years, according to Vermont
Public Radio. Two of Dean's predecessors had sealed their
records for six years. "Well, there are future political considera-
tions," Dean said. "We didn't want anything embarrassing
appearing in the papers at a critical time in any future endeavor."

In 2002, Dean's last year in office, when Vermont reporters
asked Dean to include his presidential campaign trips on his
daily schedule, Dean invoked executive privilege. Three Vermont newspapers filed a lawsuit to force the governor to open
his travel records. According to Dean, the controversy "wasn't
only about my presidential trips," he told *Editor & Publisher*
magazine. "They wanted me to identify the union leaders and
corporate leaders I was meeting with. I wasn't about to give them
that. No one would meet with me if I did. At one point, they were

arguing that if I went to watch my son play hockey, that should be on the schedule. But I didn't mind the suit. The press properly gets really crazy about anything they can't get their hands on."

On November 1, 2002, a few days before the election that chose his successor, the state supreme court ruled that Dean had to disclose information on his presidential trips.

Dean was already making the information available, posting it on his campaign Web site to alert his online followers of his appearances.

Howard Dean

Top Ten Career Patrons

Ranking	Patron	Total
1	AOL Time Warner Inc., New York	$51,800
2	Maverick Farms, Sharon, Vermont	$19,500
3	Howard Dean's campaign staff	$15,994*
4	Microsoft Corporation, Redmond, Washington	$14,750
5	University of Pennsylvania, Philadelphia	$13,250
6	International Brotherhood of Electrical Workers, Washington, D.C.	$12,950
7	Goldman Sachs Group Inc., New York	$12,750
8	IBM Corporation, Armonk, New York	$12,050
9	University of California, Berkeley, California	$12,050
10	United Food and Commercial Workers Union, Washington, D.C.	$12,000

This list is based on selected contributions to Dean's gubernatorial campaigns, and individual and PAC contributions to the Fund for a Healthy America, and Dean's 2004 presidential campaign through June 30, 2003.

Source: Federal Election Commission.

*Includes employees of Dean's presidential campaign, Dean for America.

John Edwards

John Edwards, the one-term senior senator from North Carolina, most likely hopes that geography is destiny. The last three Democrats to win the White House all hailed from south of the Mason-Dixon line: Lyndon Johnson of Texas in 1964, Jimmy Carter of Georgia in 1976, and Bill Clinton of Arkansas in 1992 and 1996. And Al Gore, who hailed from Tennessee, lost in the Electoral College but still managed to win the popular vote in 2000. But Edwards, who was born in South Carolina, began his career in Tennessee, and made his fame and fortune in North Carolina, must win in the crowded Democratic primaries before he can hope to test the nation's comfort with southern Democrats. While Iowa's caucuses and New Hampshire's first-in-the-nation primary hold little hope for Southerners (in 1992, Bill Clinton finished fourth in Iowa and second in New Hampshire), a big win in the next test—his native South Carolina—would bolster Edwards's chances at the nomination.

There is just one hitch. In 1961, Governor Ernest "Fritz" Hollings, a Democrat, signed a law that called for the Confederate battle flag—the Stars and Bars—to fly over the capitol complex in Columbia, South Carolina. For the past 42 years, the flag has flown, supported first by Democrats, and lately by the state's Republican establishment. Angered that South Carolina still officially honors the Confederacy, the National Association for the Advancement of Colored People (NAACP) launched an economic boycott of the state, focusing heavily on its hotels and tourism industry.

On February 6, 2003, Edwards appeared on the cable television talk show *Hardball* and spoke about the boycott. "I believe very deeply that the Confederate flag should not be flown in front of the Capitol in South Carolina," Edwards told the show's host, Chris Matthews. "I think it's an enormous mistake to fly that flag, and it ought to be taken down." Edwards went on to explain that he would be "personally honoring the boycott as a sign that the NAACP and the way they feel about this issue should be respected."

Edwards kept his word. Technically speaking.

Several weeks after Edwards's January 2, 2003, announcement that he would seek the Democratic nomination, a South Carolina supporter arranged his first fundraiser in the state. Rather than hold the event in a hotel or restaurant—businesses which are targets of the NAACP's boycott—an antebellum mansion known as the Governor William Aiken House was chosen.

William Aiken Jr., son of the founder of the South Carolina Canal & Railroad Company (later called Southern Railway), was a South Carolina governor, an ardent Confederate, and one of the largest slave owners in the South. The family holdings included more than 700 slaves who tended a dozen plantations. The Aiken fortune was estimated at more than $1 million at the time, and the family patriarch used it generously to help finance the war against the North.

Today, the Aikens's Charleston estate, once synonymous with the Confederacy, has been restored to its original, turn-of-the-century elegance by new owners, Patrick Properties Limited Liability Company, of Charleston. For a price, Patrick Properties will open the 20,000-square-foot mansion for corporate meetings and even weddings. In February 2003, it hosted an event attended by Charleston's well-heeled political donors to meet and greet Edwards.

The Aiken House, with its rich Confederate history, might seem like a peculiar site for a candidate who opposes flying the South's colors. But something stronger than symbolism drew Edwards to Aiken House. Like Edwards, one of the co-owners of Patrick Properties, Charles W. Patrick Jr., is a prominent trial lawyer. He was one of the top attorneys in the offices of Ness, Motley, Loadholt, Richardson & Poole, the South Carolina firm that represented 25 of the states that sued tobacco companies to recover Medicaid funds paid for tobacco-related diseases. The lawsuit resulted in a landmark $246 billion settlement. Cigarette makers agreed to pay that sum to states over a period of 25 years. They also made some trial lawyers very wealthy.

In John Edwards, they have one of their own in the Senate.

A COURTROOM VIRTUOSO

Johnny R. Edwards, his given name, was born June 10, 1953, in Seneca, South Carolina. His parents eventually settled in the tiny town of Robbins, North Carolina, 50 miles south of Greensboro. The town had a population of about a thousand people. His father, Wallace, worked as a supervisor in a textile plant. His mother, Bobbie, worked at the town post office and ran a small antiques store on the side.

Edwards was a gifted athlete growing up, and lettered in high school basketball, football, tennis, and track. The six-footer was the starting point guard on the basketball team and played both wide receiver and defensive back on the gridiron, winning all-star honors. The high school star's hopes of college glory ended when Clemson University chose not to offer him a football scholarship his freshman year. Edwards transferred to North Carolina State University and pursued a degree in textile sciences.

Edwards has made his childhood a part of his standard stump speech, in which he says he was the first in his family to go to college, working his way through school by taking on jobs at the mill when he was home for the summers. He majored in textile sciences in case he did not fulfill his childhood dream of getting into law school and becoming an attorney. But he graduated with honors and promptly enrolled at the University of North Carolina Law School. It was there that Edwards met his future wife, Elizabeth Anania and his future law partner, David Kirby.

After graduating, Edwards and Anania, the daughter of a Navy ROTC instructor at Chapel Hill, got married. The newlyweds moved to Nashville, Tennessee, in 1978 where Edwards joined former Republican governor Lamar Alexander's law firm, Dearborn & Ewing, which specialized in defending banks, insurance companies, and other corporations.

Edwards and his wife returned to North Carolina in 1981. She took a job as an attorney at one of Raleigh's leading bankruptcy law firms, Merriman, Nicholls & Crampton. Edwards joined a firm known for its criminal defense work, Tharrington Smith & Hargrove. He was soon asked by Wade Smith, one of the firm's founders and a former chairman of the state Democratic Party, to take on a malpractice case. Edwards turned down several settlement offers, according to *The New Yorker*, including one for $750,000 made just before the case went to the jury. Ultimately, Edwards won a damage award of $3.7 million for his client, his first million-dollar verdict, and a record in North Carolina at the time. The following year, 1985, Edwards won a $6.5 million judgment for a 6-year-old girl who'd suffered brain damage at Pitt Memorial Hospital in Greenville.

> **Edwards and Kirby focused on medical malpractice cases, a thriving area of the law: 4 of 10 Americans said they or family members had been victims of preventable medical errors.**

Edwards left Tharrington Smith in 1993 to start his own firm with Kirby, his law school buddy. Edwards and Kirby focused on medical malpractice cases, a thriving area of the law, even today. On December 12, 2002, the *New England Journal of Medicine* reported that 4 out of 10 Americans and 1 out of 3 doctors said they or their family members had been victims of preventable medical errors. In 1999, the Institute of Medicine of the National Academies in Washington, D.C., reported that 98,000 Americans die annually from medical errors in hospitals.

Guided by Edwards, the new firm won multimillion-dollar judgments against hospitals and physicians. But by far his biggest case, the one for which Edwards was most famous, involved a 5-year-old girl named Valerie Lakey, who became caught in an uncovered pool drain that severely injured her, pulling out most of her intestines. As the *Washington Monthly* reported, she survived but for the rest of her life will need daily medical treatment to keep her alive. Edwards represented the girl and her parents. In preparing for trial, he found a dozen children who had been injured by Sta-Rite drains, and made an emotional appeal to the jurors to punish a negligent corporation for harming children.

Sta-Rite made several offers to settle, the *Washington Monthly* reported, all of which Edwards refused. The jury found

Sta-Rite liable for $25 million, the largest verdict in state history. The company chose not to appeal. Edwards's reputation among his fellow attorneys was cemented: the Association of Trial Lawyers of America awarded him and Kirby its national award for public service.

Edwards went on to try no fewer than 63 major cases during the 1990s and, according to media reports, brought in more than $152 million for his clients, almost all of whom were victims of medical malpractice. He had become so admired and so feared that doctors would settle cases for millions of dollars rather than face Edwards at trial. The high-stakes victories netted him an invitation to join the Inner Circle of Advocates, the exclusive, secretive club of 100 lawyers who have won multimillion-dollar verdicts.

But even as he gained a national reputation for his courtroom prowess, Edwards' life was touched by tragedy. In 1996, his 16-year-old son Wade died in an automobile accident en route to the Edwards family beach house in coastal North Carolina. The Edwardses started a learning center that provides tutors and computers to honor their son's memory, said the *News & Observer* of Raleigh, North Carolina. Some of the nation's wealthiest trial lawyers have contributed financial support to the Wade Edwards Foundation. Among them is Jack H. Olender, the Washington, D.C., lawyer dubbed the "King of Malpractice" and "Jack the Ripper" by newspapers and magazines for his skills as a litigator. The attorney's Olender Foundation awarded Edwards its Peacemaker 2002 award and donated $30,000 to the Wade Edwards Foundation.

After her son's death, Elizabeth Edwards left her practice as a bankruptcy attorney. In 1998, at the age of 48, she gave birth to a third child. The couple's fourth child was born two years after that, when she was 50. Edwards also decided to quit practicing law and run for the U.S. Senate. His fame and personal wealth—financial disclosures put Edwards's worth at between $13.7 million and $38.6 million—allowed him to go from relative obscurity to front-runner status against Democratic primary opponent D. G. Martin, who was well established in local politics as a former lobbyist and two-time congressional candidate. The political greenhorn won the primary and won again against his Republican rival, incumbent senator Lauch Faircloth. Edwards loaned his campaign $3.2 million from personal funds.

During the political campaign, the hugely successful silver-tongued barrister in a Brooks Brothers suit was nowhere to be found. Rather, Edwards projected the image of a humble, small-town lawyer with an earnest desire to go to Washington to fight for the "regular" North Carolinians, people like the ones he grew up with deep in Piedmont country. It was a theme he returned to four years later when he began his run for the White House. "These people are entitled to a champion in the White House," Edwards said when announcing his candidacy. "Somebody who goes to work every day seeing things through their eyes, and who provides real ideas about how to make their lives better, not somebody who's thinking about insiders or looking out for insiders."

THE INFLUENCE OF THE PLAINTIFFS' BAR

Yet Edwards is a member in good standing of a group of political insiders. His deep-pocketed supporters have been drawn from the ranks of his professional brethren, America's personal injury lawyers. Edwards displayed throughout his political life the willingness to use the powerful resources, connections, and riches of his fellow trial lawyers to his advantage. His campaign against Lauch Faircloth in 1998 was financed largely through

two sources: the wealth Edwards won in the courtroom and contributions from attorneys around the country.

Trial lawyers—who represent plaintiffs in personal injury
and other civil suits—number among the most powerful interest
groups in Washington. Since 1990, the 56,000-member Association of Trial Lawyers of America, or ATLA, and its political
action committee have given more than $21.6 million in politi-
cal donations, according to the Center for Responsive Politics,
giving 89 percent or more of their contributions to Democrats.
In 2002, ATLA spent more than $3.4 million on in-house and
outside lobbyists to influence Congress and the executive
branch on issues, not surprisingly, of interest to personal injury
and plaintiffs' attorneys, and their clients. ATLA has lobbied on
the way the tax code treats damage awards from discrimination
claims, on the way the bankruptcy code treats damages awarded
to workers exposed to asbestos, and on whether businesses
attacked by terrorists will be liable for damages from those
injured or killed.

> Since 1990, the Association of Trial Lawyers of America
> and its PAC have contributed more than $21.6 million,
> giving 85 percent or more of their contributions to
> Democrats.

Their influence in Washington is proportionate to the growing importance of trial lawyers nationally. The plaintiffs' bar
has become a multibillion-dollar industry in its own right. Litigation over asbestos, the fire-resistant mineral used in construction and manufacturing that can cause lung cancer,
mesothelioma, and asbestosis when inhaled, may ultimately
result in $275 billion in damage awards to workers and their
families, according to Milliman USA, an actuarial consulting

firm. A portion of those damages—perhaps billions of dollars—will end up in the pockets of trial lawyers. In 1998, tobacco companies entered into a landmark settlement with state governments in which the cigarette makers pledged to reimburse states more than $246 billion over 25 years. Some trial lawyer firms, who teamed with state attorneys general in the case, have pocketed at least $10.7 billion in fees.

Like any other industry, trial lawyers oppose measures that will affect their bottom lines. In 1999, President Bill Clinton attempted to seize control of the $246 billion in payments from the tobacco companies to the states. Such federal intervention would have meant Washington bureaucrats rather than state-level officials would dole out legal fees—a scenario that trial lawyers, one of the Democratic Party's most faithful and largest benefactors, were loath to see. Edwards was among those who opposed the initiative; and the states kept control of settlement proceeds.

Generally, Republican lawmakers in Congress and the states, and those who have occupied the White House, have favored tort reform—which would limit the kind of multimillion-dollar verdicts that fuel the industry—and other initiatives that would make it harder for plaintiffs to sue. Democrats have been attentive to the legal community's legislative desires. President Clinton, for example, vetoed bills that supporters claimed would have protected corporations from a spate of investor lawsuits that had made trial lawyers millions of dollars but had become problematic for businesses, particularly in the high-tech industry.

Edwards vehemently opposed a Patients' Bill of Rights backed by President Bush in 2003 because, among other things, it would have limited jury awards to victims of medical malpractice. He proposed his own bill, which opens new avenues for lawyers to file state and federal claims against health maintenance organizations that deny claims and to more easily sue doctors accused of malpractice. "We need a real solution that frees doctors from crippling insurance costs without preventing the most injured victims from receiving the compensation they deserve," Edwards said after the Senate rejected the White House proposal.

Since 1997, the year Edwards began raising money for his Senate run, he has collected more than $23.5 million, including money donated to his political interest group, the New American Optimists, one of the loosely regulated organizations that fall under Internal Revenue Service rules rather than those of the Federal Election Commission. In the presidential race, Edwards has raised well over $11.9 million, with at least $6.8 million of that coming from fellow trial lawyers or their firms. Like Charles W. Patrick Jr. of Charleston, many of the lawyers who have backed John Edwards's bid for the presidency are some of the most aggressive in the country.

No single law firm contributed more money to Edwards's campaigns than the Dallas, Texas, firm Baron & Budd, PC, which has donated at least $407,000. Frederick M. Baron, the name partner of the firm, is a former president of ATLA and a past president of the Trial Lawyers for Public Justice. He was a former Democratic National Committee Trustee and one of the party's biggest soft-money donors, giving more than $1 million to DNC committees since 1998. Appropriately enough, he is also the national finance cochairman of the Edwards campaign, helping the candidate to exploit the community of wealthy attorneys.

Baron & Budd earned millions of dollars representing clients who filed suit against manufacturers who used asbestos in their products. Asbestos is a naturally occurring mineral that was widely used in the United States until 1979. The fiber is resistant to heat, making it useful as an insulator used in everything from kilns to power plants. It is also deadly—which the manufacturers knew. Some hid early evidence of the dangers of asbestos, thereby exposing countless workers to severe health risks. Thousands of American workers died gruesome deaths caused by asbestosis, which scars the lungs and leaves victims gasping for breath, or mesothelioma, a painful form of lung cancer.

Baron was among the trial lawyers who represented such workers. He discovered documents that showed how asbestos makers concealed the evidence of the health risks of those who inhaled the fiber. Lawyers around the country targeted asbestos makers by the dozens in what *The New Yorker* magazine once described as the "greatest avalanche of toxic tort litigation in history."

But critics of the lawsuits have noted that the number of defendants, originally limited to companies that manufactured products containing asbestos, has expanded to include companies only peripherally responsible for exposing workers.

While the lawsuits have won millions in damages from companies that exposed their workers to asbestos, they have had negative consequences. A 2002 study by the Rand Institute said that some 56 companies, including the largest asbestos makers in the world, like U.S.-based Owens Corning, were forced into bankruptcy. Some 52,000 workers, many of them in unions, lost their jobs when their employers were bankrupted by millions of dollars in damage claims, according to the American Insurance Association.

The flood of asbestos litigation has created a number of problems, not the least of which is that the companies responsible for paying judgments are going bankrupt in the attempt. There are roughly 600,000 plaintiffs who have filed asbestos-related claims, and perhaps as many as 27 million Americans who were exposed to the carcinogen. As more companies are forced into bankruptcy by successful lawsuits, future victims will be unable to recover damages for the injuries done to them. In a 1999 Supreme Court decision, Justice David Souter, a Republican appointee, called for congressional action to address "the elephantine mass of asbestos cases" that was swamping courts around the country. "This litigation defies customary judicial administration and calls for national legislation," Souter wrote. His words were echoed by Justice Ruth Bader Ginsburg, a Clinton appointee, in a 2002 decision.

> **Trial lawyers opposed a bill to reform asbestos litigation, arguing that plaintiffs (and, though ATLA didn't say so, their attorneys as well) were awarded far more by the court system.**

In the spring of 2003, the Senate Judiciary Committee, of which Edwards is a member, held hearings on the topic of asbestos litigation, and whether Congress should move to stem the flood of suits. Lawyers, doctors, and industry experts testified before the committee. The hearings revealed a rare split between two of the largest organizations of lawyers, the American Bar Association, which backed litigation reforms, and the Association of Trial Lawyers of America, which opposed congressional interference. The chairman of the Senate Judiciary Committee, Orrin Hatch, a Utah Republican, tried unsuccessfully to push through an industry-backed bill that would have created a $108 billion national trust fund to compensate asbestos victims and would have capped payments to individual plaintiffs at $750,000. The bill met resistance. To date, various proposed reforms have stalled; some are still pending in the House and Senate.

ATLA argued that the compensation offered by the bill was too low, and that plaintiffs (and, though ATLA didn't say so,

their attorneys as well) were awarded far more by the court system. As for Baron, the past president of ATLA and the pioneer of
asbestos litigation, he told the committee on September 25,
2002, that a legislative remedy was out of the question. "Thirty
years of actual experience in the state tort law systems, where
over 500,000 asbestos victims have sought and obtained compensation for their injuries, is conclusive evidence that there
is . . . no more effective mechanism for ensuring that victims
get compensation than the tort system."

BENDING THE RULES

ATLA argues that it "promotes justice and fairness for injured
persons, safeguards victims' rights—particularly the right to
trial by jury—and strengthens the civil justice system through
education and disclosure of information critical to public health
and safety." Yet some prominent trial lawyers, including those
who have supported Edwards, have been accused of undermining the integrity of the civil justice system that those victims
depend on.

A Texas weekly newspaper, the *Dallas Observer*, uncovered a
20-page document that Baron's firm prepared for its clients,
called "Preparing for Your Deposition." Among the advice the
document offered was "to maintain that you *never* saw any labels
on asbestos products that said 'Warning' or 'Danger'" and "You
may be asked how you are able to recall so many product names.
The best answer is to say that you recall seeing the names on the
containers or on the product itself. The more you thought about
it, the more you remembered!" Baron, who declined to be interviewed for this book, told the publication that clients were
always told, orally and in written instructions, to tell the truth.
He said the document was genuine and prepared by a paralegal

at the firm, and added, "I would never sanction any of our people using a written document like that to give to a client, because
it can be misinterpreted a million ways. . . . So, we don't use
written material when we prepare clients."

Paul Minor was made a multimillionaire by the tobacco lawsuits, which netted his firm $70 million for its role in the nego-
tiations in the states' settlement with Big Tobacco. Minor, along
with his partners, ranks high among Edwards's career patrons
with $129,000 in contributions to the senator. On July 25, 2003,
the federal government indicted Minor, a state supreme court
justice, and three others. Minor allegedly funneled hundreds of
thousands of dollars in loans and gifts to Justice Oliver Diaz Jr.
Minor and the others were accused of scheming "to defraud and
deprive the state of Mississippi and its citizens of their right" to
an honest judicial system. Minor, Diaz, and the others indicted
have all entered not guilty pleas; the case was still pending at the
time of this writing.

Some trial lawyers have preferred to bypass the civil justice
system altogether. In their most famous case, the Girardi &
Keese law firm chose that route. The name of the firm might
not ring a bell outside of legal circles, but the legal work they
did for a small California town that sued electric utility giant
Pacific Gas & Electric was made famous in the 2000 movie *Erin
Brockovich*, starring Julia Roberts. Edwards has certainly heard
of the firm; Girardi & Keese's senior partners and staffers
donated at least $362,475 to Edwards and his New American
Optimists organization.

Thomas Girardi and Robert Keese, both powerful and politically connected, joined up with Brockovich, then a down-on-
her-luck law clerk at a small firm run by lawyer Ed Masry, to
represent 650 plaintiffs from Hinkley, California, a small town
in the Mohave Desert, 120 miles northeast of Los Angeles. Back

in 1952, Pacific Gas & Electric built a pumping station near the town, as part of a natural gas transmission system that piped natural gas from the Texas Panhandle to the San Francisco Bay area. In 1987, the company discovered that chemical runoff disposed of in unlined wastewater ponds had leaked. Chromium, used to prevent rust in the transmission lines, had contaminated Hinkley's water supply. That, in part, explained the host of ailments townspeople had suffered.

Backed up by the big-time firm from Los Angeles, Brockovich helped residents win a $333 million award. Pacific Gas & Electric and the plaintiffs' lawyers agreed to private arbitration before a panel of for-hire judges, some of whom had socialized with the powerful attorneys of Girardi & Keese. After they had ruled, the arbitrators in the case, who had retired from the bench, were among 10 current and former judges treated to an extended Mediterranean cruise organized by something called the Foundation for the Enrichment of Law. Thomas Girardi and other lawyers involved in the case ran the foundation. Girardi told the *Los Angeles Times* that the cruise included a "professional program," making it permissible under California judicial rules.

INFLUENCE FOR INJURY

Law firms have played pivotal roles in Edwards's campaigns. For example, Ness Motley (which has since changed its name to Motley Rice LLC) allowed Edwards to use its corporate jet and pay just $2,532 for the privilege. Federal election law allows candidates to campaign with private jets and then reimburse their patrons for the cost of a first-class ticket instead of actual costs incurred flying the candidate around the country. Between January 1, 2000 and December 31, 2002, Edwards reported that his campaign paid up or treated as an in-kind contribution more than $14,000 for services rendered by his fellow trial lawyers, mostly catering for campaign events. Edwards also took air charter services from Charlotte-based Hendrick Motorsports, the NASCAR racing team that includes Winston Cup racers Jeff Gordon, Terry Labonte, and Jimmie Johnson. The campaign paid out $5,292 to Hendrick for "airfare."

Trial lawyers have also been his most generous contributors. Of Edwards's top 25 career patrons, 22 are law firms. (The remaining three are soft-money mogul and movie producer Stephen Bing, Goldman Sachs Group, and Wakefield Development, a real estate developer.) But in his early fundraising for his White House run, Edwards has relied heavily on his fellow lawyers. Some have been generous beyond what federal election law allows.

> **Of Edwards's top 25 career patrons, 22 are fellow members of the plaintiffs' bar.**

C. "Tab" Turner of Turner & Associates, a Little Rock, Arkansas, firm that made a name for itself suing Ford Motor Company and Bridgestone/Firestone when faulty tires on Ford's Explorer SUV caused a number of accidents, is the subject of a U.S. Department of Justice investigation into alleged campaign finance law violations. Turner & Associates donated at least $198,000 to Edwards's campaign and to his 527 committee, the New American Optimists. Turner and four legal assistants from the firm each gave Edwards's presidential campaign the maximum $2,000 contribution in early 2003. One employee told the *Washington Post* that Turner had promised to reimburse the employees for their donations. A lawyer for Turner was quoted by the Raleigh, North Carolina, *News & Observer* as saying Turner did not know it was illegal to funnel political contributions through another person, a trick that enables individual donors to exceed the $2,000 limit on contributions to candidates for federal office. As of this writing, the investigation was still ongoing.

Edwards has put the money he's received to good use. During his 1998 run for the Senate, he hired a 26-person campaign staff that included all-star Democratic strategists, among them Bob Shrum, a former Clinton advisor and media consultant; Gary Pierce, a media strategist and advisor; and Harris Hickman, a top Democratic pollster. Their handiwork was apparent from the start. The Raleigh, North Carolina, *News & Observer* described the event during which he kicked off his campaign, at a Methodist church social hall in Robbins, North Carolina, as a scene right out of a Norman Rockwell painting. "The old high school basketball coach. The parents. The family minister. The barber. And the candidate—John Edwards, the small-town boy who became a big-time lawyer in the state capital."

There to capture the moment was a camera crew that his Washington, D.C., media consultants sent to film the event. That kind of footage became a staple for Edwards. As his ambitions rose and the campaigns moved quickly from his North Carolina Senate seat to the national stage, the image of the small-town all-American boy became a recurring theme. He reminded voters of Moore County and places like it, where the folks still know him as Johnny, the son of a factory worker. "If you know where I come from, you know who I am," Edwards told the rally in his hometown that day in 1998.

But Edwards has also been willing to fund groups whose tactics are far less sentimental. Since 2000, he paid $7,500 in "Web consulting" fees to Democrats.com, a stridently anti-Republican Web site that, among other things, compares

President Bush to Adolf Hitler. The site sponsored a petition drive to have Bush removed from office by invoking the Twenty-fifth Amendment, arguing that the President was "demonstrably insane."

Edwards is no stranger to outside advocacy groups that support Democratic candidates by purchasing advertising and conducting other political work that benefits candidates, directly or indirectly. During the 1998 Senate race against Faircloth, an organization called the Alliance for Good Government was established in Raleigh. The North Carolina Academy of Trial Lawyers—of which Edwards was a one-time board of advisory member—and the North Carolina Association of Educators funded it, according to reports.

The group provides political consultants to candidates, collects voter lists, and does mailings, mainly on behalf of Democratic candidates. Molly Freeman, the director at the time and now a lobbyist for the state teachers union, said the alliance was established as a counterbalance to the conservative business interests that had launched their own issue advertising campaign, some of which demonized trial lawyers.

In 1999, the alliance trumpeted its role in the state elections. In a year-end review, the group contended that it had sent out nearly 1 million pieces of direct mail and made about 200,000 phone calls to get out voters. It also claimed to have provided political consulting services to 36 Democratic candidates and 2 Republicans in the general elections. The group targeted minority voters statewide and 25- to 45-year-old white women known to vote only in presidential elections.

Some of the most effective pieces of campaign literature used during that race were flyers that targeted women and African American voters. One featured a Black man with his mouth bound by tape. The words "Speak for yourself, or someone else will" were printed across the bottom. Similarly, the second flyer featured a woman with her mouth taped shut, and the same phrase printed beneath. "It was race-baiting, plain and simple," complained Chuck Fuller, a North Carolina political consultant who was Faircloth's campaign manager.

As a senator, Edwards has opposed tort reform efforts and provisions in various health care–related bills that would have hindered plaintiffs' ability to sue and, something he didn't mention, the ability of his supporters to share in the damages they win. He speaks regularly at local and national chapters of the Association of Trial Lawyers of America, touting his accomplishments in Congress and the courtroom.

At the ATLA convention in Montreal, Canada, in 2001, he told the assembled crowd that "for twenty years I fought for the rights and dignity of ordinary people, just like everyone in this room. I make no apologies for what I spent my life doing. I am proud of what I did: leveling the playing field."

The convention crowd buzzed with talk about the new avenues for lawsuits that a patients' bill of rights which Edwards had proposed would open, should it become law. And, from the back of the room, as John Edwards left the podium, came shouts that were sure music to his ears.

"Edwards for president! Edwards for president!"

His number one constituency had spoken.

John Edwards

Top Ten Career Patrons

Ranking	Patron	Total
1	Stephen Bing, Los Angeles	$907,000
2	Baron & Budd PC, Dallas	$407,000
3	Girardi & Keese, Los Angeles	$362,475
4	Motley Rice LLC, Mount Pleasant, South Carolina	$244,350
5	Turner & Associates, North Little Rock, Arkansas	$198,000
6	Goldman Sachs Group Inc., New York	$166,250
7	Williams & Bailey, Houston,	$165,250
8	Wilkes & McHugh PA, Tampa, Florida	$134,000
9	Law Offices of Wade Byrd, Fayetteville, North Carolina	$129,600
10	Minor & Associates PA, Biloxi, Mississippi	$129,000

This list is based on individual, corporate, and PAC contributions to the New American Optimists-Nonfederal through December 31, 2002, and on individual and PAC contributions to Edwards's 1998 senate campaign, the New American Optimists-Federal, and Edwards's 2004 presidential and senate campaigns through June 30, 2003.

Sources: Federal Election Commission, Internal Revenue Service.

Richard Gephardt

For a politician able to claim more than a quarter century in Congress, much of it spent at the forefront of his party's leadership, Representative Dick Gephardt faced an unnerving problem in the spring of 2003: how to distinguish himself from a packed field of presidential hopefuls, some of them comparative political neophytes who had thus far stolen much of the campaign-trail limelight.

So in late April of that year, as the quest for attention (and, more important, donations) turned into the inevitable make-or-break crusade, the veteran Missouri Democrat unveiled a proposal that presumably might knock the competition off stride: a $700 billion initiative—in its first three years alone—designed to both stimulate the sputtering economy and provide nearly all Americans access to health care insurance. And if the plan itself wasn't bold enough to guarantee Gephardt the sought-after media coverage, his funding scheme certainly was: he proposed to pay for at least part of his ambitious plan by scrapping the Bush administration's controversial tax cuts.

The 62-year-old Gephardt, who had first tested the presidential waters 16 years earlier, found a receptive audience that day. Speaking to a New York City gathering of union health care workers, he minced no words in his condemnation of George W. Bush's policies, most notably the president's health care record. "Forty-one million Americans have no health insurance," he told the crowd, who punctuated the half-hour speech with generous applause. "That's 41 million reasons why the George Bush economy and the George Bush indifference have got to go."

If the message was well received that day, so was the messenger. After all, few presidential hopefuls can boast a more pro-union record than Dick Gephardt. The former Democratic Party leader has been a passionate advocate of workers' rights over his 14-term House career, and his union roots run deep. His late father was a milk-truck driver and proud member of the Teamsters. He was a boyhood friend of Joe Hunt, president of the Iron Worker International Union (which has endorsed Gephardt's 2004 bid). He's a longtime friend of James P. Hoffa, president of the International Brotherhood of Teamsters. And he shares a close relationship with John Sweeney, president of the AFL-CIO.

Not surprisingly, big labor has been a reliable and generous benefactor to Gephardt's political career. For example, Center for Public Integrity analysis of campaign finance records reveals that labor unions account for 13 of his 25 largest career donors, giving more than $1.9 million. All told, Gephardt has received $2.1 million from labor unions throughout his House career.

The Teamsters union, Gephardt's third largest career donor, has given him more than $223,000. Following closely behind are the International Brotherhood of Electrical Workers, with $209,502; the United Auto Workers, with $160,725; and the Seafarers International Union, with $158,000. The Service Employees International Union, whose New York local hosted the April 2003 unveiling of Gephardt's ambitious health care proposal, is his seventeenth largest career contributor, with donations totaling more than $127,000.

What's more, unions have paid Gephardt's way on a significant number of trips, a Center analysis shows. Between 1996 and 2000, for instance, Gephardt reported taking more than 20 such excursions, with seven unions paying $29,320 to fly him (and sometimes his staff) around the country.

In return, Gephardt has toed the union line. In 1993 he supported unions' objections to the North America Free Trade Agreement and led the opposition to it in the House. In 1996 he pushed for passage of the union-backed Small Business Job Protection Act, which increased the minimum wage to its current level of $5.15 an hour. In 2001 he introduced the Displaced Workers Assistance Act, which the Teamsters openly advocated to address airline workers' dire economic conditions. And in 2003 he pressed for the creation of an international minimum wage. He also continues to push for union-supported pension reforms.

Such legislative support has earned Gephardt high approval ratings from the International Brotherhood of Teamsters, which represents more than 1.4 million workers throughout the United States and Canada. His fourth largest contributor, the International Brotherhood of Electrical Workers, gave him a lifetime approval rating of 91 percent on a recent legislative scorecard.

But as Gephardt knows, earning the Democratic nomination will require more than high marks from avowed supporters. By unveiling a bold health care initiative, he clearly sought to elevate this issue as one that would help define the campaign, and in the process help him break from the pack. "I challenge every candidate for president to offer a health care plan that covers every American, stimulates the economy and creates jobs," he

declared toward the end of his New York speech. "And I challenge them to tell us exactly how they'd pay for it."

The strategy worked: for days, the media pressed Gephardt's
Democratic opponents to detail their health care plans, thereby
letting the veteran congressman—if only briefly—dictate the
campaign agenda. And if Gephardt has his way, it's another
passage that the public will ultimately embrace—a few reflec-
tive lines near the conclusion of his speech that spoke to
the puzzling question of why it's taken the nation so long to
"reach out the hand of healing care" to millions of uninsured
Americans.

"Well, when I'm president," he declared, pausing ever so
briefly before finishing the thought, "the wait will be over."

HOME SWEET HOME

Richard Andrew Gephardt was born in St. Louis, Missouri, on
January 31, 1941, in the very neighborhood—as he is fond of
pointing out—he represents today. He earned a bachelor of science degree at Northwestern University, in Evanston, Illinois
(where he was elected student body president during his senior
year), and in 1965 he was awarded a doctorate from the University of Michigan Law School. Following graduation, Gephardt
went to work for a St. Louis law firm. At the same time, he began
a six-year stint with the Missouri National Guard, where he
served as a captain and legal professional.

Gephardt's political career began modestly enough in 1968,
when he became a Democratic Party committeeman in St. Louis,
Missouri. In 1971 he was elected to the first of two terms as a city
alderman, and in that capacity he emerged as leader of the
"Young Turks," a group of aggressive, fresh-faced reformers.
Thanks to this experience and grassroots support, in 1976

Gephardt was easily elected to fill the open seat of Missouri's Third Congressional District.

During his first term in Washington, Gephardt landed a spot on the tax bill–writing Committee on Ways and Means—a coveted assignment not ordinarily doled out to freshmen. He earned a reputation for independence, bucking his party on budgetary issues and taxes (he voted for President Ronald Reagan's 1981 tax cuts, for instance), and by 1984—in his fourth term in Congress—his climb through the party ranks earned him the chairmanship of the House Democratic Caucus.

> **Gephardt was so busy running for president that he missed 85 percent of the votes in the House of Representatives.**

Gephardt's rise in stature, coupled with his mounting opposition to Reagan's policies, nudged him toward his party's mainstream and the values of traditional New Deal Democratic constituencies. As a result, he became an advocate for issues concerning organized labor, the elderly, minorities, and the poor—an agenda that became the cornerstone of his lengthy political career. For example, Gephardt favors legislation to maintain the current Social Security program through at least the middle of this century. He has historically supported efforts to increase the minimum wage. He has curried favor with Hispanic voters by trying to revamp U.S. immigration laws.

In 1987, Gephardt became the first Democrat to declare his candidacy for the 1988 presidential primaries. Although still relatively unknown to the electorate at large, he registered a first-place showing in the Iowa caucuses. But empty campaign coffers forced him to withdraw his bid after poor showings in the crucial Super Tuesday primaries, which were concentrated in

Southern states, and finishing third in the Michigan caucuses.

Gephardt's run for the 1988 nomination may have come up short, but it nevertheless provided some valuable political upside: it increased his national name recognition and secured for him a more prominent role in the Democratic Party. So in 1989, when Speaker of the House James C. Wright Jr. resigned amid charges of ethics violations, Gephardt emerged from the ensuing shakeup as majority leader—the number two position in the House of Representatives.

In 1994, Republicans gained control of the House for the first time since the Eisenhower administration, and in the process swept Wright's successor, Thomas S. Foley, from office, leaving Gephardt as that chamber's top Democrat. He tried over the next four elections to return his party to the majority, but never succeeded.

For years, it was widely expected that Gephardt would one day make another run for the White House. During his fourteenth term in 2002, he announced that it would be his last. He further fueled speculation about his presidential aspirations after resigning as minority leader—a political thunderbolt precipitated by his party's failure to regain control of the House in those same 2002 elections. But it was not until January 2003 that Gephardt formally declared his intention to seek the Democratic presidential nomination. Among his motivations: the Bush administration, he said, was leading America "down the wrong path or not leading at all."

Since entering the crowded field, Gephardt has been an aggressive campaigner. Through the first half of 2003, for example, Missouri's native son spent at least 36 days in the early primary states of Iowa and New Hampshire. In fact, he was so busy running for president during those months that he missed 85 percent of House votes, according to *The Hill*, a newspaper that covers Congress.

When Al Gore opted out of the race, in December 2002, Gephardt's prospects seemed to immediately brighten. Thanks to his House leadership positions, his national name recognition is second only to that of Senator Joe Lieberman, Gore's running mate last time around. What's more, Gephardt's vociferous opposition to the Bush administration's tax cuts and other domestic policies make him easily distinguishable from the Republican incumbent. In particular, Gephardt's anti-free-trade policies win him unique and unqualified support from organized labor.

But it may be Gephardt's extensive network of political connections—particularly in key primary states—that proves to be his greatest advantage. As one New Hampshire activist told the *Washington Post:* "I don't think there has been an election in New Hampshire since 1985 where Dick Gephardt didn't come in to help Democratic candidates. I don't think there is anybody in the past, or who is getting into this race, who has maintained that kind of a connection."

SHAKING THE MONEY TREE

One of the first times Dick Gephardt championed the cause of campaign finance reform was in 1989, when he worked on a bipartisan task force to study the issue. In 1993 he became President Bill Clinton's point man on the matter. In 1996 he advocated for a constitutional amendment to force limits on campaign spending, and in 2000, in a series of speeches, he listed this hot-button issue as a priority for the Democrats. Most recently, he fought doggedly to muster the necessary votes for passage of the Shays-Meehan campaign finance reform bill, ultimately helping to win the support of a bipartisan majority in the House of Representatives. After the Senate passed its version, the McCain-Feingold bill, President George W. Bush signed the landmark measure into law.

But despite his leadership role in trying to stanch the seemingly limitless deluge of campaign dollars, Gephardt's actions sometimes tell an altogether different story.

Consider his leadership fund, the Effective Government Committee, and the soft money that flows to the so-called 527 organization that shares its name. According to Internal Revenue Service reports, the 527 arm of the Effective Government Committee raised almost $1.5 million during 2002. Although many of the individual donations to this stealth political action committee would have exceeded Federal Election Commission rules for hard money, Gephardt neatly exploited a loophole and transferred 40 percent of the 527 organization's aggregated funds to his federal hard-money account. Then he used the remaining 60 percent as a means to garner support from other Democrats and organizations around the country. In particular, the nonfederal committee distributed more than half a million dollars in key presidential primary states, including $271,000 in Iowa, $152,000 in South Carolina, and $102,000 in New Hampshire.

The top two contributors to the 527 version of the Effective Government Committee each gave at least twenty times more than the allowable hard-money donation limit. Fred Eychaner, president of the Illinois-based Newsweb Corporation, gave $105,000, while Weitz & Luxenberg, a Manhattan law firm that uses a barrage of advertising to solicit clients for asbestos-related claims and other personal-injury lawsuits, contributed $100,000. With the luxury of such large—albeit entirely legal—contributions, Gephardt and his supporters have had the wherewithal to distribute lavish sums to fellow Democrats.

This is not the only time that campaign contributions have conflicted with Gephardt's legislative stances. In 1996, for example, Gephardt said he favored increased government restrictions on tobacco, and to demonstrate his sincerity he canceled a $1,000-a-plate fundraiser for his Effective Government Committee that was to be held in September by cigarette maker Philip Morris.

"Mr. Gephardt didn't believe the industry was doing enough to stop children from smoking," Eric Smith, former Gephardt spokesman, told the Center years ago. "Things had built up to the point where he felt [canceling the fundraiser] was an appropriate move to make."

But while hobnobbing with Philip Morris benefactors may have been inappropriate, quietly accepting their campaign cash apparently remained perfectly acceptable. Records show that on August 27, 1996, Gephardt collected 33 checks, totaling $17,000, from employees of Philip Morris. And over the next three weeks, as the scheduled date for the ill-fated fundraiser approached, another 60 Philip Morris workers kicked in $29,500 more. But if Gephardt's actions seemed contradictory, the veteran Democrat clarified matters following the November elections: henceforth, he announced, he would no longer accept money from the tobacco industry.

On the other hand, Gephardt has never shied away from the largesse of his hometown economic powerhouse, Anheuser-Busch: more than $517,000 in donations earn the beer maker the number one spot on the list of Gephardt's career donors. And the former House majority leader has reciprocated over the years with plenty of legislative favors.

In 1993, for instance, when President Clinton floated the idea of boosting "sin taxes" on alcohol and tobacco products to fund his proposed health care initiative, Gephardt registered his opposition—at least for half the equation—on a flight aboard Air Force One. Lo and behold, at a White House press conference the following month, Clinton suggested that higher tobacco taxes would be used to help pay for his health care plan. But asked whether his funding scheme also included increased taxes on alcohol, he served up an answer that a top official of Anheuser-Busch, who was standing nearby, was no doubt relieved to hear: "I specifically passed up a chance to say that today," the former president said.

> **Gephardt has tried to lower taxes and levies on alcoholic products through congressional action at least five times.**

Although this sort of arm-twisting presumably could be chalked up to good old-fashioned constituent service, Gephardt has regularly done the bidding of the entire alcoholic beverages industry—a fact not lost on the former president and CEO of Anheuser-Busch, the world's largest beer maker. "Young August Busch III sent out a letter and said let's support him, he's good for the industry," Ralph Nelles, president of an Anheuser-Busch wholesaler, told the *St. Louis Post-Dispatch* in 1995. "Gephardt really went to bat as far as the brewing industry and Anheuser-Busch on taxes. . . . He and young August are very close friends."

Indeed, the Center for Public Integrity found that Gephardt has tried to lower taxes and levies on alcoholic products through congressional action at least five times. In 2001 he cosponsored a bill to reduce the per-barrel tax on beer from $18 to $9—the lowest level since 1990. A year later, at the behest of Anheuser-Busch lobbyists, he voted to suspend a tax on a sweetener commonly used in beer.

But he has done far more than support tax breaks. From sponsoring a bill celebrating the Great American Beer Week to helping pave the way for increased overseas commerce,

Gephardt has been a reliable advocate for both Anheuser-Busch and the industry at large.

But it's hardly been a one-way street: analysis by the Center for Responsive Politics reveals that the alcoholic beverages industry has donated at least $1.25 million to Gephardt over his legislative career, making it second only to law firms on the list of top industries supporting him. In fact, the industry easily earns the runner-up spot even without factoring in the substantial donations of Anheuser-Busch.

And they have indeed been substantial. Over the years, the company's political action committee has not only given Gephardt $34,000, but it has actively raised funds for him from the entire industry. What's more, company chairman August Busch III, whom Gephardt counts as a close friend, cohosted a $1,000-a-plate fundraiser in the summer of 2002 that brought in $1.7 million for a quartet of Gephardt campaign committees. Along with dozens of Anheuser-Busch executives, who gave more than $40,000 that day, was a contingent of beer wholesalers who chipped in another $50,000, *Roll Call* reported.

The only downside to Gephardt's affinity for Budweiser is that he sometimes loses cases of it on friendly wagers. In February 2002, for example, when the New England Patriots upset his beloved St. Louis Rams in Super Bowl XXXVI, Gephardt had to make good on a bet with Representative Marty Meehan, Democrat of Massachusetts. After collecting his case of Bud, Meehan optimistically announced that he would save it for when the House passed campaign finance reform legislation the following week. And the Shays-Meehan bill did indeed win approval on February 14 by a vote of 240 to 189. Thanks to Gephardt's leadership from the minority side of the aisle, Meehan had his celebration.

HIRED GUNS

As at least a half-dozen of Dick Gephardt's staff members can attest, Capitol Hill can be an ideal springboard for a career as a lobbyist. In 1998, for instance, former legislative aide Mike Wessel left after 20 years of service to join the lobbying firm of Downey McGrath Group, whose principals, former U.S. representatives Thomas Downey and Ray McGrath, both served with Gephardt on the House Ways and Means Committee. His former projects director, Jane Arnold, is now a partner in the St. Louis office of the international lobbying firm Bryan Cave, one of Gephardt's largest patrons over the years with donations of $323,971. And his former foreign policy advisor, Joy Drucker, is now director of government affairs at Stonebridge International, a global lobbying outfit whose chairman, Samuel R. "Sandy" Berger, served as national security advisor to President Bill Clinton. And then there's former staff director Robert P. "Bobby" Koch, lobbyist and now president and CEO of the Wine Institute, which advocates on behalf of 637 California wineries and affiliated businesses. According to figures tallied by the Center, Gephardt, a founding member of the Congressional Wine Caucus, has received $36,280 in donations from Koch's organization.

But for many members of Congress, Gephardt among them, Capitol Hill is a two-way street: in 2002 the former minority leader hired Elizabeth O'Hara to be his legislative assistant on matters dealing with defense, government reform, and taxes. Her former employer: the Democratic-leaning lobbying powerhouse of Patton Boggs, whose 200-plus clients include the Association of Trial Lawyers of America.

Lawyers and law firms, it turns out, are unmatched in their giving to Gephardt, with career contributions exceeding $4 million. (The alcoholic beverages industry, which earns the runner-up spot, has given the Missouri Democrat about $2.8 million less.) ATLA, for its part, claims the number eleven spot on the list of Gephardt's most generous career patrons, with more than $157,000 in donations. What's more, the association has spent thousands on trips by Gephardt and former chief of staff Steve Elmendorf.

> **Lawyers and law firms, it turns out, are unmatched in their giving to Gephardt, with career contributions exceeding $4 million.**

Following the 2002 elections, when Gephardt stepped down as minority leader, Elmendorf swapped government service for two other positions: senior advisor to his boss's presidential campaign and lobbyist for that generous trial lawyers association. Not surprisingly, ATLA's support for Gephardt did not wane. In July 2002, for example, the association recruited Gephardt to give the opening speech at its annual convention, in Atlanta, where he was given a standing ovation. In press materials, the association referred to Gephardt as "a true ATLA hero" and "a great friend of the trial bar."

That friendship is evidenced by some of Gephardt's actions in the House. During the 103rd Congress, for example, Gephardt introduced a health care plan seen as such a boon for plaintiffs' attorneys that the insurance industry dubbed it "the Trial Lawyers Protection Act of 1994." In 1999 he hewed to ATLA's position and opposed a bill that would have sent most class action lawsuits from state courts to federal courts. The following year he sponsored a bill designed to allow victims of automobile accidents to forgo arbitration—which usually favored insurance companies—and instead pursue litigation.

And then there was September 2001, when ATLA lobbyists in search of a favor sought out Gephardt and a like-minded group of his legislative colleagues. With the public reeling from the attacks on the Pentagon and World Trade Center, legislation was hurriedly crafted to both bail out the crumbling airline industry and limit lawsuits stemming from the infamous suicide missions. In a bid for national unity, ATLA urged—for the first time in its history—a moratorium on civil lawsuits that might arise out of the tragedy, and it publicly demanded that any post–September 11 bailout package also include compensation for victims' families. But the association also urged sympathetic lawmakers to ensure that any such bill be enacted without a draft provision capping attorneys' fees on behalf of victims at just 25 percent of court-ordered damages—well below the industry standard. With Gephardt in charge on the minority side of the aisle, the final bill included no such language.

FUNDRAISING FOLLIES

Deft as he may be at raising money and navigating legislative waters, Gephardt has at times crossed ethical boundaries in his quest to advance his career. One notable misstep began to unfold in mid-August 1987, when officials of Gephardt's first presidential campaign met with officials from Federal City National Bank, in Washington, D.C., to negotiate a $125,000 "bridge loan" to finance the campaign's first direct-mail fundraising piece.

According to Federal Election Commission documents reviewed by the Center, two bank officials, including its senior vice president for lending, were joined that day by Boyd Lewis, finance director of the Gephardt for President Committee, and Charles Curry, president of the firm hired to prepare the fundraising solicitations.

On August 28, the bank cut a check for $125,000 on little more than the promise that another bank was about to issue the fledgling campaign a $400,000 line of credit.

While corporate contributions to political campaigns are illegal, loans are another story: candidates may borrow against future fundraising, provided such loans are made in the regular course of business. One caveat, though: candidates are supposed to meet the same standards that a businessperson or home owner would have to meet.

But Gephardt had an advantage over a cash-strapped entrepreneur: Terrence McAuliffe, the chairman of Federal City National Bank, also served as the finance chairman of Gephardt's presidential campaign. McAuliffe, who was elected chairman of the Democratic National Committee in February 2001, was also a member of the bank committee that reviewed Gephardt's loan application. But bank officials later told the Federal Election Commission that McAuliffe had abstained from voting on the matter.

When the $400,000 line of credit from the other bank wasn't forthcoming, Federal City stepped in, rolling into this new loan more than $90,000 still owed by Gephardt's committee on the original $125,000 loan.

These dealings earned Gephardt FEC scrutiny—one of at least four commission investigations into possible wrongdoing since the late-1980s.

Three of those investigations involved relatively insignificant matters. First came a complaint from a fringe candidate that televised debates during the 1988 Democratic primaries illegally excluded him in favor of Gephardt, Michael Dukakis, and other mainstream Democratic hopefuls. Second came questions about whether Gephardt properly filed the 48-hour notices required for large contributions in the days immediately preceding the

1990 election. Finally, there was a question whether Gephardt's leadership PAC, the Effective Government Committee, improperly hosted a fundraiser for Patrick Kennedy—who today serves as a Democratic representative from Rhode island—prior to his formal candidacy.

In the end, the first case was dismissed, the second was settled for a $1,750 civil penalty, and the Kennedy matter was dropped as a matter of prosecutorial discretion.

But Gephardt's 1988 bid for his party's presidential nod was another story. Hundreds of pages of FEC documents reviewed by the Center show apparent misconduct that included questionable contributions disguised as "settlements" of committee debts, misuse of federal matching funds, shady bank loans, and a campaign staff that routinely stonewalled and subverted document requests from federal investigators. The investigation into the 1988 election remained ongoing until May 1995, when Gephardt's campaign admitted extensive violations of the law. He eventually settled the outstanding charges, and FEC lawyers dismissed other allegations that had been brought by commission accountants.

> FEC documents show questionable contributions
> to Gephardt's 1988 presidential campaign
> disguised as "settlements" of committee debts,
> as well as the misuse of federal matching
> funds and shady bank loans.

Among those accused of aiding Gephardt with his campaign finance shenanigans was McAuliffe, who by then had become one of President Bill Clinton's closest confidantes and most accomplished financial patrons. After the questionable loan from Federal City National Bank, which appeared to have violated both campaign laws and federal banking rules, FEC auditors and investigators singled out several other banking transactions as possibly being improper.

As part of the 1995 settlement agreement, Gephardt's campaign paid a fine of $80,000 and refunded $70,000 worth of excessive contributions. In return, the FEC dropped its investigation into Federal City and a variety of questionable banking transactions.

The commission also decided to forgo separate punishment for excessive spending in Iowa from Gephardt's publicly subsidized campaign account. Because Gephardt received federal matching funds, which ultimately provided a considerable portion of the money used for his presidential bid, he was legally barred from spending more than $775,000 on his Iowa effort. The campaign had argued that since success in Iowa was important to Gephardt's national chances, a large proportion of its spending there—everything from staff salaries to withholding taxes—should be considered a "national" campaign expense, and therefore not subject to the federal limits for candidates accepting public financing.

But the FEC rejected this tortured logic, and the Gephardt campaign eventually conceded it had spent $457,000 more than legally allowed.

On top of that, the FEC investigated a dubious scheme whereby money owed to other political committees and politically connected lawyers was paid off with "debt settlements" of 10 cents on the dollar. This arrangement effectively allowed additional contributions to the cash-strapped campaign from Gephardt's top supporters, who had already given the maximum allowed under federal law.

In early 2003, with his 14-term congressional career starting to wind down, Gephardt again focused on Iowa: in February alone, his presidential campaign committee listed expenditures there totaling more than $77,000, including a single payment of $65,000 to the Iowa Democratic Party.

In fact, Gephardt has been a continual presence in the Hawkeye State since 1988, when he won the all-important caucuses in his failed bid for president. And he's clearly again made Iowa a focus of his strategy, as his spending in such key early-primary states as New Hampshire and South Carolina has been anemic by comparison.

But given the results of his early-round fundraising efforts, he may not have enough money to spend. Over the second quarter of 2003, Gephardt's campaign reported taking in $3.8 million, well short of its announced goal of $5 million. While Gephardt and his campaign advisors dismissed the shortfall as insignificant, Democratic opponents happily fueled media speculation that the retiring House stalwart, who had once been cast as a likely front-runner, should now be regarded as a certain also-ran.

The day that his second-quarter report was filed, the Associated Press reported that Gephardt met with Gerald McEntee, president of the American Federation of State, County and Municipal Employees, and other presumed supporters in hopes of convincing them to stick with his candidacy. A week later, a *Washington Post* story included a few ominous lines: "At least one labor president voiced the belief that Gephardt's fundraising problems could make some unions reluctant to endorse him, according to a Democratic source. If that happens," the *Post* continued, "Gephardt's rivals will redouble their efforts to win those endorsements and to stop Gephardt from winning the Iowa caucuses next January, where he is favored."

If his lagging fundraising has dampened the enthusiasm of his longtime union supporters, they can not have been reassured

by an August 14, 2003, item in the *Washington Post*. August Busch
III, chairman of Anheuser-Busch, Gephardt's top patron, sent
out a letter, also signed by the company's president, Patrick T.
Stokes, urging friends to donate $2,000 to the candidate who
would benefit "the business community as well as the entire
country." The *Post* reported that they hoped to raise $100,000—
but not for Gephardt.

"We appreciate the opportunity to conduct our business in a
positive governmental environment," Busch and Stokes wrote,
which would be accomplished by "electing George W. Bush to a
second term."

Richard Gephardt

Top Ten Career Patrons

Ranking	Patron	Total
1	Anheuser-Busch Inc., St. Louis, Missouri	$517,750
2	Bryan Cave LLP, St. Louis, Missouri	$323,971
3	International Brotherhood of Teamsters, Washington, D.C.	$223,967
4	International Brotherhood of Electrical Workers, Washington, D.C.	$209,502
5	American Hospital Association, Washington, D.C.	$200,324*
6	Boeing Company, Chicago	$188,375†
7	SBC Communications Inc., San Antonio, Texas	$185,500
8	Monsanto Company, St. Louis, Missouri	$160,825
9	United Auto Workers, Detroit	$160,725
10	Seafarers International Union, Camp Springs, Maryland	$158,000

This list is based on individual, corporate, and PAC contributions to the Effective Government Committee-Nonfederal through November, 2002, and on individual and PAC contributions to Gephardt's congressional campaigns from 1977 to 2002, Gephardt's 1988 presidential campaign, the Effective Government Committee, and Gephardt's 2004 presidential campaign through June 30, 2003.

Sources: Federal Election Commission, Internal Revenue Service.

*Includes employees of the AHA and its state affiliates.

†Includes employees of Boeing and the companies it has acquired including McDonnell Douglas Corporation.

Bob Graham

Bob Graham was worried. The information that the Florida senator had seen while serving on the Senate Select Committee on Intelligence had convinced him that terrorists in hidden sanctuaries are primed to attack Americans, repeating or perhaps surpassing the horrors visited on September 11, 2001. The only hope, he said, would be to use whatever force necessary to eradicate terrorist organizations—wherever they might be.

So on October 10, 2002, a day he predicted that Americans would soon regret, Graham made his intentions clear. He voted against the resolution to use force in Iraq.

"The president should be in the most advantageous position to protect Americans—to launch pre-emptive strikes and hack off the heads of these snakes," he said on the Senate floor. "With the resolution before us, we are denying the president that opportunity."

Graham had unsuccessfully submitted an amendment that would have given President Bush the authority to use whatever force necessary on countries harboring five specified terrorist groups, the Abu Nidal Organization, Hamas, Hizballah, Palestine

Islamic Jihad, and the Palestine Liberation Front. Some of those groups, according to the U.S. State Department, drew support from Iran, Lebanon, Sudan, and Syria, as well as Saddam Hussein's Iraq.

"The resolution I had hoped we would pass would contain what the president has asked for relative to the use of force against Saddam Hussein's regime in Iraq and more," Graham said on the floor of the Senate. "It also should provide the president all necessary authorities to use force against the international terrorist groups that will probably strike the United States as the regime of Saddam Hussein crumbles."

But because he voted against authorizing the use of force in Iraq, Graham has painted himself as an opponent of the war, even though his failed amendment would have authorized it—along with conflicts in other countries.

In the wake of the September 11, 2001, terrorist attacks on New York and Washington, Graham, who served as Senate Intelligence Committee chair for two years, saw his profile rise. A man who was well known for his peculiar habit of meticulously recording even the lackluster minutes of his days was suddenly among those at the center of the question gripping the nation: How did this happen, and how should the United States respond? In more than three decades as a politician, Graham had earned respect in his home state, but this was his first dose of major national attention.

In the months since, Graham has been a critic of the president's policies in the war on terror. He has demanded additional funding for the protection of U.S. ports and infrastructure, and he criticized Attorney General John Ashcroft for exercising the powers granted him by the USA Patriot Act, the controversial legislation passed in the wake of September 11 to expand the Justice Department's powers to fight terrorism.

Graham, incidentally, was one of the main authors of the act he criticized.

That's typical of Graham. Over the years, he's cultivated a reputation as a friend of the environment and a fighter for the interests of the common person. But Graham's image is at odds with his background as a millionaire developer and his career as a long-serving, skillful politician who has taken money from a host of special interests.

DEVELOPING IN FLORIDA

Sugar brought the Graham family to southern Florida. In 1921, before Graham was born, Pennsylvania Sugar Corporation recruited Graham's father, Ernest "Cap" Graham, to run a new sugar cane operation—built by draining and otherwise demolishing the Florida Everglades.

Ten years later the sugar operation failed, and Ernest Graham acquired 7,000 acres in northwest Dade County as severance pay. He used the land to start a dairy farm, a venture that would eventually make millions for his family. He also entered state politics.

D. Robert Graham was born November 9, 1936, in Coral Gables, less than a week after his father was elected to the state senate. He grew up on his father's dairy farm, which by that time had expanded to include beef cattle. He attended high school in Miami, where he was elected student body president. In 1944, he won the title of Dade County's "Best All-Around Boy." He then left home to attend the University of Florida. After graduating Phi Beta Kappa in 1959, Graham went on to follow in his older brother Phillip's footsteps and earn his law degree from Harvard University.

By the time Graham left for law school, big-time developers were offering to buy the land owned by the Graham family, which had by that time started the Graham Companies. Development had crept to the edge of their property, which was now in a prime location. But instead of selling out, the family decided to create a planned community—Miami Lakes. When Graham returned from law school, he took an active role in its development. The Graham Companies, run by Graham's brothers and their children, would continue to operate the family's real estate and agriculture venture empires.

Miami Lakes, which opened in 1962, has now reached a population of 23,000 and is Graham's Florida residence. Though many of the pastures were converted into shopping malls and apartment complexes, there are still two dozen cows grazing in a vacant area across from Miami Lakes' Main Street—the Grahams pay lower taxes because they are using some of the land for grazing.

Though they transformed most of their farmland into a bustling suburb, the Graham family continues to make millions in the dairy business. The Graham Companies runs a dairy farm in Highlands County that produces more than 13,000 gallons of milk a day. The family also profits from growing and selling sugar.

Graham, who has been a Florida politician for much of his life, first entered the government as a state representative in 1966, serving two terms before moving on to the state senate in 1970. In 1978 after completing his second term in the Florida Senate, Graham ran for governor. To warm his image, Graham started his workdays series, in which he worked in a variety of jobs such as a police officer and a construction worker. He even hit the street with $15 in his pocket and spent two days as a "homeless" person in the Tampa area.

"These nonworkdays, if you will, were extremely rough," he wrote.

When he decided to run for governor, he said he stopped participating in the Graham Companies' business decisions. He continued to attend meetings but had no vote in operations. He told the *St. Petersburg Times* he didn't "want any questions either about conflicts of economic interest or conflicts of loyalty and time commitment."

> Graham strongly supported the death penalty.
> During his watch as Florida governor, the state sent 16
> people to the electric chair—more than under
> any other governor at the time.

Helped by $500,000 of his own money, mostly from the Graham Companies' agriculture and real estate profits, Graham won 56 percent of the electorate and was elected governor. Voters reelected him in 1982 with 65 percent of the vote. As governor, Graham stressed education and the environment. Although he failed to fulfill promises to vastly increase teachers' salaries, standardized test scores for Florida's schoolchildren increased during his tenure. Also as governor, he doubled the size of Florida's budget.

In 1983, Graham initiated the Save Our Everglades program, which was designed to restore the Everglades and protect Florida's wetlands and endangered species. He also brought environmentally endangered lands into public ownership, including vulnerable lands surrounding rivers, beaches, and barrier islands.

Graham strongly supported the death penalty. During his watch, the state sent 16 people to the electric chair—more than under any other governor at the time—and he signed at least 153 death warrants. One of the first he signed was for convicted murderer Willie Jasper Darden—a man whose guilt Amnesty

International and the Northwestern University Center on Wrongful Convictions came to question. A federal judge ended up granting Darden a stay, and he lived on death row through another six death warrants before the state executed him. "I don't believe any justice is served by procrastination or timidity," Graham said of his legal philosophy. By the time he left the governor's mansion, the prison system was overcrowded; his successor, Bob Martinez, freed thousands of inmates before building new penitentiaries.

In 1986, after serving his second and final term as Florida's governor, Graham decided to run for the U.S. Senate. He faced Senator Paula Hawkins. President Ronald Reagan supported Hawkins, a first-term legislator, in an attempt to keep Republican control of the Senate. In the most costly Senate race in Florida history to that time (they spent more than $12.6 million) Graham won with 55 percent of the vote. He was reelected in 1992 and 1998. To this day, he has never lost an election.

On Capitol Hill, Graham became known for his personal eccentricities. Along with his polyester neckties speckled with little pictures of Florida—he owns about four dozen—Graham keeps meticulous notes on all of his activities. He records these in a succession of red, yellow, blue, and green notebooks, each color pertaining to a different season. Not a journal in the traditional sense, these notepads contain records of everything he does during a day—even the time spent writing notes. Graham has also continued his "workdays" program and has now completed over a year's worth. For his 365th day, he helped to check in customers and handle baggage for US Airways.

Graham also founded and currently chairs the Senate New Democrat Coalition, a group of probusiness Democrats most visibly represented by former president Bill Clinton.

SUGAR'S SWEETHEART

The Florida Everglades is a unique ecosystem blending tropical and temperate flora and fauna, boasting wood storks and great blue herons. It is the only place in the world where crocodiles and alligators live side by side. And over the last century, it has taken a beating. Development has reduced the unique natural treasure to half of its original size and drained and polluted its water. Dozens of plants and animals are now near extinction.

"The east is moving west. The west is moving east," Mel Martinez, President George Bush's housing secretary and a Floridian, told the *Washington Post* in June 2002. "Unless you can contain all that, forget the Everglades."

Developers have not been the only threat to the Everglades. The sugar industry is also partially to blame. There are currently 450,000 acres of sugar fields blocking the natural flow of water through the Everglades. The sugar industry uses phosphorous to fertilize its crops even though the Everglades are phosphorous-intolerant. The phosphorous pollution has destroyed and altered parts of the fragile ecosystem.

Yet in May 2003, when a controversial bill landed on the desk of Governor Jeb Bush that would push back plans to clean phosphorous pollution until 2016, Graham did not join environmentalists in opposing the measure.

That might have been because at the time Graham was in a mad dash to obtain the money he would need for his late-start campaign, which he had joined several months later than his competitors due to double-bypass heart surgery on January 31, 2003. The former governor had to balance his image as an environmentalist with his loyalty to his top career patron—Florida Crystals, a West Palm Beach–based agribusiness that runs three sugar mills and farms 180,000 acres of cane.

Graham has taken in more than $92,000 from the company. Florida Crystals made a $50,000 contribution to the Bob Graham Leadership Forum, which was organized under Section 527 of the Internal Revenue Code and can legally take contributions in any amount directly from individuals, corporations, or labor unions. Several members of the Fanjul family, which owns Florida Crystals, made $2,000 personal contributions to Graham's campaign. Pepé Fanjul, one of the brothers who runs Florida Crystals, is a longtime friend to Graham. Fanjul is also a longtime Republican. He was vice chairman of the finance committee of the 1988 campaign of George Herbert Walker Bush, a member of the Republican Team 100 soft-money donors—those who kicked in $100,000 or more—and a guest at the Bush White House in 1990. He was a large contributor to Bob Dole's 1996 presidential campaign and contributed to the campaign of George W. Bush in 2000.

> In addition to accepting tens of thousands of dollars in contributions from the sugar industry, Graham's family business sells the sugar it grows to the U.S. Sugar Corporation.

In the Senate, Graham is a member of the Committee on Environment and Public Works and sits on its Subcommittee on Fisheries, Wildlife and Water. He is in a position to influence the fate of the Everglades. It's an odd place for a son of the sugar industry to be. In addition to accepting tens of thousands of dollars in contributions from the sugar industry, Graham's family business sells the sugar it grows to the U.S. Sugar Corporation.

In 2003, Florida's sugar industry, spearheaded in part by the Florida Sugar Cane League, a political action committee, pushed the bill to delay pollution clean up through the Florida legislature. Democratic presidential rivals John Kerry and Howard Dean had already demanded that Jeb Bush veto the bill. But Graham waited until it was already signed and then faxed a letter to Bush.

Graham denounced Jeb Bush's environmental policy and accused both him and the president of "malfeasance" because they catered to big business. He called the bill Jeb Bush had signed a "grave injustice." In a June 2003 op-ed in the *Boston Globe*, Graham criticized Bush's environmental policies, questioning the administration's commitment to "real environmental protection."

"The silence of the EPA and the Department of the Interior is not the only threat to the Everglades," he wrote. "The comprehensive lack of action by all federal agencies on a variety of pending issues that affect the Everglades is more problematic."

In response, Governor Bush said Graham's interest came too late, if it was actually sincere to begin with. "With all due respect to the senior senator, I got a faxed letter from him 30 minutes after I signed the bill, urging me to veto the bill," Governor Bush said. "And he says, 'I look forward to talking to you about this and I'm going to call your office,' and he didn't call."

Graham's reluctance to join the environmentalists on this issue was by no means exceptional. In fact, he has a history of siding with the sugar industry. In 1995, he voted against ending the price support program for sugar, a quota on imports that guarantees growers a higher price for their crop than the prevailing world market will bear. Opponents of the bill argue that the program leads to higher food prices and doesn't help small farmers—just a few large producers. When the Clinton administration suggested taxing Florida sugar to clean up the Everglades, Graham opposed it. He suggested instead that sugar growers be required to pay fees to participate in the price support program. Graham explained that he was looking for a compromise, where the sugar industry and environmentalists could coexist.

POWERING THE SUNSHINE STATE

Part of the rationale for Graham's candidacy is the notion that Florida decided the last presidential election, and that he can win Florida. His base of support in the state is strong, particularly when it comes to money. The Bob Graham Leadership Forum, his 527 committee, took in more than $218,000 in 2002, about half of that from contributors in Florida. And more than 90 percent of the Forum's reported expenditures went to beneficiaries inside the state.

Miami-based Greenberg Traurig, one of the country's biggest law firms, is Graham's second largest contributor. The firm and its employees have given Graham $88,766. Graham is connected to the firm on several levels. Not only does the firm represent the Graham Companies, but Graham has also hired people who have ties to Greenberg Traurig for his campaign.

In June 2003, Graham tapped Marvin Rosen, a Miami lawyer, to be his national finance chairman. Rosen, a former partner at Greenberg Traurig, worked on the presidential campaigns of Bob Kerrey, Gary Hart, Ted Kennedy, and Bill Clinton. He is perhaps best known for his part in planning the Clinton administration's White House coffees and sleepovers, in which large soft-money donors were granted access to top administration officials, including Clinton himself, to discuss their interests before the federal government.

As he did as governor, Graham has battled for the interests of his Florida constituents. In June 2003, Graham attempted to amend the Energy Policy Act to block the secretary of the interior from conducting an inventory and analysis of gas and oil resources off the U.S. coasts. Proponents of the amendment said the inventory was just a step toward exploration, then drilling. Many Floridians fear that offshore drilling would harm the state's tourist industry, dependent in part on miles of sandy beaches that can be visited year-round.

Though Graham says he opposes oil and natural gas offshore drilling in Florida, his wife owns stock in a petroleum company that does just that, according to Graham's financial disclosure forms. In December 2002, Adele Graham, who has an investment portfolio worth millions of dollars, bought between $15,001 and $50,000 in petroleum stock in a holding company that owns majority interest in Royal Dutch/Shell Group, which drills for both oil and natural gas. About a year before, Shell Offshore, a subsidiary of the company, was the top bidder for permits to drill on a stretch of ocean floor in the Gulf of Mexico, not far from the Florida coast.

Graham's financial disclosure forms also show that he owns between $62,000 and $232,000 of stock in energy and utility companies. He has bought and sold stocks or bonds in Exxon, Florida utilities, and Halliburton, the oil field services company that Vice President Richard Cheney headed from 1995 until he was tapped to be George Bush's running mate.

Graham's eighth largest patron in contributions is Florida Power & Light, which generates 25 percent of its power from nuclear fuel. Since 1998, Graham has cosponsored three bills in which Florida Power & Light expressed an interest. He has supported legislation that would benefit Florida Power & Light at the expense of the environment while also taking in $64,605 from the company.

In 2002, Graham voted to extend the Price-Anderson Act, originally passed in the 1950s, which caps the liability for a potential nuclear accident from utilities like Florida Power & Light and their insurers. In May 2001, Cheney told *The Economist* that without Price-Anderson, "nobody's going to invest in nuclear power plants." Graham also voted to create a repository for the nation's nuclear waste at Yucca Mountain in Nevada. Both bills helped Florida Power & Light, which was running out of space to dump its nuclear waste in Florida.

> **Graham's support of Florida Power & Light is longstanding. In 1990, he sponsored an amendment to the Clean Air Act that permitted the utility to emit more pollutants than the original act allowed.**

Graham's support of the company is longstanding. In 1990, he sponsored an amendment to the Clean Air Act that permitted Florida Power & Light to emit more pollutants than the original act allowed. The bill passed, but not without criticism from environmental groups. In response, Graham praised Florida Power & Light, saying the company had cleaned up its power plants years ago and should not be punished just because other companies had not.

SOFT MONEY AND WEAK PROMISES

The savings-and-loan debacle of the 1980s and early 1990s affected nearly every state in the union, as high-flying thrift institutions proved anything but thrifty. Various S&L executives had solicited the aid of members of Congress to avoid federal regulators. Charles Keating, who ran Lincoln Savings and Loan into the ground, became emblematic of the political elements of the scandal; a group of congressmen that included Senator John McCain and was later dubbed the Keating Five, took tens of thousands in campaign contributions and ran interference with banking authorities in exchange.

In Florida, 39 savings and loans with deposits of nearly $15 billion collapsed in the course of the scandal. One of the biggest was CenTrust Savings and Loan, an institution whose failure cost taxpayers $1 billion. Its chairman, David Paul, was a politically connected wheeler-dealer who was ultimately convicted of improperly investing his depositors' money in junk bonds and using the bank's money to finance his luxurious lifestyle.

As governor of Florida, Graham met several times with the CenTrust chairman, and in 1987 Graham's special counsel— who had also done work for CenTrust—arranged a private meeting between a CenTrust lobbyist and federal regulators and urged them to go easy on CenTrust.

Also while he was in the U.S. Senate, Graham signed a letter complaining that regulators were being too aggressive in their investigation of the Florida savings and loans. One regulator later said that David Paul, during one discussion, "threw Graham's name at me maybe eight to 10 times" in an attempt to show he had supporters in Congress. In response to questions about his relationship with Paul, Graham said the meetings were "limited" and "appropriate."

Graham's ties to the bank and savings-and-loan industry continue to pose problems, even after the CenTrust scandal. He sits on the Senate Finance Committee while at the same time accepting tens of thousands of dollars from the banking industry.

On March 6, 1991, Graham announced to the press and public that he would stop taking money from PACs representing federally insured banks, savings and loans, and credit unions in order to avoid a conflict of interest. He said he would continue, however, to take money from individual bankers. Federal Election Commission records show that at least 42 executives from Florida's Barnett Bank each gave $250 or more to Graham at a fundraiser in Jacksonville in 1991.

Graham's pledge to forgo contributions from banking PACs came at a time when the Senate Banking Committee was considering legislation to overhaul the nation's banking system. He told the *Orlando Sentinel* that he did not want to "create some inappropriate perception if we're accepting and soliciting contributions from the PACs of those institutions." For good measure, he refunded nearly $60,000 dollars he had already taken in from those bank-related PACs for his 1992 reelection bid.

But the pledge lasted about two weeks. On March 20, 1991, while he was refunding donations from NationsBank, Bank of America, and others, he accepted $1,000 from SunTrust bank. Then on March 28, he accepted $2,000 from the America's Community Bankers' PAC. On April 14, he accepted $1,000 from the Consumer Bankers Association.

When asked why Graham continued to take money from bank PACs after promising not to, staffer Jay Howser told the Center for Public Integrity that Graham intended to honor the pledge during the 1992 reelection cycle because Graham didn't want "even a hint of impropriety during his campaign and during his work in the Senate."

While the pace of bank PAC donations diminished somewhat until 1997, Graham has since returned to full swing. Even with the six-year hiatus, Bank of America and Citigroup, who contributed heavily to Graham's campaigns in earlier years, remain among his biggest career patrons.

Since 1998, Graham has sponsored two bills and cosponsored three in which Bank of America expressed an interest. On

February 4, 1999, Graham introduced a bill aimed at "relief" for Central American and Caribbean countries hit by Hurricane Georges and Hurricane Mitch in 1998. The bill would have lowered tariffs charged on products from the blighted counties, and encouraged them to join the proposed Free Trade Area of the Americas or strike other NAFTA-like trade deals with the United States.

Called the United States–Caribbean Basin Trade Enhancement Act and Central American and Caribbean Relief Act, the bill also provided humanitarian and agricultural aid for the countries hardest hit by the hurricanes. But that wasn't all. The act would have encouraged the federal Overseas Private Investment Corporation, which gives loans and insurance to U.S. firms investing abroad, to support the activities of its customers in Central America. Bank of America, which lobbied on the bill, is among OPIC's customers.

Bank of America and its employees have given Graham more than $72,000.

As for Citigroup, the world's second-largest financial services firm, its leading credit card issuer, and the first U.S. bank with more than $1 trillion in assets, Graham has sponsored 5 bills and cosponsored 12 others on which the firm has lobbied. Citigroup and its employees have given Graham $70,500 since 1985.

THE IRAQI CONNECTION

Graham has made much of the intelligence failures that led to September 11 and criticized Bush and his administration for its reliance on intelligence reports suggesting Saddam Hussein attempted to purchase uranium from Africa. "President Bush should come clean with the truth," he said of the uranium claim. "Unfortunately, he continues to display an arrogant pattern of hiding information from the American people and ducking questions that need to be answered."

That's advice Graham may want to consider taking himself. During his 1986 race for the Senate, Graham sold his Miami Lakes residence for $575,000, about the going rate for the market at the time. The buyer, who purchased it through an intermediary, turned out to be Carlos Cardoen, a Chilean national in the arms-trading business. Cardoen and his business associates, including Anthony Mijares, Abbey Kaplan, and Augusto Giangrandi, organized a fundraiser for Graham that raised about $29,000, according to Graham's campaign. Cardoen attended the fundraiser; he was invited by Bob Graham.

In 1992, *Roll Call*, the respected Washington, D.C., publication that covers Congress, reported that on November 21, 1986, Graham invited Cardoen to a dinner, asking him to attend "the first event for a select group of supporters who have in large measure made our success possible." The letter went on to say that the supporters would "act as my core group of key advisors on critical issues we face in the United States Senate."

> Graham has sponsored five bills and cosponsored
> 12 others on which Citigroup has lobbied; the financial
> services giant has given Graham
> $70,500 since 1985.

Graham's opponents for his Senate seat and the Republican Party of Florida tried to make an election issue of the contributions. The state GOP went so far as to file a complaint against Graham with the Federal Election Commission, charging Graham with soliciting illegal donations from Cardoen. Foreign nationals are prohibited from donating to political candidates, and the Republicans argued that Cardoen's support was illegal. The FEC ruled that there had been no violation; Cardoen had not written a check.

Cardoen's name was in the news for more than just campaign contributions. In May 1993, the government indicted him for illegally selling arms to Iraq. Cardoen, who fled the country and is believed to be in Chile, allegedly sold cluster bombs to Iraq during the Iran-Iraq war and allegedly continued to deal in arms with the Iraqi regime as late as 1990. The Bureau of Industry and Security, a government agency that ensures U.S. industry complies with arms control laws, has a picture on its Web site showing Cardoen shaking hands with Saddam Hussein.

Graham told the *St. Petersburg Times* that he had dropped Cardoen from his core group of supporters in April 1992, when he first learned of the allegations against him. "If there are people who are known to have relationships that are suspect, we do not accept their contributions," said Graham. "But that was not the case with Mr. Cardoen in 1985 and 1986."

But Cardoen's role as an arms dealer was widely known by 1984, when NBC News aired a story showing he had sold U.S. weapons to Iraq. Cardoen's business dealings with that country continued over the years, and on June 4, 1990, *U.S. News & World Report* published an article saying that Cardoen's companies were suspected of shipping oscilloscopes used to test nuclear detonators to Iraq.

Apparently, Graham's continuing association with Cardoen was just an intelligence failure.

Note: Graham formally announced his decision to bow out of the race on October 6, 2003.

Bob Graham

Top Ten Career Patrons

Ranking	Patron	Total
1	Florida Crystals Corporation, West Palm Beach, Florida	$92,000
2	Greenberg Traurig LLP, Miami	$88,766
3	Walt Disney Company, Burbank, California	$80,150
4	Holland & Knight LLP, Lakeland, Florida	$77,578
5	Bank of America, New York	$72,148*
6	Citigroup Inc., New York	$70,500†
7	Vivendi Universal, Paris, France	$68,000‡
8	Florida Power & Light, Juno Beach, Florida	$64,605
9	Steel Hector & Davis, Miami	$59,650
10	Searcy Denney Scarola Barnhart & Shipley, West Palm Beach, Florida	$59,500

This list is based on individual, corporate, and PAC contributions to the Bob Graham Leadership Forum through December 31, 2002, and on individual and PAC contributions to Graham's Senate campaigns from 1985 to 2002 and contributions to his 2004 presidential campaign through June 30, 2003.

Sources: Federal Election Commission, Internal Revenue Service.

*Includes contributions from employees of companies acquired by Bank of America including NationsBank and Barnett Banks.

†Includes contributions from Citigroup and employees of Citigroup and the companies that have contributed to the creation of Citigroup, including: Citibank; Citicorp; Travelers Corporation; the Copeland Companies; Salomon Smith Barney (and its predecessors, Salomon Brothers and Smith Barney); and Shearson Lehman Hutton (and its predecessors, including Shearson, Hayden & Stone and EF Hutton). From 1981 to 1993, Shearson was owned by American Express. Contributions from individuals who identified themselves as Shearson employees during this time period are also included in the Citigroup figure. Contributions from individuals who identified themselves as American Express employees are not.

‡Includes employees of the companies that make up Vivendi including: Universal Music Group, Vivendi Universal Entertainment (formerly Universal Entertainment), and Vivendi Universal Games. Contributions are from U.S. employees.

John Kerry

John Kerry has made campaign finance reform an issue ever since he first ran for the Senate in 1984. The Massachusetts Democrat is probably the most outspoken critic of political action committees in Congress. Decrying the influence of PACs on the nation's political system, Kerry refused to accept donations from the organizations during all four of his senatorial campaigns. In his very first year in the Senate, Kerry sponsored a bill for the public financing of campaigns by eliminating the tax credit for political donations. Since then, he has cosponsored at least a dozen bills to check the flow of money into American politics. He was a staunch supporter of the reform measures pushed by colleagues John McCain and Russ Feingold and passed into law in early 2002.

"Everyone knows what the money chase and the money game in Washington is all about," he said in a June 1996 debate in the Senate over campaign finance reform. "We would all be better off if we were to reduce that." That was a theme Kerry repeated often on the floor of the Senate. In March 2001, for example, he warned his colleagues that taking money from special interests created the perception that Congress was for sale. "When somebody sitting on a particular committee has to go out and raise money from people who have business before that committee, or when someone in the Senate has to ask for money from people who have legislative interests in front of them on which they will vote, there is almost an automatic cloud," he said.

Kerry should know. Over the course of his Senate career, he has not been averse to taking campaign cash from companies and firms with a direct interest in his work. Federal Election Commission records reveal that their money has been as much a part of his campaign as it has been of anyone in U.S. Congress. Since 1995, he raised more than $30 million for his various campaigns, most of it from industries such as finance and telecommunications companies—which are overseen by the Senate committees he serves on—and the law and lobby firms that represent them.

Currently, Kerry serves on the Commerce, Science and Transportation Committee, the Finance Committee, and the Foreign Relations Committee. He is the ranking member on the Small Business and Entrepreneurship Committee. Kerry's committees oversee communications, aviation, highways, consumer products, railways, buses, interstate commerce, taxes, federally financed health care, international trade, the Social Security system, and small businesses.

FEC records show that "people who have business" before Kerry's committees, or "people who have legislative interests in front of them" have pumped millions of dollars into his campaigns over the years. Overall, he has raised roughly $5 million from lawyers and lobbyists, nearly $3 million from financial interests, and more than $1 million from the telecom sector. Of the senator's top 15 contributors, five are law firms that represent clients from the telecom, financial, and health care sectors. They include law firms Mintz, Levin, Cohn, Ferris, Glovsky and

Popeo, the number one donor to Kerry; Hale and Dorr; Foley Hoag; and Nixon Peabody. All of these law firms have at least one client whose business is affected by the decisions made by committees on which Kerry sits. Among Kerry's top career patrons is Skadden, Arps, Slate, Meagher & Flom—the largest law firm in the country, which has lobbied for the likes of media conglomerates News Corp. and AOL Time Warner, transportation firms US Airways and Union Pacific, manufacturers Milliken & Company and Bethlehem Steel, and ad hoc groups fighting for corporate tax loopholes and cuts such as the NOL Coalition (NOLs, or net operating losses, are a generous corporate tax break) and the Ax the Double Tax Coalition. Apart from taking money from law firms, Kerry has also relied on industries themselves for campaign money. Five of the top 20 Kerry donors are from the financial sector, while 4 of the top 25 are from the telecommunications industry. The second largest donor to Kerry is the FleetBoston Financial Corporation, the largest financial institution in New England.

For someone who has claimed the political high ground on the issue, Kerry has been spattered by the mud of some of the best-known campaign finance scandals of recent years. David Paul, a Florida banker Kerry handpicked as the head of an elite Democratic fundraising club during his tenure as chairman of the Democratic Senatorial Campaign Committee in the late 1980s, was indicted and convicted in the savings-and-loan scandal. More recently, Kerry took money from the Taiwanese American businessman Johnny Chung, who was later convicted of making illegal campaign donations. During his 1990 and 1996 reelection bids, opponents pummeled Kerry for such "ethical lapses."

While Kerry has called for campaign finance reform, in practice he's been a prolific fundraiser and spender. In his unsuccessful 1972 bid for a congressional seat, the Democrat's first foray in electoral politics, he spent more than $279,000. The amount, approximately $1.2 million in today's dollars, was a whopping sum for a House race at the time. It was, in fact, the most expensive campaign of the year. As an incumbent senator, Kerry has raised more than $34 million for his three reelection efforts. His 1996 race against Weld, in which the two spent approximately $16 million, was one of the most expensive senatorial campaigns in Massachusetts history. In 2002, when the only challenger on the ballot was Libertarian Michael Cloud, who raised less than $185,000, Kerry raised more than $15 million and spent more than $10 million.

> **While Kerry has called for campaign finance reform, in practice he's been a prolific fundraiser and spender.**

And the deep-pocketed interests that have funded his campaigns have had plenty of business before the Senate, and John Kerry.

WELL BRED AND WELL FUNDED

Kerry's patrician upbringing has invited comparison with fellow Yale graduate and the man he seeks to replace at the White House. "On paper . . . Kerry's background doesn't seem all that different from that of George W. Bush," *Rolling Stone* magazine proclaimed in a profile. "Like Bush, Kerry is a son of the Eastern establishment, with deep roots in the exclusive institutions that have traditionally produced those who wield power in America." While Bush was schooled at the prestigious Phillips Academy (Andover), Kerry had his primary and high school education from Swiss boarding schools and the elite St. Paul's School near

Concord, New Hampshire. Though he lacked the president's political pedigree—the Bush family has so far produced a U.S. senator, two presidents, and two governors (including George W.
Bush)—Kerry also hails from the New England aristocracy and
had a childhood of privilege.

The second of four children of Rosemary and Richard Kerry,
John Forbes Kerry was born at the Fitzsimmons Military Hospital in Denver, Colorado, on December 11, 1943. His father, then
a pilot in the Army Air Corps, was undergoing treatment for
tuberculosis at the hospital. His maternal grandfather was James
Grant Forbes, who supplied Kerry's middle name: the Forbes
family's ships once carried tea and other goods from Asia.
Kerry's father, the son of a Jewish convert to Catholicism, also
belonged to an affluent family.

Richard Kerry became a diplomat after the war—he wanted
to be "part of the process of building peace in Europe," his son
told an interviewer decades later—which would take the family
to the Old World. The father's postings in various European
capitals gave the son an opportunity to experience Europe.
Years later, Kerry would recall his childhood with fondness. "I
had some great childhood experiences in those years—I
remember walking the beaches of Normandy with my father
just a couple years after Americans had stormed the beaches
there to liberate Europe. I remember playing as a kid in blown-
out bunkers in Berlin—and my family really gave me a great
sense of history."

Once back in the United States, Kerry entered St. Paul's for
the eighth grade. At the school, he was involved in sports and
the literary and drama clubs. Kerry also honed his public speaking skills, which would help him in his future career. In his first
political speech in the fall of 1960, he urged his classmates to
vote for John F. Kennedy.

Kerry enrolled in Yale University in 1962. His social activities at New Haven included membership in the Skull & Bones Society, the secretive, invitation-only club of upper-class students. Bush entered Yale two years after Kerry enrolled there and also joined Skull & Bones. While Bush famously distanced himself from campus political activities, Kerry demonstrated a keen interest in them. Kerry even became the president of the Yale Political Union, the oldest campus political forum in the country and hub of school politics. When he graduated in 1966, the country was already at war in Southeast Asia. Like many from his generation, Kerry had some reservations about Vietnam; nevertheless, he donned the uniform and headed to the war front.

In a sense, Kerry's political career began soon after he returned from Vietnam in 1970. The young lieutenant, who commanded a swift boat, had received a Silver Star, a Bronze Star with Combat V, and three Purple Hearts for service in combat. But the battles of the Mekong River delta transformed Kerry's doubts about the morality of war into intense opposition. He threw himself to the forefront of the budding antiwar movement by cofounding the Vietnam Veterans of America. "Because of all that I saw in Vietnam, the treatment of civilians, the ravaging of their countryside, the needless, useless deaths, the deception and duplicity of our policy, I changed," Kerry wrote in a book he authored with some other disgruntled veterans. Soon after his return from the war, the 28-year-old ran for Congress in the Massachusetts Third District, but he did not survive the caucus of party activists. Nevertheless, Kerry succeeded in making his antiwar voice heard on Capitol Hill. His high-profile testimony before the Senate Foreign Relations Committee on April 22, 1971, created political ripples in Washington. Speaking on behalf of the Vietnam Veterans Against the War, a nationwide movement that would play a huge role in mobilizing public opinion against the war, he termed the war "barbaric" and accused the Nixon administration of lying. In a sentence that would become a slogan for the antiwar protesters, he said: "How do you ask a man to be the last man to die in Vietnam? How do you ask a man to be the last man to die for a mistake?"

The next year, Kerry made another unsuccessful attempt to enter Congress. His switch to the Fifth District, Lowell, where his parents had a home, provoked charges of carpetbagging. But this time, an incident involving Kerry's younger brother may have also contributed to his electoral defeat. Days before the election, Cameron Kerry and another campaign aide were arrested inside the building that housed a primary opponent's campaign office, as well as Kerry's. The two claimed that they were trying to prevent Kerry's phone line from being cut; the charges were dropped a year later. Kerry did win the primary, but he lost the general election by nearly 9 percentage points.

The false starts meant a decade-long political hibernation, during which Kerry earned a law degree from the Boston College Law School and joined the Massachusetts bar. From 1976 to 1979, he was a senior prosecutor of Middlesex County, Massachusetts. He also had a brief stint as a commentator with a Boston television station. Kerry and wife Julia Thorne, whom he married shortly after returning from Vietnam in 1970, had two daughters, Alex and Vanessa, during this period. Their marriage did not last, however; the two separated in 1982 and divorced six years later.

Kerry could not be kept away from electoral politics forever. In 1982, Michael Dukakis was trying to recapture Beacon Hill after losing it to another Democrat four years earlier. Kerry defeated Evelyn Murphy, a former state environmental secretary who would later become a lieutenant governor, to take the number two spot on the ticket. The Dukakis-Kerry team won easily. In 1984, when a cancer-stricken Senator Paul Tsongas announced his decision to retire, Kerry entered the race. In the primary, he faced a formidable opponent, James Shannon, who had completed three terms in the House of Representatives. Kerry portrayed himself as a Washington outsider and defeated Shannon in a bitterly fought primary. In the November race, he defeated millionaire businessman Raymond Shamie, despite the coattails of President Ronald Reagan, who was reelected that year in a 49-state landslide.

Since then, Kerry has been reelected three times. In 1990, he warded off a challenge from businessman James Rappaport in a race marked by negative campaigning from both sides. Kerry won with 57 percent of the vote. In 1996, he faced a more serious opponent in Weld, a popular governor who had won his reelection the previous year with more than 70 percent of the vote. Nevertheless, Kerry defeated Weld by 52 percent to 45 percent in what was termed by many as the best-run race of the year. His third reelection campaign, in 2002, was the easiest one for Kerry because a Republican opponent who announced his candidacy failed to gather the required 10,000 signatures necessary to be on the ballot. It was the first time in eight decades that a senator from the state did not have major-party opposition. Kerry whipped Libertarian Michael Cloud by securing more than 80 percent of the vote.

On the Same Frequency

In the Senate, Kerry has taken an interest in issues such as health care, education, the environment, foreign relations, small businesses, and affordable housing, to name a few. He has spearheaded a couple of landmark investigations. His probes into the genesis of a fraudulent international bank and narcoterrorism were praised for their thoroughness. In the 1980s, his Subcommittee on Terrorism, Narcotics, and International Operations established the link between drug traffickers and international crime that ultimately led to the capture of former Panama dictator Manuel Noriega. During one hearing he found that the Bank of Credit and Commerce International facilitated "Noriega's criminal activity." Later, he teamed up with Senator Hank Brown, a Republican from Colorado, to probe BCCI, also known as the "Bank of Crooks and Criminals International." They found that the bank had systematically bribed political leaders worldwide. A few years later, Kerry investigated an emotionally charged topic: the Vietnam prisoners of war issue. For decades, it was believed that American POWs were alive and in Vietnamese custody. The issue was one of the impediments to normalizing relations with the former archenemy. Kerry and other fellow veterans of the war, including John McCain, conducted an investigation and concluded that the POWs weren't alive.

> As critics point out, in spite of his expertise
> in so many issues, Kerry hasn't authored
> any signature legislation.

During his years in the Senate, Kerry stood with the Democratic Party on social, labor, and women's issues most of the time. On abortion, he has said that support for women's right to choose would be a requirement for any Supreme Court judge under his presidency. His voting record is quite similar to his senior colleague, Senator Kennedy, on most social issues. However, Kerry, unlike many of his party colleagues, is a gun owner and hunter and is critical of the party's position on the issue. "I think sometimes the perception is that every time there's an issue, Democrats blame it on guns rather than on human behavior," Kerry told CNN in August 2001.

Kerry has also at times adopted probusiness positions. He has, for example, introduced legislative measures such as tax breaks that would benefit real estate, insurance, banking, and other financial groups. In the mid-1990s, he supported welfare reform, which provoked allegations of flip-flopping from his opponent in the 1996 Senate race, then governor Bill Weld. As critics point out, in spite of his expertise in so many issues, the senator hasn't authored any signature legislation. He has, however, frequently sponsored legislation that aided those who paid for his expensive campaigns.

Though Kerry warned his colleagues about the "automatic cloud" that accompanies campaign donations from interests that have businesses before their committees, the senator has not only taken money from such interests, but he has even advanced their agendas in some cases. As the Center for Public Integrity reported in May 2003, Kerry has, in recent years, pushed the legislative priorities of the wireless telecommunications industry on several occasions. He sponsored or cosponsored a number of bills favorable to the industry and wrote letters to government agencies on its behalf. Cellular Telecom and Internet Association, the industry's lobbying arm, is represented by the Boston-based Mintz, Levin, Cohn, Ferris, Glovsky and Popeo, which, in addition to being Kerry's largest donor, also employs his brother Cameron. David Leiter, who was the senator's chief of staff for six years, is a vice president at the Washington office of ML Strategies, a Mintz Levin affiliate that provides consulting and lobbying services.

Mintz Levin is one of the nation's top law firms representing telecommunications issues. According to American Lawyer Media's LegalMarketInfo.com, it was ranked seventy-first among U.S. law firms in 2002, generating gross revenue of $229 million. One of its partners, Charles D. Ferris, was the chairman of the

Federal Communications Commission during the Carter years. During his tenure, Ferris took measures that reduced regulation of the cable, satellite, telephone, and radio industries.

Besides CTIA, the firm also lobbies on behalf of AT&T Wireless Services, a leading mobile phone service provider. CTIA has more than 320 members including carriers, manufacturers, and wireless Internet providers. Both AT&T Wireless and CTIA have been Mintz Levin clients since 1998. Another client is the now-bankrupt XO Communications.

Kerry sits on the Commerce Subcommittee on Communications, which oversees the FCC, the telecommunications industry and spectrum allocation. Cameron Kerry is in the litigation section of Mintz Levin; he is not a registered lobbyist, but he does represent clients before the FCC. Among his practice areas listed by the firm are "the Federal Communications Act and other laws; rate regulation proceedings; franchising and renewal proceedings; FCC rulemakings and licensing; regulatory aspects of mergers and acquisitions; counseling regarding regulatory and legal developments; and state common carrier proceedings."

In recent years, Kerry's positions on telecom issues closely followed CTIA's legislative agenda. Since 1999, he sponsored at least two bills and cosponsored six more on issues that were lobbied by CTIA. He also pushed amendments and issued statements on the floor that were favorable to the wireless industry. The issue where the positions of Kerry and the industry were almost identical was the auctioning of the spectrum, the range of electromagnetic radio frequencies used in the transmission of voice, data, and video. The spectrum, sometimes called the airwaves, is owned by the public; the government, through the Federal Communications Commission, auctions off portions of it to private companies. The FCC, which regulates broadcast and communications companies, started auctioning spectrum licenses in 1994. The wireless industry has been lobbying for years to have access to sufficient quantity of spectrum, which is considered critical to its future. The commission has conducted more than forty auctions, selling more than 50,000 licenses and raising tens of billions for the Treasury.

When the FCC scheduled an auction of the upper and lower 700 MHz bands on June 19, 2002, CTIA wanted to delay the sale indefinitely. Currently, television broadcasters are using the 700 MHz band; they are not expected to relinquish it until 2006, when they complete their switch to digital signals. As of May 1, 2002, less than a quarter of the television channels had begun the process; wireless companies were not eager to shell out billions for an asset they would not be able to use for another four years, at the earliest, especially given the financial stress within the industry. The high-tech bubble, which saw stock prices of such firms go through the roof, had long since burst, leaving wireless companies in a cash crunch.

"The Commission is asking bidders to swing blindly at a spectrum piñata, not knowing the contents," CTIA president and CEO Thomas E. Wheeler wrote FCC commissioner Michael Powell in a letter dated April 3, 2002. "While a June auction might be called an 'auction,' in reality it would be the U.S. government opening a casino and collecting the ante for a much bigger private auction to enrich broadcasters at the expense of rational spectrum policy and the welfare of American taxpayers." Wheeler cited the Bush administration's suggestion, in the 2003 White House budget proposal, to shift the auctions to 2004 and 2006. Consumers Union, a public interest group, and the New America Foundation, a think tank, opposed the auction, arguing that money raised would go, in part, to compensate broadcasters. The FCC argued that the money was an incentive to encourage station owners to make the digital switch sooner.

Kerry and Senator John Ensign, a Republican from Nevada, swung into action on CTIA's behalf after the FCC claimed it did not have the authority to delay the auctions. The senators wrote a letter to Powell on May 2, 2002, requesting a delay and introduced a bill to that effect on the same day. "To proceed with the auction at this time would be a terrible example of budget politics taking precedence over sound spectrum management," Kerry said at the time. "I hope that the Congress will act soon to enact this bill and protect the interests of consumers of wireless services and the American taxpayer." The Senate passed a compromise bill in June and the FCC delayed the auction in the upper 700 MHz category (777–792 MHz bands) until January 14, 2003. (In July 2002, the commission postponed the auction indefinitely.) Auctions of the lower 700 bands went ahead as scheduled. "We are extremely grateful to Senators Ensign and Kerry for defending the precious national resource of spectrum, serving American consumers, public safety and our global competitiveness," Wheeler said when the Senate bill was introduced. "Actions on both the House and Senate sides were bold and promising steps in the right direction."

Kerry has acted on behalf of the industry on other occasions:

- In August 2002, Kerry introduced a bill—some 58 of his colleagues cosponsored it—to return money to firms that bought spectrum licenses that once belonged to NextWave. The FCC reauctioned NextWave's licenses after the mobile wireless data network operator, which filed for Chapter 11 bankruptcy reorganization in 1999, failed to make payments. A court ruling had given the licenses back to NextWave, leaving the winning bidders unable to use the spectrum and still owing billions to the FCC. The legislative move forced the FCC to grant relief to the companies.

- In July 2001, six senators, including Kerry, wrote a letter urging the Bush administration to allocate in a speedy manner some of the spectrum used by the federal government for a "third-generation" wireless system, which would allow users to send voice and data at high speed. This has been a CTIA priority in Washington in recent years.
- A year earlier, Kerry introduced a bill, along with Senators Ernest Hollings (D-S.C.), Daniel Inouye (D-Hawaii), Jay Rockefeller (D-W.Va.), and Byron Dorgan (D-N.Dak.), to prevent firms that have more than 25 percent foreign government—ownership from buying U.S. telecommunications companies. CTIA had lobbied on that bill as well.

Kerry's office maintained that his actions were "based on what is sound policy and what is best for the people he represents." Including, apparently, the Boston-based firm of Mintz Levin.

> **Kerry appears to have a number of friends at CTIA. Member companies of the trade group and their employees have contributed at least $152,000 to Kerry.**

Cameron Kerry, a lawyer, joined Mintz Levin in 1983, shortly after successfully managing his elder brother's campaign for lieutenant governor of Massachusetts. Records obtained by the Center show that the firm's attorneys first opened the check book for Kerry six months later. The firm's two principals, Richard G. Mintz and R. Robert Popeo, each contributed $500 at the time. Since then, Mintz Levin employees have been the biggest financial backer of the Massachusetts Democrat's political career, bankrolling various Kerry races, including the current presidential campaign, to the tune of $222,546. Kerry has received at least $101,000 from Mintz Levin since 2000 alone.

Kerry's office defended the Mintz Levin contributions, saying that they reflected nothing but personal and political ties he had to several of the firm's employees. "Senator Kerry has friends and family who work at Mintz Levin, ranging from his brother to former classmates who work in this Boston-based firm. In addition to having been elected to the Senate four times, John Kerry has been lieutenant governor and run for Congress in Massachusetts, so a lot of these folks go way back with him. It should come as no surprise that they would be supportive of his campaign for president and any effort to make anything more of it is sorely misguided."

Leiter, Kerry's former chief of staff who now works for a Mintz Levin subsidiary, echoed those comments. "These are the people who went to school with him," he told the Center. "C'mon, this is Massachusetts. They are all Democrats." Cameron Kerry, while admitting that his presence at the firm was a factor in its contributions, offered the same explanation: "Apart from my being here and having been involved in his campaigns over the years, he's got a number of other friends here."

Kerry appears to have a number of friends at CTIA as well. Member companies of the trade group and their employees have contributed at least $321,000 to Kerry. The amount includes contributions made to his presidential campaign and his previous election efforts, his political action committees and the 527 group that Kerry formed. Verizon employees donated more than a quarter of that amount ($73,570).

Kerry's work for the industry, at least for those companies from his own state, was recognized when the Massachusetts

Telecommunications Council, which represents 300 companies, chose him as the Policy Maker of the Year in 2002.

Mintz Levin is not the only law and lobby firm whose clients represent interests that have business before Kerry's committees. Hale and Dorr, the senator's fourth largest career patron having contributed more than $123,258 to various Kerry campaigns, represents several telecommunications and biotechnology clients. Foley Hoag, Kerry's thirteenth largest contributor, lobbies on behalf of at least 10 different biotech, health, or pharmaceutical firms that are overseen by the Finance Subcommittee on Healthcare. Skadden, Arps, which gave more than $73,000 to him in 2003, has more than 100 clients in the Fortune 250 industrial and service corporations. Kerry's third largest donor is the media giant AOL Time Warner, which has given him more than $134,960 in contributions. (Skadden, Arps lobbies on behalf of the media giant.) In the past two years, AOL paid the firm $200,000 in lobbying fees.

Cable behemoth Comcast gave Kerry more than $54,000, while another telecom powerhouse, AT&T, donated $21,300. In all, various media organizations, including Walt Disney Corporation (which owns ABC), Viacom (which owns CBS) and News Corporation (which owns Fox), have contributed more than $300,000 to Kerry.

Those companies all have a vested interest in the rules the FCC makes that limit the number of broadcast outlets any single company can own. On June 2, 2003, the day the FCC weakened those rules in a move that would allow media conglomerates like Disney, Viacom, and News Corporation to grow even larger, Kerry said of the commissioners, "With today's vote, they shirked [their] responsibility and have dismissed any serious discussion about the impact of media consolidation on our own democracy."

Yet when the sweeping rewrite of the rules governing the

FCC, the Telecommunications Act of 1996—which demanded that the FCC revisit and modify ownership rules every two years—was before Congress, Kerry voted for it.

Trading In Favors

If Kerry wins the Democratic nomination, he will be anointed the party's standard bearer at the 2004 Democratic National Convention on his home turf. Kerry, senior colleague Senator Kennedy, and Mayor Thomas M. Menino had lobbied the DNC for months to bring the convention to Boston. But the efforts of these politicians would not have borne fruit without the financial muscle provided by some of the region's businesses. According to DNC chairman Terry McAuliffe, the city's bid included a financial package of more than "$20 million in cash from private sources, the first time a city ever put money on the table before being awarded the convention."

Many of the private interests that have pledged to bankroll the convention are longtime Kerry patrons. John Hancock, whose employees have given more than $53,000 to Kerry over the years, has committed $2 million for the political gala. State Street Bank & Trust, Raytheon, and Fidelity Investments, three Boston-area firms that are among the senator's top 30 patrons, will spend $1 million each. Another Kerry donor, Liberty Mutual Group, has pledged $1 million.

Kerry has done favors for many of the donors. For example, he wrote a letter, dated April 26, 2001, to the Office of U.S. Trade Representative, the executive branch agency that negotiates international trade agreements, seeking the office's assistance for Liberty Mutual in China. At the time, U.S.-China relations were at a low point. Kerry sent the letter about a week and a half after the Chinese government released the illegally detained crew of an American EP-3E surveillance plane that a Chinese jet fighter had intercepted in international airspace and forced to crash-land on the island of Hainan.

Liberty Mutual had applied for a non–life insurance license to do business in the lucrative Chinese market. With consolidated revenue of nearly $15 billion, the firm is one of the largest workers' compensation insurers in the country. "Liberty Mutual is headquartered in Massachusetts and I know its chairman, Ted Kelly, and many of its employees very well," Kerry wrote in the letter. Kelly and many Liberty employees have contributed more than $38,000 to the senator's election campaigns.

> **Though he cautioned against the consolidation of "banking power," Kerry supported the merger of contributors Fleet Financial Corporation and BankBoston in 1999.**

The Kerry donor that may get the most attention for its role in the convention is FleetBoston Financial Corporation, New England's largest and the nation's seventh largest financial institution. The company's executives and employees have contributed more than $172,000 to various Kerry campaigns, making them his second largest donor. And should Kerry win the nomination, the convention will have an added significance to both the senator and Fleet: the Democratic delegates will nominate their candidate at an arena named after the financial giant, the FleetCenter, home to the NBA's Celtics and the NHL's Boston Bruins. "It doesn't hurt our feelings that we are going to see 'Fleet' all across the television," Chad Gifford, the bank's president, told WCVB-TV in Boston. Fleet has also pledged at least $1.25 million for the political festival.

Fleet's help to Kerry wasn't limited to campaign donations.

In the mid-1980s, the bank gave the senator a $473,000 mortgage loan to buy a Washington town house which was valued at $175,000. Kerry used the remaining amount for paying off campaign loans and personal debts. The loan was arranged by developer and Kerry fundraiser Wesley Finch.

FleetBoston was formed when the Fleet Financial Corporation merged with BankBoston in 1999. Menino, the Boston mayor, opposed the merger, saying that he was concerned the city might face "a reduction in home mortgage loans, and a reduction in community development loans and small business loans." In his prepared testimony July 7, 1999, before the Federal Reserve, he said, "I am concerned that the new bank will not act as if its life depended on the health of our neighborhoods."

Though he cautioned against the consolidation of "banking power," Kerry supported the merger. "In an economy where the rules of engagement have changed affecting financial institutions competing for market share in New England, the Fleet-BankBoston marriage is an important step toward fending off the challenges of outsiders and keeping our home-grown industry strong," he wrote in a commentary that appeared in the *Boston Globe.*

The merger was ultimately approved, but not without conditions. Because the new company owned two-thirds of the bank branches in New England, the two banks were forced to sell about 300 branches in Massachusetts, Connecticut, and Rhode Island. Following the merger, the new bank announced it would lay off approximately 2,500 workers. The Sovereign Bancorp of Pennsylvania, which bought the bulk of the branches Fleet sold, laid off about another 500 employees, about 6 percent of the workforce in those branches.

Fleet was just one of the financial institutions that financed Kerry's political career. His membership on the Senate Finance

Committee, which oversees various aspects of the banking, accounting, and securities industries, has brought him large amounts of campaign donations from employees of other large financial institutions as well, especially those from Massachusetts and Wall Street. (Such interests generally give heavily to panel members from both parties.) Among Kerry's top contributors from the world of high finance are Citigroup Inc., whose employees have given the senator more than $89,000, Goldman Sachs ($100,000), and Fidelity Investments ($52,725).

RELYING ON THE KINDNESS OF INSIDERS

A few weeks before his 1996 reelection, the senator raised $10,000 from a group of businessmen in Los Angeles whom he met with privately. The group included Johnny Chung, a Taiwanese-American who was later found to have made illegal contributions to the Democratic Party to the tune of more than $350,000. In return, he gained access to the White House on 49 occasions. Chung, who famously remarked that the White House was like a subway turnstile—you just put money in to get inside access—instructed his employees and friends to make campaign contributions for which he reimbursed them. Chung later pleaded guilty to charges of violating federal election law, including funneling $8,000 into Kerry's campaign. Kerry returned the money.

In a similar, but much less publicized incident, a San Diego—based defense contractor was charged in July 2002 of making illegal contributions to Kerry and four other lawmakers. Parthasarathi "Bob" Majumder and the company he headed, Science and Applied Technology, were charged with forty counts of conspiracy, illegal campaign contributions, witness tampering, fraud, and tax evasion, according to the *San Diego Union-Tribune*.

Kerry received about $13,000 from the employees of the company. The case against Majumder and Science and Applied Technology Inc. was still pending in September of 2003. Majumder, like Chung, allegedly asked friends and employees to make contributions. "Majumder would reimburse straw donors who were unwilling to utilize their own funds to make campaign contributions by providing them with cash payments and writing checks drawn on his personal checking account," according to the indictment. The donations, it was alleged, were made to obtain more federal contracts. The company received more than $150 million from the federal government to develop missile technology.

In 1996, in the middle of his second reelection battle, the senator was attacked for his ties to another businessman who had run afoul of the law. One of the banks that collapsed amidst the widespread failures of savings and loans in the late 1980s was Miami-based CenTrust Savings, the largest S&L in the Southeast. David Paul, its high-flying chairman, was indicted after the bank went bust in 1990 under the burden of his mismanagement and financial improprieties. Among the charges leveled against Paul were improper investment of his depositors' money in junk bonds, and using the bank's money to finance his luxurious lifestyle. In 1994 he was convicted of 97 counts of banking fraud and sentenced to 11 years' imprisonment. The banker was ordered to pay restitution of $65 million and a fine of $5 million. The federal government seized the bank in 1990; its failure cost taxpayers approximately $2 billion.

Paul gave more than $300,000 to various local and national candidates, according to the *Wall Street Journal*. As chairman of the Democratic Senatorial Campaign Committee in the 1987–1988 election cycle, Kerry appointed the CenTrust chief as head of the Democratic Trust, a fundraising group affiliated with the DSCC. The bank's executives and its political action committee contributed more than $30,000 to the DSCC, for which Paul was recognized at the 1988 Democratic National Convention held in Atlanta. Later that year Kerry attended a party at Paul's palatial mansion on Biscayne Bay Island near Miami. Cooking for Paul's 60 guests on that day were six of the top chefs of France. The food and entertainment, which included a 10-piece orchestra, cost CenTrust $129,000, a column in the *Journal* reported. Also, the senator reported using Paul's jet three times. (Senator Bob Graham of Florida, another candidate for the 2004 Democratic nomination, also flew on the banker's plane.)

In the 1992 campaign, Kerry's Republican opponent, Jim Rappaport, accused the senator of shielding Paul in the initial days of the controversy and demanded an inquiry to determine whether the senator had any connections with the banker. Kerry denied the charges. "John Kerry never accepted a nickel from David Paul, and the one time David Paul and [the bank he headed] asked for help from Congress, John Kerry voted against that request," his spokesperson told the *Boston Herald*.

Similar allegations of questionable conduct in incidents involving donors and friends dogged Kerry during his next reelection bid as well. In the middle of his tough battle with Weld, the *Boston Globe* reported that the senator had received lodging assistance from three friends—two real estate developers and one lobbyist—in the late 1980s. Kerry lived for periods totaling a year in two Boston condominiums provided for him by developers Wesley E. Finch and Edward W. Callan. Kerry did pay rent for the condominium, but only for the nights he spent there. By his own account, the senator used Callan's condominium for eight or nine months. The senator paid the developer a total of $2,000, considerably less than the market price, according to the *Globe*, which determined from real estate listings that "furnished one-bedroom apartments in the Back Bay rented for $750 to $1,200 a month." By contrast, Kerry paid no more than $250 a month. That wasn't the only time Kerry relied on the kindness of insiders for his lodgings. In 1989, during a three-month period, the senator stayed at times, for free, in a Washington apartment leased by Democratic fundraiser Robert A. Farmer, who was a lobbyist with the Washington-based Cassidy & Associates.

Kerry said he did not do anything unethical. Farmer was a close friend and the lobbyist did not try to influence him in any way during the period, the senator maintained. Friend, he was; but also a fundraiser for Kerry, as well as the presidential campaigns of Michael Dukakis and Bill Clinton. He currently serves as treasurer of Kerry's presidential campaign. Employees of his former firm, Cassidy & Associates, have given Kerry more than $33,000 so far. Finch was the treasurer for the senator's campaign committee twice, in 1984 and 1986. The developer and his wife have contributed more than $15,000 to various Kerry campaigns.

> **Allegations of questionable conduct in incidents involving donors and friends dogged Kerry during his reelection bids in 1990 and 1996.**

The *Globe* found no evidence of any quid pro quo, but said Kerry "had taken steps in the 1980s to effectively conceal the information." It wrote: "In several interviews, Kerry insisted that he had no obligation to report the value of the subsidies as gifts on his Senate disclosure forms, which require members to list gifts valued at $250 or more. And the senator said he did not violate a Senate rule that bars any gift of more than $100 from anyone with a 'direct interest' in legislation." It added that Finch had "substantial real estate holdings that are affected by congressional action."

ACUMEN FOR MAKING APPOINTMENTS

Before a single vote is cast in a primary, candidates for a party's presidential nomination compete in two other contests: first, to lure the high-priced political consultants, media managers, and resourceful fundraisers, and second, to raise enough money to pay for them. Kerry scored an important early victory in January 2003, when he enlisted Luis Navarro as the political director of his campaign. Navarro's last job was as political director of the Service Employees International Union, one of the largest unions in the AFL-CIO. Initially, it did not seem like a politically significant move, but the timing of the union operative's entry aided Kerry, since it came just before a February AFL-CIO meeting in Florida. AFL-CIO endorsement rules for presidential candidates require the approval of at least two-thirds of its board members. With SEIU and another powerful union, the American Federation of State, County and Municipal Employees, also deciding to withhold endorsements, it became unlikely that labor would throw its weight behind any candidate in the primary.

The candidate banking on the coveted and rarely awarded AFL-CIO primary endorsement was Dick Gephardt. The coalition's wholehearted backing would have given the Missouri congressman a potential advantage over his rivals, including Kerry. With a membership of more than 13 million men and women, its endorsement brings money, organization, and resources—especially supporters—beyond the scope of anything a campaign can hope to procure on its own. The former Democratic House leader has a long-standing relationship with unions. If he doesn't get the endorsement, one of the factors could be Kerry's presence in the field.

Like the House veteran, the senator has an impeccable record on labor issues. He has voted with SEIU nearly as often as labor hero and senior Massachusetts senator Ted Kennedy. A Center analysis shows that, since 1999, Kerry has backed SEIU positions on issues 94 percent of the time and voted against it just three times. The union put a star on Kerry's report card last year when he pushed for legislation to help cash-strapped states with their budgets to prevent the layoffs that they could entail. Kerry also intervened to help end a three-month strike by SEIU nurses at a Massachusetts hospital, who won concessions from administrators on the issue of mandatory overtime. The negotiations were held at his Boston office.

Kerry wooed Luis Navarro for months. According to news reports, the union official was one of the 40 Democratic insiders Kerry tried to cultivate during a cozy May 2002 get-together over caviar at the senator's Washington home. After successfully recruiting Navarro, Kerry followed up by hiring an array of experienced political managers and fundraisers with proven track records. This past winter the senator snatched a high-profile strategist, Bob Shrum, from the campaign of Senator John Edwards. The battle between the two Democratic Senate colleagues for Shrum—who managed the failed presidential bid of Senator Kennedy in 1980 and worked for Al Gore's campaign in the last election—was dubbed the "Shrum primary." Kerry also landed Chris Lehane, another veteran of the Gore campaign, as senior advisor for communications. Lehane has since left the campaign. To run his campaign, Kerry lured two top Democratic operatives: Jim Jordan, as the campaign manager, and Marcus Jadotte, as his deputy. Jordan, executive director of the DSCC during the 2002 cycle, also worked for several Democrats in Congress, including Kerry himself, while Jadotte ran the Florida campaigns of Clinton-Gore in 1996 and Gore-Lieberman in 2000.

Taking a page from the book of President Bush, who built his presidency on a vast network of A-list fundraisers, Kerry has employed some proven money men. His finance director is Peter Maroney, a former chief fundraiser for Massachusetts representative Joseph Kennedy. Kerry pal and legendary fundraiser Robert Farmer, who provided free housing for the senator in the 1980s, is the campaign treasurer. Farmer's fundraising prowess landed him the job of finance director of the 1988 Dukakis presidential campaign; later, he raised money for Bill Clinton. In March 2003, Lou Susman, vice chairman of Salomon Smith Barney, joined Team Kerry as the national finance chair. Susman was a fundraiser for Bill Bradley's 2000 presidential campaign. Susman's entry may increase the money flow from the financial sector.

The talents of these men are visible in the campaign's account books. Through the second quarter of 2003, Kerry led his Democratic opponents in fundraising, having collected almost $13 million. By mid-July, he had a little less than $11 million in the bank. The Center's analysis showed that, besides his traditional home-state patrons, Kerry's presidential campaign has tapped California and New York, home to Hollywood and Wall Street, respectively, and seemingly bottomless sources of political money.

Throughout the spring and summer, the Kerry campaign has tried to project itself as the leader in fundraising. Despite spirited challenges from John Edwards in the first quarter and Howard Dean in the second, which saw both overtaking the Massachusetts senator in quarterly collections, Kerry has managed to remain at the top of the pack in the overall money race. Should he lose the edge in this area, there is another source Kerry can potentially tap in a limited way: his wife's wealth.

A MOST FORTUNATE UNION

John Kerry married Teresa Heinz in May 1995, barely six months after their engagement, in a civil ceremony at the bride's Nantucket Island, Massachusetts, vacation home. The two had known each other since the early 1990s and had been dating since 1993. The wedding, ahead of Kerry's 1996 reelection campaign, made the senator an overnight, Cinderellaesque multimillionaire. In the year before the marriage, Kerry had reported only one asset, a trust fund valued at no more than $100,000. The first disclosure forms he filed after tying the knot suggested the Democrat could be worth more than half a billion dollars, though virtually all the money belonged to his wife.

Teresa Heinz inherited a vast fortune after her first husband, Senator H. John Heinz III, a Republican from Pennsylvania, was killed in April 1991, when his twin-engine Piper Aerostar collided with a helicopter in a Philadelphia suburb. Senator Heinz was the lone heir of the Heinz Company food empire and the great-grandson of Henry John Heinz, founder of the 135-year-old business. H. J. Heinz Company sells thousands of products, including ketchup, condiments, sauces, and frozen foods. It controls 60 percent of the U.S. ketchup market, according to Hoover's Online, a business information service. Until 1987, the company's management was in the hands of the Heinz family.

Kerry's marriage to Teresa Heinz vaulted him into the ranks of the super rich, and his newly acquired financial status was immediately noticed in Massachusetts political circles, especially by likely challengers. "Heinz's millions are casting a long shadow over the potential field of GOP contenders for his seat," the *Boston Globe* reported. "I can think of 675 million good reasons not to run against John Kerry," Mitt Romney told the paper. Romney, who had run against Kennedy the previous year and is now the governor of Massachusetts, was, of course, referring to Heinz's wealth, which was then estimated to be $675 million. Pundits also viewed the wedding as strengthening Kerry politically, and some even suggested that the Democrat would use his wife's wealth to "bankroll his political dreams." The senator's camp, however, maintained that the Heinz fortune had no significant bearing on his political career and disputed the notion that he was trying to benefit from the wedding.

But in reality, Kerry found political value in the Heinz millions—then as now. In the 1996 campaign, after challenging opponents not to use their personal wealth, the senator suggested that his wife's personal fortune was available in case he needed it. "I'm not going to be outspent," he told *USA Today* in April 1996. Kerry dipped into the family riches during the course of that campaign, when he used a Boston home, jointly owned by the Kerrys, as collateral for a bank loan to infuse some much-needed cash into his coffers. Kerry spent that money in the crucial last days of the race, when Weld, his Republican opponent, began running a negative campaign. The two candidates had earlier agreed on a comprehensive spending cap, including a $500,000 limit on personal funds. But the senator freed himself of the agreement after accusing Weld of violating it.

Kerry made similar pronouncements at the beginning of his presidential campaign late in 2002. When the senator entered the fray, his wife's wealth became the most talked about aspect of his campaign, overshadowing his senatorial record and his positions on issues. As in 1996, he tried to douse talk about using his wife's money. "I said to people long ago and I held to this during my Senate campaign, I came to politics based on my own initiative and my own effort to raise money and that's the way I want to finish my life in politics," he said in a March 2003 interview with the *Washington Post*. "Teresa's money is Teresa's money and I've declaratively stated that." But he would not say whether the money was available for his use or if he could legally use it.

In the recent past, at least two candidates used their personal fortune to underwrite their presidential campaigns: Ross Perot in 1992 and Steve Forbes in 2000. The former spent $60 million in 1992 and garnered 19 percent of the vote, more than any other independent candidate in history.

> **When the senator entered the fray, Heinz Kerry's wealth became the most talked-about aspect of his campaign, overshadowing his senatorial record or his positions on issues.**

However, this time around there is a potential impediment: the Bipartisan Campaign Reform Act of 2002. The legislation, which is in effect pending a U.S. Supreme Court review, allows a candidate to use only, in the impenetrable language of federal statutes, "a portion of assets that are jointly owned by the candidate and the candidate's spouse equal to the candidate's share of the asset under instrument of conveyance or ownership, but if no specific share is indicated by an instrument of conveyance or ownership, the value of one-half of the property." In other words, Kerry can spend on his campaign only half of the assets he jointly owns with his spouse (and all of the assets for which he has sole title). The senator's disclosure records show the only property of any value in joint ownership is a painting; they also jointly own the Boston home that Kerry used as collateral to secure a loan after the 1996 election. The Kerry campaign did not acknowledge the fact that the new laws limited its ability to use Teresa Heinz Kerry's wealth until early June, when an aide revealed it to the Associated Press.

Campaign finance experts, however, have pointed out that it is still possible for Heinz Kerry to use her money in the 2004 election cycle. Legally, she can give an unlimited amount to a political 527 group, which in turn can run issue ads attacking Kerry's opponents. Political organizations formed under Section 527 can raise and spend unlimited amounts of money to run so-called issue ads, which must stop short of endorsing a particular candidate (but can attack an opponent). Political scientists believe the Kerry campaign can also make use of Teresa's money in other ways. "They could use it in travel, they could use it in [organizing] events, in soliciting more money, they could use it in building a network," James Thurber, a political science professor at American University in Washington, D.C., told the Center.

Many continued to speculate that Kerry's wife—who was a lifelong Republican until she switched her registration in January 2003—would spend on behalf of her husband if he gets the Democratic nomination. So far, she hasn't ruled out pumping money into her husband's campaign. Chris Black, her spokeswoman, told the Center that the millionaire philanthropist might spend on her husband's behalf under "extraordinary circumstances." If her "integrity" and "honesty" are under attack, "she will set the record straight," Black said. "Hopefully, it won't happen."

The exact size of Heinz Kerry's fortune is not known. Various news media estimates valued it between $500 million and $760 million, which might make her one of the richest women in the United States. In its first list of wealthy politicians, *Forbes* magazine ranked Kerry as the richest member of Congress. According to the magazine, Kerry's net worth is an estimated $550 million. *Roll Call* estimates put the combined wealth of the couple at $675 million. The Center's analysis of the 2001 personal disclosure documents show that he and his wife have between $196 million and $688 million in assets, most of them belonging to Heinz Kerry. Of the 933 assets listed in Kerry's disclosure report, he has sole title to 87, valued at up to $6.8 million. (Disclosure forms that members of Congress file value their assets in broad ranges: from 0 to $1,000; from $1,001 to $15,000; $15,001 to $50,000; and so on.)

Those figures do not include the value of the many homes the couple own because congressional rules require members to list only income-producing assets. According to news accounts, the Boston home the two jointly own is valued at up to $7 million. Separately, Kerry's wife owns at least four homes across the country: a mansion in the glitzy Georgetown area of Washington; an estate near Pittsburgh, home to the Heinz family; and two vacation homes in Nantucket and Idaho.

Teresa Heinz Kerry holds government and municipal bonds and mutual funds worth anywhere between close to $100 million to more than $400 million. Other big investments are in the telecommunications sector, where she has investments between $18 million and $46 million and the financial sector (between $8 million and $19 million), health care companies ($2 million and $6 million); pharmaceutical stocks ($3 million and $11 million); insurance firms ($4 million and $8 million); medical services providers (between $3 million and $9 million); and media companies ($4 million and $8 million).

> **Kerry serves on committees that have oversight of virtually all areas of the country's financial system, while his wife has stakes in companies in literally all sectors of the economy.**

Kerry serves on committees that have oversight of virtually all areas of the country's financial system, while his wife has stakes in companies in literally all sectors of the economy. Kerry must frequently vote on bills that directly affect his wife's interests. Kerry's positions on telecommunications issues can affect the performance of the up to $47 million his wife holds in telecom company stocks. (Of those holdings, between $3.9 million and $13.9 million are in companies that are members of CTIA, the wireless telecom industry trade organization whose position Kerry took in various disputes with the FCC.) Kerry has held seats on both the Banking Committee, which oversees housing loans, and the Finance Committee, which controls funding for health care research. His wife has between $7 million and $35 million invested in real estate and medical industries.

Since Kerry started courting his wife, she has been more than willing to aid his campaigns. The Heinz family contributed just under $12,000 in hard money to the senator, a negligible amount. But Kerry gained other benefits, such as access to the family jet. He has been using a Gulfstream II jet, owned by the Pittsburgh-based Flying Squirrel, a Heinz family venture. Heinz Kerry has stakes worth between $1 million and $5 million in the charter company.

There are strong indications that John Kerry had been using the jet even before his engagement to Teresa Heinz. Documents reviewed by the Center reveal that, between 1993 and 1996, the Senate Ethics Committee granted Kerry several waivers to receive gifts of "transportation aboard a plane" by one or more unidentified individuals. The name of the person or persons giving the gift was redacted for privacy reasons. Kerry requested ethics waivers to use the transportation at least 15 times, and the committee ruled favorably on all occasions. Newspaper accounts said the individual paying for his trips was Teresa Heinz. The senator's aides told the media that he used the plane only "infrequently."

Kerry has used the plane for campaign purposes as well. Between June 2001 and his successful reelection in 2002,

Kerry's Senate campaign paid Flying Squirrel at least $24,900, according to the Center's analysis of Federal Election Commission filings. The campaign reimbursed Heinz Kerry personally more than $3,000 for phone and catering expenses. It also reimbursed an employee of the Heinz family offices for travel expenses. Kerry's presidential campaign made 15 travel payments to Flying Squirrel totaling $39,780 in just the first three months of 2003. The senator is required by law to pay for any use of the plane for campaign purposes, but those payments do not necessarily cover the costs to Flying Squirrel of flying the candidate around the country. And with an hourly rate of nearly $2,000, the plane is one of the more expensive jets to operate.

Kerry used the jet for campaign trips even before his wedding. According to the *Boston Herald*, he paid Flying Squirrel $1,078 for two fundraising trips—one to California and the other to New York—made in October 1994.

PUBLIC SERVICE, PRIVATE MOTIVE

John Kerry, who refused to take contributions from PACs, began his quest for the presidency by forming one. In December 2001, as a prelude to his presidential run, the senator created a federal PAC named the Citizen Soldier Fund. A number of influential members of Congress, including most of the presidential candidates, have such PACs, commonly known as "leadership committees." Politicians use the leadership committees to win political support by distributing money among various party organizations and candidates across the country. They also use PAC resources to foot travel bills. Kerry also set up a nonfederal 527 committee, which went by the same name as his leadership PAC.

Kerry's PAC raised roughly $1 million through the end of 2002 and disbursed nearly all of it. At the time it was formed, the Citizen

Soldier Fund's nonfederal account could theoretically have accepted any amount from a donor. But Kerry, perhaps as a concession to the reform constituency of which he was a part, said the fund would not take donations of more than $10,000 from one individual or organization in any year. Just before the McCain-Feingold legislation was to take effect consigning soft money—at least some types of it—to history, the senator couldn't resist taking the political money that he voted to ban one last time. By the end of October, the self-imposed cap was gone.

Before Kerry closed the account some time before the end of 2002, the Citizen Soldier Fund raised approximately $1.35 million in soft money, thanks mainly to a series of big checks written by some of his long-time patrons. The largest donor to the fund was Miami lawyer Milton Ferrell, who gave $59,000. Other big givers included the CEO of Boston Capital, John P. Manning, who contributed $55,000, International Data Group chairman Patrick J. McGovern ($50,000), and the American International Group ($30,000). The committee spent nearly $1.3 million, which is virtually everything that it raised. Though its stated aim was to help Democrats across the country, two-thirds of the soft money contributed to the Citizen Soldier Fund was channeled to its federal account and to candidates in a handful of states, among them Iowa, New Hampshire, and South Carolina. Records show that the nonfederal committee distributed close to $147,000 in Iowa, more than $120,000 in New Hampshire, and $58,000 in South Carolina. It spent $89,000 in Florida, the state that decided the last presidential election. Among the other big contributions the committee made were for two Senate colleagues who were facing tough reelection campaigns. Kerry gave $181,000 to Senator Tim Johnson of South Dakota, who won his race, and more than $81,000 to Senator Max Cleland of Georgia, who lost.

The purpose of Kerry's playing good Samaritan was purely political. It is not a coincidence that he doled out a quarter of the total amount raised through the soft-money account in Iowa, New Hampshire, and South Carolina, the states that are crucial to presidential primaries. Understandably, he needed allies there ahead of the early 2004 primaries, and the senator, like some of his presidential opponents, was using the PAC money to help build support for the campaign. Nonetheless, Kerry's distribution of campaign cash across the country is seemingly at odds with his oft-stated position on campaign finance reform, which is posted prominently on his Web site: "Elections must be more than auctions, and money must no longer drown out the role of citizens in our democracy."

Kerry maintained that he hasn't changed his long-held view on the pernicious influence of PAC money, arguing that the Citizen Soldier Fund was necessary for the sake of a Democratic majority. "I've come to acknowledge the unpleasant and unfortunate truth that campaign finance and other critical political reforms will remain stymied in Congress until Democrats obtain real working majorities in Washington and in state legislatures across the nation," he said. "It's become necessary, I believe, for every leader of this party to employ all legal and appropriate means to assist Democratic candidacies at all political levels."

In other words, the dark cloud of special-interest money that hangs over the political process won't be lifted until it elects politicians like Kerry to majority status in every legislature in the country, all the while being granted the favors it seeks.

John Kerry

Top Ten Career Patrons

RANKING	PATRON	TOTAL
1	Mintz, Levin, Cohn, Ferris, Glovsky and Popeo PC, Boston	$223,046
2	FleetBoston Financial Corporation, Boston	$172,387
3	AOL Time Warner Inc., New York	$134,960
4	Hale and Dorr LLP, Boston	$123,258
5	Hill, Holiday, Connors, Cosmopulos Inc., Boston	$119,300
6	Harvard University	$108,700
7	Skadden, Arps, Slate, Meagher & Flom LLP, New York	$105,150
8	Robins, Kaplan, Miller & Ciresi LLP, Minneapolis	$103,450
9	Goldman Sachs Group Inc., New York	$100,000
10	Piper Rudnick, Baltimore	$92,300*

This list is based on individual, corporate, and PAC contributions to the Citizen Soldier Fund-Nonfederal through December 31, 2002, and on individual and PAC contributions to Kerry's Senate campaigns from 1984 to 2002, the Citizen Soldier Fund-Federal, and Kerry's 2004 presidential campaign through June 30, 2003. Sources: Federal Election Commission, Internal Revenue Service.

*Includes employees of Verner Liipfert, which merged with Piper Rudnick in 2002.

Dennis Kucinich

According to a congressional trip disclosure form, filed by members when they or their staffers travel at the expense of private interests rather than the taxpayers, the Praxis Peace Institute paid almost $6,000 to fly Ohio congressman Dennis Kucinich to Dubrovnik, in Croatia, in June 2002. Praxis, which promotes "world and community peace through education and informed action" and seeks to link "spiritual perspectives and practice to informed civic responsibility," chose Kucinich to deliver the keynote address at the group's Dubrovnik conference, whose theme was the "Alchemy of Peacebuilding." They got what they paid for.

"As one studies the images of the Eagle Nebula, brought back by the Hubble telescope from that place in deep space where stars are born, one can imagine the interplay of cosmic forces across space and time, of matter and spirit dancing to the music of the spheres, atop an infinite sea of numbers," the representative of Ohio's Tenth District said.

"Spirit merges with matter to sanctify the universe," he continued. "Matter transcends to return to spirit. The interchangeability of matter and spirit means the starlit magic of the outermost life of our universe becomes the soul-light magic of the innermost life of our self. The energy of the stars becomes us. We become the energy of the stars. Stardust and spirit unite and we begin: one with the universe."

Kucinich's alchemical musings may not read like the typical political speech, but then Kucinich is trying to sell himself as an atypical candidate. "I offer a different vision for America, one which separates me from the other candidates," his campaign Web site announces. The most distinctive plank in his campaign platform is the creation of a "Department of Peace," a federal bureaucracy that would negotiate international disarmament treaties and also involve itself in domestic disturbances— between spouses.

Yet for all his quirkiness—*The New Republic* summed up the opinion of many by judging him "truly a fringe candidate"— Kucinich has found a base of donors and a message to appeal to them. Though his fundraising lags far behind the Democratic front-runners, he's nevertheless managed to perform a new variation on the old alchemist's trick: he's turned his positions into gold.

RESILIENT CHAMPION OF THE "LITTLE GUY"

The oldest of seven children, Dennis Kucinich was born in Ohio on October 8, 1946, near Cleveland's West Side, an area dotted by gritty ethnic neighborhoods and blue-collar suburbs. His Croatian father, Frank Kucinich, drove a delivery truck; his Irish mother, Virginia, cared for the children. Like many other working-class people in the city, Kucinich's family lived through hard times. With his father's meager income as the only means of support, the family frequently couldn't pay rent, and Kucinich lived in 21 different places by the time he was 17.

Raised as a Roman Catholic and educated in the Cleveland public school system, the slightly built youth showed an early appetite for competition and participated in high school football and baseball. After he graduated in 1964, Kucinich first attended Cleveland State University from 1967 to 1970, then enrolled in Case Western Reserve University, where he majored in speech and communications. He received both his B.A. and his M.A. degrees in 1973.

Even before finishing college, Kucinich wasted no time in pursuing a career in public service. At 21 he waged a campaign for a seat on the Cleveland City Council. Although he lost that election, two years later Kucinich ran again and was elected to the 33-member body.

He served three terms as a councilman, reveling in his self-appointed role as the champion of the "little guy." He aggressively advanced a populist agenda and attacked initiatives he thought were in favor of special interests. He didn't hesitate to change political alliances if he thought it would advance his own initiatives and soon acquired a reputation as a real firebrand, someone whose radical methods and barbed wit drew the ire of many of his colleagues.

In 1976 Kucinich ran successfully for municipal court clerk, the second-highest elective post in Cleveland. He had served one year of his term when he announced his intention to run for mayor. Kucinich entered the 1977 race as a political maverick. State representative Edward Feighan had already secured the Democratic Party endorsement and Cleveland's business and political elite in large part opposed Kucinich's campaign.

But the 31-year-old self-declared populist wasn't deterred. He engineered a grassroots campaign, vowing to promote the interests of the blue-collar workers of the city and institute far-reaching reforms, from cleaning up corruption at city hall to cleaning up the sewers in depressed neighborhoods. The campaign worked; Kucinich became the youngest mayor of a major U.S. city in history.

But Kucinich faced a difficult job as Cleveland's mayor. The city was running major deficits, almost $20 million at that time, and Kucinich had inherited tens of millions of dollars in debt from his Republican predecessor, Ralph Perk. Kucinich's confrontational political style did not help either. He antagonized many of Cleveland's business elite and quickly found himself at odds with the Democratic-dominated city council. The hostility between established city council representatives and Kucinich's 20-something mayoral staff, mockingly called the "Kiddie Corps," was deep and would occasionally devolve into personal insults and accusations.

By the spring of 1978 a coalition of critics and staunch political opponents had aligned themselves against Kucinich. The enmity betweens the two groups made governing Cleveland nearly impossible and the city's budgetary outlook became all the more bleak. When Kucinich unceremoniously fired police chief Richard Hongisto on live television that March, his rivals used the wave of public outrage to lodge a recall campaign to remove Kucinich from office. Although the recall election failed, it marked the beginning of Kucinich's precipitous fall from municipal grace. During the remainder of his term, Kucinich presided over a city that became known as the "Crisis Capital of the U.S." Cleveland became the first major American city to default since the Great Depression. Its bond rating was lowered twice by Moody's Investor Service, and the police force went on strike in response to proposed budget cuts. Not surprisingly, Kucinich lost the 1979 mayoral election.

When Kucinich left office in defeat, many observers reasonably assumed that his career in politics was over. In 1982, after he lost the Democratic primary for Ohio secretary of state, their evaluation indeed seemed justified. But after four years, Kucinich returned to the political arena when Cleveland Councilman Joseph Kowalski died with two years left in his term. Kowalski represented a district with some of Kucinich's most dedicated supporters in the mayoral election, so it was no surprise when Kucinich was elected to fill the vacancy.

> In 1988 and again in 1992, Kucinich ran for a seat in the U.S. House of Representatives, losing both times. He was more successful as a businessman.

It was widely thought that Kucinich would easily win reelection to the City Council in 1985. Instead, he embarked on a yearlong effort to become Ohio's governor. At first intending to challenge Democratic governor Richard Celeste for the party nomination, he later pledged to run as an independent. But lacking funds for his campaign, Kucinich made little progress and withdrew altogether in August 1986.

In 1988 and again in 1992, Kucinich ran for a seat in the U.S. House of Representatives, losing both times. He was more successful as a businessman. In 1987 he founded K Communications, later renamed Kucinich Communications, which provided consulting services, produced industrial videos, and brokered media time for its clients. In the early 1990s, Kucinich worked as the international marketing director for a start-up software business named CRC International Business Solutions, which dealt in multilingual accounting software.

Then in 1994 Kucinich challenged state senator Anthony Sinagra for his Twenty-third District seat. The district was composed of Cleveland neighborhoods that had historically responded positively to Kucinich's blend of progressive populism, and the election quickly became a lively and spirited race. Although he was outspent by his Republican rival two to one, Kucinich emerged as the victor in the race.

One year after his return to political life Kucinich already had designs on higher office. In January 1996 he entered the Democratic primary for Ohio's Tenth District seat in the House of Representatives. Kucinich, who had significant name recognition among voters, easily defeated his less well known Democratic rivals in the primary and went on to challenge Republican representative Martin Hoke in the general election.

Kucinich faced a difficult campaign running against the two-term representative. He once again relied on a grassroots campaign with ties to lower- and middle-class communities. And he received decisive support from environmental groups and labor unions, including the AFL-CIO, which poured more than $1 million into ads attacking Hoke, who was an ardent supporter of Newt Gingrich's Contract with America. After a bitter battle Kucinich managed to defeat Hoke in a close race.

In Congress, Kucinich made good on the AFL-CIO's investment. He emerged as a vocal critic of the North American Free Trade Agreement; as a presidential candidate he has called for U.S. withdrawal from both NAFTA and the World Trade Organization. Of Kucinich's top 20 career patrons, 18 are labor unions (the other two are the Association of American Trial Lawyers and Forest City Enterprises); as a member of Congress, he has consistently voted in favor of union causes, opposing free trade and favoring protectionism. In 1999, for example, the Associated Press reported that, when union representatives for the steelworkers were lobbying Congress for tariffs to protect them from imports, Kucinich led them in a chant of "Steel helped to build America" in a House conference room.

AN ANTIWAR ALCHEMIST

While his support for labor unions has provided a steady source of campaign funds, Kucinich has stressed his antiwar views in his run for president. On February 17, 2002, he delivered his pacifist "Prayer for America" to a group of Democrats in California. Following President Bush's "Axis of Evil" State of the Union address, the speech protested the war in Afghanistan and warned of the dangers of an economy on a permanent war footing. The address was circulated widely on the Internet, and almost exactly a year later Kucinich announced that, in response to "tens of thousands of e-mails and countless phone calls, letters, and personal appeals," he was entering the presidential race.

> Kucinich, who has warned of the "undue influence by powerful corporations and wealthy individuals" inherent in the campaign system, touted the surprising $1.5 million his campaign raised.

Kucinich's opposition to war was longstanding. During the closing days of the war in Kosovo, in which the United States intervened to prevent the forces of Slobodan Milosevic, the president of what remained of Yugoslavia, from carrying out a program of ethnic cleansing against the predominantly Albanian population of the region, he demanded an end to hostilities, telling the *Cleveland Plain Dealer* that the United States, and the people of Kosovo, should pin their hopes for peace on "whatever sense of humanity remains" in Milosevic. Milosevic, who is currently on trial at the Hague for war crimes, was forced from office only after NATO's military intervention drove his forces from Kosovo.

Kucinich opposed the war on Iraq, saying it "violates the Constitution and international law." On April 1, 2003, just 11 days before Saddam Hussein's Ba'athist regime collapsed, the Ohio congressman took to the House floor to call for a ceasefire. "Stop the war now. Before we send our troops into house-to-house combat in Baghdad, a city of five million people. Before we ask our troops to take up the burden of shooting innocent civilians in the fog of war." Kucinich also called for the United Nations to return weapons inspectors to the country. "As Baghdad will be encircled, this is the time to get the U.N. back in to inspect Baghdad and the rest of Iraq for biological and chemical weapons. Our troops should not have to be the ones who will find out, in combat, whether Iraq has such weapons."

Kucinich's consistency in opposing the war has led to some high-profile endorsements and donations. "There is one candidate running for president who supports the values most important to me, and most critical to the country," announced Ben Cohen, a progressive activist and one of the two founders of Ben & Jerry's, which is now a subsidiary of the global consumer products conglomerate Unilever. "That candidate is Congressman Dennis Kucinich, the co-chair of the Progressive Caucus, and the leader on Capitol Hill in challenging Bush administration foreign policies that make Americans less—not more—secure." Cohen contributed the maximum $2,000 to the candidate.

Kucinich, who has warned of the "undue influence by powerful corporations and wealthy individuals" inherent in the campaign system, touted Cohen's contribution and endorsement, and the surprising $1.5 million his campaign raised in the second quarter of 2003. Hollywood celebrities, including actors Ben Affleck, Jeff Bridges, Larry Hagman, and Edward Norton, singer Bonnie Raitt, and talk show host Jerry Springer, also gave to his campaign. "Our campaign has been surging in recent weeks," his Web site proclaimed, adding that the influx of donors gave it "the biggest percentage jump in fundraising of any presidential campaign. Our fundraising climbed this quarter to more than $1.5 million, and we ended with over $1 million cash on hand."

In his Dubrovnik speech, Kucinich said, "I have seen groups of people overcome incredible odds as they become aware they are participating in a cause beyond self and sense the movement of the inexorable which comes from unity. When you feel this principle at work, when you see spiritual principles form the basis of active citizenship, you are reminded once again of the merging of stardust and spirit. There is creativity. There is magic. There is alchemy."

And apparently, there are a few people willing to pay for it.

Dennis Kucinich

Top Ten Career Patrons

Ranking	Patron	Total
1	International Association of Machinists and Aerospace Workers, Washington, D.C.	$45,000
2	United Auto Workers, Detroit	$43,534
3	International Brotherhood of Teamsters, Washington, D.C.	$41,000
4	United Food and Commercial Workers Union, Washington, D.C.	$40,500
5	Association of Trial Lawyers of America, Washington, D.C.	$40,000
6	International Brotherhood of Electrical Workers, Washington, D.C	$36,600
7	Communication Workers of America, Washington, D.C.	$36,500
8	American Federation of State, County, and Municipal Employees, Washington, D.C.	$35,000
8	Service Employees International Union, Washington, D.C.	$35,000

| 8 | Sheet Metal Workers International Association, Washington, D.C. | $35,000 |

This list is based on individual and PAC contributions to Kucinich congressional campaigns from 1988 to 2002, and Kucinich's 2004 presidential and congressional campaigns through June 30, 2003.

Source: Federal Election Commission.

Joe Lieberman

The June 26, 2000, ribbon-cutting ceremony for the state-of-the-art facility that the pharmaceutical giant Pfizer Inc. built in Groton, Connecticut, celebrated progress and the hope of a brighter future. The company billed the new drug research center as the largest in the world dedicated to developing new medicines. The 535,000-square-foot building boasted 120 new labs, where some seven hundred scientists would work developing cures and treatments for diseases and disorders that afflict both animals and humans. To benefit their own species, some of the researchers would make use of the latest discoveries on the brave new frontier of human genome research. The ceremony was held in the facility's atrium, where scientists can mingle over cups of espresso from a built-in coffee bar.

In addition to the company employees, some of Connecticut's leading political figures attended the affair. Governor John G. Rowland, who helped pave the way for the new building with $80 million of state aid (part of which was spent on improving the area's housing and infrastructure) and 23 acres of state land on the Thames River, was on hand. So too were Representative Sam Gejdenson and Senator Chris Dodd, both Democrats. The state's other senator, Joseph Lieberman, attended the event as well. He hobnobbed with Pfizer's chairman William C. Steere Jr. and addressed the gathered employees. In his remarks, Lieberman was effusive in his praise for the high-tech miracles that the scientists would undoubtedly discover, and for the company that employed them. In a nod to faith and family values, he said Pfizer was "doing the Lord's work."

For his part, Lieberman had done a good bit of work for Pfizer. The Center found that between 1998 and 2003, Lieberman cosponsored nine bills that Pfizer directly lobbied, varying from tax breaks to patent extensions. The latter legislation, on which the pharmaceutical maker spent much of its more than $20 million lobbying budget, is crucial to the profits of the company whose revenues topped more than $32 billion in 2002. Some of the bills Lieberman sponsored dealt with research and development, one of the largest expenses that pharmaceutical companies face in the United States. Pfizer, the world's second-largest drug company, spent $5.1 billion developing new drugs during 2002 alone—Pfizer's highest reported cost.

Pfizer has been a generous supporter of Lieberman and his "New Democrat" approach to politics; with contributions of $50,700 the pharmaceutical giant is his twelfth largest career contributor. Most large drug companies like Pfizer tend to lean toward Republicans, because many Democrats favor restricting the prices pharmaceutical companies can charge for drugs, resulting in lower profits and smaller research budgets. In the 2002 election cycle, for example, more than 70 percent of Pfizer's money went to GOP candidates. Lieberman is the exception. During that period, the company increased its donations to Lieberman even though he wasn't up for reelection. In 2000 media reports credited Pfizer's donations to Lieberman as the "highest total of any Democratic member of Congress."

When asked why the Connecticut senator was so favored, Pfizer spokesman Andy McCormick said that the company contributes to those who are responsive to them.

Over the years, Lieberman has been responsive to a number of companies. He has supported international trade agreements and voted to make permanent China's status as a most favored nation. He has favored tax cuts and incentives for pharmaceutical firms and telecommunications companies. He supported privatizing the Social Security system and providing vouchers for parents to send their children to private schools. His efforts did not go unnoticed. Lieberman's top donors comprise a who's who of the financial and Fortune 500 elite, making the Connecticut senator one of the business community's favorite Democrats.

STRONG BUT SHIFTING CONVICTIONS

Lieberman was born in Stamford, Connecticut, on February 24, 1942. His father, Henry, went from driving a bakery truck to owning a liquor store—or as they call them in New England, a "package store." Lieberman attended local public schools and went on to Yale University, where he received his bachelor's and law degrees. After graduation, he practiced law for two years before deciding to pursue a political career. In 1970, at the age of 28, Lieberman was elected to the Connecticut State Senate. In his 10 years as a state senator, six were spent as Democratic majority leader. All the while, Lieberman steadily grew in popularity.

In 1980 Lieberman decided to run for the U.S. House of Representatives when Robert N. Giaimo, the incumbent, announced that he would not seek reelection after 22 years in office. Lieberman quickly secured the Democratic nomination and challenged Republican Larry DeNardis. Lieberman secured Giaimo's endorsement and seemed to be the favorite, but national politics figured heavily in Connecticut's state elections. Ronald Reagan won a landslide victory over Jimmy Carter, and his coattails were long enough to sweep DeNardis into office.

> **While he had no specific plans, public office was "still where he wanted to be," Lieberman said. By the 1982 elections, he was running again.**

Shortly after the election, Lieberman invited a group of reporters to a "not so much a farewell but a see-you-later address," during which he confirmed that while he had no specific plans, public office was "still where he wanted to be." Indeed, Lieberman wasted no time. By the 1982 elections he was running again, this time for state attorney general.

During his campaign, Lieberman courted Hadassah Tucker, the director of policy, planning, and communications for Pfizer. When they met, she was helping to launch an $11 million health care initiative. About a year later, in March 1983, they were married. Hadassah Lieberman stayed at Pfizer for three years, serving on the company's executive board. She still owns stock in the company.

Lieberman won the election by a wide margin and was easily reelected again in 1986. During his successful terms as attorney general he earned statewide recognition as an effective advocate on behalf of consumers and the environment. By the time the 1988 U.S. Senate elections were coming around, Lieberman was a favorite candidate for the Democratic nomination to run against Republican senator Lowell P. Weicker Jr. After being pushed by Democrats, including Senator John Kerry, who had been a classmate at Yale, Lieberman threw his hat into the ring, saying: "I feel from my research that there is a case to be made here—it's time for a change." Lieberman's 1988 Senate campaign ended in a close race. Weicker, the thrice-elected incumbent, was both well funded and well liked in Connecticut. But Lieberman triumphed, managing to secure victory by just 10,000 votes.

In August 1990, when Lieberman was still a freshman senator, Iraq invaded Kuwait. When the first president George Bush asked Congress for an authorization to use force to expel Iraq, Democrats were hesitant to commit the country to war. Though he had only been a senator for less than two years and risked falling out with his party, Lieberman supported military action in Iraq. He proclaimed, "You can't let a bully like that overrun a neighboring country." He was one of only 10 Democrats in the Senate to support the campaign against Iraq. He was such an outspoken advocate that President Bush asked him to be the Democratic cosponsor of the resolution to use force. His unflinching support for Operation Desert Storm—helped no doubt by its subsequent success—won Lieberman a prominent position among legislators in both parties and cemented his popularity among his constituents. When he ran for reelection in 1994, he won by a margin of more than 350,000 votes, which at the time was the largest margin of victory in history for a Connecticut Senate race. (He topped that total in 2000, winning by a margin of 379,000.)

Over the course of his Senate career, Lieberman has consistently supported an interventionist foreign policy, including the 1983 invasion of Grenada and the 1986 bombing of Libya. He also supported efforts to nullify the potential threats posed by Saddam Hussein, whom he has called "a ticking time bomb." When the second Bush administration asked Congress to authorize the use of force against the Iraqi regime, Lieberman again was a proponent of action. "We gave him 12 years and tried everything short of war to get him to keep the promises he made to disarm at the end of the Gulf War," said Lieberman defending his stance during the 2003 Democratic debate in South Carolina.

"We did the right thing in fighting this fight, and the American people will be safer as a result of it."

Lieberman has not shied from invoking his faith and his moral views on Capitol Hill. *The Almanac of American Politics* states that Lieberman has an "influence that came from respect for his independence of mind, civility of spirit and fidelity to causes in which he believes." He was an outspoken critic of Bill Clinton's personal behavior in the Oval Office. Lieberman asserted that Clinton's actions were "inappropriate," "immoral," and "harmful," but voted against removing Clinton after the House had impeached him.

In the summer of 2000, Al Gore, the sitting vice president and Democratic nominee, gave Lieberman national prominence when he chose the Connecticut senator as his running mate, making him the first Jewish vice presidential candidate. An Orthodox Jew, Lieberman refused to work or campaign on the Sabbath. In 1998, he began a bipartisan campaign, along with former secretary of education William Bennett, targeting the entertainment industry for what they saw as its flagrant marketing of violence and sex to children. Together they created the Silver Sewer Award, which they gave to "cultural polluters" with particularly egregious records that capitalize on the degradation of society. Lieberman was also a cosponsor of the V-chip legislation, which mandated new television sets carry a device that allowed parents to screen out violent and offensive programs. It passed as part of the Telecommunications Act of 1996.

Gore, seeking to distance himself from the scandals that had tarnished Bill Clinton's presidential record, chose as his running mate a man who had stressed morality and family values and repudiated Clinton during the impeachment proceedings. Yet Gore picked not only someone with a reputation for personal morality but also the chairman of the Democratic Leadership

Council and a cofounder of the New Democrat Network, groups that have been able to raise large amounts of money from corporate interests. As a senator, Lieberman had criticized affirmative action, supported experimenting with school vouchers, and favored partially privatizing Social Security. He was forced to abandon many of those positions to conform to the populist campaign rhetoric that Gore chose to emphasize in his race for the White House. Indeed, Ari Fleischer, the Bush campaign spokesman, sarcastically hailed the Lieberman selection, saying, "Governor Bush and Secretary Cheney respect Joe Lieberman for his intelligence, his integrity, and for many of the positions he has taken, positions which Governor Bush and Secretary Cheney support but Al Gore has attacked. From Social Security reform to missile defense, tort reform to parental notification [for a minor to have an abortion], and from school choice to affirmative action, Al Gore has chosen a man whose positions are more similar to Governor Bush's than to his own."

> As a senator, Lieberman criticized affirmative action,
> supported experimenting with school vouchers, and
> favored partially privatizing Social Security.

During the campaign, Lieberman had to promise the Congressional Black Caucus that "he would stand firm in support of affirmative action and civil rights," a distinct change for the politician who, in 1995, said affirmative action was "patently unfair." On August 7, 2000, Lieberman's office produced a previously unpublished article entitled *My Private Journey Away from Privatization*, which renounced his support for partial privatization of Social Security, a measure that he once said "has to happen." In the article, he claimed that he had only been intrigued by the program and had since changed his mind; his campaign claimed the article was written that June, before his selection as the vice presidential candidate.

Lieberman also abandoned one of his signature issues, his criticism of the sex and violence in movies and television. He discontinued the Silver Sewer Award and eased his rhetoric. As late as April 1999, Lieberman declared, "We're coming dangerously close in the entertainment industry, much as we prize our liberties, to the point where they're going to invite legal restrictions on their freedom." But at a September 2000 Democratic Party fundraiser in Beverly Hills, California, his tune had changed. Before an audience of entertainment industry leaders, he said, "I promise you this, that we will never, never put the government in the position of telling you by law, through law, what to make. . . . We will nudge you, but we will never become censors."

In one of the closest elections in American history, Gore and Lieberman won the popular vote but lost the electoral vote after the controversial Florida recount. Lieberman did not seem discouraged by the results, however. As he did after his failed election in 1980, Lieberman put a proud face on his defeat. He proclaimed his great respect for Gore and announced that he would not challenge Gore if he ran in 2004. When Gore announced in December 2002 that he would not seek the presidency in 2004, Lieberman was freed from his promise, and entered the race himself.

Since his near loss in the 2000 election, he has returned to his New Democrat roots.

FUNDING FOR A NEW DEMOCRAT

Lieberman has long been a member of the Democratic Leadership Council, founded in 1985 by a group of moderate Democrats who hoped to craft a centrist platform for the party, then reeling from President Reagan's 49-state drubbing of Walter Mondale.

Over the years, its chairmen have included Senator John Breaux of Louisiana, Sam Nunn, former senator of Georgia, Representative Richard Gephardt of Missouri, and Bill Clinton, while he was governor of Arkansas. Lieberman also served a term as the group's chairman. On its Web site, the DLC says that in the 1990s, its policies "helped to produce the longest period of sustained economic growth in our history, the lowest unemployment in a generation, 22 million new jobs; and helped to cut the welfare rolls in half, reduce the crime rate for seven straight years, balance the budget and streamline the federal bureaucracy to its smallest size since the Kennedy administration."

On August 1, 2000, the DLC issued its "Hyde Park Declaration," a statement of New Democrat principles. Among them are commitments to free enterprise, trade, and investment; support for international bodies like the World Trade Organization to oversee global markets; fiscal discipline in government; welfare reform; policies that reinforce marriage and demand parental responsibility; and the involvement of voluntary groups, including religious institutions, in government efforts to aid the destitute. The DLC and its various affiliated and like-minded organizations have sought aid for themselves from America's corporate elite.

Consider the New Democrat Network, a joint fundraising committee that Lieberman and Breaux founded in 1996 to raise money for the benefit of candidates that advance their brand of Democratic principles. The contributors to the soft-money component of his political action committee included telecommunications companies like AT&T and SBC Communications; banking firms such as Capital One and Citigroup; and high-tech companies like Microsoft and Nortel Networks. While many of the New Democrat Network's contributors had given directly to Lieberman as well, the collaborative creation of the PAC gave Lieberman a new avenue to raise money from the firms. He and

Breaux, who have collectively served in the Senate for more than 30 years, collaborated as a tag team supporting legislation lobbied by its top contributors.

Since 2000, Lieberman and Breaux have cosponsored legislation affecting eight of the largest soft-money donors to the New Democrat Network, the Center for Public Integrity has found. Those eight companies have given the PAC a total of almost $880,000 in soft money. Lieberman and Breaux cosponsored bills for which the companies lobbied, ranging from measures to increase Internet access to cutting taxes and expanding foreign trade.

AT&T is the New Democrat Network's third largest soft-money donor, having contributed $175,070 since 2000. In 2001, when the communications giant sought legislation in the Senate to aid its expansion of high-speed Web access to potential customers, it got a push from Lieberman and Breaux. The two cosponsored the Broadband Internet Access Act of 2001 to provide tax cuts and expansion of high-speed Web access to potential customers. The bill, which did not pass, called for a series of financial incentives in the form of tax credits for Internet providers like AT&T to make broadband services available in rural communities. It had another provision that made these companies eligible for a 10 percent tax credit for broadband services they already offered. In a legislative session in which members of Congress introduced a slew of broadband bills, Lieberman and Breaux's effort, laden with tax cuts, may have been the most industry-friendly.

AT&T wasn't the only New Democrat Network donor that would have benefited from the bill. Another large donor to Lieberman and Breaux's joint fundraising committee—SBC Communications, which gave $42,535 in contributions—also lobbied directly for the legislation. On another bill in 2001, when SBC and Microsoft, the PAC's seventh largest donor, lobbied for a bill that would provide them with expanded tax credits for research, the two again stepped in to cosponsor the legislation. Nortel, the fifteenth largest donor to the New Democrat Network, is a Canadian communications company with extensive operations in Bolivia, Chile, Colombia, Ecuador, and Peru. Nortel lobbied for the Andean Trade Preference Expansion Act with the United States, which would include those countries in the North America Free Trade Agreement, which lowered tariff barriers between the United States, Canada, and Mexico. During the lobbying effort, both Lieberman and Breaux stepped up to cosponsor the Andean Trade Preference Expansion Act.

> **Since 2000, Lieberman and Breaux have cosponsored legislation affecting eight of the ten largest soft-money donors to the New Democrat Network.**

The New Democrat Network continues to raise soft money, more than $4.8 million since it started reporting its contributions in mid-2000. It has done so through its Section 527 committee. That its donors were disclosed was in part due to the efforts of its cofounder.

In 2000, Lieberman sponsored an amendment to a defense bill that required the disclosure of the soft money flowing to Section 527 committees. When the measure passed, Lieberman released a statement celebrating its enactment. "A gaping loophole has developed through which political committees can provide safe haven to their donors, raise limitless amounts of cash, and spend it all without public knowledge" Lieberman crowed. "Already 527 groups have spent millions of dollars to influence 2000 election-year campaigns."

Including, of course, the New Democrat Network. Lieberman has been a savvy fundraiser throughout his career. According to

New Democrat Network-Nonfederal

Top Ten Donors

Ranking	Patron	Total
1	PhRMA	$220,035
2	Aetna Inc.	$200,000
3	AT&T Corporation	$175,070
4	Capital One Financial Corporation	$135,000
5	Intuit Inc.	$125,200
6	Pfizer Inc.	$125,000
7	Microsoft Corporation	$106,035
8	Citizens for Asbestos Reform	$100,000
9	Pacificare Health	$100,000
10	American Standard Development Company	$ 95,000

This list is based on individual, corporate, and PAC contributions to the New Democrat Network-Nonfederal PAC from October 1, 2000, through June 30, 2003.
Source: Internal Revenue Service.

reports by the *Hartford Courant*, he routinely solicits and spends soft money even though he has been a critic of the practice. He has admitted to making fundraising phone calls where he discussed soft money as far back as 1996. "I regret it," Lieberman said. "What can I say? I regret it, even though it was a small amount of money." But he didn't regret it enough to stop raising the cash in innovative ways. The New Democrat Network was one. He found another when he was tapped by Al Gore for the 2000 Democratic ticket.

When he ran as Gore's running mate, Lieberman became one of the few vice presidential candidates to create a separate fundraising committee for his office. On August 11, 2000, he formed Lieberman for Vice President, which collected a slew of $1,000 contributions from individuals. The committee gave Lieberman another way to raise money in addition to his senatorial campaign committee, Friends of Joe Lieberman. In March 2001, he created yet another fundraising vehicle, a leadership PAC he called Responsibility Opportunity Community PAC, which has collected more than 1,400 donations totaling $2.9 million through the end of 2002.

In 2002, Lieberman voted for the Bipartisan Campaign Reform Act, better known as McCain-Feingold, which among other things bans the national political parties from raising soft money (it still allows contributors to make large contributions to 527s). Earlier that year he cosponsored an amendment with Senator Fred Thompson, Republican of Tennessee, to aid prosecutors in enforcing campaign finance laws. "We have passed another important milestone in the long overdue effort to enact campaign finance reform," Lieberman said, referring to the large donations some interests give to politicians and parties. "Because of the collapse of the Enron Corporation, the credibility of the democratic process is once again being challenged."

Lieberman, who presided over one of the Senate inquiries into the Enron scandals, was among those challenged. In 2000 and 2001, Enron contributed a total of $50,000 to his joint leadership committee, the New Democrat Network.

DON'T ASK, DON'T TELL

The December 2, 2001, bankruptcy of Enron—at the time of its collapse the nation's seventh largest corporation—sent shock waves through both the financial and political worlds. The diversified energy firm owed some $30 billion and numbered among its creditors financial institutions like Citibank (which had loaned the company $3 billion), J. P. Morgan Chase and Crédit Suisse First Boston. The contributions of Enron and its employees made the company the top donor to President George W. Bush; some 71 senators and 187 members of the House had taken Enron contributions as well. The company, which ran a formidable lobbying machine in Washington and state capitals, gained favorable treatment from Congress, federal and state governments, and various regulatory agencies on at least 49 occasions from the late 1980s to the company's collapse, the Center found.

A procession of executives from Enron, its accounting firm Arthur Andersen, and top Wall Street firms were called in to testify before congressional committees to explain the debacle. Some asserted their Fifth Amendment rights against self-incrimination and refused to explain how it was that earnings reports in the late 1990s, which showed profits piling up with no end in sight, turned out to be little more than wishful thinking. Those who testified faced heated questioning from members of Congress, who demanded to know why their constituents' 401(k) retirement plans had gone from nest eggs to empty nests in the blink of an eye.

On January 3, 2002, Lieberman, then the chairman of the Senate Governmental Affairs Committee, joined those looking for answers and announced an investigation of Enron. "The focus is, how did this corporation collapse, and what can we do to make sure that something like this never happens again?" he told the *Washington Post*.

Yet Lieberman chose not to ask that question of one individual who could have shed some light on how Enron collapsed. Robert Rubin, the Clinton administration's treasury secretary who went on to become chairman of Citigroup's executive committee, tried to intervene on Enron's behalf in the days before the corporation collapsed into bankruptcy. He called a former subordinate at the Treasury, asking him to pressure credit-rating agencies not to reduce Enron's debt to junk bond status. Many thought it worth asking why Rubin lobbied his former colleagues to save the energy firm.

"He may be one guy we're going to talk to," Lieberman said when asked about Rubin during a morning talk show. "There is some evidence that has been public that Bob Rubin did call someone in the Treasury Department in the final weeks before Enron bellied up on December 2 and went into bankruptcy."

But Lieberman never called Rubin to testify during his fact-finding mission, ultimately deciding that the high-ranking Citigroup executive was not able to shed any light on the scandal. Lieberman's Senate Governmental Affairs Committee concluded that Rubin did not violate any laws by pushing for governmental intervention on Enron's behalf. Perhaps not coincidentally, the Center found that Rubin's employer is Lieberman's largest career donor, giving more than $122,396 over the years.

Citigroup was not the only large money donor to Lieberman that had helped build the house of cards that was Enron. Goldman Sachs, the senator's fifth largest career patron, did more business with Enron than any other Wall Street brokerage. Merrill Lynch, Lehman Brothers, and J. P. Morgan Chase were all financial backers of Enron and were Lieberman's sixth, seventh, and thirty-fourth top patrons, respectively.

On July 28, 2003, Citigroup and J. P. Morgan Chase reached an agreement with the Securities Exchange Commission and the Manhattan district attorney's office to pay about $300 million in fines for their role in misleading investors over Enron. The two firms admitted no wrongdoing for their role; indeed, the settlement stipulated that the deals the two firms arranged with Enron were within the prevailing legal and accounting standards.

Over the years, Lieberman has been a faithful steward of his patrons' interests in Washington. Between 1998 and 2002, he sponsored or cosponsored 21 bills for which Citigroup lobbied. In 1997, he was among the first lawmakers to add his name to a bill that promised to "limit the conduct of securities class actions under State law," making it harder to sue high-flying companies whose profits were mostly on paper. The bill, signed into law on November 3, 1998, limited the amount of information that plaintiffs could obtain in the discovery process, making it harder for plaintiffs alleging corporate wrongdoing to get a look at the books.

A FAVORITE SON

Just as bankers like Citigroup and brokers like Goldman Sachs have been generous patrons of Lieberman, the insurance industry has found the Connecticut senator to be an ally worth investing in. Insurers have given the candidate more than half a million dollars over the years. So frequent are his actions on behalf of Connecticut's indemnity companies that Lieberman has been described by an insurance company representative as the industry's "go-to guy on the Democratic side of the aisle."

Lieberman has had a long history of support for insurance companies. In 1994, when President Clinton proposed his universal health care plan, Lieberman broke with the Democratic president and many others in his party to back a conservative plan favored by insurance interests. In 2001, he cosponsored a bill to repeal the provision taxing policyholder dividends of mutual life insurance companies. Over the years Lieberman has taken care of his state's industry and his contributors by working on legislation to limit auto accident lawsuits by permitting lower rates for drivers who forfeit their right to sue for pain and suffering. He has sponsored and cosponsored legislation to limit damages against tobacco producers, HMOs, and drug companies, damages that are often paid by insurers.

> **Lieberman has been described by an insurance company representative as the industry's "go-to guy on the Democratic side of the aisle."**

Connecticut has long been home to a number of insurance firms, dating back to the nation's earliest days, and insurance is one of the dominant industries in the state. And like any senator, Lieberman is not above taking care of his constituents. Though he favors gun control, on June 26, 2000, Lieberman wrote a letter asking the Bureau of Alcohol, Tobacco and Firearms to expedite a federal firearms license for a Connecticut gun dealer. More often, where his contributors are concerned, his record in Washington reflects his political views.

Consider his number eight career patron, the Connecticut-based manufacturing conglomerate United Technologies Corporation. Fighting for UTC's interests coincides with Lieberman's hawkish views on defense and his conservationist stand on energy issues. Over the course of his career, Lieberman, who has collected more than $61,000 from the company and its employees, has either sponsored, cosponsored, or voted for 11 bills that UTC lobbied on between 1999 and 2002. Most did not pass, but three that did paid off in billions to UTC and its subsidiaries.

In May 2003, the senator announced a plan that would reduce U.S. dependence on foreign oil by two-thirds in a decade, in part by developing a new technology, the hydrogen fuel cell, which some believe could replace gasoline in the near future. Fuel cells would combine hydrogen and oxygen to produce enough electricity to power a car.

Lieberman's plan proposes spending $6.5 billion for fuel cell research—more than five times what President Bush, who endorsed the technology in his 2003 State of the Union speech, has proposed. Lieberman believes that by 2020, 2.5 million fuel cell–powered cars could be running on the nation's roads, provided enough is spent now to develop the technology. Many private companies are doing just that. For example, UTC has a subsidiary, UTC Fuel Cells, that is one of largest players in the development of fuel cell technology in the world. UTC Fuel Cells has already received a government contract to design a hydrogen-fueled power plant at a cost to the government of $2.6 million. The program was put in place by an amendment Lieberman slipped into the Department of Transportation's 2002 budget.

Lieberman also increased his profile as an environmentalist by sponsoring and cosponsoring three other energy bills that UTC lobbied for between 2000 and 2002. All three bills were aimed at creating tax incentives to companies that reduce energy consumption and increase efficiency.

By far, UTC's biggest interest in Washington is the defense budget. The 2002 Defense Authorization bill, which netted the defense and energy company $10.3 billion, included funding for UTC to build airplane parts for the C-17 strategic airlift aircraft, the F-22 Raptor fighter jets and the F-35 Joint Strike Fighter. The federal appropriations are equivalent to almost a third of the company's revenues from the prior year. Not only did Lieberman vote in favor of the bill; he was one of the conferees who negotiated the final legislation with the House.

Lieberman also voted for the National Defense Authorization Act of 2003. Lieberman, who was then chairman of the Senate Armed Services Subcommittee on Airland Forces, lauded the bill's passage, which gave another $4.1 billion to UTC subsidiary Pratt & Whitney to work on 23 F-22 Raptor advanced tactical fighter planes. It also included $530 million to purchase 35 Black Hawk helicopters from UTC.

OLD MEDICINE FOR THE NEW ECONOMY

New Democrats have gone to great lengths to associate themselves with progress, whether in government or the private sector. One of the largest priorities of this new breed of Democrats can be summed up in two words: tax breaks. While Lieberman has been one of President Bush's harshest critics on his tax cuts for upper-income individuals, he has often tried to give corporate America a fatter bottom line by trimming its tax burden. A Center analysis found that Lieberman introduced at least 32 bills to cut taxes, many of them targeted toward high-tech industries.

The DLC is enthusiastic over the new economy, fueled by the Internet and the increased worker productivity that computers have spurred. Lieberman shares this passion for high-tech. On his campaign Web site, Lieberman boasts that he earned a "100 percent lifetime rating from the Information Technology Industry Council," and "the Founders Circle Award from Tech-Net, a leading tech industry group, for his leadership on tech issues." Lieberman supports tax cuts directed at high-tech companies and has supported an increase in the H1-B visa program for the tech sector. Critics contend that H1-B visas, granted to foreigners with a demonstrated skill, depress wages of high-tech workers already in the United States. A powerful coalition of Fortune 500 companies has long supported the H1-B visa program.

In a May 21, 2003, address at George Washington University in Washington, D.C., Lieberman outlined an ambitious agenda for another industry promising high-tech miracles, the pharmaceutical industry. The senator proposed creating an American Center for Cures, a government-funded effort to find treatments for diseases that afflict humanity. In the speech, Lieberman talked of a woman whose daughter suffered from juvenile diabetes and noted that embryonic stem cell research—which theoretically can make use of tissue from human embryos to develop cures for several diseases—might ease the girl's affliction. Lieberman blasted the Bush administration, which limited the controversial research to stem cells that had already been harvested. "As president, on the first day I am privileged to enter the Oval Office, I will rescind President Bush's restriction on stem cell research," he promised. "And that will be a big, real step on the road to curing more diseases."

Lieberman has paid fairly close attention to the biotechnology industry. In June 2001, he hired Chuck Ludlam, the principal lobbyist for the Biotechnology Industry Organization, to advise him on legislation affecting the field. The members of BIO, a well-funded and powerful advocacy group representing

1,000 biotech and pharmaceutical companies, research institutions, and others advancing the biotech industry's agenda, have given Lieberman at least $407,000 over the years, the Center found. Some of them are among Lieberman's top-tier donors, including Pfizer and GlaxoSmithKline.

Hiring Ludlam may have turned out to be the biggest boon the industry received from Lieberman. After seven years of running BIO legislative affairs, Ludlam had become the industry's go-to guy and lobbied Congress on nearly a hundred bills. The Washington lobbyist turned legislative assistant now counsels Lieberman on issues such as taxes, insurance, and trade—issues his former employer tried to affect when he lobbied for BIO. In the past Ludlam would make donations, lobby, and testify before Congress as vice president for government relations for BIO; now he works inside the Senate.

> **Lieberman showed an increased interest in legislation that could affect BIO's members after hiring their former lobbyist for his staff.**

With Ludlam on his staff, Lieberman has shown an increased interest in legislation that could affect BIO's members. From 1997 until 2000, the Center found, Lieberman cosponsored 10 BIO-lobbied bills in the two congressional sessions immediately prior to Ludlam's arrival. But in the congressional session after Lieberman hired Ludlum, the senator went on to cosponsor 9 bills on which BIO lobbied and was the primary sponsor on 2 other bills that the trade group favored. Lieberman took legislative actions on 7 of these 11 bills after hiring the former BIO lobbyist.

Lieberman pushed the interests of BIO and its members to respond to bioterrorism. In the fallout after the September 11 attacks in New York and Washington, the subject became an increasing concern. When envelopes containing lethal doses of anthrax were mailed to members of Congress and media fig- ures, killing five people, and when news analysts regularly spec- ulated on terrorists using smallpox and other pathogens, federal lawmakers attempted to address the nation's fears. Many con- gressional leaders in turn looked to Lieberman, who was one of the initiators of the legislation that led to the creation of the Department of Homeland Security. Lieberman turned to Lud- lam. The industry expert went to work and developed S. 3148, the Biological Countermeasures Research Act, which Lieber- man introduced in the Senate on October 17, 2002.

The bill provides many of BIO's company members with generous tax incentives, guaranteed markets for successful products, and special patent protection. His former clients rec- ognized Ludlam as the architect of the legislation. One month after working on the bill, he was asked to deliver the keynote address at a bio-security seminar held at the MGM Grand Con- ference Center in Las Vegas. In press releases publicizing the event, Ludlam's biographical brief makes specific mention of his contributions to Lieberman's bill.

"The key question is whether or not the administration, and particularly the new secretary of Homeland Security, will develop a plan for involving biopharmaceutical companies in countermeasure research," Ludlam told a biotech trade publi- cation. While the seminar's attendees were in no doubt as to what the answer to that question should be, in Washington the incentive-laden bill had run into problems. With a Republican Congress and administration, few Democratic initiatives were likely to pass. So Lieberman cosponsored three similar bills lobbied by BIO, all of which aimed to deliver similar incentives to the biotech industry. One that had bipartisan and BIO sup- port finally passed in 2002.

Lieberman backed bills favored by BIO before its lobbyist joined his staff. In 2000, he cosponsored the Biomass Research and Development Act, which has provisions that could create new avenues of potential income for BIO members. The bill would forge a relationship between the secretary of agriculture and the secretary of energy to coordinate research and development activities leading to the production of bio-based industrial products, including renewable energy sources.

On the issue of embryonic stem cell research, Lieberman's legislative actions have run parallel to the interests of BIO. On January 17, 2001, the trade group and many of its members signed an open letter to President-elect Bush, saying, "Given the great hope that stem cell research provides to those who are suffering or dying from devastating illnesses, we urge you to allow this research to move forward with federal support." The group lobbied the administration and Congress for that support as well. Lieberman cosponsored a bill to pay for it. The legislation, the Stem Cell Research Act of 2001, was overshadowed by Bush's August 2001 decision, televised live from his Crawford, Texas, ranch, in which he announced that stem cell research could go forward, but only on the limited number of cells already in use.

Finding Cures, Fishing for Dollars

In May 2003, when Lieberman announced his campaign health care and drug plan, he mentioned those who are afflicted with disease but without a cure. At the center of his plan, delivered at George Washington University in Washington, D.C., was the creation of a new federal plan to invest $150 billion in drug research over 10 years.

"For millions, that pain of course is nonstop," he said. "Kids and grownups whose lives are compromised or cut short by diabetes. Seniors who can't walk to the mailbox without feeling the deep ache of arthritis . . . For all of these men and women, for their children and for generations to come, it is time to say: treatment is not enough. We need cures." Lieberman has not been above criticizing Pfizer, or the pharmaceutical industry in general. In the 2000 campaign, when he ran as Al Gore's running mate, Lieberman followed Gore's lead in arguing that drug companies charged too much, impoverishing seniors who lacked insurance coverage to pay for life-saving and life-extending medications.

In his May 21, 2003, speech outlining his plan for an American Center for Cures, he pointed to the deaths and suffering caused by heart disease and cancer, and said, "Some say that we can depend on pharmaceutical companies to deliver the life-saving cures we need. But we can't. These companies often invest most heavily in the next big-ticket blockbuster drugs and they don't always have the market." The fact sheet that Lieberman's campaign issued on the proposal names Viagra, the impotence treatment made by Pfizer, as just such a blockbuster drug that diverts the research and development efforts of pharmaceutical giants from deadly diseases.

Pfizer's stock-in-trade is its blockbuster drugs—medicines that have more than a billion dollars in annual sales as of late 2002—such as Viagra, its painkiller Celebrex, and its anticonvulsant Neurontin. The company—which has also seen recent increases during 2001 and 2002 in sales based on its recent merger with Warner-Lambert, maker of the blockbuster cholesterol drug Lipitor—has spent millions lobbying Congress on several bills aimed at creating research tax credits that could fatten its bottom line and at extending its patents on—and profits from—its blockbuster drugs.

Lieberman has backed bills that would establish a permanent tax credit for research-based companies, including pharmaceutical firms, for the costs they encounter when developing new products and increase the amounts those companies could write off. Lieberman's legislation would have benefited companies like Pfizer while placing a costly burden on the backs of the American taxpayer. Pfizer lobbied for both bills.

In May 1998, Lieberman took a trip to White Sulphur Springs, West Virginia, home of the tony Greenbrier resort, which boasts a championship 18-hole golf course, indoor and outdoor tennis courts, a spa, a Land Rover driving school, and Olympic-sized indoor and outdoor pools. Pfizer paid almost $1,000 for Lieberman to travel and deliver a speech to PhRMA during its annual meeting.

A month later, Lieberman pushed a plan that would have extended the length of time a drug company could hold a patent on a medicine. By 2006, almost 200 U.S. pharmaceutical patents will expire, meaning that U.S. pharmaceutical companies like Pfizer can lose a majority of their $36 billion market share overnight to companies that can make "generic," and less expensive, versions of the blockbuster drugs.

While Lieberman has been close to the company doing "the Lord's work" for years, the politician most closely connected with Pfizer in the public's mind is probably former senator and 1996 Republican presidential nominee Bob Dole. In a series of advertisements, the septuagenarian genially pitched the company's impotence treatment, Viagra. Though Lieberman never appeared in a commercial for Pfizer, he has made an endorsement of the company's most famous product. During a speech at the Gridiron Club Dinner in December 1998, Lieberman made a quip about Viagra while discussing campaign finance reform. "I've turned to biotechnology," he told the group "and I'm asking Pfizer to turn soft money into hard money."

That's a trick Lieberman may need more companies to perform. Despite the front-runner status conferred on him by the name recognition he gained in the 2000 presidential campaign, Lieberman trails his rivals in fundraising. By honoring his promise not to run against Al Gore for the nomination, Lieberman got a late start on soliciting donors and organizing a campaign, which he made something of a family affair. He put his children, Matt and Rebecca, on the campaign staff, and, during the second quarter of 2003, paid them each $2,500 every two weeks. If Lieberman's campaign went the distance, they might pull down around forty checks that would net them about $100,000. The compensation he paid his children became a source of friction among his campaign employees and led two of his top fundraisers to quit their positions. After his children's salaries became public, Lieberman said he would reduce their pay.

Joe Lieberman

Top Ten Career Patrons

Ranking	Patron	Total
1	Citigroup Inc., New York	$122,396*
2	The Hartford Financial Services Group Inc., Hartford, Connecticut	$ 78,650
3	Irell & Manella LLP, Los Angeles	$ 75,950
4	Chase Enterprises, New York	$ 75,500
5	Goldman Sachs Group Inc., New York	$ 72,250
6	Merrill Lynch & Company Inc., New York	$ 68,400
7	Lehman Brothers Holdings Inc., New York	$ 64,800
8	United Technologies Corporation, Hartford, Connecticut	$ 61,000
9	Crédit Suisse First Boston, New York	$ 58,750
10	GAF Materials Corporation, Wayne, New Jersey	$ 56,500†

This list is based on individual, corporate, and PAC contributions to the Responsibility Opportunity Community PAC-Nonfederal through December 31, 2002, and on individual and PAC contributions to Lieberman's 1980 congressional campaign, Lieberman's Senate campaigns from 1987 to 2000, Lieberman's 2000 vice presidential campaign committee, Responsibility Opportunity Community PAC, and Lieberman's 2004 presidential campaign through June 30, 2003.

Sources: Federal Election Commission, Internal Revenue Service.

*Includes contributions from Citigroup and employees of Citigroup and the companies that have contributed to the creation of Citigroup, including: Citibank, Citicorp, Travelers Corporation, the Copeland Companies, Salomon Smith Barney (and its predecessors, Salomon Brothers and Smith Barney), and Shearson Lehman Hutton (and its predecessors, including Shearson, Hayden & Stone, and EF Hutton). From 1981 to 1993, Shearson was owned by American Express. Contributions from individuals who identified themselves as Shearson employees during this time period are also included in the Citigroup figure. Contributions from individuals who identified themselves as American Express employees are not.

†Includes employees of the GAF Materials Corporation and the Heyman Family of New York and Connecticut.

Carol Moseley Braun

When Carol Moseley Braun announced her candidacy for the Democratic nomination for president in February 2003, she said she was running on a platform of "peace, prosperity, and progress." She would conduct a grassroots campaign to "generate the kind of support that will make this . . . a viable campaign," she said. Shortly thereafter she kicked off a speaking tour to Iowa, New Hampshire, and South Carolina and quickly discovered how hard her "grassroots" support would be to find. In Des Moines, Iowa, for example, the woman who had gained fame as the first African American woman to win a seat in the U.S. Senate formally addressed an audience made up of a former college classmate, a conference hall filled with empty chairs, and a C-SPAN camera.

Her problems went beyond a lack of attendance in the Hawkeye State, however. While her competitors were raising millions of dollars, the former senator was able to muster only slightly more than $200,000 over the first six months of 2003. Weak fundraising and poll numbers in the low single digits convinced some political commentators to write her off as a serious challenger.

The inability to raise funds also took its toll on her campaign staff. By mid-June, five staffers had left. Moseley Braun characterized this as a reorganization of her campaign, claiming that she was consolidating because "I don't have money to burn." However, sources familiar with the campaign told the Center for Public Integrity that some of the departures reflected employee discontent over late and missing paychecks, rather than a strategic move on the part of the campaign.

Owing to the campaign's outstanding debts, staff members went from being paid monthly to semimonthly—and then not at all, according to several sources familiar with the campaign. One check to an employee bounced. Expenditure records filed with the Federal Election Commission list a total of $77,900 in debt, of which nearly three-quarters represents money owed to campaign staffers, consultants, and lawyers. As of July 15, 2003, more than $17,600 was still owed to departed staffers.

Not surprisingly, the financial shortfalls have compelled Moseley Braun to make other concessions that upset her staff. A Center investigation found that payroll taxes withheld from four employees were never sent to the Internal Revenue Service. Instead, five days before the end-of-quarter tax deadline, the withheld funds were sent to these staffers, along with a letter explaining that they had been changed from "employees" to "consultants." The shift in job status would presumably save the campaign money in personnel costs, but it added to a feeling of discontent among some staffers, who now were responsible for filing additional taxes in a very short window of time.

This is not the first time that a Carol Moseley Braun campaign has had problems with accounting or campaign finance. In fact, charges of ethical improprieties have dogged her throughout her career in government service.

FROM SOUTH SIDE TO STATE HOUSE

Carol Moseley Braun was born the eldest of four children on August 16, 1947, "the very day that Jackie Robinson signed with the Brooklyn Dodgers," as she likes to recall. The daughter of a police officer and a medical technician, Moseley Braun grew up in a segregated neighborhood on Chicago's South Side. Her father was at times violent. "It was not really a happy childhood," Moseley Braun told the *St. Louis Post-Dispatch*. "I had to grow up fast."

And grow up fast she did. Moseley Braun did well enough in school to enroll at the University of Illinois at Chicago and, after graduation, went on to the prestigious University of Chicago Law School. While pursuing her law degree, she met Michael Braun, whom she would later marry. The couple had one child before divorcing in 1986.

Soon after graduating from law school, Moseley Braun became an assistant U.S. attorney. During her four years as a prosecutor, she won the U.S. Department of Justice Special Achievement Award for superior performance. In 1978 she successfully ran for the Illinois House of Representatives and took her seat in the state legislature.

Among her colleagues, the young representative soon acquired a reputation as both a tough debater and a skilled conciliator. She sponsored a host of education bills, including landmark legislation in 1985 that created parents councils at schools across Chicago. Her success in the legislature earned her the post of assistant majority leader, making her the first Black and the first woman in Illinois history to hold that position.

In 1988, after 10 years in the legislature, Moseley Braun ran successfully for Cook County recorder of deeds, where for four years she oversaw a staff of 300 employees and earned praise for her efforts to modernize the office. Moseley Braun's political prospects were on the rise.

THE YEAR OF THE WOMAN . . . AND CONTROVERSY

In 1992—the so-called Year of the Woman—a record-setting number of women were elected to national office. Carol Moseley Braun was the star of the group.

In November 1991, outraged by the vote of an all-male, all-White Senate Judiciary Committee to confirm Supreme Court nominee Clarence Thomas despite allegations of sexual harassment, Moseley Braun decided to challenge two-term Senate veteran Alan J. Dixon, who had voted in favor of Thomas's nomination.

Dixon, a Democrat known as "Al the Pal" for his congenial demeanor, had served 42 years in government without losing an election and was viewed as such a strong incumbent that no prominent Republican planned to oppose him in the general election. But running on a promise to reform the government and inject the voice of the disenfranchised into the overwhelmingly White and male Senate, Moseley Braun was able to compete.

> **In the March 17, 1992, primary, Moseley Braun won a surprising victory in a three-way race, despite being vastly outspent.**

In the March 17, 1992, primary, she won a surprising victory in a three-way race, defeating Dixon and Albert Hofeld, a wealthy Chicago attorney, despite being vastly outspent. Her opponents spent a total of $6.8 million on the campaign; Moseley Braun managed just $440,000. The *Washington Post* called her 38 to 35 percent win over Dixon "a stunning upset." However, when she moved on to the general election against Republican challenger Richard Williamson, Moseley Braun faced another challenge.

On September 28, 1992, Chicago TV station WMAQ reported that three years earlier Moseley Braun had improperly deposited a $28,750 check for her mother, Edna Moseley, a 71-year-old Medicaid recipient. Edna Moseley had received the windfall from the sale of timber rights on land she had inherited after going on Medicaid and had given the check to her daughter to deposit. Because her mother's medical care was being subsidized by the state, the income should have been reported to the Illinois Department of Public Aid, which might have required a portion of the check to be used for reimbursement.

Moseley Braun vigorously defended herself in public and eventually repaid the state $15,240, but the issue dogged her throughout the remainder of the campaign, even cutting into her sizable lead over Williamson. Her actions also damaged the public's confidence in her: an exit poll taken during the election found that slightly more than half of the voters—including a third of her supporters—doubted her honesty because of the event.

Despite this controversy, and troubles within her campaign, Moseley Braun won with 53 percent of the vote to Williamson's 43 percent. It was a historic event, and Moseley Braun received national attention. But before she could take her place as the first Black woman to serve in the Senate, she again found herself under public scrutiny.

This time, the controversy swirled around Kgosie Matthews, Moseley Braun's campaign manager, whom she had begun dating during her run for the Senate (they would be engaged the following spring). Moseley Braun credited Matthews with turning her campaign around and keeping her in the race. She called him her "knight in shining armor," but his personality clashed with other campaign workers, leading to the departure of several staffers during the primary.

In early December, the *Chicago Sun-Times* reported that a few staffers had anonymously accused Matthews of sexual harassment during the campaign. Moseley Braun stood by her man, saying that an investigation she had commissioned from outside lawyers "concluded there was no foundation to these anonymous allegations." The event still played poorly in public, however, as Moseley Braun's actions were perceived as being much too similar to those that she had so vehemently protested during the Clarence Thomas hearings.

Shortly after dealing with the sexual harassment allegations, Moseley Braun found her judgment questioned when she took a 27-day vacation to Africa with Matthews and her son. At the time, most other new senators were moving to Washington, compiling their staffs and planning their legislative agendas. She was also questioned about paying Matthews a salary of $15,000 per month while other staff members saw their paychecks delayed because of more than $400,000 in campaign debt. What's more, Moseley Braun admitted to poor judgment when, in an apparent act of political patronage, she gave 10 people—including some campaign workers—jobs in her old office shortly before leaving. Her successor promptly fired them.

DIVERSIFYING THE SENATE

Despite the rough transition to her new job, Moseley Braun showed a willingness to make waves in Washington. Perhaps the high point came in late July of her first year, when the United Daughters of the Confederacy applied to Congress for a renewal of the trademark on its insignia, a laurel wreath surrounding a

Confederate flag. Renewal of such a trademark is an honorific title bestowed on patriotic groups; Jesse Helms, the conservative Senate veteran from North Carolina, was a fervent supporter. Helms described the UDC as a group of "delightful gentleladies" who performed charitable deeds, and a test vote on the subject narrowly passed.

Moseley Braun didn't find the insignia so benign. She threatened to filibuster "until this room freezes over" and deemed any congressional sponsorship of the Confederate symbol an "outrage" and an "insult." "It is absolutely unacceptable to me and to millions of Americans, Black or White, that we would put the imprimatur of the United States Senate on a symbol of this kind of idea," she said.

> Sloppy bookkeeping during her 1992 campaign, along with allegations that she and Kgosie Matthews spent campaign funds on personal luxury items, resulted in an FEC audit and an IRS inquiry.

Her impassioned oratory changed the mood of the Senate, sparked a discussion of racism, and convinced many of her colleagues to change their votes and defeat the proposal 75 to 25. Even Alabama senator Howell Heflin, who said his family was "rooted in the Confederacy," conceded the point to the senator for Illinois. "We must get racism behind us," said Heflin. "We must move forward. We must realize we live in America today." The national media was also impressed. The *New York Times* called it "Ms. Moseley Braun's Majestic Moment."

During her single term in the Senate, Moseley Braun supported or sponsored civil rights and educational initiatives. She sponsored legislation offering tax incentives for businesses to reclaim and redevelop contaminated industrial sites. She also cosponsored a balanced-budget amendment in 1994 and voted for the North American Free Trade Agreement, despite opposition from labor unions.

Still, Moseley Braun couldn't distance herself from controversy. Sloppy bookkeeping during her 1992 campaign, along with allegations that she and Matthews spent campaign funds on personal luxury items, resulted in an FEC audit and an IRS inquiry. Problems with employee turnover—she had five chiefs of staff in five years, including one who reportedly quit before officially taking the job—led *The Economist* to quip: "She has a reputation for turning out staff faster than she turns out legislation." There were also allegations that a Senate staffer was fired after returning from maternity leave.

In the midst of this, Kgosie Matthews surfaced at the center of another Moseley Braun political headache. Although the couple had broken their engagement in early 1994, the two traveled to Nigeria in 1996, where they met with Sani Abacha, the country's ironfisted dictator. Although human rights groups accused Abacha of killing democracy activists and opposition leaders, Moseley Braun opposed sanctions against the West African nation. Controversy was especially intense because the trip was made without the knowledge or approval of the State Department, and Matthews had previously been a paid lobbyist for the Nigerian government.

The senator's trip was immediately condemned by critics, including the Congressional Black Caucus. Edith Wilson, her chief of staff, abruptly quit after she learned of the visit. Moseley Braun, who had made six previous trips to the country, offered a variety of defenses, claiming, at different times, that the trip was to console Abacha's wife, whose son had recently died; that it was a form of quiet diplomacy; and that she had done no worse than other senators who had met with questionable dictators.

The public was unconvinced, and so were Illinois voters during her 1998 race for reelection. Her opponent, Peter Fitzgerald, used an advantage in campaign spending to focus the race on Moseley Braun's ethical lapses, which had been further spotlighted by her Nigeria trip. Unable to bring the focus back to her legislative record, Moseley Braun lost to Fitzgerald, 51 percent to 47 percent. But her political career was not over.

In 1999, Bill Clinton nominated Moseley Braun to serve as ambassador to New Zealand; she was confirmed despite the efforts of her old nemesis, Jesse Helms. Moseley Braun served as envoy to the South Pacific nation and earned praise from the prime minister, who called her "the modern face of America."

STRATEGIC MEDICINE

In the spring of 1992, after Moseley Braun had gained national attention for winning the Senate primary, she was contacted by GlaxoSmithKline, the U.K.-based pharmaceutical giant. For giving a series of speeches to the company's Chicago convention in June, the future senator was paid $15,000—more than a fifth of her earnings for the entire year. Senate rules prohibit the acceptance of money for speeches, but since Moseley Braun had yet to win the general election, no sanction applied.

Glaxo was generous to Moseley Braun in other ways, as well. The company and its employees have donated nearly $25,000 to her campaigns, making Glaxo her eighth largest career donor. When Moseley Braun took her seat in the Senate, the support appeared to pay off for the drug maker.

In 1995, the Senate considered whether to amend the General Agreement on Tariffs and Trade, or GATT, treaty to close a loophole that extended Glaxo's patent on Zantac, a popular anti-ulcer drug. David Pryor, a Democrat from Arkansas, argued that the loophole enriched drug companies at the expense of consumers and said that if it was not closed, "Consumers lose, taxpayers lose, and the ideas of competition and free trade lose."

Moseley Braun felt otherwise. She was the only Democrat on the Finance Committee to vote against closing the loophole, and she voted against it in a full session of the Senate, when a motion to close the loophole failed by two votes.

A spokesperson for the senator denied that her actions had anything to do with support from Glaxo. Rather, Moseley Braun acted based on "the policy aspects" of the issue, which she felt would benefit the United States.

DISCREDITING CREDIT

Moseley Braun's current financial problems are nothing new. In fact, her 1992 run for the Senate was plagued with allegations of misspent funds and unbalanced ledgers. Although she was able to raise more than $6 million, her campaign ended up deeply in debt. The debt stood at $544,000 in February 1993, and rose to a high of nearly $700,000 in 1995, despite additional fundraisers.

In January 1994, the Federal Election Commission began an audit of her campaign and uncovered a host of bookkeeping problems. The campaign had $249,212 of unaccounted-for expenditures, more than $80,000 in individual contributions that exceeded the legal annual limit, and multiple failures to properly itemize contributions and credit card payments.

According to Billie Paige, who became the campaign treasurer in 1996, it cost more than $1 million in accounting and legal fees to fix these problems. In addition, tens of thousands of dollars in excess contributions were returned. By 1996, the campaign had filed 42 amended reports—one ran over 1,300 pages—to resolve the initial problems found by the auditors. The FEC could still have fined the campaign for its original misstatements, but due to an impending expiration of the statute of limitations, combined with other factors, declined to take action.

Still, Moseley Braun had to deal with her creditors. Kezios Properties, a Chicago real estate company that leased space to the campaign, went to court and won a $56,000 judgment. Earl Hopewell, Moseley Braun's treasurer from 1992 until 1996, sued his former employer in September 1996 for nearly $200,000 in fees and salary. The suit claimed that the campaign had funded unnecessary luxuries, including $110,000 for private jet charters. A month later, Hopewell ignited further controversy by alleging that Moseley Braun and Kgosie Matthews had spent $39,000 of campaign funds on personal items, including jewelry and designer clothing.

Similar allegations had surfaced before, and the Department of Justice had twice rebuffed requests from the Internal Revenue Service to convene grand jury hearings on the matter. Later, in 1997, information surfaced indicating that the IRS had launched a criminal probe of Matthews for improper use of campaign funds.

> "I don't know what it takes to put a stake in the heart of that kind of a nasty rumor," Moseley Braun said. "But I can tell you, it's been seven years of a smear campaign around that issue."

In 1999, at her ambassadorial confirmation hearings before the Senate Foreign Relations Committee, Moseley Braun was given the opportunity to clear her name. The nominee proclaimed her innocence and cited the FEC report, which she said debunked charges that she spent campaign funds on personal purchases. "I don't know what it takes to put a stake in the heart of that kind of a nasty rumor," she said. "But I can tell you, it's been seven years of a smear campaign around that issue, and I just hope that this hearing and the documents that have been filed with this committee . . . will finally put the stake in the heart of something that wasn't true when it was first said."

RUNNING ON EMPTY

Given Moseley Braun's past—and current—problems with campaign financing and her bitter Senate defeat after just one term, why is she running again? Some have suggested that she was asked to run in order to steal some thunder from the controversial Reverend Al Sharpton, who, like Moseley Braun, is Black. Both the candidate and the Democratic leadership have derided this allegation as mere Washington gossip.

Others speculate that Moseley Braun may be running to clear her record and burnish her nationwide image, in the hopes of a future political post.

Whatever her motives, Moseley Braun faces a series of obstacles. University of Maryland political scientist Ron Walters notes that because of her gender and race, Moseley Braun has "at least two strikes against her. The third strike is some of the baggage that continues to follow her."

Carol Moseley Braun

Top Ten Career Patrons

Ranking	Patron	Total
1	EMILY's List, Washington, D.C.	$89,739
2	United Airlines, Chicago	$44,944
3	Corboy & Demetrio, Chicago	$29,650
4	Bank of America Corporation, New York	$29,550
5	HSBC Holdings Inc., Hong Kong, China	$29,250*
6	Jenner & Block LLC, Chicago	$27,782
7	Service Employees International Union, Washington, D.C.	$25,000
8	GlaxoSmithKline, Brentford, Middlesex, United Kingdom	$24,999†
9	Waste Management Inc., Houston	$24,300
10	Sidley Austin Brown & Wood LLP, Chicago	$23,350

This list is based on individual and PAC contributions to Moseley Braun's Senate campaigns from 1991 to 1998 and to Moseley Braun's 2004 presidential campaign through June 30, 2003.

Source: Federal Election Commission.

*Includes employees of companies that have been acquired by HSBC, including Household International of Prospect Heights, Illinois; ACC Consumer Finance;

and Beneficial Corporation. In 1997 Household acquired Transamerica Financial from Transamerica Corporation Individuals who identified themselves as working for Transamerica Financial are included in HSBC's total. Individuals who identified themselves as working for Transamerica Corporation are not.

†Includes contributions from GlaxoSmithKline employees and employees of the companies that later became parts of GSK, including Glaxo, Inc.; Burroughs Wellcome; Glaxo Wellcome; SmithKline Beecham; SmithKline Beckman; SmithKline Corporation; Beckman Instruments, Inc.; Norcliff Thayer; Diversified Pharmaceutical Services, Inc.; Beecham Group plc; and Meyer Laboratories, Inc. Contributions are from U.S. employees.

Al Sharpton

In 2001, Edison Schools, the controversial for-profit company that takes over troubled public schools and promises to turn them around, reached a preliminary agreement with New York City to run five failing schools that served predominantly minority children. The company, which had the blessings of Rudolph Giuliani, then the mayor of New York, would receive $250 million of taxpayer money to run the schools. There was one hitch, however. The local teachers union opposed the move and community parents were deeply skeptical. Edison needed the parents' support. To try to get it, the company turned to an unlikely source: the controversial, self-styled civil rights leader, the Reverend Al Sharpton.

In a scant 15 years, Reverend Sharpton had gone from a street preacher, would-be entertainment mogul, and media grandstander to a force to be reckoned with. Although he had been publicly branded a slanderer and faced numerous civil suits and a few criminal charges for flouting tax laws, refusing to pay bills, and mismanaging his nonprofits in the 1980s and early 1990s, by 2000, Democratic politicians like Al Gore and Hillary Rodham Clinton were paying him visits, seeking his support in their election bids. Those who ran afoul of him, like mayoral candidates Ruth Messinger and Mark Green, regretted it on election day.

Sharpton promised Edison's executives a fair hearing but ultimately decided to oppose the plan. He and his National Action Network joined a lawsuit that sought to bar Edison from running the schools. In the end, Edison lost the referendum.

National Action Network boasted on its Web site that, along with the parents and some of the other groups that opposed the company, it had "defeated Edison's attempt to operate five charter schools." Sharpton said that for him, using public money to fund private schools was simply wrong. He told the *New York Daily News* that "people who want private situations should pay for it."

The donors to his nonprofit might have been surprised to learn that they had been paying for Sharpton's private situation. Sharpton, who sends both his daughters to private school, borrowed money from the National Action Network to pay the girls' tuition, even though nonprofits are prohibited by law from extending loans to officers. The organization extended an interest-free loan for $17,220.

Sharpton has built, with the aid of a core of wealthy contributors, a small empire of tax-exempt and for-profit companies and mingled their finances to confuse creditors and tax collectors alike. When called to account, he conflates his personal travails with his civil rights crusading, turning his own questionable practices into a vehicle for self-promotion and raising his political clout.

"Always in the Public Eye"

Sharpton was born in 1954 into a comfortable middle-class home, though circumstances changed when his father abandoned the family and his mother moved Al and his older sister to a Brooklyn housing project, where she raised them while working as a domestic and receiving welfare. Sharpton became involved in the church early on, delivering his first sermon at the age of 4 and becoming ordained as a junior pastor at age 10 at the Washington Temple Church in Brooklyn. Sharpton became a preaching prodigy and toured with gospel singer Mahalia Jackson. "I did some of the normal kid things, but I was always in the public eye," he wrote in his 1996 autobiography. "I never had a private life. But I always knew how to attract attention; I grew up attracting the attention of the crowd. I grew up understanding the psychology of standing out. And I understood the emotions of the people."

Sharpton experienced the hottest days of the civil rights movement through a television set in his living room. Though the movement is a constant reference in his speech and identity, his age placed him a good decade younger than those who marched on the streets of Selma. It also imparted a heroic glow to the movement's figures whom the young Sharpton, already extraordinarily attuned to matters of image and mass appeal, would worship and emulate.

When he was 11 years old, Sharpton went to the Abyssinian Baptist Church in Harlem to hear a sermon by the man who would become the first of a series of father figures and mentors, Congressman Adam Clayton Powell Jr. Sharpton vividly recalls Powell's "magnetism" and "majestic air," his elegance and self-assurance. Powell adopted him as a young sidekick, allowing him to observe Powell holding court with various politicians and personalities, wielding an influence that inspired him.

Sharpton has said, "You can't understand Al Sharpton until you understand Adam Clayton Powell." Reared in turn-of-the-century Harlem, Powell followed his father into the clergy, entered politics as a New York City councilman and was elected to the House of Representatives in 1945. Though he succeeded in passing progressive legislation, including an antidiscrimination rider known as the Powell amendment, his flamboyance and arrogance earned him many enemies. In 1963, he was found guilty of defamation and slander but refused to pay the judgment, resulting in a contempt of court citation. That citation, as well as allegations that Powell misused House funds, led to his expulsion from Congress in 1967. The Supreme Court eventually ruled the decision unconstitutional, and Powell was reelected to the House in 1968, though he lost his seat in 1970. "What I learned from Powell about leadership . . . is that you can't care what people think," Sharpton wrote in *Al on America*, his campaign manifesto. "Adam Clayton Powell did not care about being accepted by society."

> **In a string of incidents with racial overtones, Sharpton assumed a role as public advocate, honing his special brand of protest-cum-rally-cum-sermon.**

One year after meeting Powell, Sharpton went to work at Operation Breadbasket, an arm of Dr. Martin Luther King Jr.'s Southern Christian Leadership Conference that used nonviolent protest to lobby corporations for Black jobs. There he met his second principal mentor and influence, Reverend Jesse Jackson. When Jackson left Operation Breadbasket in 1971 to start his Operation PUSH, Sharpton founded a nonprofit of his own, the National Youth Movement, which adopted a similar program of voter registration and corporate protest.

However, the man Sharpton says had "more impact on my life than any civil rights leader" was entertainer James Brown. Brown's son worked in the National Youth Movement, and when he was killed in an auto accident Brown adopted Sharpton as a surrogate son. After graduating from Tilden High School and spending two years at Brooklyn College, Sharpton went on the road as Brown's road manager. Sharpton's years with Brown showed him the ins and outs of show business, a world for which Sharpton had a natural affinity. Brown also introduced him to his wife, backup singer Kathy Jordan. In the 1980s Sharpton created Hit Bound, the first in a series of entertainment promotion businesses. He also decided that the National Youth Movement would switch its focus to the entertainment industry, lobbying Black artists to use Black promoters and management.

Sharpton first came to national prominence in 1984, when a White man named Bernhard Goetz shot four Black teenagers on a Manhattan subway. Goetz, who claimed that the four boys were about to mug him, was ultimately acquitted of all charges save one, for gun possession. Sharpton led efforts to indict him on federal civil rights charges and landed himself on newspaper pages and television screens across the country. The event was the first in a string of incidents with racial overtones in which Sharpton would assume a role as public advocate, honing his special brand of protest-cum-rally-cum-sermon.

What crystallized Sharpton's public image, however, was the case of Tawanna Brawley. On November 28, 1987, Brawley, a Black high school student from Wappingers Falls, New York, was found in a plastic bag, covered in feces and with racial epithets written on her skin. When questioned by police, she said she had been abducted and raped numerous times by a team of White law enforcement officials over a period of four days. Sharpton, along with attorneys C. Vernon Mason and Alton H. Maddox Jr. (who were later disbarred for unethical practices), became an advisor to the Brawley family.

The tactics that worked for Sharpton in the street did not go over as well in the courtroom. During a grand jury hearing on the case, Sharpton, Maddox, and Mason leveled wild accusations at local law enforcement officials and even accused Steven Pagones, then an assistant district attorney in Dutchess County, New York, of being complicit in the alleged assault and rape. The grand jury concluded that Brawley's charges were a hoax; Pagones sued Sharpton, Maddox, and Mason for defamation, and prevailed in his case against Sharpton in July 1998.

In 1991, during one of a series of marches protesting the death of Yusuf Hawkins, a 16-year-old Black teenager shot in a dispute with White teenagers in the Brooklyn neighborhood of Bensonhurst, Sharpton was stabbed in the chest by an onlooker. The knife came within inches of Sharpton's heart, and he was taken to a Coney Island hospital, where he held a press conference about nonviolence from a wheelchair. Sharpton cites the incident as a turning point at which he decided to cool his overheated rhetoric and concentrate on more tangible political achievements. "I decided to try to begin acting out of resolve, out of an overall plan, to become proactive. That's why I entered electoral politics: I realized that running around from problem to problem, chasing phone call after phone call, would never move society," he wrote in his autobiography. Sharpton maintained some of his old ways, however: the hospital filed a lawsuit against him months later for skipping out on his $7,400 bill.

In addition to running for elected office, Sharpton decided while in the hospital to establish a new nonprofit organization. In 1994, he founded the National Action Network, a civil rights organization with a network of national chapters whose mission is to be "the voice of empowerment for the disenfranchised throughout America." NAN was a replica of Jesse Jackson's Rainbow Coalition, which established chapters across the country to work on issues such as racial profiling and voter registration—neither the first nor the last initiative of Jackson's that Sharpton would imitate. "[Sharpton] is obsessed with Jesse Jackson to a point almost everything he does is patterned after him," said Frank Mercado-Velez, a former Sharpton backer and CEO of the Heritage Networks broadcasting company. "He knew what he wanted to be most was president of Black America, and the one guy standing in front of him was Jesse Jackson."

Sharpton's selection for chairman of the board was civil rights veteran and former King chief of staff Wyatt T. Walker, now pastor of Canaan Baptist Church of Christ in Harlem. NAN's office at 1941 Madison Avenue in Harlem became known as the House of Justice, where Sharpton preached sermons each Saturday broadcast on local radio station WLIB.

Sharpton began pursuing a seat in the U.S. Senate soon after leaving the hospital. It was not his first try at elected office: he ran for New York state senator in 1978, though his candidacy was later disqualified because he did not meet residency requirements. In his 1992 run, Sharpton's polling numbers surprised many; though he won only 14 percent of the vote statewide, he won roughly 20 percent of New York City votes. More importantly, he won 67 percent of the Black vote statewide, in addition to 16 percent of the Hispanic and 20 percent of the union vote. He tried for the Senate again in 1994 against incumbent Daniel Moynihan, winning 25 percent of the statewide vote and more than 30 percent in New York City.

In 1997, Sharpton ran in the New York City mayoral race. When he lost the Democratic nomination by a slim margin to Ruth Messinger, he chose to declare the election corrupted by voting irregularities rather than back Messinger against Republican incumbent Rudy Giuliani. Sharpton pursued his case for weeks in the state supreme court—which eventually ruled the election valid—rather than campaign in the Black community for Messinger, who lost in a landslide to Giuliani.

Sharpton's growing influence was duly noted by Democratic Party operatives, but it was a series of shootings that gave him the platform he needed to move forward. On February 4, 1999, Amadou Diallo, an unarmed immigrant from Guinea, was shot 19 times in the doorway of his Bronx apartment building by four White police officers when they saw him reach for what they thought was a gun but turned out to be his wallet. The incident occurred 18 months after the brutal assault on Haitian immigrant Abner Louima in a New York police station, and would be followed by three more fatal police shootings of unarmed Black men over the next year.

Suddenly, the dire gospel of police brutality and racial profiling that Sharpton had preached for years seemed to have its day of judgment. "Those [events] added as much to Sharpton's credibility as anything," David Bositis of the Joint Center for Political and Economic Studies, a Washington, D.C., think tank that analyzes policies affecting African Americans and other minorities, told the Center. "Sharpton . . . was accused by White politicians of being a rabble-rouser out on the streets, making things happen. When things happened, more Black people said Sharpton was right."

> White politicians said Sharpton was "a rabble-rouser out on the streets making things happen.
> When things happened, more Black people said Sharpton was right."

Sharpton sprang into action immediately after the Diallo shooting, leading daily protests in front of police headquarters. More protests followed the Diallo officers' acquittal and the three other police shootings. The protests attracted thousands and featured the arrests of former mayor David Dinkins, Representative

Charles Rangel, and Reverend Jesse Jackson. Sharpton became an advisor to Diallo's parents, and the National Action Network paid their travel expenses from Africa. Along the way, he became a touchstone for critics of Guiliani. Politicians like former mayor Ed Koch, who had once called him "Al Charlatan," now sought Sharpton's counsel.

Sharpton wielded his new clout to great effect in the 2001 New York City mayoral race, backing Bronx borough president Fernando Ferrer against fellow Democrat Mark Green. When Green won the mayoral nomination, Sharpton refused to endorse him against Republican Michael Bloomberg because of flyers that appeared in neighborhoods hours before the runoff bearing a caricature of Ferrer kissing Sharpton's ample posterior. The Democratic Party dispatched foot soldiers to stop the bleeding, but Sharpton refused to budge, and Bloomberg won the election.

Sharpton, who made his decision to back Ferrer while sitting in a jail cell, was already looking beyond New York. In April 2001, Sharpton traveled to the Puerto Rican island of Vieques to protest U.S. Navy bombing exercises there after hearing that Puerto Rican activists in New York who backed Sharpton during the Diallo and Louima protests had done the same. Sharpton and several others were arrested for trespassing on the Navy base, and Sharpton was sentenced to 90 days in jail. While in prison, Sharpton pondered his future and plotted his next move. When he emerged from the jail to a party and press conference, he had a new message and a new ambition—the nation's highest office.

PERSONAL FAILINGS AS POLITICAL FODDER

Sharpton has skillfully turned his scofflaw habits to his political advantage. At a March 8, 2003, "action rally" at his Harlem headquarters, Sharpton compared his own travails, particularly the defamation suit he lost in 1998, to those of past civil rights leaders. "Don't get confused when they keep bringing up defamation suits with Sharpton," he told the crowd. "They used a defamation suit on [Adam Clayton] Powell; they used a defamation suit . . . on the King movement. We have seen these tactics before."

Upon learning of his indictment on tax evasion charges in 1989, Sharpton declared that it was time to "join the Black leader tax indictment Hall of Fame." He's made return visits to that hall. Between 1993 and 2002, the New York State Department of Taxation and Finance filed eight complaints against Sharpton and his wife totaling more than $75,000, while the federal government leveled $37,449 in liens. As of March 2003, those bills remained unpaid.

In June 1988, the owners of Sharpton's Crown Heights apartment began eviction proceedings against him, claiming Sharpton owed them nearly $6,000 in rent. A housing court ordered Sharpton to pay the back rent, but he was back in court six months later after the owners complained he had failed to pay another $11,000 in the interim. He attributed the lapses in rent to his increased advocacy activities, which demanded money and time that prevented him from preaching, his main source of income.

More serious charges were leveled against Sharpton in 1989 when a grand jury indicted him on 67 counts of fraud, grand larceny, and falsifying business records, among other charges. Prosecutors alleged that Sharpton stole some $250,000 from the National Youth Movement by writing checks for cash out of the organization's bank account or soliciting money from donors that never made it into the account at all. However, a jury found Sharpton not guilty of all charges in July 1990. "I'm a working man," said one juror after the decision. "I've written checks for cash myself. I don't see anything wrong with that."

His tax troubles continue even as he campaigns for president. When he filed his financial disclosure form with the Federal Election Commission on June 30, 2003, Sharpton's attorney, Michael A. Hardy, disclosed that Sharpton faced potential federal, state, and city tax liabilities, the amount of which would be determined by an audit. But Sharpton will likely get by with a little help from his friends: nearly $18,000 in tax liens have also been paid on Sharpton's behalf by NAN and others.

Sharpton has mocked the liens, saying the government should pay him reparations instead—a position that turns his troubles into a political protest that resonates with supporters. "There's a difference between people who have money and people who don't. People who don't do not view taxes in the same way," said Bositis of the Joint Center for Political and Economic Studies. "He's a street politician, advocating a Black point of view, and I think his supporters see him as the subject of persecution."

Sharpton's personal and public finances have always coexisted closely: alongside his nonprofit organizations, Sharpton operated several private music and entertainment promotion businesses. Hit Bound worked with acts like Jermaine Jackson and contracted with record companies, including RCA and Polygram. Sharpton asked National Youth Movement employees to encourage radio stations to play Hit Bound records and plugged the records at the organization's events without disclosing his interest, according to prosecutors in his fraud trial.

Sharpton's second venture was Raw Talent, which was incorporated in 1991. In addition to outside acts, Raw Talent booked all of Al and Kathy Sharpton's public appearances, including preaching dates and singing jobs. In 1999, the Sharptons and a third partner created Rev. Als Productions, which handles the same business as Raw Talent. Sharpton operates Rev. Als Productions out of the house he moved to in 1996, a two-story home in Brooklyn's Flatbush neighborhood.

Sharpton's personal business dealings came under intense scrutiny when Pagones, the New York prosecutor who had won a $65,000 slander judgment against the civil rights figure, filed suit after receiving little of the damages that were supposed to come from garnishing Sharpton's wages. In a December 2000 deposition, Sharpton testified that the last time he filed a U.S. personal income tax return was for the calendar year 1998, and that he could not remember whether he had sent his accountants any of the information necessary to request an extension for filing his 1999 return, at that time 7 months and 21 days overdue. His attorneys stated for the record that he had no savings accounts, no checking accounts, no stock certificates, no U.S. savings bonds. In fact, Sharpton claimed, his only personal property was a watch and a wedding ring.

> In a December 2000 deposition, Sharpton claimed that his only personal property was a watch and a wedding ring.

"Let me just ask a question," opposing counsel asked him. "Other than a watch and wedding ring, do you own any personal property?"

"That's about it," Sharpton replied.

He also claimed he didn't own the clothes on his back. "I debate whether I own it because a lot of that is a business expense," he said of his suits, "but I have—I have access to about ten or twelve."

At his deposition, Sharpton said his $73,000 annual salary from NAN went directly into a Rev. Al's bank account, and that his daughters' tuition as well as the $1,500 monthly rent and utilities for his house—owned by E. Bernard Jordan, pastor of Zoe Ministries and Sharpton campaign contributor—were paid by Rev. Als Productions against his and Kathy's future earnings. Though tax returns showed Sharpton received a $40,000 salary from Raw Talent in 1998, he refused to hand over the 1999 tax returns detailing the first year of Rev. Als Productions because his accountants were "in discussion" with the IRS. Financial disclosure forms filed in June 2003 state that Sharpton received $120,000 from Rev. Als in 2002, though his lawyers could not name the individuals who contributed the money to Rev. Als because they said the records were lost in a February 2003 fire in National Action Network's offices.

Sharpton also testified that his monthly household expenses came from "love offerings," untaxed cash donated to him when he preached at various churches, which by his estimate totaled approximately $10,000 per year. "A friend of mine says, 'Would you come by Tuesday night and preach?' I go by, there's no arrangement for everything, and he says, 'I think that they want to give Reverend Sharpton a love offering, a gift,' and they pass the plate and give it to me," said Sharpton in the deposition. Soon after, Pagones felt the love of Sharpton's support network when the judgment—which had grown to $87,000 with interest—was paid off by a coterie of wealthy Sharpton friends.

"I believe [Sharpton] believed the way he was running his financial world was a legitimate way to operate—he had the right lawyers, the right accountants, set up in a way in which he was protected from creditors and the IRS," Gary Bolnick, the attorney who represented Pagones in the suit to satisfy the judgment, said. "He set up his empire in such a way that he gets the benefit of the wealth without the money passing directly into his hands."

THE INNER CORE

Many in the group that paid off Sharpton's judgment constitute the inner core of supporters that have financed his campaigns—and lifestyle—for years. Rallied by Inner City Broadcasting cofounder Percy Sutton, the group included *Black Enterprise* magazine chairman Earl Graves Sr. and *Essence* magazine publisher Ed Lewis.

These names also appear on the campaign contributor lists and board rolls of the National Action Network. In its early days, Sharpton had to extend credit to the struggling organization as it built its donor and membership base, but between 1994 and 2001, the organization's revenues swelled from $200,000 to more than $2 million. Only a fraction of this revenue came from membership dues, however. Most came from wealthy donors, including broadcaster Radio One Inc.; Byron Lewis, owner of UniWorld Group Inc., the country's largest Black-owned advertising agency; Comer Cottrell, CEO of Texas-based hair product brand Pro-Line International; and BET Holdings Inc., the media conglomerate based in Washington, D.C.

NAN's biggest benefactor by far, however, is boxing promoter Don King, who gave NAN $245,000 in 1999 and $175,000 in 2000. Sharpton met King while on the road with Brown.

NAN's rapid growth is largely attributable to another page stolen from Jesse Jackson's playbook: the Madison Avenue Initiative. Two years earlier, Jackson created the Wall Street Project to lobby corporations to expend more advertising dollars on minority markets and hire minority-owned advertising and marketing firms. The Madison Avenue Initiative employed a similar strategy but targeted the advertising industry.

National Action Network

Top Donors

Ranking	Patron	Total
1	Don King Productions	$420,000
2	African Heritage Network	$177,000
3	The Word Network	$151,000*
4	Prudential Financial Inc.	$ 63,500
5	Spanish Broadcasting System	$ 50,000
6	Afeni Shakur	$ 50,000
7	*Black Enterprise*	$ 42,000
8	*Essence*	$ 42,000
9	Radio One Inc.	$ 25,000†
10	Byron Lewis	$ 25,000
11	Viacom Inc.	$ 25,000

This list is based on individual and corporate contributions to the National Action Network from 1999–2000 as reported in confidential tax documents made available to the Center, which identify top donors to the group in each year.

Source: National Action Network.

*Includes contributions from affiliated companies.

†Viacom contribution came from subsidiary Black Entertainment Television Inc.

"The initiative was magnificently structured; it brought in a lot of money, and it gave Black businessmen a common cause where they were usually competitive with each other," Mercado-Velez said. "The second-richest guys in New York City are on Wall Street, and Jesse already had them, but the richest were in media, so we got them." Suddenly Sharpton was appearing on the covers of Black-owned magazines and garnering interviews, generating enough exposure so that "when Diallo happened, he was set with a league of constituents, a pile of cash, and a bunch of ready media outlets," says Mercado-Velez. "That's when I realized I was dealing with a genius."

Many members of the Madison Avenue Initiative went on to fund Sharpton's campaigns, including Graves; Essence Communications, publishers of *Essence* magazine; UniWorld; radio broadcasters Radio One, Spanish Broadcasting System, and Inner City Broadcasting; and BET. Inner City also paid Sharpton nearly $30,000 in the early stages of his presidential campaign for "fee payments," while PepsiCo, SPN Broadcasting, and campaign donor Hawkins Food Group gave him another $80,000 for "consultation," according to financial disclosure reports.

Of the 47 board members listed on tax forms as serving NAN since its inception, at least 21 have donated to Sharpton's campaigns—including his accountant, Bart Mitchell, of Mitchell & Titus, LLP. Expenditure disclosure forms filed with the FEC during Sharpton's previous runs for public office show more than $600 paid out for parking tickets. The same documents show that the campaign extended two personal loans to Sharpton worth $9,000 and $1,900 each. As with NAN, Sharpton's campaigns demonstrate another facet of his genius—the permeable membrane between his private and public finances.

Al Sharpton

Top Ten Career Patrons

RANKING	PATRON	TOTAL
1	Inner City Broadcasting Corporation, New York	$27,300
2	Rev. Al Sharpton, New York	$23,552
3	Don King Productions Inc., Deerfield Beach, Florida	$15,400
4	Zoe Ministries, Tuxedo Park, New York	$15,400
5	Raw Talent, New York	$14,200
6	American Federation of State, County and Municipal Employees, Washington, D.C.	$14,100
7	Essence Communications Partners, New York	$12,000
8	Maravilla Productions Inc., New York	$10,000
9	Canaan Baptist Church, New York	$ 9,050
10	UniWorld Group Inc., New York	$ 8,700

This list is based on individual, corporate, and PAC contributions to Sharpton's 1997 mayoral campaign, and on individual and PAC contributions to Sharpton's Senate campaigns from 1992 to 1994, as well as Sharpton's 2004 presidential campaign through June 30, 2003.

Sources: Federal Election Commission, New York State Board of Elections.

Conclusion

When Senator Russell Feingold, Democrat of Wisconsin, gave hundreds of speeches nationwide about campaign finance reform throughout the 1990s, he told us that what "hit home the most was when I looked at the kids in the audience, 17 and 18 years old, and I'd say, you know, you're really not welcome to the table of American politics, and that's wrong because that's a denial of the American dream."

For any prospective candidate pursuing the American dream, the numbers are truly daunting. With or without a ban on soft money in politics, the average amount of cold cash raised by an incumbent seeking reelection to the U.S. Senate in 2002 was nearly $5.7 million; the average amount for a U.S. House of Representatives incumbent to stay on the job was almost $900,000. As we noted earlier in this book, at the White House level, in 1999, the crucial year before the presidential election, Governor George W. Bush raised an average of $230,360 *per day*; and though Vice President Al Gore raised substantially less, it still amounted to an average of $84,320 a day.

That's not the kind of money ordinary folks have lying around. Nor do they have the slightest idea of where or how to get it.

Successful candidates must know where to get it or how to make it. Look at the U.S. Senate, of which 40 of 100 members are millionaires (in 1997 there were 36). A candidate who is not a millionaire (and more than 99 percent of Americans are not) and doesn't have the option of using his or her own money to run for office has just one option: dialing for dollars. That means calling and schmoozing with people most of us would rather not hang out with.

Representative Jim Leach, a Republican from Iowa who has been in Congress for 26 years and is the former chairman of the House Banking Committee, talked to the Center for Public Integrity about the pernicious effect big money can have on the political process.

"The most stifling effect of the large amounts of money being played with is not near so much one candidate versus another candidate," Leach said. "It's with the extraordinary scorching effect of candidacies emerging. People don't want to run for office, (a) if they have no money, (b) if they have to raise money, and (c) if they have to put up with the effects of what other people's money says about them. . . . People don't want to go through the rituals of raising money when the end reward is to have other money negatively used against you. . . . When [large amounts of money] are used for negative campaigns they put a pall that is quite chilling on the political process. It is not only the amount of money, [but] it is the use to which money is applied that is so destructive."

A lot of people would agree, including some of the most successful players of this not-so-clean game. Take Bob Dole, for example. Few American politicians have raised more campaign cash in their careers than the former Senate majority leader and Republican presidential candidate. By our calculations from Federal Election Commission and other records from 1973 through 1996, Dole, before the much-vaunted Bush Pioneers and their numerical tracking system, raised a whopping $78 million. Like Leach, Dole spoke candidly with us about the sordid business of asking for money.

"There's something about it that's so demeaning," Dole told us. "To get on the phone and say, you know, 'This is Bob Dole—you know, the majority leader? And I know you've been thinking about my campaign, and I know you want to make a good contribution, don't you?' Ah, with the poor guy yah-yah-yah-yah-yah trying to find out 'What bill do I have pending up there?' [It's] torture. . . . But it's pretty obvious what you are doing. It's a shakedown, you know. . . . It's not rocket science. . . . It doesn't mean they are buying anything, but the guy on the other end doesn't know that," he said, laughing.

Like Dole, anyone who has participated in hundreds of fundraising events over decades, from one-on-one meetings to large ballroom dinners with those willing to write checks, necessarily has to overcome ambivalence early on and develop a rationale for the relentless, demanding, abnormal activity. Dole appears to have managed by reducing to straw-man status any other alternative to fundraising—with his usual wit, of course.

"I wish that I knew a perfect way," he said. "I think you have to be born in an isolation booth and not let out until you are of constitutional age to be president and then suddenly have an infusion of all the knowledge you need to be president. And you don't take any money, and you're elected. I don't know—you wouldn't have any common sense, but you'd be virtuous."

Dole, of course, can speak from long experience. He was first elected to office in 1950 as a Kansas state legislator, where he served for a decade before his election to Congress in 1960. The former Senate majority leader's public service career only ended in 1996, when he lost the presidential election to incumbent Bill Clinton. Now he has the luxury of observing the political process from a relaxed, though still close, perspective: the longtime senator has become a Senate spouse; his wife, former two-time cabinet secretary Elizabeth Dole, won the race to become the junior senator from North Carolina.

> **"You've got so much money in politics now that the incumbent almost has to fall out of a ten-story building with somebody else's wife to be defeated."**

"I think the one thing you're missing is the lack of competition," Dole said, when asked about how politics had most changed over the past half century. "You've got so much money in politics now that the incumbent almost has to fall out of a ten-story building with somebody else's wife to be defeated. Maybe that's all right, but I think I became a better senator when I almost lost my Senate seat in 1974 to Bill Roy. And I'd been this [Republican] national chairman; I'd been doing a lot of things; running around the country, but I'd forgotten that my first responsibility was Kansas. So there is something about competition, I think, that helps."

What's happening to competition goes beyond money in politics. In 2002, in the U.S. House of Representatives with its 435 members, only *four* challengers defeated incumbents, the fewest in the history of our country, according to the Center for Voting and Democracy. Fewer than one-tenth of the races were won by competitive margins of less than 10 percent. And in state legislative elections in 2002, 37 percent of the races were uncontested by a major party.

What is it about our democracy that is causing this serious outbreak of "choiceless" elections?

Redistricting run amok is part of the story. Dan Rostenkowski, the ex-con former chairman of the House Ways and Means Committee, wrote in the *Chicago Sun-Times* of an "elite, more powerful and less public [than political fundraisers], who have played a much larger negative role. These are the redistricting pros who use computers to artfully draw maps carefully calibrated to solidify the power of the party they are working for. . . . That protects incumbents. Trust me, I know. It is a technique I used. But it also creates a take-no-prisoners legislative style that makes compromise very difficult and progress nearly impossible."

The take-no-prisoners technique Rostenkowski talks about has been much on display in recent months, especially with the in-your-face power grabs in Texas and Colorado. In Texas, Governor Rick Perry (urged on by U.S. House majority leader Tom DeLay) tried to ram redistricting changes favorable to Republicans down the throats of Democrats. He brought the Republican-controlled Texas legislature into special session, only to be thwarted when a dozen Democrats bolted from the state senate. Eleven headed for a motel in New Mexico, with security provided by Governor Bill Richardson, a Democrat, and caused a brief media firestorm. That kept redistricting temporarily at bay, since Texas Senate rules require that at least two-thirds of the 31 state senators be there to vote.

Texas Republicans complained that the congressional districts as they stood, drawn by a three-judge panel in 2001, unfairly favored Democrats. Of course, Richardson's Democrats had tried to pull the same thing in New Mexico in 2003, following a 2002 election in which judges had also drawn their congressional districts.

Colorado Republican legislators made their effort as well, hoping to shore up a freshman congressman of their party by shifting the boundaries of his district.

In other words, the hope for partisan advantage led to efforts by legislators to make sure that November elections are a done deal and that their guys would win.

In the U.S. House of Representatives, in each election cycle between 1990 and 2000, more than 90 percent of incumbents won; in the past three congressional elections through 2002, the incumbent reelection rate was more than 98 percent. These are the kinds of numbers we expect to see in countries like North Korea, Cuba, or China, not the United States.

Of course, no one wants to participate in a rigged game in which the outcome has already been orchestrated. Not surprisingly, studies have shown a strong correlation between voter turnout and competitiveness, according to the Center for Voting and Democracy. And the predictability of elective races plays beautifully into the hands of special interests.

"Redistricting makes the inequities in campaign financing even worse," said political science professor Douglas Amy. "Most elections are so noncompetitive due to how the lines are drawn that big donors already know who's going to win. So they give to the likely winners to curry favor."

There are other reasons for the lack of serious competition. For one thing, the political parties have tightened their grip in recent years on the presidential debates. They ousted the League of Women Voters in 1988 after creating the Commission on Presidential Debates, which doesn't disclose its corporate sponsors, prevents nationally known third-party candidates from appearing, and carefully orchestrates and manipulates the actual debate format to such an extent that TV audiences can be heard snoring everywhere. Control and predictability once again serve the political parties and their politicians well, but they are deadly to participatory democracy and public discourse.

But if there is a fait accompli, "choiceless" aspect to American politics—with the public understandably tuning out—why are the campaigns to mostly reelect incumbents so expensive?

"The money I have never figured," Dole said. "When I first ran for Congress in 1960, I spent $19,000 total." That works out to roughly $118,000 today, in 2003 dollars. But the average House race in 2002 cost incumbents $898,382 to gain reelection, and $414,478 for a candidate seeking an open seat. Millions of words have been written examining why campaigns and elections are so expensive. To former president Carter, it is painfully clear why American politics has become prohibitively expensive.

"I think that our political system has been subverted in a very damaging way," he said in an interview with the Center, "by the greed primarily of the news media, television stations, who demand in our country, almost uniquely among great democracies, that candidates have to pay for their presentation of their own campaign platforms and promises through extremely expensive news media. And this is a basic fallacy of our system now."

Through an organization called the Alliance for Better Campaigns, Carter, former president Gerald Ford, and former CBS News anchorman Walter Cronkite have been advocating for years to get free television airtime for all candidates. "So far as I know, there are no European countries and very few countries in which the Carter Center is involved in other parts of the world where we don't require that every qualified candidate have equal access to the major news media. And our country is dependent on how much money you can raise."

What Carter described is yet another special interest getting its way in Washington and, worse, interfering with a candidate's ability to speak directly to the people. It is what the Alliance for Better Campaigns has called "profiteering from democracy."

All these are formidable challenges to a democracy. But they are not intractable. American history is full of stories of people who defied expectations, who through courage, or persistence, or faith, or even just plain orneriness prevailed. As Margaret Mead put it: "Never doubt that a small group of thoughtful, committed citizens can change the world. Indeed, it is the only thing that ever has."

> "I think that our political system has been subverted in a very damaging way by the greed primarily of the news media."

Who would have thought, for example, that a young Black minister named Martin Luther King Jr. would help to lead a national movement for civil rights and, years later, not only secure passage of the Civil Rights Act and the Voting Rights Act, but change the way Americans thought about race, equality, and freedom. Representative John Lewis marched at King's side for years and was arrested and beaten numerous times. In an interview with the Center, he said: "I am deeply concerned about the future of our democracy. Sometimes, I think about the warning you see on cigarette packets that says, 'This could be dangerous to your health.' Well, I think we need to put a warning. . . . The lack of political participation, the lack of political involvement on the part of the American people is dangerous to the future of our democracy. You cannot have a viable, democratic society with hundreds and thousands and millions of our people not participating, just sort of standing on the side. That is not healthy, that is not good. . . . Somehow and some way, we have to find a way to get people off the sidelines, to get people to have a sense of faith and confidence."

But we can't do anything, if we are not alert to the threat. Despite the many warnings about the vulnerable state of our democracy today, including *The Buying of the President* books we have produced since 1996, most Americans are woefully un-informed or unconcerned about their *decreasing* access to political power and the government decision-making process that affects their daily lives. In every election cycle that process becomes more exclusionary, more expensive, more secretive, and a little less *of the people, by the people, and for the people*. And yet each assault on the ingenious ideal of representative democ-racy is quietly countenanced, however outrageous or offensive, as though our "truth, justice, and the American way" of life are completely impervious to change from outside or from within.

We are hustling and bustling along in our daily lives, com-placent and oblivious to politics generally. We seem little con-cerned by what is not just intelligence but in fact hard evidence of the various menacing forces daily eroding our democracy. The loss of citizen rights, voter involvement, and civil liberties can take literally years and can abrade so gradually as to be imperceptible. For our democracy, the skies are anything but blue, but for most of the American people this might as well be anytime on or before September 10, 2001. If there is an aston-ishing wake-up-call moment, apparently more astonishing than the bizarre 2000 election—perhaps the figurative, democratic equivalent of large commercial airplanes flying full-speed into famous buildings—we will rise to the challenge, as we have throughout our history.

Like Todd Beamer, Thomas Burnett Jr., and the other 43 doomed passengers on United Airlines Flight 93, on Septem-ber 11, 2001, who, stuck on a hijacked airplane, learned from their cell phones that other airplanes had been hijacked that morning and flown—catastrophically—into the World Trade Towers and the Pentagon. Flight 93 had been turned around and was now headed for Washington, to do what, the passengers could imagine.

Burnett called his wife from the plane that fateful morning, told her the grim facts, and then said that he and the other passengers were "going to do something." What they did next was storm the hijackers and take the plane down, into a field in rural western Pennsylvania, very possibly saving hundreds, perhaps thousands, of lives.

As he said, it was time "to do something."

Acknowledgments

Watch what they do, not what they say.

These simple words have been the modus operandi for us here at the Center for Public Integrity since we opened our doors back in May 1990. It's not that we don't care what public officials say—of course we do—or that we are cynical enough to believe that no one in politics is capable of a thoughtful, sincere, and, yes, truthful and accurate, utterance. Of course they are. But in a highly politicized, polarized city dominated by spin, truth becomes more elusive every day and mere words can sound hollow and divorced from real events. The old saw, "Actions speak louder than words" has real meaning for us and for investigative journalists everywhere.

Over the years, we have investigated the powerful and produced more than 225 reports and 11 books; our work has been honored a total of 15 times by both the Society of Professional Journalists and Investigative Reporters and Editors. The Center is nonprofit and nonpartisan: we are not selling anything, we don't lobby for or against legislation, and we alienate both political parties equally with our research. Therefore we harbor no illusions about being invited to dinner at anyone's White House anytime soon. We also don't have to worry—thank God—about Nielsen ratings or finding people to cry on camera. We have internal deadlines, yes, but generally we operate without the usual daily time or space limitations—certainly when compared to most newsrooms. What we write is more substantive than most journalism, and more interesting than most political science. We are, in other words, researchers who recognize the enormous responsibility we bear to balance fairness and the right to privacy with the broad public interest and the public's right to know. We are ever mindful of a quote from Albert Einstein that is on our office wall: "The right to search for truth implies also a duty; one must not conceal any part of what one has recognized to be true."

That's why, in late 1995, when we learned that the Clinton White House was rewarding major donors to the Democratic Party with overnight stays in the Lincoln Bedroom, and later obtained secret "usher records" that listed every guest for an entire year, we cross-checked the list against Federal Election Commission campaign contribution records and then published an investigative report, *Fat Cat Hotel*, listing those lucky 75 men and women, each of whom we had contacted by phone or letter. The Clinton White House was silent, and the Democratic Party spokeswoman called our report "ridiculous." Subsequent internal White House records that were released the following year confirmed everything we had written and more—the personal, enthusiastic approval of the president of the United States. The Center received SPJ's Sigma Delta Chi "Public Service in Newsletter Journalism" award for the report.

In early 2003, we obtained a copy of secret draft legislation for the Domestic Security Enhancement Act that the Bush administration had quietly prepared as a bold, comprehensive sequel to the USA PATRIOT Act, giving the government broad, sweeping new powers to increase domestic intelligence-gathering, surveillance, and law enforcement prerogatives and simultaneously decrease judicial review and public access to information. We also learned that this major, historic "Patriot II" legislation had been written *without consulting or informing* Republican or Democratic leaders in Congress, who actually had never heard of it, much less read it. As a result, the Center for Public Integrity took the unprecedented (for us) step of posting the entire 120-page bill on our Web site. Attorney General John Ashcroft's aides had tried to talk us out of posting it and, having failed, unpersuasively downplayed the document to reporters as an "early discussion draft." Nearly every major print media outlet in the nation—and many around the world—covered it, and more than 325,000 "unique visitors" came to our site in the first week alone.

We wrote *The Buying of the President*, published in 1996, *The Buying of the President 2000*, and now *The Buying of the President 2004*, because we believed that Americans have a right to know who's behind our presidential candidates, the *real* price of power and the alliances that have been made. This kind of information is not in TV commercials or on candidates' Web sites, and is present only in sporadic bits and pieces, if at all, in the news media. It was amazing to us, then and now, that prior to 1996, no one had ever written an investigative book about the major presidential candidates and their parties, published before the first votes are cast in the primaries and caucuses.

There is good news and bad news about investigating major presidential candidates and their parties in three straight elections. The good news is that we know what to look for and have developed and executed an unprecedented, elaborate methodology. The bad news is that all of the political "players" would rather personally fight in Iraq than talk to anyone from the Center for Public Integrity. Despite repeated requests, via telephone, e-mail, and letter, over many months, none of the major presidential candidates in this book would subject themselves to our probing questions about the grubby matter of their political survival and who has made it possible. For the first time, the political party chairmen also declined to speak with us. And the congressional leadership was also mum, despite our requests—Senate majority leader Bill Frist, Senate minority leader Tom Daschle, House speaker Dennis Hastert, and former House speaker Newt Gingrich, to name a few.

We do appreciate the time and big-picture insights about the state of democracy that former president Jimmy Carter, Senate Commerce Committee chairman John McCain, former Senate majority leader and GOP presidential nominee Bob Dole, Senator Russell Feingold, Representatives John Lewis, Jim Leach, Marcy Kaptur, and AFL-CIO president John Sweeney shared with us. Chamber of Commerce president Thomas Donahue, who has spoken with us in the past, declined our request for an interview.

Over the course of a year, 50 researchers, writers, and editors investigated the candidates and the political parties, contacting or interviewing more than 600 people and systematically gathering hundreds of thousands of federal and state records and secondary source material. As part of the Center's exhaustive, "leave-no-stone-unturned" approach, we examined the biographical history of each of the candidates. We sifted through thousands of documents and articles to trace each politician from childhood to power. We delved into their education, their professional lives, and sometimes even their military service.

From these materials, we created and updated comprehensive one-of-a-kind databases. To discern their personal financial holdings we culled all available financial disclosure statements and created a database that detailed every cent owned by each politician, along with their incomes. Only by knowing each candidate's financial holdings could we analyze potential conflicts of interest.

The next step was to collect every available contribution record for each politician during his or her entire government career. To reach this goal, Center data analysts spent months gathering and coding donations made on the federal level going back to 1978. To truly examine the financial histories at play, researchers compiled additional documents including state campaign contribution records and the underreported contributions of soft money going to candidate committees through the 527 system. The result was a truly unprecedented database containing 1,834,513 campaign finance records of the presidential candidates that allowed us to convert federal, state, and soft-money records into single lists, ranking each candidate's top career donors.

In addition to campaign contributions, researchers followed the money trail to analyze candidates' campaign expenditure records and look for the connections between politicians and interested parties. We checked documents detailing any all-expense-paid trips or use of corporate jets by the candidates, as well as any federal election law "matters under review" by the Federal Election Commission. We also systematically compared past and current congressional staff listings with lobbying records to identify postemployment, "revolving-door" practices. Center researchers studied federal and state lobbying records, legislative voting records, and sometimes committee hearing records to explore what legislative favors had been granted to large campaign donors. In addition, we examined and analyzed litigation and legal records, as well as Securities and Exchange Commission annual reports, proxies, and other company-related documents involving many of the candidates and political parties.

The Center filed the most Freedom of Information Act requests on a single investigative project in its nearly 14-year history, requesting all correspondence for the last six years between those seeking the White House and more than 100 federal agencies. Many of the more than 10,000 documents that the Center received have shown servicing-the-donor connections between these candidates and their largest contributors.

In addition to *The Buying of the President 2004*, the Center has created a special Web site (www.bop2004.org), which can also be linked from the Center's homepage (www.publicintegrity.org), offering continuing investigative coverage of the presidential election, including short candidate biographies and periodic new campaign developments. The site also features a "document warehouse," which includes the candidates' most recent financial disclosure forms, trip reports, IRS 527 reports, databases of assets, and links to their campaign contribution reports, Web sites, and political action committees.

Recall that in the summer of 2002, in the midst of the media frenzy over the epidemic of corporate irresponsibility, the Center for Public Integrity was the *only* organization anywhere that posted internal Harken Energy documents regarding the Securities and Exchange Commission's investigation of George W. Bush and the company; in fact, we ended up putting up almost a thousand pages on our Web site. We have also gathered tantalizing documents about specific candidates that we will make available on the Web.

Regrettably, we once again made the painful choice to use up our valuable "word count" space for this manuscript with narrative about the candidates and parties, saving details such as our source notes for *The Buying of the President 2004* for our Web site.

Obviously, the preparation of this book was a massive operation. The 50 members of the investigative team are listed in the front of the book, and brief biographies of many are listed on the Center's Web site. I gratefully acknowledge the devoted efforts of each and every person. It is a truly inspiring and humbling experience to be around so much dedication and talent, day after day. I must single out a few of the stars of this show.

Bill Allison is the managing editor of the Center, editorially responsible for everything we produce. Coauthor and project manager of *The Cheating of America* in 2001 and senior editor for *The Buying of the President 2000*, he has a phenomenal, boundless talent. Consider that in the seven months prior to completion of this manuscript, besides this massive undertaking, the Center produced 30 news-making investigative reports on topics ranging from global water privatization to the Patriot II legislation, from media ownership and regulatory conflicts of interest to prosecutorial misconduct. No one else produces original investigative reporting of such range and quality, weekly, along with a 120,000-word book.

He couldn't have done it without the Center's superb new deputy managing editor, Teo Furtado, whose editing skills, exuberance and first-rate professionalism are infectious. Allison and Furtado are easily the best one-two editor combination we've ever had here at the Center. Research Editor Peter Smith coordinated the mind-numbing fact checking, and production editor M. Asif Ismail helps keep the trains running on time.

But the real force-of-nature, day-to-day leader was Center veteran Alex Knott, the project manager for *The Buying of the President 2004*. Thanks to Alex, we had an intricately systematic methodology the likes of which I have never seen on a Center project, with checklists of every conceivable investigative document that ought to be pulled and two- to three-page progress memos at each weekly meeting he chaired for more than six months. He kept us on track, to the minute.

Special thanks to Senior Writers Alex Knott, Robert Moore, and Alan Green, all three of whom have won national journalism awards for their Center work in recent years. I am especially grateful to Alan, who kindly agreed to come back and help us out, writing three fine chapters. Ben Coates, M. Asif Ismail, Laura Peterson, and Brooke Williams each wrote a chapter, and performed exceptionally well under enormous pressure.

As you might expect, our methodology is data-intensive, and we were extraordinarily fortunate to have Aron Pilhofer and Derek Willis as the project database editors. How they balanced the sheer volume of what was required for this project with their other Center work will always confound me. Web Developer Han Nguyen makes the Center's award-winning Web site sparkle.

Ben Coates, a Stanford grad bound for the Columbia University Ph.D. program in history, was a star both as senior researcher working with Alan Green and as writer of a chapter himself. Former Daytona-Beach *News-Journal* reporter Daniel Lathrop contributed great research and worked the phones as hard as anyone. Soles Fellow Adam Mayle, who coauthored the Patriot II report, wrote 10,000 words worth of candidate biographies for the Center's special Web site tied to *The Buying of the President 2004.*

Adam was one of what we internally referred to as "The Fantastic Four," my phenomenal team of researchers, led by respected Center veteran and former Soles Fellow, the brilliant and personable Katy Lewis, who, sad to say, is going off to law school at the University of North Carolina. Besides a heavy research load, Aubrey Bruggeman had the unenviable task of requesting interviews with people who didn't want to be interviewed, almost daily, which she handled with grace and aplomb. Rounding out the "Fantastic Four," intern Mark Reading-Smith helped us get to the finish line in his memorable summer stint with us.

We are especially grateful to veteran award-winning investigative journalist Steve Singer, who lives in Austin, for providing useful information to us about George W. Bush's record as governor.

Special thanks to Professor Wendell Cochran of American

University in Washington, whose 23 journalism graduate students assisted in the research as part of his class.

To them and to the entire "BOP" team, I am deeply appreciative.

We would have neither a team nor a Center for Public Integrity without philanthropic support. Our development director Barbara Schecter and her fine staff of Sugesh Panicker and Julie Mañes do a magnificent job. I am very grateful to the Victor Elmaleh Foundation, Henry and Edith Everett, the Popplestone Foundation, and the Hafif Family Foundation for specifically supporting this book. We also want to acknowledge the other funders ($10,000 and over) who provide the much needed general operating support for the Center for Public Integrity: the Arca Foundation, the Around Foundation, the Atlantic Philanthropies, the Carnegie Corporation of New York, the Nathan Cummings Foundation, the Everett Philanthropic Fund, the Ford Foundation, the David B. Gold Foundation, the John S. and James L. Knight Foundation, Arthur D. Lipson, the John D. and Catherine T. MacArthur Foundation, the S. R. Mott Charitable Trust, a Rockefeller family member, the Park Foundation Inc., the V. Kann Rasmussen Foundation, the Rockefeller Family Foundation, the Sandler Family Supporting Foundation, the Scherman Foundation, and the Streisand Foundation. The Center for Public Integrity is fortunate to have many other funders who provide support for specific projects in addition to thousands of members who contribute annually.

I want to thank our literary agent, Esther Newberg, of International Creative Management (ICM) in New York, for her wonderful efforts on our behalf. And, as always, we are indebted to our indefatigable and always reliable libel lawyer Marc Miller, who has been vetting our copy since day one.

490 Acknowledgments

It is difficult to imagine an executive director of an organization having a more supportive or encouraging board of directors and advisory board, and I want to acknowledge their important leadership of the Center for Public Integrity, led by cofounder and chair Charles Piller. Aided by the remarkable generosity of the MacArthur Foundation, our biggest single benefactor, the Center has made very exciting, recent strides toward long-term security and institutionalization.

This book is dedicated to my daughter, Cassie, who was present at the creation of the Center for Public Integrity, from its first office in our house when she was 10 years old, to the first P.O. box, to all three downtown Washington offices, and who even attended a few of the earliest news conferences. She, more than anyone else, endured those difficult years of my travel and 80-hour weeks and, through it all, could not have been more supportive.

Finally, I am truly blessed to be surrounded by so many splendid people who have done so much to enable me to do this strange work. But, in addition to Cassie, no one has been more caring, long-suffering or just plain wonderful than my mother, Dorothy Lewis; my wife, Pamela Gilbert; and my son, Gabriel Gilbert Lewis.

Charles Lewis
September 2003
Washington, D.C.

Index

About the Center for Public Integrity

The Center for Public Integrity began operation in May 1990. It is a nonprofit, nonpartisan research organization founded so that important national issues can be investigated and analyzed without the normal time or space limitations. Described as a "watchdog in the corridors of power" by the *National Journal*, the Center has investigated and disseminated a wide array of information in more than 225 published Center reports since its inception. Nearly 9,000 news media stories have referenced the Center's findings or perspectives about public service and ethics-related issues. The Center's books and studies are resources for journalists, academics, and the general public, with databases, backup files of government documents, and other information available as well.

As with its previous books and reports, the views expressed herein do not necessarily reflect the views of individual members of the Center for Public Integrity's Board of Directors or Advisory Board.

To access the most recent findings of the Center, including additional or updated information about the presidential campaign not contained in this book, you can visit the Center's Web site at www.publicintegrity.org, or subscribe to *The Public i*, the Center's award-winning newsletter.

For more information, to buy books and other publications, or to become a member of the Center, contact the Center for Public Integrity:

The Center for Public Integrity
910 Seventeenth Street, N.W.
Seventh Floor
Washington, D.C. 20006

E-mail: contact@publicintegrity.org
Internet: www.publicintegrity.org
Telephone: (202) 466-1300
Facsimile: (202) 466-1101

Perennial

Books by Charles Lewis:

THE BUYING OF THE PRESIDENT 2004
The Authoritative Guide to Where the Presidential Candidates
Get Their Money—and What Strings Are Attached
ISBN 0-06-054853-3 (paperback)

The Buying of the President 2004 continues the quadrennial "outing" begun with
the well received volumes for the 1996 and 2000 elections. Lewis reveals and
investigates the sponsors and the known (and not-so-known) conflicts of interest
entangling each of the aspirants of the White House.

"A gloriously detailed account of the candidates' finances and friendships."
—*The Economist* (on *The Buying of the President 2000*)

THE CHEATING OF AMERICA
How Tax Avoidance and Evasion by the Super Rich
Are Costing the Country Billions—and What You Can Do About It
ISBN 0-06-008431-6 (paperback)

An entertainingly written anecdotal expose of the millions of well-heeled
individuals and corporations in America that dodge their taxes.

"Fascinating, highly readable. . . . Little guys everywhere will read this book with
righteous indignation." —*Publishers Weekly* (starred review)